P9-CMZ-756

305.800973 Gol

Goldfield, Michael.

The color of politics :

DISCARD

MAR 01 2010

Please Do Not Remove Date Due Slip
From Book Pocket

 Palm Beach County
Library System

3650 Summit Boulevard
West Palm Beach, FL 33406

DEMCO

The Color of Politics

Also by Michael Goldfield

The Myth of Capitalism Reborn, A Marxist Critique of Theories of the Restoration of Capitalism in the Soviet Union (with Melvin Rothenberg)

The Decline of Organized Labor in the United States

The Color of Politics

Race and the Mainsprings of American Politics

Michael Goldfield

the new press — new york

PALM BEACH COUNTY
LIBRARY SYSTEM
3650 SUMMIT BLVD.
WEST PALM BEACH, FLORIDA 33406

© 1997 by Michael Goldfield

All rights reserved. No part of this book may be reproduced, in any form,
without written permission from the publisher.

Published in the United States by The New Press, New York
Distributed by W.W. Norton & Company, Inc., New York

The New Press was established in 1990 as a not-for-profit alternative to the large,
commercial publishing houses currently dominating the book publishing industry.
The New Press operates in the public interest rather than for private gain,
and is committed to publishing, in innovative ways, works of educational, cultural,
and community value that might not normally be commercially viable.
The New Press's editorial offices are located at the City University of New York.

Book design by Ji Lee *and* Hall Smyth
Production management by Kim Waymer
Printed in the United States of America

9 8 7 6 5 4 3 2 1

PALM BEACH COUNTY
LIBRARY SYSTEM
3650 SUMMIT BLVD.
WEST PALM BEACH, FLORIDA 33406

To Roslyn and Joe, Evi, and Karl, Greg, and Gabe

We are not afraid to follow truth wherever it may lead, nor tolerate any error so long as reason is left free to combat it.

—Thomas Jefferson, 1820, quoted by Lynne V. Cheney, former chair of the National Endowment for the Humanities, front page of *Telling the Truth*, 1992

In its grand outlines, the politics of the South revolves around the position of the Negro....In the last analysis, the major peculiarities of southern politics go back to the Negro. Whatever phase of the southern political process one seeks to understand, sooner or later the trail of inquiry leads to the Negro.

—V. O. Key

I might say...what has Mississippi got to do with Harlem? It isn't actually Mississippi; it's America. America is Mississippi. There's no such thing as a Mason-Dixon Line—it's America. There's no such thing as the South—it's America.

—Malcolm X

Contents

Preface and Acknowledgments

This extended essay attempts a reinterpretation of U.S. political history, showing the centrality of race at all the critical turning points from colonial times to the present. When I was originally approached by André Schiffrin of The New Press and asked if I would be willing to expand a lengthy essay on the subject into a book, I seized the opportunity. It seemed a welcome break from another book on which I had stalled in the middle of writing. Further, in a moment of unrealism and quite possibly intellectual conceit, I figured I could accomplish this task in two to three months maximum, then return to the half-written book. A year and a half later, a much revised and greatly expanded work emerged.

To the extent that I have gotten any of the details and stories right, I have received help and advice from hundreds of friends, colleagues, and scholars, some of whom I did not know before I approached them. Many who have helped me I have undoubtedly forgotten. Among those I remember, I wish to thank Chuck Alston, Numan Bartley, Beth Bates, Tim Bates, Robin Blackburn, Tim Bledsoe, Barry Bluestone, John Bracey, Walter Dean Burnham, Dan Buck, Dan Carter, Ken Casebeer, Eric Davin, Micaela di Leonardo, Elizabeth Faue, Kathleen Frankovic, Richard Freeman, Alan Gilbert, David Gordon, Jackie Hall, Herbert Hill, Michael Honey, Ron King, Peter Lange, Ken Lawrence, Jesse Lemisch, Richard Lewontin, Ted Lowi, Staughton Lynd, Walter Mebane, Larry Mishel, Karen Orren, Kevin Phillips, Jonas Pontusson, Marcus Rediker, Joel Rogers, George Ross, Ellen Schrecker, Constance Schulz, Steve Skowronek, Jim Stimson, Tom Sugrue, Ruy Teixeira, Rick Vallely, Michael Wallerstein, Margaret Weir, Warren Whatley, Nat Wood, Gavin Wright, Lamont Yeakey, Alfred Young, and Maurice Zeitlin. In addition, a number of other friends and colleagues read all or part of the manuscript at various stages and gave me important feedback and suggestions.

They include: Bob Brenner, Michael Brown, Ed Cliffle, William Domhoff, Eric Foner, Michael Hamlin, Ira Katznelson, Robin Kelley, Howard Kimeldorf, Seymour Martin Lipset, Michael Martin, Wendy Mink, Frances Fox Piven, Jill Quadagno, Peter Rachleff, Adolph Reed, David Roediger, Alan Wald, Sherri Wallace, and Robert Zieger.

In my work at Wayne State University's College of Urban, Labor, and Metropolitan Affairs, I have been blessed with superb graduate research assistants. At the early stages of my work on the manuscript Brad Markell provided me with yeoman's work, before being recalled from a layoff at General Motors and returning to his other vocation as a Detroit area leader of the United Auto Workers. Rob Gordon has been so intimately involved in every aspect of the book that he has almost been my coauthor. His research skills, acumen, and knowledge have been so superb and have so humbled me at times that I am tempted to say that any problems and errors that remain must be his responsibility. Thus absolved, I invite the reader to join me in an intellectual journey that I hope conveys some small amount of the excitement and absorbtion that it has given me.

Finally, I wish to thank several sources of support including fellowships and grants from Wayne State University's College of Urban, Labor, and Metropolitan Affairs and the the Wayne State Humanities Council, as well as a fellowship from the German Marshall Fund.

Michael Goldfield
Detroit, 1997

Introduction

One thing people, I want everybody to know
You gonna find some Jim Crow everyplace you go.

I'm gonna tell you people something that you don't know
It's a lotta Jim Crow in a moving-picture show.

I'm gonna sing this verse—I ain't gonna sing no More,
Please get together—break up this old Jim Crow.
—*Jim Crow* by Leadbelly

This is the United States of America, the U.S.A., the land of the free and the home of the brave, the land of equality and opportunity for all. Yet, race consciousness and racism pervade every fiber of our social existence. It is, as Studs Terkel notes, "the American obsession" (Terkel 1992). One sees and hears it everywhere. There is hardly a contemporary political issue that is not imbued with racial overtones: welfare reform, drugs, crime, punishment, and the death penalty, immigration, and of course, affirmative action—these being only some of the most obvious.

Long before I attempted to engage in research or writing about the subject, I was, like most Americans, experiencing, reacting to, and thinking about it. Although I did not know it at the time, I attended my first two grades in a segregated grammar school in Maryland, a border state whose separate restaurants, hotels, and general social space only barely qualified it at the time as Up South. During the 1960s, when I was active in the civil rights movement, we would stop—in integrated groups—at the still-segregated eating places in Maryland along Route 40 on our way to Washington, D.C., passing by the apartment complex where my family and I used to live. When my family moved to New Jersey in the early 1950s, I belonged to a racially integrated Boy Scout troop with a Native American scoutmaster, a janitor at the local high school whose Leni-Lenape heritage made him a fount of wisdom on our many hikes and outings. Our assistant scoutmaster was a southern-born white truck driver whose frequent vulgarity, racist and anti-Semitic remarks were combined with a generosity to all of us. Our troop was filled both with conviviality and bouts of racial tension, as when we whites would be chased home by our Black fellow scouts. The shadow of the plantation, however, still reached deep into North Jersey during the 1950s. This became clear in 1956 when Plainfield High School's former All-State football star and national high school multiple track record-holder Milt Campbell, an African-American, won the gold medal in the decathalon at the Olympics in Melbourne, Australia. The city fathers quite naturally planned an elaborate homecoming celebration. It was discovered that the Park Hotel, Plainfield's finest, was racially segregated. This being the North, not Mississippi, segregation in this small venue quickly gave way to civic pride as the whole area shared in the triumph of one of its native sons. White gentile housing covenants and country club exclusions, no less job and education discrimination, of course, remained intact.

While I was growing up, white racism was continually on display. As a child in the 1950s, I used to listen to Jewish adults (a group rightfully considered more liberal and tolerant than most other whites), many of whom, like my own family, had lost relatives in Nazi concentration camps. They would often denounce Naziism and anti-Semitism as racism but, in the next breath, make racist remarks about Blacks, or *schwartze*, as they called them. Although I had no political consciousness at the time, the hypocrisy of my *lantsman* repulsed me greatly. In the early 1960s, I worked in a machine shop, earning money for college. The workplace was all white, most of the workers were from Eastern Europe; many had never met, no less had extensive contact with, African-Americans. Yet, the vehemence with which they repeated the most bigoted of stereotypes and my inability to sway them with facts or rational argument troubled me.

The civil rights movement of the 1960s, of course, brought many changes in the old Jim Crow. Yet, racial issues and racial cleavages are more pivotal to national political campaigns today than they were in the decades immediately before the 1960s. The centrality of these racial issues in current politics and the deep emotions that they stir sometimes appear baffling, even irrational. Yet, their dominance, even in defiance of elementary facts or logic, is undeniable. Let us briefly rehearse some highlights.

The economy has been uneven; wages and family incomes are not growing for the vast majority of the population; college education and housing for first-time buyers are being priced out of reach. Although there are strong complaints about taxes and government spending, the objects are peculiar. The extraordinary peacetime military buildup under Presidents Carter, Reagan, and Bush hardly stirs emotions, although many view it as unnecessary. Yet, the several decades-long expansion of social welfare programs is a political issue for which the drums beat loudly. But it is not just any social welfare program. The biggest focus is on Aid to Families with Dependent Children (AFDC), whose real benefits contracted greatly in the decades prior to 1995 (some estimate that the level had fallen back to the 1967 level) and make up barely 1 percent of the total federal budget. The stereotyped, stigmatized face of the welfare mother in political imagery is young and African-American (see Piven 1996:61–67).

The stagnating and reorganized domestic economy has led to downsizing and layoffs of people previously thought secure. With some notable exceptions, job opportunities for young people have diminished, especially for those with low education. Resentment, however, is not directed strongly at those who are managing the economy, at those who are reaping enormous profits and benefits, or at the system as a whole, but at affirmative action, at nonwhite foreign (especially Asian and Mexican) competition, and at immigrants. As I will argue later, this is nothing if not irrational. Affirmative action is one of those programs that is much talked about but has had little effect in all but a small number of venues. As Louisiana Governor Edwin Edwards stated in his 1991 gubernatorial campaign against former Ku Klux Klan leader David Duke, "I don't think there are 500 people in Louisiana that have either been adversely affected or benefited from affirmative action. But everyone who doesn't have a job or whose son cannot get into law school believes it's because of affirmative action" (quoted in Moore 1992:54). If affirmative action is so limited in its scope, why are so many white people so worked up about it?

Immigration also has strong racial tones. In most states, there are hardly any immigrants to speak of. In several states (California, Texas, Florida, and New York) the number of immigrants is indeed large, especially in urban areas. Yet, studies about the degree to which immigrants contribute to the economies of these states, in contrast to the degree to which they use tax-supported services (including schools, welfare, and health facilities), are inconclusive. There is also little evidence that areas of immigrant concentrations have seen either lower wages in general or greater degrees of decline in the incomes of lesser educated white males (to cite the group most often mentioned) than areas with few immigrants. What is behind the intensity of emotion many white people feel against Asian and Latino immigrants?

Most U.S. inhabitants are rightly concerned about rampant crime and the deterioration of the nation's cities. But a focus on providing jobs and rebuilding urban areas seldom gets a hearing. Few are interested in looking at the reasons why Canadian cities (nearer to many residents of the Northeast, upper Midwest, and Northwest than most of our own country's cities) are cleaner, freer of crime, and generally more livable. What gets support are more prisons and increased punishment, hardly a cost-effective method. The United States, with the highest percentage of prisoners of any country in the world, now spends over $25,000 a year per prisoner, according to conservative estimates. Prisons are now one of our fastest-growing industries, are an incredible expense, and are arguably an inefficient use of

money. Were it not for the racial agenda of those who propose harsher punishments and more prisons, many Americans would accept the old home-
spun wisdom that "an ounce of prevention is worth a pound of cure" (see,
e.g., Freeman 1994 and Shapiro 1995 for useful summaries).

Since the 1960s, we have seen the shameless and unfortunately too often
successful use of racist rhetoric in political campaigns across the country. It
is clear that the appeals to the baser and more uncharitable feelings of many
whites are no less bigoted because they have appeared in coded or indirect
form: George Wallace's and Richard Nixon's opposition to "forced" busing;
Ronald Reagan's tales of wealthy Black "welfare queens" who neither worked
nor paid taxes; his championing of the "Lost Cause" in Philadelphia,
Mississippi, the town where three civil rights workers were murdered in
1964; and perhaps the most racially incendiary of all, George Bush's use of
African-American rapist Willie Horton to influence white voters in his 1988
campaign. Such demagoguery, of course, was successful. On the fringes, not
so far from this mainstream, is Pat Buchanan, who, like David Duke, is often
explicitly racist and anti-Semitic and has had leaders of Nazi and white
supremacist organizations on his staff, including the white supremacist and
Nazi Larry Pratt as his campaign cochair, all the while claiming to be against
racial discrimination and not himself personally racist (see *New York Times,*
February 16, 17, and 23, 1996).

Democrats, too, use a brand of racial appeals to white voters, more
nuanced because they attempt to maintain African-American voting support while giving bigotted signals to whites. Jimmy Carter first won the
Georgia governorship by successfully wooing Wallace supporters in his state,
long before he emphasized his belief in "ethnic purity" during his winning
1976 presidential campaign. Bill Clinton's snubbing of Jesse Jackson and his
calculated attack on hip-hop singer Sister Souljah at a Rainbow Coalition
meeting during the 1992 campaign gave the same assurances to whites.

The increased importance of race in national politics since the successes
of the civil rights movement is paradoxical. During the 1930s and 1940s,
traditional liberals and industrial unionists believed that conservatism had
unwarranted support from poor and working-class whites in the South
because the race question diverted them from pursuing their real interests.
V. O. Key, for example, argued:

> In fact, apart from the restraint imposed by that [the race] question,
> the South ought, by all the rules of political behavior, to be radical.
> A poor, agrarian area…it offers fertile ground for political agitation.
> The overshadowing of the race question, in which the big farmers
> have the most immediate stake, blots up a latent radicalism by con-
> verting discontent into aggression against the Negro. (Key 1984: 44).

In the late 1940s, Key and others believed that the gaining of the franchise and civil rights for southern Blacks would lead to a diminishing importance of racial issues. White southerners would act like northern working-class whites, becoming more left-wing and solidaristic with blacks. With the successes of the civil rights movement, a new day seemed to have arrived. In 1964, northern senators and congressmen of both parties were nearly unanimous in their support of the Civil Rights Act; only southern Democrats opposed it in significant numbers. Instead of the class-based realignment predicted by many, however, the politics of the North and the nation as a whole since the late 1960s has become more like that of the old South. Not that race was not always there, but it is now more successfully used in defense of conservative politics in the country as a whole. How do we explain this seeming anomaly?

The really important question for us, however, is, not why politicians exploit racial prejudices and fears, but why such tactics work. Why are whites, especially lower-class, traditionally working-class whites so easily taken in by those who seem to offer little to solve their deepest problems? What is behind not merely the racial animosity but the moral righteousness that often accompanies it? Are they being snookered, are their prejudices that important to them, or is there something more? The answer to this question, I will argue, is both important and complex. We must dig deeper than merely looking at present racial attitudes. Although the current racialized politics has its own unique characteristics, in its main contours it is not new; it is also the product of a long process of American social and political development. A clear understanding of the role of race in the contemporary United States requires an analysis of the role that race has played historically. A large part of this book is devoted to such an analysis.

Before proceeding in this endeavor, however, I beg the indulgence of the reader. I propose to sharpen our focus by initially looking at two sets of questions and a range of answers that have been given to them. First, what is race, and what is the root cause of racism? How permanent and immutable is it (can it be changed, and if so, how?), and why has it been the vehicle for so much divisiveness and conflict? Second, how central has race been to our social, political, and economic life? Exactly what role has it played in American political development? What is distinctive, special, or exceptional about the United States, and what if anything does race have to do with it? So let us take our first cut at these questions.

THEORIES OF RACE

Theories of race, racial inequality, and racism may be distinguished for our purposes by two related criteria: (1) what they propose as the causes of racial inequality and racial discrimination and (2) how immutable they consider racial differences and conflicts to be.

Throughout the nineteenth century and up to the 1920s, biological theories of racial superiority, inferiority, and hierarchy were dominant in this country and elsewhere. These theories posited that certain races (as well as males) were biologically superior in intelligence and other important characteristics. If this theory were true, racial and gender differences would be permanent; inequalities would be based on inherent differences in capacities; equal opportunity for all and selection of people for education and employment based on merit (rather than discrimination) would produce dominant positions for white males and subordinate positions for non-whites and females. By the 1930s, however, biological theories of human racial and gender differences in intelligence were largely discredited among serious scholars and intellectuals. Certain key studies that supposedly proved the biological inferiority of women, African-Americans, and other non-white males turned out to be fraudulent, based on fake data (e.g., Paul Broca's famous experiments on brain sizes). Others had omitted unfavorable data, made unwarranted assumptions, or made elementary, yet decisive, mistakes in logic or scientific method. Recent theories of white male biological intellectual superiority and African-American inferiority, including the much publicized *Bell Curve*, by Richard Herrnstein and Charles Murray (1994), are similarly flawed, although their serious discussion today suggests that a sizable number of people are still influenced by sheer quackery. The bottom line on these questions seems to be that expressed forcefully by Richard Lewontin and others in the early 1970s: So-called racial and ethnic groups throughout the world have a common gene pool, and the variation within groups is far larger than that among groups. Recent anthropological studies only seem to confirm what we know from genetics. All Homo sapiens may have a common origin that is far too recent for there to have been any significant evolutionary differences between differing groups of people.[1]

Although biological theories of racial differences are taken seriously only by the most extreme of racists, they do little to explain the hostility of dominant groups to subordinate groups. Suppose prehistoric peoples or life on other planets were found that really did have lesser or greater mental capacities. For what reason might we feel antagonisms toward them or they toward us? What if future research were to reveal differences in the brain structures of men and women, giving each different capacities in one area or another that were, so to speak, hardwired rather than enviromental. None of this would obviate treating people as equals, giving all persons equality of opportunity, even if the end result were, for example, more women psychiatrists and more male mathematicians. Thus, the discriminatory attitudes held by those who still cling to biological theories of race are quite inconsistent with their premises.

Another older theory suggests that racial antagonism is based on deep-seated psychological needs, perhaps instincts. All groups allegedly feel allegiance to their own kinship networks and broader communities and have deep antagonisms to outsiders. Although this theory does not posit any racial hierarchy, it does suggest that racial and ethnic antagonisms are intractable, incapable of change, that it is a waste of time to try. Such theories, although they may have had some partial validity in the precapitalist epoch, are too narrowly based to accord with present-day facts. Immigrant groups do become assimilated. Over time, ethnic groups and nationalities have merged, absorbed each other, and diminished or lost their former antagonisms or, conversely, have gone from peaceful relations to deadly conflict. (For a fascinating discussion of the broader development of solidarity and altruism in both animals and humans and their possible biological basis, see de Waal 1996.)

A more prominent view, until recently the most common among both conservative and liberal intellectuals, is that racism is a set of individual attitudes, or prejudices, based on ignorance or bad taste. Conservative free market economists, in a position elaborated most fully by Gary Becker in his *The Economics of Discrimination* (1971), argue that employer preferences for white rather than non-white employees are irrational in that they diminish the employer's potential profits. A rational, profit-maximizing employer would hire the cheapest, most qualified workers, regardless of their color or racial identity. The solution to racial discrimination (on the presumption that reducing it in the workplace would go a long way to reducing it in society in general) is a freer market (which would financially punish employers with racist tastes) and education. Similarly, certain liberal theorists, perhaps epitomized by Gunnar Myrdal in his *An American Dilemma* (1964), attribute racial discrimination to ignorance and a certain type of provincialism, especially among lower-class whites. The heritage of slavery and the backwardness, isolation, and low levels of education in the South until recently made this region the most racially prejudiced. The changing of discriminatory laws and rising education levels would reduce and eventually eliminate racial discrimination. Both the liberal and the conservative versions of this theory—that racism is basically a problem of individual attitudes rooted in ignorance and narrow-mindedness—are highly optimistic about the degree to which racism would be (one almost wants to say "automatically") eliminated by the normal workings of social development and enlightened leadership. It is, of course, clear that ignorance, prejudice, and bad taste play some role in the history and practice of racial dominance, that individual experiences, education, and insights have at times changed individuals dramatically from racists to antiracists. Nevertheless, these theories, in either their liberal or their conservative versions, are insufficient as general theories because they tend to minimize the deep historical roots of racist practices, the degree to which these practices are embedded in modern institutions, and the interests that support them. (For an incisive critique of these views, see Cornel West 1987:75–78).

A commonly argued, more nuanced contemporary view is that which Theodore Allen calls the "psycho-cultural approach" (Allen 1975:19; 1994, 4) and George Fredrickson refers to as "liberal pessimism" (Fredrickson 1996). Although race prejudice by groups may not be natural or instinctual, it is nevertheless allegedly rooted in deep-seated psychological needs for cultural identity; although racism may be a set of attitudes, it is inexorably transmitted. Hence, white racism and racial slavery in the United States were the somewhat inevitable consequences of centuries of British and European racist culture and the search by displaced Europeans for a new colonial identity in the Americas. Racist attitudes by whites are in this view deep-seated indeed, incapable of changing in significant ways on a permanent basis. Among historians, Carl Degler and Winthrop Jordan are representative of this approach.[2] Likewise, Derrick Bell, Herbert Hill, and Andrew Hacker, among more recent authors, while being strong defenders of the rights of Blacks in contemporary U.S. society, are extremely pessimistic about whether whites in general will ever change. All these authors believe that racial identities are primary and fundamental; they are rather dismissive of arguments that white racism may be changeable or that other interests may be dominant at times. Each of these scholars has done important research, some of which, in my opinion, casts doubt on their central thesis.

A more sophisticated version of the psycho-cultural view, quite influential, especially in the field of cultural studies, is that of Michael Omi and Howard Winant (Omi and Winant 1986; Winant 1994). Rather than representing a stable feature of Anglo-American identity formation, race in the United States for them is an unstable "decentered," complex of social meanings over which dominant and subordinate racial groups continually struggle (Omi and Winant 1986:68). Unlike the liberal pessimist view, Omi and Winant's theory of racial formation sees the possibility of large-scale transformation of racial identities by both dominant and subordinate groups. They also persuasively extend their theory of racial formation in the United States to include a number of non-white groups. They argue that different types of racial oppression are based on a "unique form of despotism and degradation" (Omi and Winant 1986:1). Native Americans faced genocide; African-Americans were enslaved; Mexicans were colonized; Asian-Americans were excluded. And one should add that women, even of the dominant groups, were considered private property of men and restricted to the private sphere. Like some of the best analyses of race in the cultural studies field, Omi and Winant's work shows a sensitivity to the ubiquitousness of racial systems of oppression and their social dimensions. In comparison with the liberal pessimists, Omi and Winant stress racial oppression's fluidity. The weakness of this approach as a total theory, however, is its limited analysis of the causes and roots of racial formations and how these systems actually change. Their unwillingness to look at economic factors and social class leads Omi and Winant to give no priority to different types of struggles. Linguistic and cultural criticism may be just as important as broad social struggles. No one group or segment of society is more important than another in transforming racial identities. Their stance also leaves them unable to analyze which groups may actually benefit materially from systems of racial hierarchy and, thus, who might have strong economic and social interests in preserving the racial status quo. Their theoretical weakness in this regard is also suggested by their ambiguous relationship to the Marxist tradition and the crude attempts to distance themselves from it.[3]

The most sophisticated and penetrating analysis of racial identity formation is that of David Roediger, many of whose insights are being appropriated in recent cultural analyses of race. Like Barbara Fields and Theodore Allen, Roediger argues pursuasively that race, though central and important, is a social construction in a way that social class is not. He gives many intriguing examples. One of the most stunning is that Ghanaians—who regarded Africans as Black and people of mixed race as white in the 1960s —who had heard Malcolm X speak in Ghana in the early 1960s, described him as a *white man* with astonishing ideas (Roediger 1994:4). Roediger's project is to analyze why white working-class racial identity was formed in the United States, how this identity was shaped from causes inside the working class as well as from outside, and how the identification as whites has held back white workers from understanding their class interests. With a set of more Marxist concerns than Omi and Winant and a determined use of the class-based insights of Du Bois, Roediger is sensitive to a whole series of causal issues that they miss. He states that one cannot understand racism without understanding its class and economic context (Roediger 1986:8). He is also optimistic that certain types of class struggles in which antiracism is prominent will help lead white workers to abandon their identity as whites for one as workers. He often gives intriguing and highly nuanced analyses of the contradictory historical cases of interracial unity among labor organizations (including the Knights of Labor, the National Labor Union, and the Industrial Workers of the World). However, despite his schematic statements about the importance of external contexts, Roediger is primarily concerned with the psychological and cultural roots of white working-class identity. He limits his investigations to one historical period —circa 1800 to 1865—that he sees as critical, leaving little room for the immense changes in the systems of racial domination that have taken place since then. Without a more complete analysis, it is never clear how these processes and products relate to the socio-economic context in which Roediger claims they are rooted.

While attempting to incorporate the best insights from the cultural and attitudinal analyses of race and racism into a broader perspective, I will argue that these theories are not fully informative without a clear analysis of the class and economic roots of racial formation and systems of racial oppression. As with cultural and psychological theories, there is also a wide array of socio-economic analyses. One approach, for example, argues that racial discrimination and white racial identity originate among white workers who benefit materially by the exclusion of their nonwhite competitors in the labor market.[4] If this theory were accurate, racism would be highly intractable and not likely to be changed because it would be in both the immediate and the long-term interests of most white workers. Yet, although the material benefits of racial exclusion may be quite real in certain venues for white workers (as in some elite and tightly controlled skilled trades such as printing pressmen, electricians, and plumbers and even occasionally, if less frequently, for lower-skilled workers such as New York City's Irish longshoremen during the 1850s), for most white workers, especially those with the more typical, limited ability to control the labor market in their occupations and industry, the opposite has most often been the case. As Reich (1981) argues pursuasively, in job situations where discrimination is most intense and racial income differentials have been most extreme (e.g., historically in Mississippi), white workers have often been among the least well paid in the nation. In those parts of the country and those industries where interracial unions have narrowed racial income differentials (e.g., in the automobile industry in the North), white workers have been among the best paid in the United States. Thus, a weakening of racial discrimination at the workplace is often in the immediate interests as well as the long-term interests not only of African-American workers but of white workers as well. So although white workers' defense of racial privileges in hiring, job placement, and promotion is an important part of the racial system in this country, by itself it is insufficient to explain patterns of racial discrimination as a whole. Further, most patterns of racial discrimination in the workplace in hiring, placement, and promotion have been set by employers, not by white employees, who in general have had little leverage to influence these patterns. One must look, therefore, to more powerful, society-wide interests to explain the class and economic bases for racial domination and subordination.

A view that looks to employers, rather than white workers, as the source of racial discrimination and animosity is the divide-and-conquer approach. In this analysis, racism is instilled by employers who attempt to forestall solidaristic, class-based organization on the part of their own employees and workers in general. This view has been argued by Marxists (e.g., Roemer 1979), but it has also been a common one among liberal unionists. It was the argument put forward by racially and economically liberal Alabama Governor "Big Jim" Folsom during the late 1940s and the 1950s. He claimed that "race was a phony issue, a ploy used by the rich and powerful to divide poor people and blind them to their common interests." (Carter, 1995:73). (See also Sims 1985:161–188 for a more detailed account of Folsom's racial views.) Clearly, racially divisive tactics by employers have been an important part of the system of race and class relations in this country, but the theory leaves many forms of racial discrimination unexplained. It also fails to elucidate why the tactic has at times been so successful and how it relates to broader socio-economic questions.

Much criticism by recent analysts has been made of so-called class-reductionist positions. This classification, however, is quite broad and is difficult to analyze as one position. Virtually all analysts who attempt to distinguish themselves from this label include a whole variety of differing views, all of which stress class. It is, however, crucial to make more fine-grained (although not necessarily very subtle) distinctions. At one extreme is the position argued by the early Socialist Party (SP) in this country. The SP policy ranged from the benign neglect of Eugene Debs, who said, "We have nothing special to offer the Negro and we cannot make separate appeals to all races," to the undisguised white chauvinism of Wisconsin Congressman and SP leader Victor Berger (Spero and Harris 1968:405). Racial discrimination supposedly would automatically disappear when the class system of capitalism was overthrown. This position not only provided an excuse not to deal with central issues of racial discrimination but was also at times a cover for racist behavior and statements. On the other hand, some theories that emphasize the class roots of racial identity and racial discrimination in this country have argued for its centrality in understanding virtually every aspect of social and political life in this country. I will comment on some of these various positions in my later discussions.

One highly sophisticated socio-economic approach is that of Stanley Greenberg, who argues that the racial systems of discrimination in the United States, as well as in South Africa, did not originate in the modern workplace

nor in individual attitudes, psychology, or culture; rather, they were originally rooted in the economic needs and desires of large agricultural producers
to have highly exploited and controlled Black labor forces. The social and political structures and the racial identities that were required to sustain such a
system were by necessity codified and extended to the societies as a whole.
The agricultural interests were supported by other economic elites whose
interests were parallel to or at least not incompatible with those of the agri-
culturalists. The existence of racial oppression and racial attitudes among
whites stem from this dominating racial system. Both the difficulty of overcoming racist attitudes among whites and the problems faced by racially solidaristic labor movements must be explained within this context. Changing
the systems of racial domination and subordination ultimately requires the
challenging and overthrowing of those economic interests that gain the most
(Greenberg 1980). If one can identify those social and economic interests that
benefit from the systems of racial domination and how they support it, one's
strategy for eliminating racism can be more highly focused.

As I mentioned before, certain analysts have stressed that a clear understanding of the system(s) of racial domination in this country must account
for the varieties of subjugation faced by non-white peoples in the United
States. Much of this domination is, of course, related to economic interests,
including the expulsion of Native Americans from their historical lands,
often justified by crude racist views; the seizure and subjugation of former
Mexican territories also has a clear economic basis. A full understanding of
race and race relations in this country surely requires that the situations of
all non-white peoples be taken into account. As we begin to move more
dramatically to an increasingly multi-racial (rather than biracial) society, this
point becomes even more important. Yet, racial discrimination and domination of other non-white peoples in the United States can only be understood in the context of the historical enslavement and oppression faced by
Black people in this country, which has played a central and continuing role
in the country's development from the very beginning. For this reason, while
trying to examine the full range of racial dominance and subordination in
the United States, my account will center on the system of domination of
Blacks. Why this remains central can be fully explained only by a detailed
socio-economic analysis.

Much of what has been raised as central by psychological, cultural, and
socio-economic theories of race and racial discrimination must be taken into
account in any full theory. The racist attitudes of whites, the creation of racial
identities, the resilience of culture and its ability to structure interpretive
questions of stable worldviews and traditional patterns of economic and
social relations, the immediate interests of workers and employers, and a

number of other features need be analyzed. Yet, in the end, I hope to demonstrate that these must be tied to deep-seated socio-economic factors whose analysis is necessary to fully understand not only the creation of racial identities and systems of racial oppression but ultimately how such subordination will eventually be overcome. This will be one of the continuing threads of this book on which I will elaborate.

RACE AND AMERICAN POLITICAL DEVELOPMENT

It is, of course, important to understand the roots of racial oppression and the tractability of racial attitudes and structures of domination. Whatever the underlying causes of racial divisions, racial domination, and racial subordination, however, it is at least as important to know how central these phenomena have been throughout American political history. Is the present focus on race in American politics new, or does it have a long history; are the roots of the present racial politics largely current, or are they at least partially based in the past? It is instructive to look at different views about the role race has played. In short, what is distinctive or exceptional about the United States, and what if anything does race have to do with it?

One perspective on American political development focuses on the actions, statements, and ideas of elites and government bodies—sometimes referred to by its critics as "elite history." American history for some is a struggle among leaders over the role and policies of the U.S. government: the constitutional debates, the role of the Supreme Court, secession by the Confederacy, whether to go to war, how to solve the Great Depression. Elite history has many variants, both methodologically and across the political spectrum. Methodologically, perhaps the most extreme position sees the ideas of political elites and the working out of these ideas in ideological conflicts among these elites as the key factor in American political development. This position is displayed in its most one-dimensional form in the work of Gordon Wood on the American Revolution and the formation of the Republic. For Wood, race is hardly a factor, if at all. A more nuanced version of this methodological stance is found in the works of Bernard Bailyn, who discusses race and racial slavery but clearly regards these issues as secondary. For others such as Charles and Mary Beard, governmental policies reflect, not ideas, but the conflict and resolution of battles between powerful economic elites. Economic interests, not ideas, are the motor forces of history. More recent adherents to this methodological orientation are the corporate liberal historians, represented by James Weinstein, who regard the economic interests of elites as responsible for virtually all government policies, including even those liberal reforms, such as unemployment insurance and the National Labor Relations Act, that others have attributed to the pressure on the government from popular movements. For all these views, race and racial discrimination are secondary issues in American political history. At most, they are merely regional problems of the South, historically the most backward and supposedly least important section of the country.

The political views expressed in elite histories vary widely. Corporate liberal theorists place themselves on the left. There is also a highly conservative version of elite history, in some cases largely establishment history, often bordering on national chauvinism. Such an approach tends to exaggerate certain of our unique qualities as a nation, to glorify our traditions out of all reasonable proportions, especially in comparison with those of other lands, and to omit many of our outstanding defects. At the extreme end, one has not only the deification of the colonialists and Founding Fathers but also a claim that our culture, politics, and society are God-given and superior to all others. Such accounts can only be made plausible by vastly exaggerating the degree of consensus that has existed historically in our society, minimizing the number of individuals and groups that America has not served well, and omitting those aspects of American society that do not compare favorably with features in other developed capitalist countries.

Perhaps the most prominent historian in this genre is Daniel Boorstin, extolled by Newt Gingrich and other conservatives. Boorstin's work is characterized by one fellow historian as "strident conservativism, boosterism, and unabashed patriotic celebration" and by the somewhat conservative Bernard Bailyn as an "apologia," Not only are sympathetic discussions of Native Americans, women, Blacks, labor, radicals, and dissidents of all sorts missing, but any people or groups slightly outside the mainstream, including Tom Paine and the Quakers, are dismissed as irrelevant.5 Race is, of course, not very important at all in this conservative account.

The challenges to elite history have come from several quarters. One such view sees social and economic development as central to political development. This approach is, quite naturally, taken by a number of Marxist writers, many of whom regard race as central. Various works by W. E. B. Du Bois, Oliver Cox, Herbert Aptheker, Philip Foner, and Eric Williams fall into this category. There are also those who look to the centrality of economic factors, including Gabriel Kolko and William Appleman Williams, for whom race hardly plays a major role.

The current most popular challenge to traditional elite history today, however, comes from those practitioners of the "new social history" who argue that a full picture must describe the lives and activities of ordinary people. History must be studied, not from the top down, but from the bottom up. The new social history includes detailed narratives of social movements, particularly those by the lower classes, and rich discussions of the plight and accomplishments of Native Americans, African-Americans, Latinos, Asian-Americans, women, and the labor movement. Also contained are fascinating discussions of family and community life, embracing much that was at one time considered outside the purview of historians. The new social history thus presents a more inclusive—and, one might add, more accurate—view of the American experience. Among those who may be considered part of this approach, there is a large variance in the attention given to race. Gary Nash, one of the most eminent of the new social historians, goes to great lengths to examine the importance of people of color in early American history. For others, including Sean Wilentz (whose account of early nineteenth–century New York City white working men has been widely criticized for its blindness to questions of race), race and racial hierarchy hardly come into play at all.

Recently, there has been a public battle over general conceptions of American history taking place between defenders of conservative elite history and advocates of the new social history (battle is perhaps a misnomer in that this chapter of the cultural wars has mostly involved conservatives attacking and crushing their opponents). The struggle emerged into public view over the 1995 publication of the National Standards for United States History by the National Center for History in the Schools at the University of California at Los Angeles. Although nominally independent, the report was funded by both the National Endowment for the Humanities and the U.S. Department of Education and has been viewed by both critics and proponents as an integral part of the program of Goals 2000: Educate America Act, which was passed by Congress in 1994. The standards reflect a certain amount of the themes of the new history mentioned above, although the National Standards are rather circumspect in this respect. Further, the recommended supplemental sources cover all the traditional materials, including The World's Greatest Speeches; a biographical encyclopedia of great Americans, material on the U.S. constitutional debates, including the Federalist papers—contrary to the implications of Lynne Cheney in her widely reprinted and circulated piece, "The End of History" (Wall Street Journal, October 20, 1994); and a large array of other standard and important materials.

Conservatives have attacked the National Standards outline as an orgy of political correctness, trashing America, giving a history of victimization, rather than accomplishments, "loaded up with crude anti-Western and anti-American propaganda" (Leo 1994). Yet, when one gets behind the rhetoric and examines the detailed criticisms, it is surprising how little is there. There is supposedly too much discussion of "pre-literate" Native Americans and Africans and not enough of Anglo-white males (who still, incidentally, make up the bulk of the discussion and references). Lynne Cheney decries the dropping of the picture and mention of Robert E. Lee—many of his current champions seem to lose sight of the fact that he was the military leader of the war to defend African-American slavery—and the failure to emphasize leading congressional figures, including Henry Clay and Daniel Webster.[6] The recommended supplementary readings, of course, include ample material along these lines. The right-wing Republican Family Research Council attacks the National Standards for not underscoring the landing on the Moon "as *the* most significant event of our time" and for neglecting "to mention that the United States won the space race," finding it "hard to overstate the magnitude of the failure." (Gary Bauer, N.D.: Family Research Council circular) On the basis of these and other alleged historical atrocities, the U.S. Senate on January 18, 1995, voted its disapproval of the standards by 99 to 1.

The disjunction between what Garry Wills describes as the "storm of vituperation" from conservatives about political correctness and the new McCarthyism, and the nitpicking nature of the actual criticisms forces one to only one conclusion: Many conservatives do not seem interested in obtaining an accurate, inclusive picture of the American past nor in having historians engage in serious investigations; rather, they want the "reinforcement of old myths" and the celebration of the type of life and values they mythologize as having existed in the 1950s (Wills 1995). On one level, of course, the conservative attack can be rightfully written off as an attempt to stifle critical discussion (the search for truth that Lynne Cheney supposedly cherishes) and to glorify business leaders and other, even more dubious establishment figures.

Yet, the story as often told in the new social history is also wanting in important respects. Virtually all the conflicts of importance in their accounts seem to take place between people on the top (i.e., various elites in control of society) and those on the bottom. The virtuous, democratic masses, the many, versus the corrupt, self-aggrandising, undemocratic, greedy few. Many accounts, of course, rescue from historical oblivion important struggles of ordinary people. In the process, however, the most prominent accounts tend to stress the nobility of the participants, especially of white working-class people, and the solidarity between them and non-white, oppressed peoples. They thus give an overly romantic view of the racial and ethnic comity that has existed throughout American history and of American political development in general, leaving us little in the way of explanation of why these supposedly unified and inclusive social movements failed at all. The sometimes violent conflicts between various groups, the exclusionary attitudes of some at times, and the fact that these groups were often unable to sustain unified struggles, are downplayed. Why were the ruling groups able to dominate so thoroughly in the United States? Why were the struggles of people at the bottom so much less successful in the United States than in other developed capitalist countries? These questions are difficult to address in the context of much of the new historical writing. This issue appears in particularly problematic form in the fascinating, highly informative, ultimately unsatisfactory monument to the new social history, the two-volume work *Who Built America*. In the end, this romanticized view of American political development, although it is an important corrective to some of the more traditional views, ends up downplaying the role of race, racial identities, racial discrimination, and racial conflict.

Thus, in a somewhat perverse way, the conservative critics do have a point. The "consensus" seen throughout American history by certain historians is not pure fantasy, although they almost certainly have its contours wrong. The dominance and ideological hegemony of the ruling classes in the United States is a phenomenon that is central to American political development. This hegemony must be understood, not dismissed. I wish, therefore, to proceed neither by denying it, as do many current social historians, nor by uncritically glorifying it, as do the establishment historians.

In order to get an initial grasp on the uniquely long-term, exceptional history of ruling-class hegemony in the United States, let us return to the more traditional views and see what we can learn from them in conjunction with the insights from the new social history. It is interesting and a sign of the times (as well as amusing) that House Speaker and former history professor Newt Gingrich (in his course "Renewing American Civilization") explicitly presents us with a caricature of the consensus view of American political development. In his class, Gingrich raises the issue of American exceptionalism, claiming that it is the defining concept around which to understand the history and present of our society. He mistakenly states that this concept was coined and elaborated by Everett Carll Ladd, a contemporary conservative political scientist. He also mistakenly takes the notion to mean that scholars have used the term to mean that this country was both unique and superior to others. Nevertheless, the notion of American exceptionalism provides us with a convenient starting place to deepen our discussion of race and U.S. political development.[7]

American Exceptionalism

An enormous, long-standing literature, popular as well as academic, has developed over the last century and a half that purports to discover and explain the nature, essence, or mainspring of American politics.[8] Much of this extensive body of writing focuses on what is peculiar or exceptional about the United States in comparison with other economically developed capitalist countries, (viz., Japan, Australia, New Zealand, Canada, Britain, and those in Western Europe. The topic itself is usually referred to as American exceptionalism.

The main focus of the American exceptionalism literature historically has been to answer the question of why the United States has no substantial, independent working-class party.[9] In times when social movements and labor organizations are strong and radicalism is influential, much of the emphasis has been on those factors that kept the movements from being more radical, their organizations from becoming more permanent, and a stable third political party from emerging.[10]

In those times, however, as in the present, when social protest is at a low ebb or is fragmented, when labor organizations have become less radical or have been weakened, a whole new thrust in the analysis of American exceptionalism often emerges. The study of American politics and political development either ignores social movements, labor organization, and radicalism or at most views them as marginal sideshows (or curiosities) to the main drama of American politics. Not only mass mobilizations but also class and racial divisions are conveniently ignored in such times. The 1950s and early 1960s, shaped by Cold War imperatives, the crushing of dissent, and the destruction of radicalism in the labor movement, ushered in an intellectual climate in which society was viewed as homogenized (and generally seen through white blinders). Class conflict had supposedly ended, labor was at most a pluralist interest group, consensus reigned, and America was on its way to becoming a happy, middle-class society (see Boorstin 1958; Bell 1960; Kerr et al. 1960).

In the 1980s, with conservative, probusiness Republican administrations in Washington, with Democrats seeking ways to recapture the seemingly conservative white vote in the South and the apparently racially antagonistic urban white Catholic working-class vote in the North, with organized labor declining in strength, class politics and class analysis hardly seemed appropriate to many people. Social movements and even race were also downplayed. One expression of this orientation perhaps is the fashionable view that the state and the main arena of politics are largely autonomous from social forces (for a critique of this perspective, see Goldfield 1989b). Another indicator is that various views from the 1950s (most prominent of which is Louis Hartz's (Hartz 1955), which stresses the individualism of American culture) have become popular again, along with an uncritical nostalgia for that decade. This trend has continued into the 1990s unabated, if anything in ever cruder form, finding expression in the popular writings of Lynne Cheney, Newt Gingrich, and Rush Limbaugh.

What Is Distinctive About America?

THE WEAKNESS OF U.S. LABOR Still, the central starting point of the more substantive American exceptionalism literature has been the organizational and political weakness of American labor. Ours is the only economically developed capitalist country with no major working-class party, no labor, social-democrat, socialist, or communist party. All other comparable countries have or have had such parties. Further, and not unrelated (since working-class parties are often to a significant extent based on the trade unions), is the general weakness and recent decline of trade unions in the United States. The percentage of the civilian labor force in trade unions in 1997 was less than 15 percent. This figure is far lower than that in other developed countries. Canada has 37 percent, Germany and the United Kingdom have about 40 percent, while Sweden and the Netherlands have over 90 percent. Japan, the second-lowest country, has approximately 25 percent.[11]

From the last peak of approximately 35 percent union membership in 1953 to the present, union density (the percentage of union members in the labor force) has declined continuously. No other developed country has had such a continuous decline in the post–World War II period. Attempts to find an explanation for these trends in the relative affluence of our society or in changes in the industrial or occupational structure are clearly misplaced because all other developed countries have undergone similar transformations and development (see Goldfield 1989a for a more detailed discussion of this question).

Despite the recent weakening of trade unions and the lessening political influence of labor parties in many European countries, the historical weakness of labor in the United States and the lack of political influence of working-class organizations are relatively unique features of U.S. society and cry out for an explanation.[12] The weakness of U.S. labor has also had a tremendous impact on virtually all aspects of society, especially those that most people regard as troublesome.

THE RESULTS OF WEAK WORKING-CLASS ORGANIZATION Comparative scholars have often focused their attentions on some of the unique or exceptional deficiencies of the United States compared with other developed countries. Despite our existence, still, as perhaps the most affluent country in the world, of all the developed capitalist countries in Asia, Europe, and North America, we have the highest crime and murder rates, the largest percentage of prisoners, the highest concentrations of poverty, and the most problem-infested cities. In some instances, the severity of these conditions approaches that in the most economically impoverished lands. Some of these problems are recent; some are quite old. Many can be traced, at least indirectly, to the weakness of working-class organization.

Our voting turnout is the lowest of any developed country and has been declining throughout the century. The percentage of eligible voters who voted in the 1992 presidential election was 55.2 percent, the highest since 1972, when an independent (John Anderson) garnered a substantial percentage of the vote (*Congressional Quarterly* 1995:80); in 1996 the figure was 49% (*New York Times* November 7, 1996) Other developed countries have much higher turnout rates, including West Germany with over 90 percent and Sweden with slightly less. Canada, at the low end comparatively, has had a 75 to 80 percent turnout rate in the post–World War II period.[13] Even more disturbing than the low turnout rates is the class skew of voting. Turnout rates have consistently been far lower in this country among poor and working people than among the more affluent. One set of figures, for example, places turnout for people with incomes of less than $15,000 per year at less than 14 percent in 1990, 11 percent in 1992, and 7.4 percent in 1994—astounding numbers for a country with democratic pretenses (*New York Times*, August 11, 1996). And since 1989, the number of people living below this poverty-level figure has increased substantially. This class skew is not evident in other developed countries. Walter Dean Burnham has concluded that we have "an essentially oligarchical electoral universe" (Burnham 1982:142), and E. E. Schattschneider in 1960 spoke of this as a "crisis in democracy," (Schattschneider 1960:109). Some have even suggested that this makes us hardly an electorally democratic country. There have been many attempts to explain what virtually all thoughtful commentators have recognized as a serious problem. Some have pointed to the many obstacles in this country that have been placed in the way of those attempting to register, especially those of the lower classes. Of far more importance, although not unrelated to the roadblocks to registration, is the lack of major electoral alternatives for the bulk of the population, especially the lack of a major working-class party.[14] This defect in American political life—a defect, of course, unless one is anti-democratic and elitist—is also exceptional among developed countries.

Our social welfare benefits are less extensive in this country than those in other developed capitalist countries. As we all know, this country has resisted a national health plan long after other comparable states have adopted one. As a consequence, we have less coverage and higher per capita medical costs than any other land. This country has less government expenditures per capita (even with a large military) than other developed countries, with less coverage rates for pensions, sickness insurance, and unemployment. Only Japan vies with us in some categories at the bottom. (See Goldfield 1989a:27–32 for an extended discussion. For more recent figures and discussion, see Stephens 1994; Huber, Ray, and Stephens 1994; Huber and Stephens 1992; Garrett and Lange 1991; P. Baldwin 1990; Esping-Anderson 1990; Janoski and Hicks, 1994; and Mishel and Bernstein 1994). Although labor movements are not the only political forces in developed capitalist countries that have striven for extensive social welfare coverage, they are by far the most powerful and influential. The weakness of labor organization is not unrelated to the weakness of social benefits in the United States.

In a recent book, Seymour Martin Lipset presents a long list of other characteristics that he sees as endemic to U.S. society, some tied to those things that many regard as positive. The emphasis on individual rights and the divided nature of national governmental institutions make ours a highly litigious society. We have many times the number of lawyers per capita and almost five times the tort costs as a percentage of gross national product (GNP)—an incredible 2.4 percent—as any other country (Lipset, 1996:50). Lipset even argues that the higher rates of teenage pregnancy and divorce in this country are a product of our historical culture and values. And these statistics are not to be explained by the existence of the African-American poor. Although the rates for Blacks are proportionately higher than those for whites, the rate of teenage pregnancy for whites is twice that of the closest European country, and divorce rates in the United States have only a modest class and racial skew (Lipset 1996:50). Finding the supposed roots of American exceptionalism has been a long-standing quest for many students of U.S. political and social life. The attempts at explanation have been both diverse and numerous, dating back well into the nineteenth century.

THEORIES OF AMERICAN EXCEPTIONALISM For over a century, the United States has been one of the most economically developed capitalist countries in the world; from the 1920s until recently, it has been the most developed. Marx's original account of capitalist development, at least insofar as it appears in schematic form in the *Communist Manifesto,* suggests that working-class movements will be most developed, most fully organized, with broader class conscious, and perhaps more radical in the most developed countries. Most late nineteenth– and early twentieth-century non-Marxist commentators had similar expectations. Yet, Marxists and others, too, have long noted that working-class politics in the United States has been decidedly less advanced along this path.[15] All have noted the absense here of a labor, social democratic, socialist, or communist party with significant electoral and organizational support. Unlike all other developed capitalist countries, the United States of America has no substantial, independent working-class party. The key question, then, is why working-class politics in the United States is so undeveloped. Attempts to explain this apparently unique feature of U.S.

society have been manifold for over a century. Analysts have ranged across the political spectrum, from Marxists (including Marx, Engels, Lenin, and Trotsky), who have tried to explain the conjunctural reasons for what they have seen as the historical, temporary retardation of the American working-class movement, to more conservative commentators who have argued that the United States is, not merely exceptional, but a permanent, enduring proof to the falsity of Marxist prognosis (Bell 1960; Kerr et al. 1960). Among a sampling of explanations for this American exceptionalism are the following:

1. Alexis de Tocqueville and Werner Sombart have identified the supposedly more democratic, egalitarian features of U.S. society as the reason for the absense of developed working-class politics.

2. Others, e.g., Stephen Thernstrom, have pointed to alleged higher rates of social mobility.

3. Geographic mobility, the uprooting of the poorest members of the working-class population, has also been cited as a key factor. The transient character of the worst-off parts of the population precluded the formation of stable working-class communities, the basis in many other countries for enduring labor politics (Karabel 1979).

4. Louis Hartz, in his *The Liberal Tradition in America* (1955) argues for the importance of a nonfeudal past in this country and the acceptance by the general population of a strong belief in Lockean individualism. These factors are sometimes said to be reflected in the frontier images and the Horatio Alger myth.

5. Conservatives, including Professor Gingrich, sometimes point to the highly religious character of large percentages of the populace. Seymour Martin Lipset argues that the historically large number and size of dissenting Protestant sects has played a significant contributing role.

6. Some assert that workers have historically had higher wages here. Or in the words of Sombart, in the United States, "All Socialist utopias came to nothing on roast beef and apple pie" (Sombart 1976:106).

7. The historian Frederick Jackson Turner and his followers have pointed to the existence of a frontier in the western United States as a "safety valve" for nineteenth century working-class frustration and discontent.

8. Political scientist Theodore Lowi has stressed the federal structure of U.S. politics as the main obstacle to the formation of an influential working-class party (Lowi 1984).

9. Others have located working-class failures in a lack of solidarity rooted in the historical (white) ethnic diversity of the country.

10. Still others have argued for the centrality of early white manhood suffrage, gained more easily here than in Europe and other countries.

11. The savage repression of working-class radicals by the state and the extreme nature of capitalist opposition to working-class politics and organization are additional reasons given by some analysts.

12. In a global, anti-Marxist argument, Kerr and his associates (1960) claim that sharp class conflict is a feature, not of developed capitalist society, but of emerging pre-industrial society. Thus, the United States may be more advanced than, not behind, comparative countries in the weakness of its labor movement.

13. And the list goes on.[16]

All these theories are, in my view, problematic; some are misleading; the best provide only partial insights. It is not my goal to delve deeply into the various positions on American exceptionalism here.[17] It is worth noting briefly, however, that social mobility studies have shown little difference between the United States and other capitalist countries during the relevant comparable historical periods despite sharp assertions to the contrary by Speaker Gingrich and others (see, e.g., Lipset and Bendix 1964). White manhood suffrage was extremely limited in the pre–Civil War period and in the South after 1900. From the dawn of the twentieth century until the 1960s, disenfranchisement affected poor whites almost as much as it did blacks in the South (see Key 1984). Even at its fullest, however, white male suffrage never touched on the disenfrachisement of nonwhites, women before their enfranchisement in 1920, and noncitizen immigrants. Feudalism was long gone in Europe before working-class movements emerged there. Finally, the frontier (whatever its impact in an earlier time—and I would argue that it is mixed) has long since departed from the U.S. landscape.

Reconceptualization of the Problem

The problem of American exceptionalism must be posed differently. An important argument can be made that politics goes through long periods in which viable political options are relatively constrained. During other shorter, often more volatile periods, the options and possibilities for change are usually much broader. These latter periods are turning points or moments whose outcomes structure and set the limits on politics during subsequent

periods. Thus, to understand the more limited, stable periods, it is necessary to examine also the previous critical turning points that shaped them.

Athough not necessarily subscribing to a theory of critical moments,
most students of American political development recognize at least three
pivotal periods. These include the founding of the Republic, the Civil War,
and the depression–New Deal era. Each of these periods, in the eyes of many
authors, was an important turning point in U.S. political history. In addition, each left a decided impact on contemporary and later political life.
There is less agreement on which other periods are turning points. There
are those who argue, however, for the centrality of Andrew Jackson's presidency (e.g., Schlesinger 1950), Reconstruction (e.g., Du Bois 1964), the 1890s
(e.g., Goodwyn 1976; Burnham 1986), the Progressive Era (e.g., Skowronek
1988), and also the present. Even the choice of period or periods often
depends on what factors are considered important, with emphasis ranging
from critical elections (e.g., Sundquist 1983) to sectionalism (e.g., Bensel
1987) and to economic interests (e.g., Beard and Beard 1944).

If one accepts this general perspective about pivotal turning points as
reasonable, however, in examining American political development, it will
not do to investigate merely the more stable periods when the United States
has seemed to many people to be relatively serene and homogeneous. Nor
is it adequate to take as a putative norm those periods in which class conflict seemed weak and fragmented. Rather, one must also examine those periods in which the situation was quite different. For as any careful examination of U.S. history will show, and as many of the new labor historians have
documented convincingly, contrary to the views of the consensus and elite
historians, class struggle and militance have been anything but mild in this
country. There have been many times when mass, radical, left-wing, broad-
based, occasionally violent working-class upheavals have taken place. These
struggles have sometimes had both the breadth and the intensity of those
in other countries that led to the establishment of independent working-
class political organization there. Later, I will refer to a number of these struggles. And contrary to received wisdom, third parties far to the left of either
the Democrats or the Republicans have at various times attained widespread
influence in the United States. The Socialist Party, with its hundreds of elected local officials before the First World War, is a case in point. During the
1920s, 1930s, and 1940s, local and state-level labor, radical agrarian, and other
third parties were a central fixture of the political landscape. The Minnesota
Farmer-Labor Party, Wisconsin's Progressive Party, the American Labor Party
of New York City, End-Poverty-In-California (EPIC), the North Dakota
Nonpartisan League, the Oklahoma Farmer-Labor Reconstruction League,
and hundreds of local labor parties all had substantial influence (Davin and

Lynd 1979–1980; Davin 1989). The real question, then, is not why such broad class struggles and the formation of independent working-class political organizations have not taken place (since, of course, they have); rather, the question is why they were so comparatively short-lived, why they were repressed or unsuccessful, why they did not lead to the formation of a more enduring national form of class-based organization. And it is from this perspective that the historical political weakness of the American working class is best examined.[18]

By what criteria can one select the critical periods or turning points in American political development. One criterion is easily agreed to: Each critical turning point must have a decisive impact on the way the country is governed and ruled and on social relations. In addition, I will argue that at each such juncture, social—usually class—conflict was at a high level. I will argue further that questions of race were central to the outcome of the struggles. The resolution of each of these conflicts led to altered social and political relations in general, new arrangements of social control, and a reorganized system of racial domination and subordination. It is important to emphasize that the identification and analysis of critical periods of American political development, as well as the configuration of the criteria used to identify these periods, are the central organizing feature and theme of much of this book. In particular, the argument that race was central to each of the critical turning points is the distinguishing—and undoubtedly the most controversial—feature of my analysis. By these criteria, I identify five periods:

The first such critical period was during the colonial era, when the southern colonies turned from indentured servitude of people of all ethnic groups and nationalities as the main source of labor to Black slaves. It was at this time that the color line was drawn and racial identities, which continue to this day, were established. A system of white supremacy in laws, customs, and social relations was established, developed, and enforced.

The second period was the Revolutionary War/constitutional period, in which the nature of what constituted political freedom and democracy was fixed. The role of slaves and slave owners within the polity was codified; and notions of states' rights, divided government, and property rights were institutionalized. In all these aspects, I will argue, slavery and race were central.

The third great turning point was the Civil War/Reconstruction era, which emancipated the slaves and destroyed the national power of the southern slave-owning class. The war was over slavery and, later, the role of the ex-slaves within the polity. The South formed a new system of labor, based on a changed white supremacy that dominated the country as a whole well into the next century.

The fourth critical moment in American political development was the Populist one, out of which came the System of 1896, which solidified the rule of northern business and the national political dominance of the Republican Party for almost four decades. Political participation for the lower classes, North and South, was restricted. Segregation became more rigid in both the North and the South. An era of conservative rule was established as America's ruling classes took up more fully the "white man's burden" at home and abroad.

The fifth critical period in the United States was the Depression/New Deal era. This period marked the rise of industrial unions, broad social policies at the federal level, and the beginning of the breakup of the old Jim Crow. Politics and social relations, however, were only partially transformed. And the contradictions and legacies, the successes and failures, of the Depression/New Deal era continue to shape the politics of the United States today despite the immense changes in the economy, culture, race and gender relations, and almost everything else.

Each of these periods installed new or modified systems of racial domination and new methods of white domination. The key to understanding and solving the old conundrum of American exceptionalism—the peculiarities of American politics and the political weakness of its working class—is the interplay between class and race. Race is the key to unraveling the secret of American exceptionalism, but it is also much more. A focus on exceptionalism only gets us so far. Race has been the central ingredient, not merely in undermining solidarity when broad struggles have erupted, not merely in dividing workers, but also in providing an alternative white male nonclass worldview and structure of identity that have exerted their force during both stable and confrontational times. It has provided the everyday framework in which labor has been utilized, controlled, and exploited by those who have employed it. And race has been behind many of the supposed principles of American government (most notably states' rights) that are regarded as sacred by some people today.

My hypothesis about the reasons for the inability of U.S. workers to develop sustained forms of class organization and consciousness focuses on white supremacy. I make several claims: First, the system of white supremacy has played a central role in all the critical turning points of U.S. politics from colonial times to the present. This, in fact, is the main thesis and continuing thread of this book. Second, the development of the system of white supremacy and the ideology used to justify it originate from and are based in the socio-economic system. Third, the primary function of both the system and the ideology has been, on the one hand, to control and exploit African-American (and by extension other nonwhite) labor; on the other hand, it has been to control white workers, isolating them from their potential allies among nonwhites. Fourth, I wish to suggest that the system of white supremacy and the ideology of white chauvinism used to justify it have not merely kept African-Americans and other nonwhites oppressed, not only weakened their organizations. The system and the ideology have also been detrimental for white workers in two ways: On the one hand, the system of white supremacy has been a major impediment to the development of a sustained, solidaristic, class-based labor movement; on the other hand, it has often hurt white workers in their immediate economic interests. Fifth, there have been many economic, political, ideological and other institutional supports for the pervasiveness of white supremacist ideology and beliefs. These factors have played a central role in keeping workers from organizing on a class basis. Sixth, even with these latter factors, the failure to recognize the importance of white supremacy and the unwillingness of white workers, white labor leaders, and all too often, white radicals to confront it head on have been a primary factor in keeping workers from organizing on a class basis. Seventh, a number of the highlights of labor struggle, however, when class consciousness and organization seemed to be blooming, have been accompanied by strong committments to placing the fight against racial discrimination at the top of the political agenda. At key junctures, I will attempt to draw some of the lessons about racial domination in the United States and the possibilities for overcoming it.

Before proceeding with this agenda, however, I must make a small caveat: All broad historical analyses are inevitably fraught with difficulties. It is unlikely that any one investigator might have detailed knowledge, even where possible, of all the periods that she or he discusses. I certainly make no such claim and am painfully aware that in certain areas, I may be skimming along on thin ice. Even less possible, however, is doing justice to the full range of issues, to various nuances and complexities with which a more detailed, limited focus would inevitably deal. Such is especially the case in a book that still bears many of the birthmarks of its origin as a lengthy article, originally based on a conference talk. One could, of course, lace one's analysis with a large number of hedges and qualifications, being noncommittal on various controversial points. My purpose, however, is to present a broad hypothesis, suggesting its wide applicability. Thus, I have deemed it better to attempt to state things sharply, to take positions on a large number of controversial issues, to range over a wide scope, and to err on the side of overstatement rather than to cover my tracks by making things even less clear, realizing that I am skipping merrily through the minefields in which more knowledgeable specialists cautiously tread, hoping not to set off too many unpleasant and potentially embarrassing explosions.[19]

How, one might ask, can such a broad, multifaceted hypothesis be carefully examined. How does one decide whether this hypothesis or one of the other hypotheses is most adequate? Here, of course, I only wish to suggest its plausibility. The proper approach to a fair evaluation, however, similar in certain respects to the method relied on in the physical sciences for confirming and rejecting broad theories and hypotheses, should be based on a comparison of this hypothesis with other plausible candidates, including those theories of race and the approaches to American political development already discussed in this introduction. We would want to know for each theory whether it is able to account for the most important facts and fundamental events of U.S. history. We would also want to assess the degree to which each candidate leads its adherents to gloss over, omit, or distort important aspects of reality. That is, does it do violence to the facts? Finally, in a fair comparison, we want to know how it fares generally in relation to its competitors, which theory makes the most sense of the problems it aims to solve.[20] My burden here will be to give sufficient facts and arguments to suggest the plausibility of each aspect of the hypothesis throughout the course of American political development.[21]

1. Biological differences in receptivity to diseases, genetic proclivities to skin cancer, or even propensities to heart disease are of a different category and are not unusual forms of within-species variations. For a penetrating analysis of the history of intelligence testing, see Stephen J. Gould's *Mismeasure of Man* (1981). For a comprehensive and perhaps exhaustive discussion of the Bell Curve, see *The Bell Curve Debate*, edited by Russell Jacoby and Naomi Glauberman (1995) as well as *Inequality by Design* by Claude S. Fischer et al. (1996). For a wide-ranging discussion of biology and human nature, see Richard Lewontin et al., *Not in Our Genes* (1984); for a classic summary of the relationship between genetics and racial and ethnic groups, see Richard Lewontin, *The Genetic Basis of Evolutionary Change* (1974).

2. For a detailed analysis and brilliant, devastating critique of both Degler and Jordan, see Allen (1994:4–14). For a somewhat surprising, uncritical acceptance of Jordan's argument, see Nash and Weiss (1970:11, 18); and Nash (1990:10–11). Tocqueville seems also to have held this

view, as Fredrickson (1971:22) incisively argues.

3. Omi and Winant are often quite favorable, for example, to W. E. B. Du Bois, even as he identified himself as a Marxist, and the Italian Marxist Antonio Gramsci. On the other hand, they attempt to sharply distinguish themselves from a crude form of Marxism that they see as class reductionist and economic determinist, rarely including more sophisticated versions in their critiques and discussions. One hardly knows what to think when Winant gives a listing of early twentieth–century activists and intellectuals who challenged race as a natural phenomenon (the list includes the Chicago school of sociology and American nationalists, of whom Marcus Garvey was one); the only group that is qualified in a negative way is "a few Marxists (whose perspectives had their own limitations)" (Winant 1994:13).

4. For the most prominent statement of this position, see Bonacich (1972, 1976, 1979, 1980).

5. See Boorstin (1958). For the quotes and discussions of Boorstin, see Novick

(1988:327–34); for a trenchant analysis and critique of Boorstin's writings, see Lemisch (1975, passim).

6. The Confederate general most forgotten in accounts of the Civil War is James Longstreet, who after the war became a supporter of Reconstruction and an outspoken champion of rights for African-Americans. When he died in 1903, the Daughters of the Confederacy refused to send flowers to his funeral. To this day, there are no statues of him in the South (Foner 1988:298).

7. Contrary to Speaker Gingrich's assertions in his recent course, the term American exceptionalism actually owes its prominence to a debate within the Communist Party of the United States (CP) and the Communist International (Commintern) during the late 1920s. Jay Lovestone and his associates, who took over the leadership of the CP in 1927, albeit with strong minority opposition, attempted to justify the weakness of their party and its need for a "non-revolutionary" American approach on the basis of the historic strength and adaptability of U.S. capitalism. His opponents in the U.S. party, eventually supported by the Commintern, accused him of a break with Marxism that they labeled American exceptionalism. During the late 1920s, the 1930s, and the 1940s, large numbers of U.S. intellectuals were involved in the radical movement in this country; many eventually became prominent, albeit often relatively conservative, academics. They did, however, provide the transmission belt for this terminology to become absorbed into the mainstream of academic social science literature.

8. For introductions to this literature, see Allen (1968), Laslett and Lipset (1974), and Lipset (1977, 1996).

9. Or, in Werner Sombart's (1976) classic formulation:"Why no socialism in the United States?"

10. The most recent period of insurgency, the 1960s, for example, brought forth a whole new interpretive literature. For works explicitly on American exceptionalism from this genre, see Allen (1968, 1994), Katznelson (1978), Karabel (1979), and Markovits (1987). For works that emphasize class possibilities in American labor history, see the extensive review in Brody (1979). For detailed reviews of recent research on the CP, see Goldfield (1980 and 1985) and Wald (1995).

11. For more detailed discussion of these and other comparisons and a discussion of the special case of France, including the comparability of the figures, see Goldfield (1989a). For the up-to-date comparative figures cited above, I have used unpublished data from the U.S. Department of Labor, Bureau of Labor Statistics, Office of Productivity and Technology, Division of Foreign Labor Statistics.

12. For critiques of the usefulness of the notion of American exceptionalism, see Zolberg (1986) and Wilentz (1984).

13. For comprehensive but slightly outdated comparative figures, see Mackie and Rose (1974); see also the discussions in Burnham (1982).

14. For a definitive discussion of the debates over these issues and a careful analysis see Chapter 4 of Piven and Cloward (1988). For further analyses, see Burnham (1982), Teixiera (1987, 1992), Conway (1991), Kleppner (1982), and Rosenstone and Hansen (1993).

15. William Z. Foster (1952:33) notes that in the 1850s, Marxists were already concerned about the lack of class consciousness of U.S. workers, especially in contrast with their high degree of trade union militancy.

16. I first became aware of the arguments over American exceptionalism from a pithy and cogent piece by Allen (1968), in which a brief analysis of some of the above explanations is presented (see also Allen 1994). A comprehensive discussion of these and other theories may also be found in Lipset (1977); convenient excerpts for many positions are available in a collection by Laslett and Lipset (1974).

17. Broad critiques may be found in Allen (1968), Lipset (1977), and

Katznelson (1981).

18. My understanding of the problem in this fashion relies heavily on Allen's seminal essay (Allen 1968).

19. For my own small part, I can only say that I am working on a much more detailed, treatment of many of the themes discussed here for one historical turning point, the 1930s and 1940s.

20. These issues are discussed in the philosophy of science literature, e.g., in Lakatos 1970, especially pp. 132–138, 154–177; Putnam 1978; and R. Miller 1988.

21. I make no claims to complete originality of this hypothesis. A compelling version was put forth eloquently and convincingly over sixty years ago by W. E. B. Du Bois in Black Reconstruction. Since the 1960s, Theodore Allen (in several articles and in one recent and another forthcoming major work), Lerone Bennett, and others have put forward chunks of this hypothesis. Yet, like the attention paid to white supremacy itself, the hypothesis and its supporting arguments

PART I

Critical Turning Points
in Early U.S. History

CHAPTER 1

Early History of the United States

THE COLONIAL ERA

> I think it was in Africa that I came more clearly to see the close con-
> nection between race and wealth.... And then gradually this thought
> was metamorphized into a realization that the income-bearing value
> of race prejudice was the cause and not the result of theories of race
> inferiority; that particularly in the United States the income of the
> Cotton Kingdom based on Black slavery caused the passionate belief
> in Negro inferiority and the determination to enforce it even by arms.
> W. E. B. Du Bois 1940:129.

The proper place to start in the examination of the first part of our
hypothesis about the central role of white supremacy is at the beginning, with the development of colonialism in the New World. During the
sixteenth and seventeenth centuries, the Portugese, Spanish, Dutch, French,
and English began to explore and settle the Americas. Supported by investors
and their respective governments, each nationally affiliated contingent of
explorers and settlers sought to discover wealth and amass fortunes, both
for themselves and for their various sponsors.

The New World was, of course, already inhabited by a diverse range of
peoples, ranging from primitive tribes of nomadic hunters to the highly
sophisticated and developed Aztec and Inca societies. At first, the riches garnered by the Europeans were gold and silver, largely stolen from the Aztecs
and other Indian peoples. It is estimated that Spain alone, between 1500 and
1650, extracted 180 tons of gold and 160,000 tons of silver from the Americas
(Levine et al. 1989:8–10).

British preconceptions about the original natives in the New World
were, to be sure, complex. There is much evidence, however, that the attitudes of the early colonists in both New England and Virginia were initially positive and not especially racist. This can be seen in the descriptions of
Richard Hakluyt, the leading publicist for British colonialism. It is also displayed in the actions of early explorers and colonists whose open-mind-
edness on such questions was reinforced by economic interests, especially
their desire for good trading relations and their frequent dependence on
the natives for food and survival.

In the long run, however, the main wealth in the New World was neither precious metals nor bartered goods. Rather, it was the vast quantities of fertile land and the timber and crops that could be taken from that land. As the British settlers began to make use of some of it and set their sights on additional territory already inhabited by earlier occupants, conflict developed. With superior weaponry and unlimited appetite, the colonists started to take this land for themselves. They were also aided by the rapid spread of European diseases against which the Indians had developed no defenses, a phenomenon referred to by some as "ecological imperialism" (i.e., disease as a means of conquest; Crosby 1986). The British colonialists justified these aggressive intrusions—the seizing of land, mass murder, and the genocidal destruction of the fabric of life of another people—by the development of a racist imagery and ideology about the Native Americans that grew out of their preexisting ethnocentrism. They also developed a supporting "myth of emptiness" that peoples who did not possess British notions of private property did not really own their land and were not therefore really being displaced (Blaut 1993:15; Cronon 1983).

The slaughter of native peoples and the stealing of their land were to be a continuous feature of U.S. history during the seventeenth, eighteenth, and nineteenth centuries, adding a violent, racist edge to our culture from the very beginning, perhaps captured in a common line from 1950s Western movies: "The only good Indian is a dead Indian." Although various images and rationales were used to explain these actions, the underlying factor was economic. Those who look primarily to cultural factors, especially certain undeniable predispositions in pre-colonial British and European culture, miss the decisive change in attitudes that took place and what motivated the transformation.[1] The land taken from the Native Americans, however, was of no use by itself. The productive use of this land required labor. Unlike the situation in England and in various parts of Europe, where a ready supply of labor was available in the form of peasants and former serfs who had been forced from their hereditary land, labor had to be imported to the Americas. This point must be underscored. The demand for exploitable labor is the continuing thread for understanding the main contours of the race question in the United States throughout its history. It is also the key to understanding the relation between race and class.

The British did make an attempt to use the indigenous Native American population for labor, but this proved unworkable. For various reasons, Indians were intractable or simply died (Mannix and Cowley 1962:61). As John Hope Franklin argues, "The greater susceptibility of Indians to diseases carried by Europeans and the simple economic background of the

37

Indians which did not prepare them for the disciplined regime of the plantation system" made them unsuitable (Franklin 1969:47). To this one might add that in many instances, the early military strength of the tribes was considerable and that those who were forced to labor might escape into areas where there were safe refuges and whose territory they knew far better than their captors did (Usner 1992). Finally, the policy of killing the Indians and driving them away from colonial settlements "proved incompatible with their widespread employment as slaves" (Kolchin 1993:8). Thus, labor had to be imported from abroad.

The Portuguese, Spanish, and Dutch, with small populations at home, could supply few laborers from their domestic reserves. They soon began to rely on Africans who had been bought, kidnapped, or stolen from their homeland. The English, with their huge surplus of unemployed laborers, dispossessed churchmen, paupers, convicts, beggars, vagabonds, thieves, highway robbers, pickpockets, prostitutes, unwanted orphans, and despised "riffraff," were the only colonizing power with a large labor surplus at home to send to the colonies. And this they did by enticement (including the promise of eventual free parcels of land or, in New England, religious freedom), trickery (adults gotten drunk and children lured on ships with candy (E. Williams 1966:11; Mannix and Cowley 1962:56), and coercion (sentencing, kidnapping, and in at least one case, sending several hundred orphans against their will). The distinctive feature of colonial labor on the Anglo-American mainland throughout the seventeenth century was that it was made up in good part of British and European indentured servants, in contrast with the primarily African composition of the labor force in other British and European colonies (Allen 1978).[2] These laborers would eventually be referred to as "white," although before 1680 the term was not a common one for racial or ethnic identification (Jordan 1977:95).

Two questions that are central for understanding race and race relations in the United States have preoccupied and divided historians of colonial North America: First, what caused racism here? Was it largely a consequence of Black enslavement, or was it a pre-existing condition that led rather naturally to slavery? Second, what factors are responsible for the rapid, large-scale change in the composition of the colonial labor force in the late seventeenth century from one consisting largely of British and European bond servants to one consisting largely of Black lifelong hereditary slaves?[3] Early attitudes of European colonists toward Blacks are a matter of some dispute. Yet, there exist clear signs that the British were willing to regard them as equals. Morgan describes the alliance of the English explorer and pirate Sir Francis Drake, who developed a long-term relation with the Cimarrons, a several-thousand-member non-white Panamanian colony of ex-slaves.

Together, Drake's followers and the Cimarrons fought the Spanish, ate and celebrated together, and in general, acted in a manner that suggested little racial prejudice. A number of historians (including the Handlins, Morgan, Bennett, and Allen) have convincingly argued that slavery, bondage, and servitude were not initially racial in the United States. Many of the original group of African bondsmen (those who first arrived in 1619 in the Virginia colony and those who soon followed them to Virginia and the other Anglo-American mainland colonies) seem to have been freed by various means, including manumission and expiration of their terms of servitude, in the same manner as their British and European brethren.

As historical research makes clear, the passage of early Irish, English, and European bond servants to the New World was often as horrific and deadly as that later suffered by African slaves (E. Williams 1966:13 and Mannix and Cowley 1962:57–58, for example, all underscore this point). The conditions of labor for the Africans and non-Africans when they arrived were equally oppressive. Even relatively short-term bond servants were held in conditions of near enslavement; with no similar protection of their rights as existed in England, servants could be mutilated, tortured, and killed with no punishment to the perpetrators (Morgan 1975:116–127 passim; Kolchin 1993:9). Scholars have pointed to a large amount of evidence that Black and white laborers in the early colonial period accepted each other as equals. As Edmund Morgan summarizes, "Black and white serving the same master worked, ate, and slept together, and together shared in escapades, escapes, and punishments" (Morgan 1975:155). In describing the working conditions of African-American bond servants, he says, "There is no evidence before 1660 that they were subjected to more severe discipline than other servants" (Morgan, 1975:154). Even sexual relations seem to have been on a relatively equal basis. "In 1649 William Watts, a white man, and Mary, a Negro servant, were required to do penance for fornication, like any other couple, by standing in the church at Elizabeth River with the customary white sheet and white wand" (Morgan 1975:155). And as Lerone Bennett argues, "It was not at all unusual for a white master to force a white woman servant to marry a Black male servant. Nor was it unusual for a white master to give a Black man a position of authority over white male and white female servants" (Bennett 1975:18). As late as 1714, one can find Irish and African servants being offered together for sale (Mannix and Cowley 1962:59).4 Breen and Innes (1980) describe relatively equal, respectful relations between free white and free Black landowners on Maryland's Eastern Shore between 1640 and 1676.

None of these facts is meant to deny that there were anti-Black sentiments among whites or that there was not some degree of differential treatment. Whether or not these attitudes were more extensive than the negative attitudes the English held toward other foreigners is the subject of scholarly debate. Further, the existence of African slavery in other colonies could hardly have been without its influence. Those who hold the psycho-cultural thesis, however, assert that these anti-Black sentiments were primary. In my opinion, the psycho-culturalists unsystematically and impressionistically look at English literature and other texts and conflate British attitudes in other North American colonies, especially Barbados, where the number of whites were few. It is important to stress that the psycho-culturalists do not deny that there was a large-scale change in the system of racial domination and subordination toward the end of the seventeenth century. Rather, they see these changes as evolving from, and an almost inevitable development out of, pre-existing racist attitudes.

In any case, it was only in the period from 1660 to 1710 that hereditary lifetime African slavery became widely utilized. In order for this slavery to become fully institutionalized, the initial English tolerance as expressed in the words and actions of explorer Sir Francis Drake and early British colonial leader Richard Hakluyt and in the easy relations between African and white bondsmen had to be defeated.

Culturally rooted explanations fail to convincingly address these issues. If cultural and psychological prejudices against non-whites were initially weak, what made them become so strong later in the United States? As Allen has argued, if long-standing racial and ethnic prejudice was central to human nature, why were Jews (who were, along with Muslims, the ultimate non-Christians) and the historically despised and abundant Irish laborers not considered viable candidates for enslavement (Allen 1994:7)? The disjunction between long-standing prejudice and eventual enslavement is a theoretical problem for the psycho-cultural view. Further, if the prejudices on the Anglo-American mainland were traceable to long-term attitudes rooted in English culture, why was the color line so sharp (and one-dimensional) in the British Anglo-American mainland colonies but so fluid (and multileveled) in the British Caribbean, where there was a clear social place for children of mixed parentage? Casting the net wider, we might ask why in Brazil did there exist social mobility for Afro-Brazilians? Again, these facts create problems for culturally rooted explanations.5

These early characteristics of race relations and servitude set the contours for much of the early labor struggles in the late seventeenth-century colonial period. Contrary to the views of Louis Hartz, Daniel Boorstin, and other proponents of American exceptionalism (in whose footsteps Newt Gingrich, Rush Limbaugh, and other current pundits march), protest and struggle by the lower classes can be traced to the very beginnings of the Anglo-American colonies on these shores. Eventually, colonial society was shaken by a series of lower-class revolts between 1660 and 1683, many of these taking place in Virginia, the wealthiest, most populous, most important colony, the home to the families of most of the future Founding Fathers (Morgan 1975:246). The underlying causes of the rebellions were the oppressive conditions of labor and life of the current and newly freed bond servants. During the early years of the colony, a majority of the bond servants died of disease and overwork before their terms of servitude were up. Their higher rates of survival after 1650 led the laboring population to chafe at their degrading working and living conditions and at their lack of opportunities for mobility once their servitude was over. Both their circumstances and their opportunities were held in check by the colonial elite, a corrupt, avaricious group of large-scale tobacco planters who completely controlled the colonial government. The most significant revolt during the early colonial period was Bacon's Rebellion in 1676. Nathaniel Bacon, himself a member of the Virginia colonial elite but involved in a dispute with the governor, was pressed by the logic of events to offer freedom to servants and slaves who would join him. Bacon forced the House of Burgesses to pass a series of democratic measures, burned Jamestown to the ground (after Governor Berkeley had accused Bacon of treason), and then temporarily forced the governor and his allies to flee the colony. Both African-Americans and whites responded to Bacon's egalitarian appeal in large numbers.[6] Even after the death of Bacon from dissentery effectively undermined the rebellion, over 100 Black and white followers stuck together to the end, refusing to yield.[7]

One of the most remarkable pieces of evidence that Virginia's leaders viewed their labor force as a whole, taking for granted the rebellious cooperation and solidarity of slaves, servants, and poor freemen, Black and white, is their lack of comment on the interracial character of Bacon's Rebellion. No attempt was made to play Black and white laborers against one another. Divide-and-conquer tactics would almost certainly have been used if the elites had believed they would work. Although Bacon was attacked for a host of sins, real and imagined, including avarice, hypocrisy, pride, and atheism, no one attacked him for the interracial character of his supporters nor made any racial slurs that survive in the records. Breen notes that Grantham, the English army captain, seemed to have been more conscious of the interracial character of the rebels than the local planters were (Breen 1973:11). Those of us who study labor and popular struggles in the nineteenth and twentieth centuries will recognize that in terms of race relations, this was a far different racial world than that which developed later. Thus, one must fairly conclude that racial attitudes prior to the 1680s were far different from those that developed later.

Edmund Morgan, in discussing the class resentment in Virginia, argues:

> It is questionable how long Virginia could have continued on this course, keeping men in servitude for years and then turning them free to be frustrated by the engrossers of land, by the collectors of customs, by the county courts, by their elected representatives, by the council, and, above all, by the king himself...." (Morgan 1975:292)

Class struggle at this time was anything but mild, and the liberal consensus was weak indeed.

Now, there are several theories about how, why, and when the transformation of the Virginia labor force took place. Each has certain loose ends and fragments that leave it open to criticism. I have already argued that pre-existing racial prejudice is insufficient to explain the early period of relative racial equality, the later rapid turn toward Black labor and racist ideology, or the reasons why other victims of prior intense prejudice, including Jews, Muslims, and the Irish were not also enslaved. Two other, not necessarily exclusive arguments bear examination. The first is a purely economic analysis. It argues that by the 1680s, there was a dwindling supply of white English bond servants available on the market because of a combination of improving wages and labor market conditions in England and declining fortunes for English servants in Virginia. At the same time, there was a lowered price for Black slaves because of both economic bad times in the Caribbean and increased competition of slave traders. This led planters reluctantly to turn to Black slave labor (see Menard 1977, 1985; Menard, Carr, and Walsh 1991; Menard and McKusker 1985; Kulikoff 1986; Galenson 1981; Kolchin 1993:11–13).

Although this economic argument has its compelling features (for surely the planters were interested in the cost of labor and continuing, if not increased, profits), there are several problematic features: First, availability of servants should not have been a problem for those forcibly obtained. Why were not the Irish, who were seized by the English for numerous other purposes and even sold in Europe during this period, shipped to the North American mainland in greater numbers, at least as a supplement to Black slaves. Second, pegging the declining supply to voluntary choice by potential immigrants assumes a knowledge of comparable labor markets in Virginia and Great Britain (or, in economic terms, perfect information on the part of the British lower classes), which is at best a dubious assumption. Nevertheless, figures do indicate an increase in the cost of indentured servants relative to Black slaves (Menard 1977:372), suggesting that economic ingredients exerted some influence.

One is struck, however, by both the timing and the rapidity of the transformation from a primarily white to a primarily Black labor force in the southern colonies. Menard looks at Chesapeake counties in both Maryland and Virginia and finds a similar pattern. He notes, following Morgan, that in York, a typical Virginia tobacco-growing county, servants outnumbered slaves in the 1670s by approximately two to one, a proportion that was reversed by the late 1680s (Menard 1977:362). Given the alleged preference for white indentured servants that the proponents of the economic argument all impute to the planters, something else besides slightly higher prices for their traditional sources of labor must have been at work. The economic argument is not strong enough to carry the burden of such a swift and dramatic trans-formation. Such an immense change suggests that some more pressing fac-tors on the part of planters existed which overcame their supposed prefer-ence for white indentured servants in the face of only slightly higher prices.

Theodore Allen, following Morgan, argues that it was the problematic feature of social control of the white labor force that led to the urgency of the transformation (Allen 1975, 1994). To maintain and increase their wealth, British colonialists, American capitalists, merchants, and plantation owners not only needed laborers but needed to control them as well. The many rebel-lions between 1660 and 1683, some interracial, many largely white (both former bondsmen, now free, and present bondsmen), of which Bacon's Rebellion was the most important, convinced the plantation owners and other elites that the labor force needed to be divided so as to be better con-trolled. The supply of Black labor was increased, and a white racial identi-ty was accentuated. It did not hurt, I might add, that there were perhaps some economic incentives involved in this switch.

Allen argues that what is needed to maintain control of the laboring population in a colony is a social buffer between the ruling classes and the most exploited laborers. It was the numerical ratio of poor whites to Blacks that led to the creation of a white social buffer and the sharp drawing of the color line (i.e., any known African ancestry made one Black) in what was to become the United States.[8] Where fewer whites existed, as in Haiti, Barbados, and Brazil, it was necessary to create other forms of social buffers, mulattoes where their numbers were sufficient, free Blacks where they were not. This I believe, following Allen and Fredrickson, is the key to some of the central differences in racial/skin color classifications in South Africa, Brazil, the Anglo-Caribbean, and various former Spanish colonies.[9] The uniqueness of the American system of racial identities, where any known African ancestry defines one as Black, along with the limited exceptions (South Carolina until the 1850s and southern Louisiana up to the present day where creoles and mulattoes have had separate places in the social struc-ture), are based on the unique compositional and control problems of the colonial labor force in the North American continental colonies (see Davis

(1991) for a highly informative, if uneven, discussion of the color line in the United States). Those who look to the cultural differences in the colonial motherland for the major explanation of the differences in the colonies give a fundamentally flawed analysis. The clue to their problems is the stress on the differences between places such as Brazil and the North American mainland (which were, of course, colonized by Portugal and Britain, respectively) while ignoring the differences among various British colonies.

The social control theory, buttressed by economic arguments, accords well with most of the facts, but it suffers certain problems with timing. Although the large-scale importation of slaves did not begin until after the major rebellions, the initial implementation of racially differential laws began earlier. One must, therefore, postulate at least some differences in the way elites viewed their different forms of labor, even before either the economics of labor supply or social control were perceived as serious problems. This important qualification, although not conducive to a neat theory, does not in my opinion vitiate the overall argument.

How the system of white supremacy was implemented is described in detail by both Theodore Allen and Edmund Morgan. Public policy was consciously designed to develop racist contempt on the part of whites for Blacks and Indians. A 1661 Virginia law stated that if an English bond servant ran away with an African slave, the English servant would have to serve time both for his or her own absense and for that of the slave (Allen 1975:6; Morgan 1975:311). In 1670, the law forbid free African-Americans and Indians, even if baptized, from owning Christian (read "white") servants (Morgan 1975:331). In 1680, it gave a penalty of thirty lashes to any slaves who hit "any christian," even if the latter were a servant (Morgan 1975:331), allowing white servants "to bully slaves, without fear of retaliation, thus placing them psychologically on a par with masters" (Morgan 1975:331). Mixed marriages seem to have not been unusual even in the 1670s and 1680s. It was only in 1691 that a law was passed limiting intermarriage; but even here, according to Morgan, the main intent was to prevent out-of-wedlock relations between white women and nonwhite men (Morgan 1975:335). In 1705, a law was passed ordering the dismemberment of unruly slaves but forbidding the whipping of naked white Christian servants (Morgan 1975:331). These laws, whose purpose was to create a sharpened color line, implementing differences in the social condition and political rights of Blacks, whose intent was to separate poor whites from Blacks by making the former feel superior, went deeply against the grain of previous attitudes and practice, according to both Morgan and Allen.

It was during this period in the late seventeenth century that the shift to African labor began in earnest. Allen argues that the change to larger percentages of African labor was accompanied by laws in the early eighteenth century requiring the importation and employment of white servants. Although white servants were still highly profitable, it was the need to have them serve in the militia, to be used as "a basic means of social control" over the African hereditary, lifetime servants that had risen to the fore. And it was, according to Allen, a main purpose of white supremacist laws to encourage the poor whites to fulfill this role (Allen 1975:7–8).

By the late 1680s and early 1690s, the rural revolts and threats to the social order from the lower classes were a thing of the past. With a stable social system based on white supremacy in place, the southern economy prospered. The centrality of slavery to the subsequent development of the early colonial economy is partially reflected in the fact that Virginia in particular and the South in general were the most prosperous, most rapidly growing part of North America.[10]

Not only was the South dependent on slavery, but a good deal of the economic prosperity of the northern Anglo-American colonies was dependent on their commercial dealings with the wealthier South (Robinson 1979:55). Thus, the economic wealth of the South and the country as a whole became dependent on the brutal forced exploitation of Black labor, and the whole system of racial slavery and white supremacy that supported it.[11] Slave patrols, the auction block, the whip, unpunishable rape and concubinage of African and African-American women by white masters, disenfranchisement and harassment of free Blacks were all rooted, on the one hand, in the need to control and exploit a cheap Black labor force and, on the other, in the need to keep Black and white labor divided and separate. Rebellions by whites in the South continued to take place in the middle decades of the eighteenth century. Unlike the seventeenth-century revolts in colonial Virginia, however, even the most violent and popular ones dissipated quickly. As Levine and his associates argue, despite the "profound tensions" dividing southern society, "Racism provided the glue that kept white southern society from flying apart. Through the Civil War and even beyond, wealthy southern landowners were able to convince poor whites that the division between white and black meant more than that between rich and poor" — an overarching view, I might add, that I will find some significant reasons to qualify at key historical junctures (Levine et al. 1989:38, 77).

Thus, white supremacy and racial slavery were developed, not primarily for cultural or psychological purposes, because of previously existing racial prejudice, but because they advanced the most powerful economic interests in the colony and the colonial homeland. As the quote from W. E. B. Du Bois at the beginning of this chapter suggests, racist theories of Black inferiority and racist attitudes were used to justify a system of racial domination and

subordination that gave power and profit to white southern plantation owners. It is this bedrock that must be kept in mind.

The establishment of lifelong hereditary Black bondage as the primary
source of labor in the southern colonies was a critical turning point in
American political development. Certain aspects of this labor system and
the ideology of white supremacy that was developed to justify it are still
with us today. Other aspects have changed, evolved, or even been eliminated. All have left their permanent mark on current U.S. society.

Economically, the system of racial slavery, designed to extract immense
profits from low-cost, coerced labor was the bedrock of the southern economy until after the Civil War. In altered form, after Emancipation, much of
the South continued to rely on subjugated, coerced, low-cost Black labor in
agriculture and related industries until the 1950s and 1960s. Despite the elimination of many of the legal and social props for this racial system of labor,
its legacy is still with us. As I will argue later, certain programs from the
New Deal era along with the manner in which the plantation system and
its associated low-wage rural industries, especially woodworking and lumber, met their demise laid the basis for the high Black youth unemployment
and the general conditions that exist in urban ghetto areas today.

The legal system was designed to keep the Black slave population in
place; laws were enacted affecting not only slaves but free Blacks as well that
included restrictions on property holding, political participation, and intermarriage; fugitive slave laws and procedures for catching escaped slaves;
denial of rights of Blacks, free or enslaved, to testify or participate in court;
and restrictions on their access to public places. Along with the laws, customs and social mores were established that mandated servile behavior and
let violence, murder, and rape by whites against African-Americans go
unpunished. Police, courts, and judges often exercised deadly partiality
against Blacks, a situation that often grew worse after emancipation, when
there were no longer slave owners who had an interest in limiting the mistreatment of their property. Although the laws have been largely repealed
and the customs undermined, their legacy continues in many respects,
including the high levels of police brutality against nonwhites, differential
drug laws, and the uneven application of the death penalty, the latter varying immensely based on the race of the victim and the perpetrator.

Plantation owners attempted to enlist the support of lower-class whites
in the control of the Black workforce, during slavery and after, hiring them
in positions as overseers, supervisors, guards, slave patrollers, and police.
Though permanent employment in these positions involved only a small
percentage of the white lower classes, at certain times larger numbers
became involved in social control. Under slavery, bounties were offered to

all whites for the capture of runaways; large numbers of poor whites were also employed periodically as members of slave patrols. The system was designed to elevate the status (if not the economic situation) of white laborers. They were granted the rights of political participation denied Blacks, treated more leniently by the police and courts, allowed social rights and public access, and generally accorded a higher position. In certain arenas, particularly after the abolition of slavery, they were given preferences for higher-skilled jobs, be it in industry, in agriculture, or as railway engineers, and even for low-skilled jobs in the textile industry, although these jobs invariably paid far less than similar jobs in other parts of the country. White lower-class poverty and misery was worse in the South, where the differentiation between whites and Blacks was most extreme.

It was not just the carrot of various privileges that divided lower-class whites from African-Americans in the South. Lower-class whites also faced numerous levels of penalties for transgressing the racial divide. They might be socially ostracized, shunned by neighbors, former friends, and kin. Their jobs, future prospects, property, and credit might be placed in jeopardy. And for those who attempted to exhibit acts of class solidarity with Blacks or, even worse, to take the lead in organizing and leading such struggles, harsher physical punishments were sure to come. White supporters of Black Reconstruction, biracial Populist and Socialist activities, interracial labor organizing in the 1930s, and the 1960s civil rights movement were among the many victims of lynching and brutal murder. Though much of this violence has been eliminated, it lives on in the form of the church burnings, vigilantism, and right-wing terror against African-Americans and other minorities that randomly rear their heads today.

The white racial identity whose formation began at this critical turning point during the late seventeenth century is alive and well today. Those who are "free, white, and twenty-one" believe that they have a moral right to racial preferences over nonwhites in every venue. Whiteness has been analyzed in detail by David Roediger and others. In filling jobs and other positions, there is always the presumption that those who are Black have less intelligence, skill, capability, and character (work ethic, reliability, loyalty). Thus, despite affirmative action programs, it is still true, as African-Americans have historically argued, that they generally have to be far better qualified than whites to obtain opportunities. Further, even when manifestly less qualified, white entitlements exist because of kinship, neighborhood, and friendship networks, as well as preferences based purely on whiteness. What few preferences African-Americans have received from affirmative action programs pale before the privileges and preferences received by whites that are hardly based on merit.

And finally, the drawing of the color line in North America, so untypical of other multiracial societies, is a product of the early colonial era. The exceptions that existed in earlier times have largely been eliminated; even (or especially) those in the Black community have come to accept (and even proclaim) the view that anyone with any known degree of Black ancestory is Black. The only exceptions today seem to be the occasional proclamation of multiracial identities that one sometimes finds on a small number of college campuses and the difficulties in classifying certain Latinos. This so-called one-drop theory (i.e., one drop of Black blood makes one Black) is not followed for any other ethnic or racial group (be it Chinese, Polish, or Mexican); it is a heritage of the context in which racial slavery was established in this country in the late seventeenth century.

The racist ideology that defined Black people as biologically inferior and socially undesirable was developed to justify Black slavery. This racist ideology, in new and contradictory forms, evolved, developed, amplified, and amended, lives on in America today.

It is worth mentioning two points that I will explore more fully later: First, if one buys even a small part of this analysis, it should be clear that whether white workers act in solidarity with Black workers and join with them in racially egalitarian organizations cannot be reduced to questions of whether it is or is not in their immediate interests. The type of hegemony that a system of racial domination exerts is reflected not merely in certain material benefits but also in a wide range of social penalties and psychological supports. Second, despite the seeming completeness of such systems, their hold is never absolute. Hegemony is hard work and rarely complete. Except under the most adverse conditions, individuals and groups of white workers sometimes break with this system; and in times of stress, they occasionally do it in large numbers and quite unexpectedly. But more on this later.

1. Nash straddles the issue somewhat by claiming that the British had dual (i.e., both positive and negative) predispositions; see Nash 1970:2).

2. Morgan notes, however, that the creation of "a sense of community" by British colonists in Virginia was complicated by the existence of a sizable minority of foreigners who included, according to colonial records, Portuguese, Dutch, Spanish, French, Turks, and Africans (Morgan 1975:153).

3. For guidance to the relevant literature, one can consult reviews by Starr (1973); Vaughn (1989), a strong proponent

of the Degler-Jordan thesis; Kolchin (1993: 14–18); and Allen (1994:2–21), a proponent of one version of the socio-economic interpretation.

4. Interestingly, Gunnar Myrdal came to similar conclusions over fifty years ago, before much of the newer historical work had appeared:

The historical literature on this early period also records that the imported Negroes—and the captured Indians—originally were kept in much the same status as the white indentured servants. When later the Negroes were gradually pushed down into chattel slavery while the white servants were allowed to work off their bond, the need was felt, in this Christian country, for some kind of justification above mere economic expediency and the might of the strong. (Myrdal 1944:I:85)

5. Oliver Cox, in a seminal, though largely ignored book, argues that nothing comparable to modern racism existed in the world anywhere prior to 1500 and the colonialization of the darker peoples of the earth (Cox 1970:321–352).

6. The initial dispute between Bacon and Berkeley was over Indian policy. Although Nash sees Bacon's Rebellion as largely fueled by anti-Indian sentiment, the evidence suggests otherwise. Rather, the "giddy multitude"—a phrase used by the Virginia Burgesses to refer to the discontented freemen, bondsmen, and slaves—seemed willing to use any opening to vent their anger against the colonial elites (Nash 1992:123–8). More likely, as Breen argues, "Whatever the aims of Bacon and his lieutenants, there is little evidence their goals were the same as those of their followers. Contemporaries, in fact, believed Bacon had aroused popular fears and frustrations to achieve his own private end" (Breen 1973:9).

7. Bacon's thousands of supporters were demobilized only by trickery. This was accomplished through the skilful and deceitful maneuvering of Governor Berkeley's representative Captain Thomas Grantham. According to Wilcomb E. Washburn, Grantham approached the last group of "400 English and Negroes in arms....Most of the men he persuaded to disperse to their homes, but eighty Negroes and twenty English refused to deliver the arms" (Washburn 1957:88). All this attests to the interracial character of Bacon's armed minions. See Allen (1975) for a detailed analysis.

8. Although some might argue that the house slaves provided such a buffer between masters and field hands, there is little historical evidence to support this supposition. There is also no evidence to suggest that the distinction between house and field slaves was based on color. As Genovese argues, "However much the quadroon and mulatto servants...dominated the Big House of the legend, they did not dominate the Big House of reality" (Genovese 1976: 327). There is also much evidence to show that runaways, rebels, and during the Civil War, Yankee spies were as likely to emanate from the house as from the fields (Genovese 1976:327–365 passim).

9. A parallel argument is given by Fredrickson (1981) in his chapter entitled "Race Mixture and the Color Line," comparing the United States and South Africa. Fredrickson argues that the most extreme contrast with the U.S. system occurred in Indonesia, where the children of Dutch males and Asian females "were officially classified as members of the European or Dutch population" (Fredrickson 1981:96–7). See also Harris (1964) and Degler (1971) for useful comparisons.

10. Virginia was soon to be displaced, but not by a northern colony. According to Donald Robinson, by the middle of the eighteenth century, "South Carolina was the richest colony on the mainland," and not fortuitously, "slavery there the harshest" (D. Robinson 1979:56).

11. There is an immense literature on slavery, much of which is extremely useful and informative. I have found helpful the historiographic essays in Elkins (1959:1–26 and Fredrickson (1988:112–124). See also the introductory essays by Ken Lawrence and George Rawick describing the historiography, collection, and editing of slave narratives (Rawick 1977).

CHAPTER 2

The American Revolution and the Founding of the Union

> The real revolution is more useful and interesting than the make believe one. S. G. Fisher (1912), quoted in Schlesinger (1955:244)

> What to the American slave, is your 4th of July? I answer; a day that reveals to him, more than all other days in the year, the gross injustice and cruelty to which he is the constant victim. To him, your celebration is a sham; your boasted liberty, an unholy license; your national greatness, swelling vanity;...your sermons and thanksgivings ...are, to Him, mere bombast, fraud, deception, impiety, and hypocrisy—a thin veil to cover up crimes which would disgrace a nation of savages. Douglass (1950:II:192)

The American Revolution of 1776–1783 and the subsequent founding of the Republic are acknowledged by virtually all students of American political history to be significant, influential moments, critical turning points in American political development, perhaps in world history. We encounter all the main theoretical approaches in this much-studied and much-written-about area.

One finds, of course, the deification of the revolutionary elites by certain conservatives, some of whom claim—contrary to all known facts—that the Founding Fathers shared their current stance about the intrusion of religion into public life. There are the far more serious scholars, including Bernard Bailyn and Gordon Wood, who see the motive forces in the ideological conflicts and public clarification of ideas by various elites, including Whigs, Republicans, and religious leaders. One also finds the Beards and various Progressive historians who see the struggles of the economic elites —merchants, shippers, bankers, slave owners, and gentry farmers—with each other and with the British as the determining forces.

It has been clear, however, for a long time that there were other major actors in the Revolution, including small farmers and evangelicals. By the 1950s, mainstream historians were emphasizing the importance of lower-class urban mobs (see Schlesinger 1955; Bridenbaugh 1955:113–118, 305–14; Morgan 1956:20–21, 39–40, 46–48,151), about whose relevance Bailyn

(1965:I:581–84) and Wood (1966) concurred a decade later. Though there has been debate about the character and composition of these mobs, it is clear that they included many nonelites. The new social and labor historians have focused on them, reconstructing the world of the urban laboring classes—artisans, mechanics, laborers, seamen or Jack Tars, and indentured servants—asserting their centrality to the Revolution's development. Others have given new details of the role played by free and enslaved Blacks. All these groups had their grievances, demands, forms of action and protest, and influence in the anticolonial movement.

In expanding our knowledge of the actors and forces involved in the American Revolution, the new scholarship has described and analyzed the complexity of the revolutionary process. Alfred Young, who follows the seminal analysis of Carl Becker (1909), in discussing the radicalism of the American Revolution, argues convincingly for distinguishing between two types of radicalism, that with respect to external issues (i.e., the relation to Britain) and that with respect to internal issues, including democratization and the reorganization of social and economic structure of society. In this typology, many wealthy merchants and slave owners, for example, were radical in their desire for a break with Britain but were happy with maintaining intact much of the other political, social, and economic relations of colonial society. At the other extreme, Black slaves were often indifferent to, or at different times and places took different sides on, independence from Britain but were radical about the extension of liberty to all persons, including themselves. Seamen, on the other hand, tended to be radical on both internal and external issues. The same might be said for yeomen farmers in some areas.[1]

The world's first successful anticolonial revolution developed almost inevitably out of the conflict over Great Britain's wish to gain maximum profits from its subservient colonies and the counterposed desire of various strata of the colonies to maintain more benefits and control for themselves. Limits on the economic independence of commercial and planter elites, indebtedness of prosperous merchants and artisans, which in hard times could land them in debtors' prisons, and the extreme economic downturns that affected all colonialists at times, resulting from their ties to the British economy and the vagaries of its colonial policies, chafed most North Americans at one time or another.

With the end of the Seven Years' War with France in 1763, which had greatly raised its debt, Great Britain attempted to increase the exploitation and control of its North American colonies. The Crown did this by limiting the independence of North American commerce, including the regulation of shipping, raising the customs and taxes on both northern goods and southern tobacco, and forbidding the colonies from issuing paper money. These policies directly affected colonial elites, as well as having an impact on the economic well-being of the rest of the population. In addition, other issues of importance to large numbers of ordinary colonists emerged in the course of the anticolonial struggle against Great Britain.

In March 1765, the British Parliament passed the infamous Stamp Act, adding new taxes and inconvenience to colonial commerce. In order to enforce this and other new laws, increased numbers of troops were sent to the colonies. The problem remained for the British to supply and house their army in a faraway land. To this end, they passed the Quartering Act in April 1765. "Americans were to lodge officers and privates in inns, uninhabited houses, barns, and other buildings; supply them with numerous articles of consumption; and furnish wagons to haul their goods," (Beard and Beard 1944:96). The North American colonists not only were subjected to control and the enforcement of unpopular taxes by British troops; they also had to house and feed their oppressors on demand. These very same troops often earned extra money by taking work at below-market wages from colonial laborers and artisans, sometimes undercutting their rates by as much as 50 percent. In Boston, a conflict over this issue led, on March 5, 1770, to British troops firing on a crowd of protesters; described by John Adams as "a motley rabble of saucy boys, negroes, molatoes, Irish teagues and out landish jack tarrs." Five of these people were killed, including Crispus Attucks, a half-Indian, half-African sailor, today honored as the first Black to die in the American Revolution, providing, according to Adams, the first martyrs who accelerated the revolutionary break with Britain (in this general account, over which there is little present dispute, I follow Lemisch 1968:399–400).

At this point, it is reasonable to ask what any of this has to do with race, the situation of Black Americans, and the question of Black slavery? I will argue that it has quite a bit to do with these issues but that the answer is by no means a simple one. There are three major dimensions to the question, each of which has been the subject of important work by recent historians—and, I will argue, often of extravagant claims: First, we want to know what the role of free Blacks and slaves was in the "urban crucible" (to use Gary Nash's poignant phrase) of the revolution; how much interracial unity there was among the urban mobs and how important this multiracial, multi-ethnic working class was in the develoment of the revolutionary struggle. Second, we want to know how important the role of the slaves was, including their activities for liberation. Third, we need to ask about the importance of the issues of slavery and race for the American Revolution.

Although few still argue that the laboring classes played no role in the Revolution, there are many who argue either that their numbers were not large (Wellenreuther 1981, 1983) or that their particular grievances were of little import (Wood 1991) or that they were not particularly disorderly (Maier 1972). Still others have argued that they played an important or even pivotal role and that the revolution which they largely created was hijacked by the elite (e.g., Rediker unpublished). These issues are worth addressing.

Hoerder, Nash, and Smith, (1983:416) define the laboring classes as "all those who work with their hands" and argue that they made up the vast majority of the inhabitants of colonial cities and towns. The laboring classes included unskilled laborers and seamen, artisans, indentured servants, and slaves. Even the latter, though they did not participate formally in the political process, were very much a part of social and political life. Nash and his associates suggest rough figures, with some variation by area, for the occupational structure of eighteenth-century colonial towns. For every twenty males, they estimate that 15 percent were slaves or indentured servants, 25 percent were laborers or merchant seamen, 35 to 40 percent were artisans, and 5 to 10 percent were merchants. Charleston and New York had higher proportions of slaves, Philadelphia more indentured servants, and Boston greater percentages of merchants and professionals.

It was the laboring classes who made up the overwhelming majority of the colonial mobs, according to all descriptions. Their central role is acknowledged by a wide range of commentators. As Schlesinger argues graphically, mobs and mass "violence played a dominant role at every significant turning point of the events leading up to the War for Independence" (Schlesinger 1955:244).

At the center of the mobs were poor seamen. The conditions of eighteenth-century Jack Tarrs, as described graphically in Jesse Lemisch's seminal article (1968), were a form of servitude (see also Rediker and Linebaugh (1993) for more detailed information). Disobedient seamen were frequently whipped and maimed. The law empowered "every free white person" to catch runaways. Strikes, called *mutinies,* were punishable by death. Pay was often held for months or occasionally years to prevent desertion. Death at sea was not uncommon; storms, malnutrition, and disease took a heavy toll. Away from land and ordinary civilization for long periods of time, seamen lived in a world of their own (Lemisch 1968).

What linked seamen to ordinary citizens in coastal towns throughout the colonies, including Boston, New York, Philadelphia, and Charleston, aside from their stays on shore, was impressment. Impressment, the method the British Royal Navy adopted to solve its manpower shortages in both America and Britain, was a form of brutal kidnapping. "Impressment angered and frightened seamen" but also affected all classes of society. Anyone could be pressed into the navy, including "legislators and slaves, fishermen and servants."

On one night in 1757 in New York City, 800 were seized, one-quarter of the adult male population. Race, nationality, class, and even age (young boys who had not even reached puberty were sometimes snatched) were not impediments. Impressment was highly egalitarian in this perverse sense, forging a certain commonality of interest among its intended victims (Lemisch 1968:383–84).

The struggles against impressment were international, taking place in ports all around the Atlantic. Their frequency and intensity increased after the British declaration of war against Spain in 1739. Seamen rioted twice in Boston in 1741 and twice more in 1745. Throughout the 1740s, seamen and their supporters attacked press gangs in Antigua, St. Kitts, Barbados, and Jamaica as well. One of the most famous early riots against impressment took place in Boston in 1747, where a group initially consisting of 300 seamen, growing to several thousand, seized the officers leading the press as hostages, then blocked the return of the press boats to the main ship. The mob, made up of "Black and white, of many ethnic and national backgrounds," took these actions in the name of "liberty" against authorities that they saw as having overstepped their bounds. Marcus Rediker argues that Samuel Adams, who watched the 1747 Knowles Riot, translated the action into political discourse. Adams claimed that the mob "embodied the fundamental rights of man" against government oppression (Rediker, unpublished; Rediker 1987:251–53; Rediker and Linebaugh 1993:135–36). Sailors were central to every port city riot for the rest of the century, regularly battling impressment in Boston, New York City, Charlestown, Philadelphia, Newport (Rhode Island), Casco Bay (Maine), and a host of other places. As Lemisch, Rediker, and others have documented, these riots were far from peaceful and accumulated a number of deaths, contrary to the images of the genteel prerevolutionary mob riots portrayed in many of the standard histories.

The tradition of mob actions laid the basis for the key protests in the revolutionary struggle against Britain in the decade after 1765. They were the most effective, perhaps the only effective, vehicle for combating the control of the British. They also had, in contrast with traditional forms of political participation (voting, serving in the legislature, speaking at town meetings), an egalitarian aspect. They were open to all, the poorest members of the population, women, free Blacks, bond servants, and slaves, as well as artisans, professionals, merchants, and the very rich. The mobs, therefore, had a universal character about them, implicitly embodying certain principles about "all men" as opposed merely to the rights of (male) Englishmen.

A number of claims are made about these mobs. Gordon Wood's claim that they had no independent class grievances or agendas does not seem to match the evidence. Yet, among those who see the importance of the lower-class goals, there is some difference as to just how central they were. Lemisch himself is quite circumspect and merely argues that the forces at the bottom of society had independent issues and activities that must be taken into account in giving a full picture of the development of the American Revolution. Rediker, however, makes a far more extensive claim. He argues that the colonial laboring classes were highly solidaristic, especially across racial and ethnic lines. They were first of all "connected by commonalities of culture...."

> A subculture of apprentices, journeymen, servants, slaves, laborers, and sailors revolved around common work experiences and a common cultural life of revels, masques, fairs, May-day celebrations, street parties, taverns, and "disorderly houses."...Black and white workers—slaves, free Blacks, soldiers, sailors, and poor working men—congregated in 1741 at John Hughson's tavern in New York, where they planned a rebellion that would do in the "white people"—by which they meant the rich white people—of New York....

> There was, therefore, a history of interracial cooperation that underlay the joint protests of sailors and slaves against impressment and other measures during the revolutionary era....

> In the process they provided an image of interracial cooperation that raises doubts whether racism was as monolithic in white society as is often assumed. (Rediker unpublished:28–29)

Although these points of contact and joint struggle are, of course, hopeful signs about the possiblity for interracial cooperation and solidarity, suggesting the limits of the psychocultural approaches, they were not as far-reaching as has been indicated. The demands by the laboring classes for abolitionism were episodic and qualified. Aside from the Quakers, the strongest attacks on slavery were indeed made by artisan spokesmen, including James Otis and Nathaniel Appleton of Boston and Benjamin Rush and Thomas Paine of Philadelphia. Their concerns, however, were clearly more motivated by a resentment of the competition of slave labor than by an egalitarian desire to see Blacks fully incorporated into society (Nash 1986:206). Highly solidaristic sentiments were more isolated, perhaps suggested by the actions of John Simmons, a white artisan in Maryland, who in 1775 refused to attend a militia muster whose purpose was to guard against rumored slave revolts. Simmons stated that he would rather join with Blacks and other nonpropertied whites to kill the "gentlemen" who monopolized the best land. Simmons was tarred, feathered, and banished for allegedly agitating a slave rebellion (P. Wood 1993:164). The interracial laboring people's struggles do not seem to have approached the racial demands of Bacon's Rebellion, in which the unfree participants were promised their freedom. Whatever the common grievances and points of social contact between lower-class whites and Blacks, the plight of most slaves and therefore the immediate problems they faced were—with the exception of these small number of urban slave artisans, North and South, whose masters allowed them to hire themselves out—decidedly different from those of even the most destitute white port-side seamen. The most immediate problem of slaves and to a lesser extent of apprentices and servants was their legal status, which made them extreme-ly dependent on their masters. This dependence placed important limits on their ability to participate in the revolutionary process—no less, I would add, play a leading role (Wellenreuther 1983:442). Although these interra-cial struggles are important to note and suggest interesting possibilites for broad solidarity, it will behoove us not to overly romanticize them.

The distinctions here, striking the right note and balance, are of the utmost importance. These interracial mobs representing all on the bottom were more than just the foot soldiers of the revolutionary movement. We can agree with Rediker that their militancy was not merely used by upper-class patriots, but that it "pushed the revolutionary vanguard to extreme posi-tions and eventually to a declaration of independence" (Rediker unpub-lished:28). To carry this argument further, however, and see post-Revolution conservative assertions of control as "part of an American Thermidor" that assumes not only an independent but also a leading role for the laboring classes in the American Revolution does not fit well with the facts.

Gary Nash gives perhaps the most balanced account of the role played by the laboring classes in the revolutionary struggle. He argues that in New York and Boston, political cleavages based on class were secondary. Those on the bottom tended to follow elite revolutionary leaders. In Philadelphia, on the other hand, independent politics by those on the bottom and a greater radicalism manifested themselves, influencing and for a while seizing the leadership of the whole movement. One key, as Nash argues, was undoubt-edly the fact that New York and Boston were occupied by troops, forcing more of a common front (something of a united front against imperialism) against the British, whereas Philadelphia was not. Although there were thus signs of an incipient independent interracial lower-class radicalism in the American Revolution, the urban laboring classes were ultimately too stratified by occu-pation and situation and of too little social weight to play a leading role (see Nash 1979, chapter entitled "The Onset of the Revolution.").[2]

Peter Wood has argued convincingly in a number of articles that Black struggles for freedom intensified as the American Revolution approached.

We wish to know how important this activity was in the development of the struggle for independence.

Despite numerous assertions in the nineteenth and twentieth centuries that Black slaves were submissive, that they acquiesced to or even positively accepted their situations, all evidence, as well as common sense, suggests that they did not. Although many white colonists doubted the ability of Blacks to govern themselves, few doubted their desire to do so. As Winthrop Jordan argues:

> The Negro as potential rebel was of course presumed to crave liberty. Indeed if there was one thing about which Americans of the eighteenth century were certain…it was that men everywhere yearned for freedom. Nothing would have surprised them more than to learn that later generations spoke knowingly of the contented slave.… (Jordan 1977:388)

William Willis (1963:159) makes an even stronger argument, as does Peter Wood (1993:150–52). The eighteenth century was punctuated not merely by many acts of defiance by slaves but also by numerous plots and rebellions, often occurring in waves.

There is, to be sure, a tremendous difficulty in ascertaining exactly how much rebellion by Black slaves actually took place in North America. In his seminal work on the subject, Herbert Aptheker discusses the "exaggeration, distortion, and censorship." Many witnesses or participants had reasons to distort the facts. Some conspiracies were nothing but the wildest rumors, "created out of whole cloth." "Fear itself, of course, created exaggeration. …Indeed, at times, entire communities were reported as wiped out, and days went by before the rumors were shown to be false. This was the case, for example, in the stories of the destruction of Wilmington, North Carolina, following the Turner outbreak" (Aptheker 1987:153–55). On the other hand, news of actual conspiracies and revolts was often suppressed or censored (Aptheker 1987:155–61). Despite these problems of discovery, it is clear that there was a good bit of resistance by slaves.

There was certainly a large amount of murder of masters and overseers by slaves, by direct physical assault, poisoning, and arson. Jordan discusses the hundreds of slaves executed for such acts in Virginia between 1783 and 1814 (a period and place for which data happen to exist), arguing that the figures greatly underestimate the acts because they do not include the hundreds transported elsewhere, those who were pardoned, those who took their own lives, those who were killed by masters or overseers, or those who were never caught (Jordan 1977:392–93).

Conspiracies, plots, and actual violence were frequent occurrences in the eighteenth-century colonies. New York State and New York City had among the highest concentrations of slaves in the North. During the first half of the eighteenth century, Black slaves sometimes made up over 18 percent of the city's population. In April 1712, twenty slaves set fire to a building, then killed nine whites who came to put out the fire. A number of slaves were taken into custody. Thirteen were hanged, one starved to death in chains, three were burned publicly at the stake, and six others committed suicide to avoid the tortures planned for them by the white authorities—all of which suggests the fear of insurrection by slaves. By 1740, a major cycle of unrest swept the eastern seaboard, affecting New York in 1741. This latter rebellion was presumably interracial, as eighteen slaves and four whites were sentenced to torture and hanging, thirteen slaves were sentenced to burn at the stake, and seventy more were shipped to the West Indies (Nash 1986:69).

South Carolina, where Black slaves greatly outnumbered whites throughout most of the eighteenth century, was the scene of both numerous acts of resistance and savage repression against alleged perpetrators. Willis argues that by the late 1720s, "Negro subversion had become the main defense problem of South Carolina" (Willis 1963:159). Peter Wood likewise documents large numbers of acts of resistance "real and suspected" during the first half of the eighteenth century (P. Wood 1974:285–307). The abortive Stono Uprising of September 1739 near Charlestown, South Carolina, in which twenty-five whites were killed, struck terror in the hearts of whites in the whole colony.

The slave rebellions during this period, like the riots against impressment, also had an international character. As Rediker summarizes:

> Their struggles included the First Maroon War of Jamaica (1730–1740), slave rebellions in New Orleans (1730, 1740), St. John in the Danish Virgin Islands and Dutch Guyana (1733), major plots in the Bahama Islands, St. Kitts, and New Jersey (1734), the great slave conspiracy in Antigua (1735–36), rebellions in St. Bartholomew, St. Martin, Anguilla, and Guadeloupe (1736–38), the Stono Rebellion (1739), the 'Great Negro Plot' of New York (1741), and a series of disturbances in Jamaica (early 1740s). (Rediker and Linebaugh 1993:136; Rediker unpublished: 14).

As Herbert Aptheker documents and Peter Wood underscores, slave resistance tends to take place in waves. Wood also argues that it frequently took place during periods when the white communities were distracted or in crisis. Times of epidemics often provided such opportunites, as was the case with the Stono Uprising, which occured while yellow fever was widespread. Stono also began the weekend that news reached Charleston that Spain and Great

Britain were at war (P. Wood 1993:152–54; 1974:312–314). The French and Indian Wars provided the context for further unrest among Black slaves, especially in Maryland and Virginia (Aptheker 1987:87). The period of conflict between the colonies and Great Britain, up to and through the Revolutionary War, seems to have occasioned a large wave of plots and rebellions, as well as other organized activities by Blacks in search of freedom.3 In 1772, a major conspiracy was uncovered in Perth Amboy, New Jersey, a center of the slave trade (Aptheker 1987:200). Before they were subdued, a group of slaves in St. Andrews Parish, Georgia, killed four whites in 1774 (Aptheker 1987:201). In September of 1774, a group of Blacks in Boston offered to fight for the British if they were freed from slavery in return (Aptheker 1987:87). In 1775, a massive uprising in the Tar River area of North Carolina was discovered just before it was to start (P. Wood 1993:165). Another serious plot was discovered in Beaufort, Pitt, and Craven counties of North Carolina in 1776 (Aptheker 1987:202). Resistance by Blacks was accelerated greatly by Virginia's British Governor Lord Dunmore's brief call for slaves to fight with the British in return for freedom. As we shall see, the yearning for freedom and the ferment among colonial Blacks were to be important ingredients in the general unrest and popular activity during the revolutionary period.

To put the liberation struggles of Blacks during the American Revolution in perspective, however, it is well to note the limits on these activities. The key place to start is with the demographics. In 1775, on the eve of white independence, England's mainland colonies had half a million Blacks, approximately 20 percent of the population, the greatest percentage before or since (P. Wood 1993:150). Ninety percent of blacks were concentrated in the five southeastern states, constituting about a third of the population of that region (Wood 1978:271). The colony with the largest Black population was Virginia, which in 1775 had over 279,000 whites, compared with 186,000 blacks. South Carolina was the one colony where Blacks constituted a majority during this period, outnumbering whites 107,000 to 72,000 in 1775. In North Carolina, the only other populous southern colony, whites outnumbered Blacks in 1775, 157,000 to 52,000 (Wood 1989:38). And there were some small numbers of counties, especially in the lowlands of South Carolina, where blacks outnumbered whites by five or ten to one (Wood 1978:271). These demographics suggest the initial difficulties—nay, the virtual impossibilities—for successful slave rebellions in the North American British colonies. Whites were armed and ready; penalities for violation of work discipline were harsh; penalities for suspected rebellion were draconian and bestial. Whites who might be overwhelmed in one area could quickly call on neighboring slave patrols and even militias to join them in suppression.

In contrast, in many other colonies, the ratios of Black slaves to whites were overwhelming. In Jamaica, Guiana, Barbados, and Haiti, not only did Blacks outnumber whites many fold, but this was also often true throughout the whole colony. In one large sugar-growing parish in Jamaica, the site of a 1776 conspiracy, Blacks outnumbered whites by twenty-six to one. When troops left the island that year to strengthen British forces on the mainland, there was little backup (Frey 1991:71–72). Even in these areas, successful slave revolts were difficult, requiring exceptional conjunctures, as was the case in Haiti in the 1790s. Yet, Caribbean slaves did not confront the impossible circumstances faced by Blacks on the North American mainland. In South Carolina, where the Black majority was slight compared with that in the various island colonies, white elites spent an enormous amount of time, energy, and resources guarding themselves against slave revolts, not only by military means and brutal police control but also by fomenting divisions and race hatred between Blacks and Indians, who might otherwise have been natural allies (Willis 1963). Here, of course, is a good example of the conscious and successful use of divide-and-conquer tactics by a ruling elite. What is thus surprising is, not the lack of more successful slave revolts by North American mainland Blacks, but the degree to which they continued to struggle and resist against impossible odds and repression.[4]

Despite the insurmountable difficulties Black slaves had in mounting an independent struggle for freedom during the American Revolution, their often dramatic resistance, the possibility that they might support the British in return for emancipation, along with the participation of many urban Blacks in pivotal anti-British revolutionary activities, pushed the issue of the abolition of slavery to the forefront.

In summary, the role of the lower-classes in the American Revolution was decisive but not dominant. Lower-class urban laborers and Black slaves helped to broaden the issues, forced a revolutionary democratic character on the struggle, and provided the motive force for resistance and acceleration of the break with Britain. Ultimately, white labor was too stratified, giving it too little social weight. Black labor, of central economic importance, was (except for the small number of free Blacks) too shackled by slavery to play a pivotal role politically. Thus, the American Revolution was largely led and dominated by the commercial and plantation elites, whose leading spokesmen included John Jay, John Hancock, Alexander Hamilton, Samuel Adams, Patrick Henry, George Washington, Thomas Jefferson, and James Madison. Yet, largely because of the role of the lower classes, in addition to the dominant bourgeois character of the American Revolution (exemplified by the demands of the northern merchants and southern slaveholders for control and increased profits from their commercial affairs), the grievances and rhetoric of the anti-British movement also had a revolutionary democratic component. In contrast with the "highly particularistic notion of the rights of Englishmen" put forward by British radicals in their own earlier political revolution, the Declaration of Independence, which declared that "all men are created equal," was "at least open to a generous and universalistic interpretation," although for most white men, of course, "all men" did not include Indians, blacks, women, or children (Blackburn 1988:111).

Yet, as Bailyn argues, once equality was declared universal and inalienable, there was a "contagion of liberty." The vast majority of people were pushed forward by the "logic of revolutionary thought," to the conclusion that "all men" really did mean *all*. However, this logic of revolutionary thought did not develop automatically (as Bailyn suggests); it was, rather, forced on revolutionary thinkers by the developing struggle. Rediker argues convincingly that Samuel Adams probably developed his more inclusive approach in response to the 1747 Knowles Riot, which heavily involved seaman and Blacks (Lax and Pencak 1976:205–06, 214; Rediker 1987:251–53; Linebaugh and Rediker 1993:135–36; Rediker unpublished:4–9). Although many southern elites responded to the increased slave resistance with increased repression, other southerners reacted more generously. In Georgia, after the burning alive of two slaves who were accused of arson and poisoning, a group of Scottish parishioners met in January of 1775 and adopted a strong resolution against the "unnatural practice" of slavery, vowing to work for the manumission of the state's slaves (P. Wood 1993:161). In 1774, Abigail Adams in Massachusetts, wrote to her husband John, in Philadelphia for the First Continental Congress, of the rumors of slave rebellions up and down the East Coast, arguing for abolition: "It always appeared a most iniquitous scheme to me—to fight ourselves for what we are daily robbing and plundering from those who have as good a right to freedom as we have" (P. Wood 1993:159–60).

Tacky's Rebellion, beginning in 1760 in Jamaica and involving thousands of slaves, led to far-reaching abolitionist pamphlets and agitation. In the wake of Tacky's Rebellion, future revolutionary leader James Otis, published his famous *Rights of the British Colonies*. Otis declared, "The colonists are by law of nature freeborn, as indeed all men are, white or Black," (Otis in Bailyn 1965:439), arguing further that slavery debased those who practiced it (Bailyn 1965:439–40; Rediker unpublished:15–17). Otis both electrified and shocked his fellow revolutionists as well as the abolitionist, yet more genteel Quakers, by calling not only for immediate emancipation but also for the use of force to accomplish it.

The concept of slavery was a common term of eighteenth-century political discourse. It was continually used to describe the effect of British domination on the largely white North American colonists. Yet, the degradation of Black plantation slavery, existing in fact and sanctified by colonial law, was the most extreme form of this slavery that the American revolutionaries claimed to oppose.

This stark contradiction—that the North American opponents of all forms of slavery and the proponents of equality for all were themselves enslavers—did not escape the notice of many revolutionaries or, for that matter, of their British and loyalist critics. This was not to be the last time in U.S. political history that the issue of freedom for Blacks would acquire importance in the international arena. Not only did the maintenance of slavery undermine the moral legitimacy of the revolutionary movement, but it held back the ability to gain allies and sympathizers around the world.

Even in the South, there was a strong impetus toward abolitionist rhetoric, including the strong remarks of Thomas Jefferson, perhaps the most enlightened leader of the Virginia slave-owning class. It was, however, in the northern and middle colonies that explicit arguments for the abolition of Black slavery were heard throughout the revolutionary period (Bailyn 1990:237). The argument was common that the tacit acceptance of slavery even by nonslaveholders in the North, degraded human life in general, leading to the barbarity and cruelty so common in the sugar islands of the British Caribbean. The hypocrisy of slavery by those who claimed to be fighting for liberty was denounced by, among others, John Allen, a Baptist preacher and pamphleteer in 1774:

> Blush ye pretended votaries for freedom! ye trifling patriots! who are making a vain parade of being advocates for the liberties of mankind, who are thus making a mockery of your profession by trampling on the sacred natural rights and privileges of Africans; for while you are fasting, praying, nonimporting, nonexporting, remonstrating, resolving, pleading for a restoration of your charter rights, you at the same time are continuing this lawless, cruel, inhuman, and abominable practice of enslaving your fellow creatures.... (Bailyn 1990:240).

Such arguments were made and heard far and wide in the anticolonial movement. The Calvinist theologian Samuel Hopkins, a former student of the well-known Jonathan Edwards, declared "the cause of the colonies and the cause of emancipation to be indissolubly united." In a widely circulated pamphlet written in 1776, entitled *A Dialogue Concerning the Slavery of Africans; Shewing It To Be the Duty and Interest of the American Colonies to Emancipate All the African Slaves...*, he vividly described the horrors of Black enslavement. He implored his fellow revolutionists that the slavery of which they complained "is lighter than a feather compared to their heavy doom, and may be called liberty and happiness when contrasted with the most abject slavery and inutterable wretchedness to which they are subjected" (Bailyn 1990:244). And thus it was, of course, no accident that in 1775, it was North American Quakers who formed the first antislavery organization in the West.

Despite the work of most earlier historians, who either denied its importance or more commonly completely ignored the issue, it is now generally accepted that there was indeed strong abolitionist sentiment in the North American revolutionary movement. How overwhelming this sentiment was and the degree to which there actually existed possibiilties for ending slavery at the time of the American Revolution are now matters of contention among historians.

Perhaps the most compelling argument that abolition was possible during the revolutionary period is given by Gary Nash (1990). Nash begins by documenting the burgeoning attention paid to abolition in the colonies, both North and South. He cites the introduction in New England of an emancipation bill in 1767, the 1773 Harvard commencement debate on the issue (Nash 1990:8–9), and the renunciation of slavery at numerous New England town meetings. He notes Benjamin Rush's account of the overwhelming antislavery sentiment in 1774 at the First Continental Congress, as well as descriptions by political leaders and foreign observers of the majoritarian opposition to slavery in all southern states except in South Carolina and Georgia. There was also allegedly widespread opposition to slavery among leaders in Virginia and Maryland, together the home of half of all North American Blacks in 1776 (Nash 1990:10–12). Evidence on manumissions is revealing. Laws prohibiting it were repealed in all states except North Carolina (Berlin 1974:28–30). Nash finds the degree of manumissions during this period especially compelling:

> The rapid growth of the free Black population in the upper South thus gives a final, if rough indication of anti-slavery sentiment. Maryland's free Black population, which was 1,817 in 1755, reached 8,000 by 1790 and nearly 20,000 by the turn of the century. In Virginia, where a census in 1782 revealed 1800 free Blacks, the number swelled to nearly 13,000 in 1800 and 20,000 a decade later. Delaware's free Black population, only 3,899 in 1790, swelled to 8,268 in 1800 and 13,136 in 1810. Even with these increases, free Blacks made up only one-twelfth of the upper South's Blacks and two percent of those in the lower South. But such figures should not be dismissed as unimportant, for they indicate that even in the absense of a compensated gradual emancipation law, thousands of slaveholders were disentangling themselves from the business of coerced labor. Such was not often the case in South Carolina and Georgia to

be sure, but throughout most of the country in the upper South as well as the North, the feeling had spread widely that slavery was incompatible with the principles of the Revolution, that it could not be reconciled with Christian morality, and that it was an unsatisfactory basis for the economy of the new nation. (Nash 1990:18–19)

If the sentiment for abolition of Black slavery was so strong in the North and the bulk of the South, why then did it not take place as part of the American Revolution? The view that Nash criticizes is the one argued most poignantly by Donald Robinson (1979). Supposedly, Georgia and South Carolina, whose opposition to any limits on slavery or the slave trade was absolute, made the abandonment of Black freedom a condition for the formation of the Union; the North acquiesced. Nash argues that these states hardly had the leverage to enforce such a demand. First, both were being seriously threatened by a pan-Indian alliance—the Creek confederacy had already driven Georgians out of all the disputed territory—and desperately needed the military aid of a federal government. They were hardly in a position to reject a national government (Nash 1990:27–28). Second, these two states represented only 5 percent of the nation's population. When a rumored peace agreement in 1780 involved the ceding of Georgia and South Carolina to Great Britain, northern delegates to the Continental Congress were not very concerned. Third, most southerners and leading economists agreed that the South could not make it on its own because of its commercial dependence on the North (Nash 1990:29).

Slavery was a national problem requiring a national solution. What kept liberation of the slaves from being part of the revolutionary establishment of the Republic, according to Nash, was not the resistance of the South but the weakness of will of the North. The anti-slavery impulse in the nation was weakened by, among other things, the failure of many northern abolitionists to free their own slaves. Several examples of such hypocrisy existed in Philadelphia for all the members of the Continental Congress to see in the 1780s. The most astounding was that of Benjamin Rush, the revolutionary leader who was the author in 1773 of one of the most damning attacks on slavery. Three years later, Rush purchased a slave, William Grubber. While keeping Grubber, Rush continued to condemn slavery as an institution as well as the individuals who owned them. In 1787, he had a vision and intensified his work for the Pennsylvania Abolition Society, serving as an officer. He was also a tireless supporter of Philadelphia's free Blacks; yet, it was another seven years before he released Grubber. Rush's was not an isolated case (Nash 1990:31–33). In 1780, Pennsylvania, the hotbed of Revolutionary War abolitionism, passed an abolition bill that was the most restrictive of the gradual abolition bills enacted in the wake of the independence struggle. It stipulated that all children born of slave mothers after the bill was passed would become free at the age of twenty-eight. Thus, it not only freed no current slaves but also consigned the next generation to slavery until most of their productive work life was through (Nash 1990:34).

Although Nash makes a number of suggestive remarks, he gives no arguments for why the North had this problem of weakness of will. He even seems to suggest that stronger leadership might have turned things around. But he leaves the question hanging. One can agree on one part of Nash's argument: If there was a moment during the revolutionary period when abolition of slavery was possible, it was in the 1780s.

The popular support for extending revolutionary democratic principles to Blacks was still strong during this period. By 1800, not only had the general revolutionary impulses of the country weakened, but anti-Black sentiment among whites had deepened. After this period, as Nash notes, virulent racism emerged in the North. In 1805, white Philadelphians drove local Blacks from the traditional Fourth of July celebrations. Within the next ten years, they were burning Black churches, a long-standing tradition in the United States. Such attacks were to spread throughout the North during this period. Thus, if abolition were possible, it was only during this earlier period, when public sympathy was extensive.

Equally important, many southern plantation owners were finding that slave-based plantation agriculture was unprofitable during the 1780s and were thus not adamant in defending it. By the 1790s, after the invention of the cotton gin, the large amount of profit available from this new commercial crop made slave owners more than a little reluctant to abandon their source of cheap labor. Simultaneously, the increasing economic entwinement of northern commercial elites, especially those in New York and Pennsylvania, with cotton production hardened their support for slavery.

Likewise, the actual course of slave liberation, beginning with the Haitian Revolution of 1791, continuing through the discovery of Gabriel Prosser's planned general insurrection in 1800, and including the 1803 St. Dominguan Revolution, undermined much of the benign, paternal, liberal attitudes of many whites. After 1791, thousands of French planters, many with large complements of slaves, fled to Virginia, where their tales of horror caused massive fright.

The seeming window of opportunity during the 1780s notwithstanding, it seems to me that Nash greatly exaggerates the possibilities. For despite the frequency and growing acceptablity of this often strident and irrefutable abolitionist rhetoric within the anti-colonial movement, the real status of the issue of slavery and Black freedom was most clearly evident in the vacillations and ambiguities around the question of the use of Black troops during the American Revolution by both the British and the North American armies. Even with the frequent shortage of recruits on both sides during the course of the war, not only slave emancipation but also the use of free Blacks were usually avoided by the British as well as the colonists.

Let us begin with the British, who were viewed by Black slaves and by many historians as more open to liberation than the colonialists. There was, to be sure, some element of truth to this claim. In April of 1775, Lord Dunmore, the royal governor of Virginia, threatened to emancipate all slaves if the colonists took up arms against King George. By November, as he was being driven from the colony, Dunmore offered freedom to all slaves who would join the British army. A number of slaves did respond, offering themselves to the loyalist cause. British policy, however, tended to be halfhearted at best, for a number of clear reasons. First, the British themselves had important slave-owning supporters who, like the rebel planters, did not wish to see slavery contested (Blackburn 1988:115). Further, Dunmore's proposals for the more extensive use of Black troops never received approval from the British government (D. Davis 1975:80). Proposals to arm slaves to fight for the British provoked vehement opposition in Parliament and in other influential spheres of English society. The highly profitable world slave trade, centered in London and Bristol, was threatened as merchants and slave traders reacted strenuously. Edmund Burke regarded such proposals as threatening the national honor and debasing "our character as a people." Most important of all for the British ruling class, North America was not the only colony where British subjects made huge profits from slave labor. Slave revolts had already taken place in Jamaica in 1776, apparently inspired by the American Revolution, and in the Guianas. Inspiring social revolution in North America or in its other colonies was not part of the British imperial agenda. Finally, there existed in England in 1772, approximately 20,000 Black slaves, most employed in the London area as servants for the aristocracy and other wealthy families. All these factors weakened the British desire to use Black troops extensively to defeat their colonial rebels.

Rumors, especially in South Carolina, of British-inspired slave revolts thus had little substance. These insurrection fears nevertheless played an important role in pushing a number of the southern states toward revolution. The Continental Congress viewed Dunmore's proclamation as "tearing up the foundations of civil authority" in Virginia, suggesting that their sympathy for slave liberation was not quite as advanced as portrayed by Nash. Despite the ambiguity (at best) of both the rebels and the loyalists, Black slaves nevertheless used every opportunity to revolt or run away. When British war vessels appeared at the mouth of the Savannah River at the beginning of 1776 to purchase provisions (not to liberate slaves, as was rumored), it led to a large number of slave desertions from Georgia plantations (Frey 1991:56, 59–60, 63, 65).

The colonialists' policy was highly ambiguous. Although Black soldiers had served with distinction at the battles of Bunker Hill and Lexington, Congress and the military leadership decided in November 1775 to exclude even free Blacks and to use an all-white army. This policy was in deference to southern opinion and reflected a fear of British retaliation (D. Davis 1975:78). Sylvia Frey argues that white colonial attitudes toward slavery had already hardened extensively as a result of British "tampering" and increasing slave resistance (Frey 1991:78). Military necessity caused the reversal of the policy on recruiting free Blacks, although some northern states, unable to fill their quotas for troops, began using slaves as well.

The reason, of course, that there was such resistance to using Blacks, especially slaves, in the military is clear. Promises of emancipation, such as those that Bacon made to his unfree followers, were intimately tied to winning the allegiance of slave troops. Thus, one of the clearest signs of the lack of sympathy for emancipation is the resistance to enrolling Blacks, free or slave, in fighting units. Despite occasional lapses because of the exigencies of war—Blacks were sometimes enlisted by Patriotic forces in the North while Black soldiers in the South were at times used by the Tories—slave emancipation was generally avoided by both sides.[5] Attitudes in the southern states toward the freedom of slaves were not always as positive as Nash suggests. Although many colonies offered white soldiers land in return for service, Virginia, the Carolinas, and Georgia promised recruits a slave to go with the land.

When the battlefields shifted to the South in 1778 and Savannah, Georgia, was occupied by the British, the South Carolinian John Laurens, an aide to General George Washington, proposed the recruiting of 3,000 slave troops who would win their freedom by fighting. The plan won the approval of Congress and even southern generals but was nixed by the South Carolina legislature (D. Davis 1975:79).

Thus, despite the rhetoric of anti-slavery and the pressures of war, there was too much resistance to giving freedom to even a small number of Black slaves, even in a period when the military situation was most dire. If abolition were to have come at the time of the Revolution, it would have had to be pressed more fully by the lower classes rather than the elites. Yet, their forces were ultimately too weak and their class demands on many other issues as well as emancipation were not well enough defined or forcefully enough presented to be a major factor in the outcome of important policy debates. With the war coming to an end, the impulses to abolitionism and more radical democratic measures, especially on the part of the colonial elites, slackened considerably.

THE FOUNDING OF THE REPUBLIC

The demands for freedom, however, did not automatically disappear from the air. The Revolutionary War had considerably weakened the hold of slavery in the North. Vermont, Pennsylvania, and Rhode Island, three states with only tiny percentages of slaves, soon passed legislation abolishing slavery. Three-quarters of the slaves in the North, however, were in New York (with 20,000) and New Jersey (with 10,000); in these states, anti-slavery measures got nowhere. Some northern leaders remained active abolitionists. Benjamin Franklin was perhaps the most important. Even Alexander Hamilton, however, who was to become a wealthy, conservative New York State landlord, freed the slaves he gained through marriage and helped form the New York Manumission Society. There were, to be sure, many others.

It is within this context that we are entitled to evaluate the status of the often ambiguous statements and consistent lack of action on the part of Thomas Jefferson with respect to slavery. Jefferson, of course, is one of those southern leaders whose anti-slavery stance is extolled by Nash and others.

First, it must be said, that Jefferson, whatever his flaws, was the author and champion of one of the most stirring, democratic, egalitarian statements of the modern age, the Declaration of Independence. One might compare him with Aristotle, whose brilliant analyses of human freedom, individuality, and notions of self-fulfillment form the basis for many contemporary, democratic, and even socialist analyses of these subjects, this despite the fact that Aristotle was an elitist and often antidemocratic and did not extend his notions to slaves and women.[6] Still, as David Brion Davis's thoughtful analysis makes clear, Jefferson comes off as weak and vacillating with respect to slavery, not merely in comparison with the more forward-looking northern elites but also in comparison with a number of southerners. In 1789, Beverley Randolph, governor of Virginia, gave open aid to the Pennsylvania Abolition Society. In 1790, James Wood was vice president of the Virginia Abolition Society while serving as governor. Although occasionally expressing repugnance for the institution of slavery, most often in private writings, Thomas Jefferson was never able to transcend being primarily an enlightened representative of the slave-owning class. In contrast, there were, during the revolutionary period, a number of prominent planters who freed their slaves and ended up leaving the South. Jefferson never considered joining them. Jefferson never approved of or even acknowledged "the existence of the Virginia Abolition Society." According to Davis, the most important constraint on Jefferson's public activities was his "continuing identification [throughout his life] with the interests and culture of a planter class" (D. Davis 1975:170, 176, 195). Thus, Brent Staples's editorial on Jefferson's racial liberalism and his alleged affair with his slave Sally, in the New York Times April 18, 1995, which claims that "Jefferson was exceptional, ahead of his time [with respect to the issue of slavery]—but not completely free of it" must be rejected as so much fanciful rubbish, an unwillingness to face the truth, warts as well as beauty (see also Conan Cruse O'Brien's October, 1996 article in the Atlantic on Jefferson).

Although the question of abolition had for the moment receded into the background, other class issues remained paramount. Grievances continued in the country after Great Britain capitulated to its former colonists in 1783. By 1786, the protest was no longer directed against Great Britain, but against members of the colonial elite themselves. Although unrest was manifest in all the colonies to greater or lesser degrees, the sharpest outbreak was Shays's Rebellion, an uprising of indebted Massachusetts farmers and military veterans led by former Revolutionary War Captain Daniel Shays. The rebellion was put down by the Massachusetts militia. Class issues and class conflict had come to dominate the social and political life of the Union. Despite having repressed and undermined the popular protests, colonial elites were still unhappy with many aspects of the life of the new nation.

In the summer of 1787, a self-selected elite met in secret sessions in Philadelphia to draft a constitution. Most delegates were merchants, lawyers, landowners, and southern planters. The many popular, democratic representatives of the common people had been clearly excluded. The elites had watched with anguish as state legislatures passed laws to protect debtors in disregard of their creditors (Levine et al. 1989:166). Few of these elites had sympathy for the more radical democratic notions of the Revolution. And fewer still gave opposition to plantation slavery a high priority. Thus, by the time of the Constitutional Convention, despite Nash's claims to the contrary, power had already shifted from those who wanted to push for greater democratic control of the new polity (the radicalism with respect to internal issues) toward those who wished to secure the property rights of the new aristocracy of wealth. Even Gordon Wood, often so unattuned to popular aspirations, notes the complete shift in ideology during this period (see, for example, G. Wood 1969:519–24, in a section entitled "The Repudiation of 1776").

Despite the growing anti-slavery sentiment in the North after the 1750s in the form of increasing activities by Quakers, growing opposition to the international slave trade, the formation of abolition and manumission societies, the increased agitation and petitions of free African-Americans, and the outspoken statements of a small number of colonial leaders, serious consideration for the plight of African-American slaves in the aftermath of the

American Revolution, as we have already seen, was slight. The spirit of 1776 had already developed what W. E. B. Du Bois called the "American blindspot" (Du Bois 1964:367) Yet, lack of consideration for the slaves did not mean that the question of slavery itself was unimportant. The issue of slavery asserted itself forcefully in postcolonial politics. Slavery was to be a pivotal issue in the formation of the Union. (See the different but parallel argument in Fields (1990)).

Slavery was central to the formation of the Union because southern elites knew that every bit of their affluence was completely dependent on African slavery. Without it, they would have been impoverished (see especially, D. Robinson 1979:210). The South Carolinans were quite lucid on this point at the Constitutional Convention. For example, General Pinckney, a representative from this former colony, stated that without slaves, "South Carolina would soon be a desert waste." Rawlin Lowndes, a delegate from South Carolina who opposed ratification because he thought that the Constitution jeopardized slave property, stated, "Without negroes, this state would degenerate into one of the most contemptible in the union...Negroes are our wealth, our only natural resource." (D. Robinson 1979:242; see also Cox 1970; 513). The enthusiastic participation of most southerners in the formation of a national government had one absolute qualification: Black slavery could not be touched. Northern political elites, of course, knew this. There could be no union without the acceptance of slavery in the South. No northern leader of any importance at the Constitutional Convention ever seriously suggested that the freedom fought for the Revolution should apply to Black people in the South (D. Robinson 1979:141).[7] The records of the Constitutional Convention of 1787 show that James Madison believed that the greatest source of division between states was based on "their having or not having slaves" (Farrand 1911:I:486). In 1830, Madison wrote to LaFayette, in reference to emancipation, "I can hardly express myself too strongly in saying, that any allusion in the Convention to the subject you have so much at heart would have been a spark to a mass of gunpowder" (Lynd 1967:159).

Although the Continental Congress rejected the South Carolinian attempt to place the adjective *white* in the Constitution, it acceded or compromised on almost every other demand.[8] Yet, this complete capitulation in accepting the legality of slavery did *not* eliminate it as a major issue. Sectional disputes on how to regard Negro slavery came up over taxation (1783) and representation (1787). The Founding Fathers made a final compromise on July 12, 1787, by assigning three-fifths representation for both purposes. The three-fifths compromise had momentous consequences.

It gave constitutional sanction to the fact that the United States was composed of some persons who were "free" and others who were not. And it established the principle, new in republican theory, that a man who lived among slaves had a greater share in the election of representatives than the man who did not. With one stroke, despite the disclaimers of its advocates, it acknowledged slavery and rewarded slaveowners. It is a measure of their adjustment to slavery that Americans in the eighteenth century found this settlement natural and just. (D. Robinson 1979:201)

The centrality of racial slavery and the growing hegemony of white supremacy throughout the land are perhaps nowhere more clearly seen than in the full acquiescence of northern delegates over the 1787 fugitive slave law. According to this law, any Black person in any state in the Union, if she or he were accused of being a fugitive slave, must be captured and sent back to the place from whence she or he supposedly escaped. Thus, the North would permit its free Black citizens to be captured by southern slave owners with the help of northern officials, to be delivered up to the whims of the slavocracy and its judicial officials. No right to a hearing prior to transfer would be provided. Robinson suggests that northern delegates might have successfully taken a stand on this and other slave-related issues if they had so desired (D. Robinson 1979:232–33). Gouverneur Morris of New York was probably the only delegate who argued against these laws on abolitionist grounds. The new fugitive slave law thus marked a distinct change from the pre-Revolution situation, when controls were less rigid and fugitive slaves such as Crispus Attucks could roam northern urban centers with a degree of impunity.

The self-confidence of delegates representing the South is reflected in another incident. Benjamin Franklin demanded in 1790, through a petition, the immediate ending of the slave trade. The vehemence of the attacks against him by southern representatives suggests that the standard interpretation of this period (which was before the invention of the cotton gin and prior to the Haitian Revolution)—that many of the Founding Fathers, including the Virginians, hoped that slavery would soon die out—is at least partially off the mark.[9]

One other issue, which many today regard as significant, caused little discussion. Conservatives commonly assert the centrality of religion (some even go so far as to say Christianity) to the establishment of the Constitution and our governmental system. The truth, however, is dramatically different. For example, when Benjamin Franklin proposed that the proceedings should open with a prayer, the motion died for lack of support. As Leonard Levy argues:

Former president Ronald Reagan, who sometimes reinvented history, mistakenly declared that as a result of Franklin's motion,

"From that day on they opened all constitutional meetings with a prayer." (Levy 1994:81)

Ronald Reagan is not the only one to have gotten things wrong. Many of the Founding Fathers were, of course, religious, although a number were deists and Unitarians, highly suspicious of all organized religion. Quite explicitly and consciously, however, the Constitution contains no reference to God. Its only reference to religion was to prohibit religious criteria from being a test of office, including the "annexation" to any oath of office, a motion that was passed unanimously with no debate (L. Levy 1994:79–80).

Thomas Jefferson, who was a leading advocate of the separation of church and state, as Isaac Kramnick notes, was "deeply suspicious of religion" and regarded the clergy as equally threatening to freedom as were kings and nobles. For his views, embodied in the Constitution, Jefferson was the object of furious attack by the Christian Right of his day when he ran for president in 1800 (Isaac Kramnick, "Jefferson vs. the Religious Right," New York Times, August 29, 1994). Thus, the equivocations by Bill Clinton, much less the more strident assertions of Speaker Gingrich, William Bennett, and others, would have been anathema to the Founding Fathers. Jefferson would have placed them all in the camp of the tyrants. And for those poor souls who still believe in strict constructionism (or the doctrine of original intent) with respect to interpretations of the Constitution, they too should be denouncing the contemporary Religious Right and most current conservative ideologues.[10]

In conclusion, the period of the Revolution and the founding of the Republic marked a critical turning point in American political development. On the one hand, the world's first anticolonial revolution inspired hopes for universal freedom and the rights of all, both in hallowed rhetoric and in action. The motive forces of the Revolution, the interracial, lower-class, urban mobs had embodied much of this universalism, which was implicitly and occasionally explicitly extended to Black slaves. The agendas of certain dominant colonial political forces, most notably in Pennsylvania, had openly included them in their demands for freedom. And the agitation of numerous clergymen from the Quakers to New England Puritans had likewise been for extending the desired liberation to the slaves; such was also the program of many radical agitators from Sam Adams to Tom Paine and James Otis. The democratic aspirations of the Revolution also were embodied in the Constitution by the absolute separation of the new state from religion. These revolutionary democratic traditions provide a rich legacy for those of us who still identify with the popular democratic traditions of the American Revolution.

Yet, in the end, this critical turning point was contradictory, for it sanctified slavery and the absolute rights of slave owners to their property within the founding constitution of the new democratic Republic. It codified the reactionary doctrine of states' rights, whose primary purpose was to shield slave-owning states from intrusion by the federal government into their control, regulation, use, and brutalization of their Black slave population. It inscribed the system of racial subordination and domination, which had previously been the hallmark of individual colonies, into a nationally recognized system. Thus was race planted in the American polity, not as a dilemma, but as the absolute contradiction and lie within its very heart.

1. Gordon Wood, on the other hand, denies emphatically that the internal issues played any role whatsoever (1991:3–4).

2. Kornblith and Murrin(1993:46–47) make a similar argument when they argue:

> In retrospect, however, what appears most notable about the Stamp Act riots is how the fears and resentments of the participants were focused rather narrowly on stamp distributors and their sympathizers, not on the rich or powerful in general. In mobilizing against the Stamp Act, urban crowds defended not only the principle of home rule, but also the prerogatives of many of those who ruled at home.

3. Gary Nash asserts that "the American Revolution represents the largest slave uprising in our history" (Nash 1990:57).

4. Large-scale political activity by slaves was, of course, an all-or-nothing game because of the presumptive denial of any rights by their masters. The most elementary political demand, that of emancipation from servitude, carried harsh penalties, often death. In general, there were few possibilities for political reform movements short of overthrowing the whole system.

5. Blackburn 1988:113–14. See Franklin 1969:131–38, for a lengthy summary of the vicissitudes of the use of Black troops by patriotic forces.

6. For a detailed and penetrating argument that Aristotle's arguments can easily be extended to embody modern notions of freedom and individuality, see Gilbert (1990).

7. Thus, the vaunted federalism of U.S. politics, including the recurring theme of states' rights, may be traced back to the the desires of the southern ruling class to preserve its particularly oppressive and remunerative forms of exploitation based on white supremacy without northern interference. These federalist stances extended far beyond the slavery era. They can be seen, for example, in the 1930s in southern political opposition to nationally uniform minimum wages and relief rates; they are also reflected in the 1950s and 1960s opposition to federal civil rights directives, including Arkansas Governor Orval Faubus's initial defiance of President Eisenhower at Little Rock in 1957 and former Alabama Governor George Wallace's long-term resistance to integration. And one could easily make a convincing argument that states' rights advocates today (who have successfully championed the dismantling of the national welfare system, shifting responsibility to the individual states) are also in good part providing a convenient cover for bigotry and the unequal treatment of African-Americans.

8. Patterson of New Jersey stated that northern delegates "had been ashamed to use the term 'Slaves' and had substituted a description" (Lynd 1967:159).

9. This standard view owes its origins, according to Eric Foner (1970), to the arguments of Salmon P. Chase before the Civil War. Donald Robinson, who argues against this view, identifies this interpretation with Lincoln in the third debate with Douglas, also noting that the view is held by prominent modern historians (D. Robinson 1979:vii, viii).

10. For a devastating and convincing critique of the doctrine of original intent, see Boyle (1991).

CHAPTER 3

The Coming of the Civil War

> ...this war...began in the interests of slavery on both sides....The South was fighting to take slavery out of the Union, and the North fighting to keep it in the Union....Frederick Douglass [1865], 1975:IV:160.

> From the first, I, for one saw in this war the end of slavery, and truth requires me to say that my interest in the success of the North was largely due to this belief. Frederick Douglass [1892], 1968:331

> History has different yardsticks for the cruelty of the Northerners and the cruelty of the Southerners in the Civil War. A slave-owner who through cunning and violence shackles a slave in chains, and a slave who through cunning or violence breaks the chains—let not the contemptible eunuchs tell us that they are equals before a court of morality! Leon Trotsky (1963)

The Civil War and Reconstruction represent perhaps the greatest turning point in U.S. history. In terms of sheer destruction of physical property and death, it was overwhelming, with over 600,000 dead combatants out of a total population of less than 32 million. The Civil War laid the basis in electoral politics for political loyalties that barely budged until the 1930s, some of which were dislodged in the 1960s, and one of whose most important remnants, the Democratic South, was eroded only in the mid-1990s. The conflict also resulted in a stronger central government from which it was no longer acceptable for a state to announce, as South Carolina did in 1832, that it would nullify a federal tariff, much less secede from the Union, as eleven Confederate states did in 1861. Yet, these important features hardly get to the essence of the matter. Most important, a social revolution was carried out, destroying the dominance of the southern capitalist class, finishing the bourgeois democratic revolution begun in the previous century, replacing —at least in the Constitution—the warped notion of racial citizenship with a more consistent (although still implicitly male) universalism. This social revolution opened the way for the unfettered national dominance of northern capital and its system of wage labor, beginning, or at least accelerating, one of the most massive and longest periods of sustained economic development the world has seen. Although interrupted by depressions and stagnation, it was to last a century. The post–Civil war Reconstruction period left unfinished a number of historic democratic tasks whose racial legacies remain unresolved today and figure prominently in virtually all aspects of contemporary life.

Every theory of American political development can be seen hawking its wares over the Civil War. The war was a battle over ideas and principles of government: states' rights versus preservation of the Union, the meaning of republicanism and freedom, or as William Miller argues, "a clash of moral ideas and loyalties, both sides claiming descent from the American Revolution," "the contradiction between slavery and America's meaning" (W. Miller 1996:4, 180).

For the Beards, it was a battle over tariffs and other economic interests of northern capitalists that, exacerbated by the degree of pro-southern Democratic Party dominance after the 1856 elections, led to the war (Beard and Beard 1944:260, 252–65 passim). In the account of the "new political history" of the 1960s, issues of religious, ethnic, and cultural conflict, often at the state and local levels, were far more important than either national economic issues or slavery itself (see E. Foner 1980:17–19 for a discussion and critique). Michael Holt, in an especially narrow view, sees slavery as hardly the cause at all, since it had always been there as a divisive sectional issue; rather, he sees the cause as the breakup of the traditional party system in the 1850s, which allowed the sectional differences to lead to war (Holt 1978:1–4). There are also those who note the importance of struggles of the masses, the general enfranchisement of white male voters under Andrew Jackson, activities of slaves (escapes, plots, and revolts), the growth and power of the abolitionist movement, and even the role of white labor organizations, all of which allegedly contributed to the sharpening conflict. One historian says it was the intense racism of both the North and the South that led to the war, as the North wanted the new territories empty of Blacks (free or slave) and the South wanted the right to subordinate them everywhere. Concluding, he stresses that "racialism as a force in American history has been too little emphasized by American historians," a point with which I would concur while disagreeing with the particular analysis (Rawley 1969:11–14:257–74).

Surprisingly, there are even those who suggest that the Civil War was not a central turning point at all, that the issues between the North and the South could have been resolved peacefully, and that the Civil War hardly needed to have taken place. Although Holt tends to this view, the most extreme formulation is that of Barrington Moore, whose static analysis dismisses one cause after another, seeing no cause as necessary, the possibilities for compromise immense, and almost no direct consequence from the war. It was all a big mistake; virtually everything of importance that happened after the war would almost certainly have happened anyway (Moore 1966:111–55).

At this point, it will come as no surprise to the reader that I will claim that slavery and questions of race were central to the causes of the Civil War, to how the conflict developed, to why it was so important, and to understanding its contradictory outcome. These issues have also played a central role in defining social struggles before, during, and after that time. Further, I will argue that the all-important abolitionist movement has been given too little weight by most other commentators.

A good place to begin in our examination of these questions is with the contradictory legacy of the Founding period. Opposition to conservative financial policies advocated by the plantation and commercial elites had been widespread in the rural areas in the years after the Revolution. The legitimacy of continued revolutionary class mobilization and mass struggle was undermined, however, with the military defeat and suppression of Shays's Rebellion in Massachusetts and the Whiskey Rebellion in Pennsylvania several years later (Slaughter 1986). The enshrinement of slavery in the Constitution marked the demise of the abolitionist thrust of the revolutionary period and the claim that freedom for Blacks was central to the idea of freedom for which the colonists had fought. The relatively voluntary subordination of the urban laboring classes to upper-class leadership (against whom they had often fiercely contested in the early revolutionary period) —in contrast with the stance of their rural brethren—also marked the end not only of the limited possibilities for revolutionary class struggle but also of broad class demands in general and laboring-class abolitionism in particular. In addition, the interracial mob struggles against impressment and for broader democracy faded into memory.

Yet, despite the disappearance of laboring-class abolitionism, interracialism, and revolutionary democratic perspectives, consensus did not reign, even in the urban crucibles. The nature of republicanism was bitterly contested, with enormous ramifications in labor relations and public policy. The economic elites viewed the Revolution/Constitution period as having first and foremost secured the rights of private property (free from Crown and government interference), guaranteeing equal opportunity for all white males (in the North, it was supposedly the chance to become a successful entrepeneur; in the South, it was the possibility for all white males to become slave owners), yet giving no surety for felicitous results for the vast majority. Activities that attempted to assure equality of results, such as union organizing and strikes, were considered heinous conspiracies, outlawed by the most extreme feudal tenets of early English common law (see Orren 1991 and Gregory and Katz 1979). In contrast, the white laboring classes, especially artisan workers, had a curious mixture of premodern and more modern (sometimes even social democratic) views of republicanism, views that have been much glorified by the new social history. Their perspective asserted the sovereignty and rights of free white male citizens whose political freedoms were captured in the Bill of Rights. This view suggested that freedom for both individuals and society would best be instituted by assuring, not the conditions for the accumulation of vast wealth, but a society of independent property-owning farmers and artisans. (For farmers, see A. Taylor 1993 and Kulikoff 1993; for workers, see Wilentz 1984.) Although not a strictly leveling approach to property, there was an assumption that a minimum equality of results was necessary for all citizens. In spite of its oppositional and political democratic thrust, this working-class republicanism, even in contrast with the democratic struggles from below during the Revolution, was narrow, exclusive, nonuniversalistic, and of course, racist. It is within this new postrevolutionary context that the sectional conflict over slavery began to grow.

Despite the demise of abolitionist sentiment and the narrow view of republicanism held by white labor, the question of Black slavery remained the central national issue from the Founding period through the Civil War. Slavery was central because it was the focal point of sectional conflict. As David Potter convincingly argues, slavery became "a transcendent sectional issue in its own right, and as a catalyst of all sectional antagonisms, political, economic, and cultural," (Potter 1976:48–49). Although the Founding and the Constitution had settled for the time being which classes would rule at home and the limits of popular democracy, they had not settled whether the plantation capitalists of the South or the merchant and industrial capitalists of the North would control the national government.[1] On a formal level, national political supremacy would be decided by what proportion of the many new states joining the Union were to be free states and what proportion were to be slave states. Though tariffs, foreign policy, and a host of related issues were involved, the key determining issue was whether slavery would be extended to the new territories, first east of the Mississippi, then to the huge expanses to the west of the great river. It would be the outcome of this struggle that would eventually determine who would control the fortunes of the nation and what would be the primary method by which labor would be exploited in the country as a whole. As Eric Foner (1970) demonstrates, abolitionism and the moral condemnation of slavery were important parts of the movement to oppose the extension of slavery. Yet, this was not the major component. It is clear that opposition to the extension of slavery did not imply, either in theory or in practice, an opposition to the already existing slavery of the South.

The issue of slavery in the territories began early. It arose in 1790 at the time of the Southwest Ordinance and again in 1798 with the organization of the midwestern territories under the Northwest Ordinance. The question was discussed with renewed vigor after the revolt of the "Black Jacobins" in Haiti led by Toussaint L'Ouverture in 1791 (James 1963). There, ruthlessly exploited Black slave laborers (whose high likelihood of death from overwork led to very short life expectancies) asserted their rights to be recognized as human beings and citizens. There were at the time some significant number of Americans who celebrated the initial revolt as a continuation of the principles of the American Revolution. For the slave owners and their allies, on the other hand, Haiti represented the horror of horrors, a justification for heightened vigilance, tighter restrictions, and no mercy for any but the most servile behavior. An extreme form of the most virulent racist reactions to Haiti is expressed in the work of Bryan Edwards, who blames abolitionists for the so-called tragedies of the French Caribbean. As David Brion Davis summarizes Edwards's fears:

> As a West Indian Virgil who had seen the outer fringes of hell, he takes us down into the pit, past the hideous tableaux: the white infant impaled on a stake; the white women being repeatedly raped on the dead bodies of the husbands and fathers; the fair eyes being scooped out of their sockets by black men's knives; and Madame Sejourné having a babe cut from her womb and fed to the pigs in her own sight, and then her husband's head sewed up in the bloody ' cavity. This Edwards tells us is the final triumph of philanthropy. It is the fruit of the doctrine that resistance is always justifiable where force is substituted for right. Edwards makes no mention of the atrocities which the white Frenchmen (and Englishmen) committed on the blacks. (Edwards, 1793:II:32–38, quote in D. Davis, 1975:193–94).

According to the reactionary Edwards, the sources of the problems of African-Americans and, more important, their threat to white society are the mushy, misguided generosity, philanthropy, and liberalism of those who sympathize with the oppressed and want to alleviate their conditions. Here we see an early historical antecedent of the type of racial analysis that has become so prevalent today in both Republican and Democratic Party circles: The source of the oppression of African-Americans today is not the legacy and continued existence of discrimination and oppressive circumstances but the misguided attempts of do-gooders, including the offering of a lavish existence on the public dole, which encourages indolence, breakdown in moral fiber, a desire to evade work and responsibilty, licentious sexual activity, large numbers of out-of-wedlock births, and unrestrained violence.

And of course, both the 1960s War on Poverty and affirmative action are allegedly major culprits. Yet, there is a further parallel, and this involves the reaction of liberals. Conditions in the Black ghettos have helped fuel an enormous increase in violent, often dysfunctional, antisocial behavior among disaffected, often downtrodden and hopeless, ghetto youths. Much of this behavior has led liberals to lose sympathy and support the calls for more police and greater repression that have been the earmark of conservatives. Likewise, when Touissant's successor Jean-Jacques Dessalines, inaugurated the massacre of the tiny white minority in Haiti that all but eliminated them from the island, many liberals quickly lost their sympathy for abolition and joined with the slave owners in placing their emphasis on what seemed to them likely to be the antiwhite resentments of newly freed black slaves. Although historical development proceeds, some things never change.

With the 1803 Louisiana purchase under Jefferson, the issue of slavery was raised again. Initial northern resentment, however, focused not merely on the territories but on the three-fifths rule compromise made at the Constitutional Convention, which allowed southern plantation owners congressional representation far in excess of their numbers. It also gave owners of large numbers of slaves in black-majority counties the ability to easily control their state legislatures, which in turn selected their state's senators. Northern resentment peaked in 1817 when President James Madison, a Virginian, vetoed the Bonus Bill, which would have led to the funding of the Erie Canal, linking Buffalo and the Great Lakes with Albany on the Hudson River and hence with New York City. The veto took place on the last day of Madison's presidency and was fully supported by his Virginian successor James Monroe (Sellers 1991:79, 130). By way of retaliation, New York Congressmen James Talmadge, Jr., in 1819, introduced antislavery amendments to the Missouri statehood bill, making a condition for admission the banning of further slave importation into the state and the eventual freeing of those already there. The vote on the Talmadge amendments displayed an extreme sectional cleavage that obliterated normal factional alignments (which usually held in a disciplined manner). Free-state congressmen backed the amendments by overwhelming margins (84 to 10 and 80 to 14) against virtually unanimous opposition from slave-state representatives (1 to 66 and 2 to 64). According to John Quincy Adams, this vote "disclosed a secret" that an antislavery political party could solidly unite the North against the expansion of slavery (Sellers 1991:130–31). Although their fundamental interests were different, the desire of northern capitalists for a wider capitalist market, a conducive culture and ideology, and the ability to freely exploit labor whenever and wherever it was profitable and the desire of northern workers and farmers for free or at least cheap, easily accessible land, along with dignity for their labor, be it urban or agricultural, fused into a powerful anti-slavery coalition. This conflict was temporarily resolved in 1820 by the Missouri Compromise, which passed the House and Senate by the slimmest of margins. The compromise admitted Missouri as a slave state but declared that no future state whose territory lay north of Missouri's northernmost latitude would be admitted as a slave state. It was also understood that Maine, originally part of the Massachusetts colony, would be admitted as a free state. Missouri thus became the fifth new state since 1816 (Indiana, 1816; Mississippi, 1817; Illinois, 1818; and Alabama, 1819; Sellers 1991:131).

Although Thomas Jefferson, in his private correspondence and conversations, was clearly tormented by the existence of slavery, during the 1819 and 1820 debates, he chose to attack those northerners who wished to exclude slaves from Missouri. Even in his old age, as perhaps the most revered of the Founding Fathers, he was unable to escape his identification with the slave-owning class. That task was left to others. During the dispute over the Missouri bill, New York Senator Rufus King denounced slavery in oratory that was considered stirring and overwhelming, according to then Secretary of State John Quincy Adams (W. Miller 1995:179), although Herbert Aptheker describes it as "rather mild anti-slavery expressions," compared with Talmadge's remarks (Aptheker 1987:47). Nevertheless, King's talk was widely publicized and quickly reprinted in pamphlet form. It is alleged that Denmark Vesey, an educated, multilingual free African-American, who was to organize in 1821 and 1822 one of the most extensive insurrectionary plots in North American history, with an underground network involving thousands, had not only read the pamphlet but had read parts of it aloud to his followers. This was mentioned at Vesey's trial; as one South Carolinian who was in Charleston at the time stated in a letter to President James Monroe, "The discussion of the Missouri question at Washington, among other evils, produced this plot" (Aptheker 1987:81). Thus, many southerners came to believe that even talk against slavery needed to be banned, not merely in the South but in the federal government and in the North as well.

The political conflict accelerated during the 1830s because of a variety of factors. One of the most important was the expansion of the franchise during the era of Andrew Jackson's presidency (1829–1837). This broader franchise (making eligible almost all white males) created the mass politics that allowed the emergence of influential sectional agitators who would attempt to mobilize public opinion either for or against slavery (Foner 1980:39).

The struggle over slavery in the country as a whole was reflected in Congress during the 1830s and early 1840s. Southern representatives argued that debate itself must be eliminated because anything but a united front in support of slavery would lead to the slaughter of their wives and children.

Hundreds of thousands of abolitionist petitions with millions of signatures poured into Congress, which initially refused even to accept them, much less discuss them. When Ohio Congressmen Joshua Giddings on the House floor defended on constitutional grounds the rights of slaves who had mutinied on the ship *Creole* while in transit from Newport News, Virginia, to New Orleans, Louisiana, he was censured by the House without a chance to defend himself. Giddings promptly resigned. Three months later, he was back, reelected by his constituents with perhaps the largest majority ever in a contested House election, 7,469 to 393 for his Democratic opponent, receiving 95 percent of the vote. For all who were listening—and it is hard to imagine that there were many in the country who were not listening to this much-publicized story—the conclusion was clear: Slave owners in the South and many citizens in the North had some extreme differences over slavery, and neither seemed about to flinch (Stewart 1976:70–78).

Slavery in the territories was debated with increased fury between 1846 and 1847 over the Wilmot Proviso. On August 8, 1846, Pennsylvania Democratic Congressmen David Wilmot, a bigot who had risked his constituents' anger to support the gag rule and oppose the tariff, offered an amendment that would forever ban slavery from any territory acquired from Mexico. The amendment passed the House, splitting the Democratic Party, whose free-state members supported it 54 to 4, while the slave-state Democrats unanimously opposed it. Wilmot, who called it the "White Man's Proviso," wanted even free Blacks excluded so that the new territories could be reserved for white freemen. As Sellers notes, this was "a fusion of antislavery with racism that proved unstoppable" (Sellers 1991:426). The question of statehood for Texas and the war with Mexico, both supported heavily by slave owners, fueled the fire.[2] The extension of slavery was settled temporarily again by the Clay-Webster compromise of 1850 and a new fugitive slave law. The conflict raged on over the 1854 Kansas-Nebraska Act and with the vehemently proslavery 1857 Dred Scott Supreme Court decision (see Fehrenbacher 1981 for a comprehensive discussion of Dred Scott).

The debates often took a far from genteel form. The pro-slavery vigilantes had been so brutal to independent white farmers in Kansas that many citizens were frozen with horror. Thus, the massacre of a group of pro-slavery thugs and mercenaries by the abolitionist, religious fanatic John Brown and his men at Oswatomie did not lead to a backlash. Instead, it reinvigorated abolitionist forces and underscored the fact that proslavery forces could be stopped only by violence. In 1858, after four years of civil war, with the decisive rejection of the pro-slavery Lecompton constitution, slavery was stopped in Kansas; it was, however, to remain a territory until 1861.

The event, however, that finally showed how irreconcilable the differences over slavery were among ordinary citizens, as well as between southern and northern capitalists, was the hanging of John Brown after his abortive raid on the federal arsenal at Harpers Ferry, Virginia, for the avowed purpose of beginning massive slave insurrections in the South. However, any discussion of John Brown that is serious must be a lesson in the historiography of American history. How else can one reconcile the divergent interpretations? David Potter, following much standard literature, describes Brown as a violent, vindictive hypocrite with "flawed judgment, homocidal impulse, and simple incompetence," who listened to no one, especially Blacks, and who failed at everything he ever tried in life except his death (Potter 1976:357; see also Filler 1986). Du Bois, on the other hand (whose biography of Brown Potter fails to cite in his copious footnotes), argues that Brown "worked not simply for the Black Men—he worked with them; and he was a companion of their daily life, knew their faults and virtues, and felt, as few white Americans have felt, the bitter tragedy of their lot" (Du Bois 1962:7). And perhaps even more extravagantly:

> Of all the inspiration which America owes Africa, however, the greatest by far is the score of heroic men whom the sorrows of these dark children called to unselfish devotion and heroic self-realization: Benezet, Garrison, and Harriet Stowe; Sumner, Douglass and Lincoln —these and others, but above all, John Brown. (Du Bois 1962:16)

How do we reconcile such divergent views? In 1859, John Brown electrified the nation. With a small band of men, he attacked the Harpers Ferry federal arsenal, seizing wagonloads of arms to begin launching armed slave insurrections in the South. Although most historians are skeptical, the plan, in my opinion, could have succeeded. If it had, African-American slaves might have been liberated in part by their own armed guerilla struggle, and the subsequent course of U.S. history would undoubtedly have been different. Instead Brown was captured. He was hanged in Charleston, Virginia, on December 2, 1859, and martyred.

John Brown's trial riveted the nation; he conducted himself with unsurpassed dignity. As the generally unsympathetic Potter writes:

> Description can hardly do justice to his conduct. He was arraigned with excessive promptness, while still suffering from his wounds, and was indicted and brought to trial, one week after his capture. The trial lasted one week, after which he was sentenced to hang.... The haste was shocking by any standards....During the trial, where Brown lay wounded on a pallet, and later, while awaiting execution, he handled himself with an unfailing dignity and composure.

Apparently he never flinched from the hour of his capture until the moment of his death. His conduct deeply affected his jailer, won the hearts of the guards, and made a profound impression on millions of people who stood the death watch vicariously with him as his execution approached. (Potter 1976:376)

John Brown's death underscored how irreconcilable the differences were between the North and the South. Organized support in the North "reached startling proportions." Memorial meetings were organized, church bells were rung, guns were fired, prayer meetings were held, a memorial volume was published, and pilgrims began streaming toward his grave in North Elba, New York. Ralph Waldo Emerson asserted that Brown would "make the gallows as glorious as the cross," and Henry David Thoreau compared him to Christ. Louisa May Alcott wrote, "The execution of Saint John the Just took place today" (Aptheker 1989:137). He was mourned "more than any American since Washington" (Potter 1976:378–82). All this for a man who would have incited the horror of horrors for southern slave owners: an insurrection of the slaves.

John Brown's last prophetic words were to serve as an inspiration to Union troops in the coming war: "I, John Brown, am quite certain that the crimes of this guilty land will never be purged away but with blood" (Du Bois 1962:365). The most popular song of the ensuing Civil War was "John Brown's Body."

John Brown—tyranical, obsessed, violent even at times to his children, at other times immensely self-sacrificing and sensitive to the plight of others, a contradictory human being—was in the words of Frederick Douglass, one of the "greatest heroes known to American fame" (Du Bois 1962:105). How do we reconcile his character? The answer is simple. We need not. Such contradictions and the using of Brown's alleged personal deficiencies to somehow undermine his historical virtue and importance or to belittle his contribution to abolitionism are pertinent only to those who are either ideological defenders of racial systems of domination, or those who foolishly believe that the 1960s aphorism that "the personal is political" has greater relevance than the particularistic venues in which it might apply. Although a dead white man and highly religious at that, John Brown, one of the most heroic and stirring figures in American history, is never mentioned by modern conservatives and is scorned by careful liberal scholars, such as David Potter, in their accounts. It is, of course, as both conservatives and liberals like to argue, a question of values.

So far, we have looked merely at the surface manifestations of the growing conflict over slavery that led to the Civil War. What exacerbated and intensified the sectional conflict was not a breakdown of the political system or an injudicious hardening of regional positions; these were epiphenomenal or at most consequences. Rather, it was changes in the underlying socioeconomic reality, the economic, ideological, political, and cultural needs of people whose prosperity, livelihoods, and survival were linked inexorably with two different social systems.

Let us begin with only one side of the equation, the growth in the system of racial slavery. At the time of the American Revolution, slavery in North America was a contradictory, frequently unprofitable institution, with the dramatic exception of certain large enclaves—the sugar-growing areas of Louisiana and the rice, indigo, and Sea Island cotton areas of South Carolina and Georgia. In most places, tobacco (the once-dominant cash/export crop) was becoming increasingly difficult to grow profitably. This situation underlay the openness of the Virginia Founding Fathers to ending slavery, the enormous increase in manumissions in the Upper South at the time, and the feeling of many that slavery would eventually die out in due course. But it was not to be. (For supplementary material, see Wright 1978:10–15 and North 1966:17–58).

All previous bets were called off with the takeoff of Black slave–grown cotton, whose importance for the development of the U.S. and world economies during the nineteenth century is difficult to exaggerate. Sea Island, long-fiber cotton, in the late eighteenth century, was a climatically sensitive crop that could be grown only along the coastal areas of South Carolina and Georgia, producing a highly desirable but limited harvest. The more hardy, ubiquitous, short-fiber, or Upland cotton was unprofitable because of the difficulty in extracting the sticky seeds from the fiber. The invention of the cotton gin in 1793 by the recently matriculated Yale undergraduate Eli Whitney changed all that. Whitney's invention was so successful and spectacular that his subsequent fate is a striking tribute to the entrepreneurial spirit and moral virtues of free market capitalism. After he demonstrated his new machine to a group of Georgia plantation owners, his workshop was broken into, his machine stolen, the design copied, and manufacturing by others initiated. When he set up a factory, it was burned to the ground. When he sought to raise additional capital, false rumors were spread that his version of the machine destroyed the cotton fibers. His patent rights were disregarded. Sixty straight cases were tried and lost by Whitney and his supporters. "Such was the importance of the machine, the extent of the infringement, and the wealth and influence of the guilty parties, that no jury could be found to return a verdict on the merits of the case" (Edward Bates in Bruchey 1967:57). As a consequence, the life of "one of the foremost figures in the history of industrial development" was filled with heartbreak, broken health, costly suits, a failed career, and penury. This story should (although it inevitaby will not)

give some pause to those ideologues who trumpet the degree to which capitalism rewards its innovators and entrepeneurs.

TABLE 4.1 *Bales of Cotton Produced Per Year*

Year	1791	1800	1822	1833	1840	1852	1859	1860
Number of Bales	9,000 bales	156,000	756,000	1.07 million	2.178 million	3.126 million	4.02 million	4.86 million

Source: Bruchey 1967, Table 3A; see also Du Bois 1964:4)

After the invention of the cotton gin, North American cotton production
expanded rapidly. Note in Table 4.1 the spectacular increases just before the
start of the Civil War. And the profits were immense. During the early boom
years, profits of South Carolina and Georgia planters doubled each year
(Sellers 1991:66). The state where slavery was harshest and most unrelent-
ing, which had the greatest head start in cotton production, was the site of
immense wealth. More great fortunes were accumulated in the low-coun-
try parishes of South Carolina during the first half of the nineteenth century than anyplace else in the country, possibly in the world (Sellers 1991:67).
By 1860, the twelve wealthiest counties in the country were all in the cotton South (Sellers 1991:407–08). As Sellers argues,

> Nowhere was American slavery more brutal or more fabulously
> profitable than in the South Carolina lowcountry. Here slightly
> acculturated, Gullah-speaking Africans outnumbered whites as
> much as eight to one in healthy months, far more when planter
> families fled summer's often fatal miasma. Here blacks—more sus-
> ceptible to malaria than whites admitted—were consigned to the
> mercies of swarming mosquitoes and fevered overseers. While other
> American slaves multiplied gratifyingly enough to cushion hard
> times for planters of tobacco and upland cotton, the blacks who
> sweated rice from lowcountry muck had to be replenished by con-
> stant slave importations. (Sellers 1991:273–74)

Cotton grown by Black slaves and the immense profits it generated were no
mere regional economic phenomena. Cotton was the bedrock for the world
industrial revolution whose center was the cotton textile manufacturing
industry in the nineteenth-century United Kingdom. Cotton products,
which made up between 32 percent and 52 percent of British manufacturing exports between 1815 and 1860, were the basis for Pax Britannica, based
on British domination of the world economy. Between 1840 and 1860, over
60 percent of the world's cotton was produced in the American South, and

virtually all of that which went to Britain came from this one region (Bruchey 1967: Tables 1A and 1D). Marx, as is often the case, summarizes this situation in a poignant manner:

> ...Without slavery you have no cotton; without cotton you have no modern industry. It is slavery that gave the colonies their value; it is the colonies that created world trade that is the pre-condition of large-scale industry. Thus slavery is an economic category of the greatest importance. (Marx 1847:112)

A similar, more contemporary assessment may be found in Douglas North (1966:62–64, 67–70).

For the United States itself, cotton exports between 1815 and 1860 accounted for over half the value of all domestic exports (North 1966:75–76). Investment capital for railroads, roads, and the development of major ports and the willingness of foreign investors to subsidize other U.S. products were all derived from cotton profits. The westward movement and expansion of cotton turned the Mississippi River into a major transportation artery, making the ports of New Orleans and Mobile the second and third most important in the country after New York (Bruchey 1967:Table 3M). The development of northern cotton textile as well as other important industries, was closely linked to southern cotton production.

Slave-grown cotton made swift tracks across the South. In 1791, 75 percent of U.S. cotton production was in South Carolina, which accounted for 50 percent in 1811 and South Carolina was still the leading state in 1821. Yet, despite continued large-scale growth, the expansion elsewhere was so rapid that South Carolina had been surpassed by seven other states by 1859 (Bruchey 1967:Tables 3C and 3D). After the 1820s, slave-grown cotton made its "lightning advance" (Sellers 1991:126) across the Gulf states, eventually including Arkansas and Texas, which were among the states that had passed South Carolina before the Civil War. The leading states by 1860 were Mississippi, with 26.4 percent of all U.S. cotton production; Alabama, with 21.7 percent; and Georgia and Louisiana, each with 15.4 percent.

The economic importance of the South was reflected in the region's national political dominance. Five of the first seven presidents of the Republic, for thirty-two out of the first thirty-six years, forty of its first forty-eight, fifty of its first sixty-four were slaveholders. The Speaker of the House for twenty-eight out of the first thirty-five years was a slaveholder. It was an anomaly if the president pro tem of the Senate was not. A majority of cabinet members and Supreme Court justices were slave owners. It was only in 1863 that Salmon P. Chase of Ohio succeeded the slave owner Chief Justice Roger Taney, who had originally been appointed by slaveholder Andrew Jackson (Miller

1996:13). With only a fraction of the population of the North and West by the time of the Civil War (even counting the noncitizen slaves), the South had an overwhelmingly disproportionate influence in national politics.

The economic importance of cotton and the influence of those who profited from it led to an intensification of the system of white supremacy for slaves in the South, for free Blacks in the slave states, and eventually for free Blacks in the rest of the country. Slaveholders in the South began to tighten the screws as soon as the abolitionist euphoria of the Revolution had worn thin and as cotton production began to expand. Manumissions, which had only recently become easier and more frequent in the Upper South, became first more difficult and then often impossible. In most slave states, slaves were forbidden to learn to read and write, supposedly so that they would be less likely to pick up subversive ideas such as freedom. Fugitive slave laws became more draconian and effective. Repression of plots, real and imagined (sometimes merely involving slaves congregating without authorization), became more widespread and brutal. Abolitionist societies, which had been stronger in many parts of the Upper South than their counterparts in the North, were being crushed by the late 1820s, their many thousands of members often physically driven from the region (Sellers 1991:127). The reason for all this, of course, is relatively straightforward: Slave owners wanted nothing to interfere with their abilities to maximize their profits by the exploitation of their unprotected laborers.

Yet, the growing restrictions on free Blacks, though often containing numerous peculiarities, contradictions, and local variations, were perhaps more complicated. Those who think that racist attitudes among whites are inherent or come with the culture give relatively static explanations that fail to account for the timing or the way the changes took place. The existence and, more important, the success of free Blacks became a growing ideological challenge to the system of racial slavery as slave labor spread across the South. As Ira Berlin argues,

> Southern race relations required that Negroes be powerless, submissive, and dependent. This allowed whites to extort slave labor and provided the basis for paternalistic rule. The free Negro's insistent drive for independence and respectability shook the ideological foundations of slave society. It challenged white racial assumptions and created doubts about the beneficence of slavery. More dangerous still, it demonstrated to slaves that blacks could be free, control their institutions, and improve their lives without whites. To meet these threats, whites continually pushed free Negroes closer to slavery and tried to keep them dependent on whites by harsh, proscriptive laws. (Berlin 1974:316)

Du Bois made a similar argument earlier:

> As slavery grew to a system and the Cotton Kingdom began to
> expand into imperial white domination, a free Negro was a con-
> tradiction, a threat and a menace. As a thief and a vagabond, he
> threatened society; but as an educated property holder, a successful
> mechanic or even professional man, he more than threatened slav-
> ery. He contradicted and undermined it. He must not be. He must
> be suppressed, enslaved, colonized. And nothing so bad could be
> said about him that did not easily appear as true to slaveholders.
> (Du Bois 1964:7)

In the early nineteenth century, numerous slave states quickly moved to dis-
enfranchise free Black voters. Only in North Carolina and Tennessee did the
franchise survive, although this omission was remedied in the new constitutional conventions of these states in 1835 and 1834, respectively. To prevent slaves from passing as free, and to dehumanize free Blacks, southern
legislatures enacted laws that required free Blacks to register and carry papers.
A North Carolina law required all urban free Blacks not only to register but
also to wear a patch which said "FREE." Free Blacks who failed to register
could be sold into slavery, a common punishment also proscribed in Virginia
for the failure to pay back taxes (Berlin 1974:91, 190, 191–93). Free Blacks
who were unemployed, even if their papers were in order, could be jailed,
bounded out, and have their children enslaved. Every slave state except
Delaware forbade free Blacks from testifying against whites in court but
allowed slaves to testify against freemen. Delaware, on the other hand, punished horse theft with sale to the West Indies. Whites who were less concerned with waiting for the law often kidnapped free Blacks and illegally
sold them into slavery, an act that was rarely punished or even reversed
(Berlin 1974:99–101).

South Carolina carried its fears that free Blacks might instigate insurrections to unusual extremes. In 1822, after the uncovering of the Vesey plot,
the legislature provided for the imprisonment of free colored seamen while
their ships were in port. If the ship captains did not pay the costs, the seamen could be sold to cover them. Several other states passed similar laws.
Following a protest by Britain about the incarceration of its Black sailors,
the State Department and attorney general ruled that such laws were unconstitutional, but the offending states continued to enforce them anyway
(Litwack 1961:51–53; Sydnor 1948:152; Miller 1996:418–19). These Black
codes, developed before the Civil War to restrain free Blacks, were the basis
for the new Black codes developed after emancipation to limit the rights of
all the newly freed African-Americans.

The control and influence that the slave states had over the national government and the limited interest that most northern politicians had in opposing such committed interests led to a large number of restrictions on the rights of free Blacks in the country as a whole. In 1790, Congress limited to whites the right to become naturalized as a citizen. In 1792, the newly organized militia was restricted to white male citizens. In 1810, Blacks were eliminated from carrying the U.S. mail. Although it occasionally made exceptions, the federal government also generally declined to issue passports to Blacks (Litwack 1961:54–56). Yet, the southerners did not invariably get their way. Blacks served in other branches of the armed forces, and 100 of Captain Oliver Perry's 400 highly decorated forces in the War of 1812 were Blacks. When the Senate in 1842 passed a southern-sponsored bill to eliminate Black troops, the House declined to take action (Litwack 1961:31–33).

To understand why southern plantation owners wished to suppress African-Americans in the South and elsewhere requires no elaborate theory. What is more complicated and difficult to explain is why white capitalists, politicians, and working-class people participated in, were the instruments of, and even at times took the lead in the racial subordination of Blacks. The question is: Why did the shadow of the plantation cast itself so fully over the North? That it did, however, is indisputable.

We might begin with Tocqueville, an observer whose perceptiveness and insights are generally overinflated by American intellectuals and academics. Although his superficiality is often overwhelming (especially with respect to issues of race), he does correctly note the existence of pervasive racial discrimination in the North (Tocqueville 1956:I:373). One can also glean something of the range of respectable white opinion in the North by looking at some of the remarks in the 1858 Lincoln-Douglas debates in the Illinois Senate race. Stephen Douglas, the Democrat who was representative of those forces in the North that would conciliate southern slave owners, expressed a typical opinion:

> I repeat that this nation is a white people—a people composed of European descendants—a people that have established a government for themselves and their posterity, and I am in favor of preserving not only the purity of the blood but the purity of the government from any mixture or amalgamation with inferior races. (Johannsen 1965:34)

It should also be noted that Douglas was a kindred soul to modern politicians when it came to playing the race card:

> ...if you, Black Republicans, think that the negro ought to be on a social equality with your wives and daughters, and ride in a carriage

with your wife, while you drive the team, you have a perfect right to do so. I am told that one of Fred Douglass's kinsmen, another rich black negro, is now traveling in this part of the State making speeches for his friend Lincoln as the champion of black men. (Johannsen 1965:92)

Lincoln, representative of those forces in the North who were opposed to slavery, took a slightly different tack. About slavery, at least in the territories, he was unequivocal, saying "I hate it because of the monstrous injustice of slavery itself" (Johannsen 1965:50). Yet, while admitting the impracticality of freeing the slaves and sending them to Liberia ("my first impulse"), he argues against making blacks "politically and socially our equals....My own feelings will not admit of this; and if mine would, we well know that those of the great mass of white people will not." And finally,

> I will say here, while upon this subject, that I have no purpose, directly or indirectly, to interfere with the institution of slavery in the States where it exists....I have no inclination to do so....I have no purpose to introduce political and social equality between the white and black races. There is a physical difference between the two, which, in my judgment, will probably forever forbid their living together upon the footing of perfect equality....I, as well as Judge Douglas, am in favor of the race to which I belong having the superior position. (Johannsen 1965:52)

Lincoln's position was eventually to become far more racially egalitarian, although even in the 1858 debates, Lincoln's racial attitudes were sharply distinguished from those of Douglas and the slave owners:

> I agree with Judge Douglas he is not my equal in many respects—certainly not in color, perhaps not in moral or intellectual endowment. But in the right to eat the bread, without the leave of anybody else, which his own hand earns, *he is my equal and the equal of Judge Douglas, and the equal of every living man.* (Johannsen 1965:50–53

These racist attitudes were expressed in public policy and social practices in the structure of white supremacy in the North. Virtually all the free Blacks in the North became disenfranchised after the Revolution. By 1840, 93 percent of Northern blacks were effectively excluded from voting; the exceptions were those who lived in Massachusetts, New Hampshire, Vermont, and Maine. After 1819, every new state that was admitted into the Union prohibited Black voting. By 1860, only Rhode Island, with its minuscule Black population, had reversed itself. Most northern states adopted provisions that prohibitted the immigration of free Blacks into their states. With the exception of Massachusetts, the one state that gave Blacks equal citizenship rights with whites, every other state proscribed Black legal rights in one way or another. In all other states, Blacks could not be jurors. In five states, they could not present testimony against whites in court (Litwack 1961:66–94). Even in Boston, prejudice often reared its head. During mid-century, student protest at Harvard Medical School forced the faculty to withdraw its admission of three Black men and one white woman. The field was so competitive that three leading doctors went insane after losing credit for anesthesia to a fourth; the cheapening of the Harvard degree by "the amalgamation of sexes and races" was thus considered too great a threat (see Takaki 1979:139–43; Sellers 1991:257–58).

Nevertheless, to equate the racial subordination in the North with that in the South for free Blacks, much less slaves, as Tocqueville does, is both preposterous and obtuse, while the claim that Blacks had equal rights in the North would likewise be farfetched (de Tocqueville 1956:373–4). The laws, social customs, and racist attitudes ultimately flowed from the need to harmonize and justify the huge profits from degraded, superexploited African-American labor. In the South, the connection was direct, although even there, conditions were sometimes moderated by conflicting interests. The oppression of slavery was sometimes lessened and the system of control weakened when slaves were rented out by their masters in urban areas. Some slaves were even free laborers in all but name, causing protests from the guardians of the white supremacist order, who were nevertheless unable to stop it. Such practices, however, were often extremely profitable for large slave owners, who, like the proverbial 800-pound gorilla, usually sat where they wanted. In addition, free Blacks often played an indispensable role, performing critical tasks in the urban economies and being available for hire as seasonal labor in the rural areas. Because of their necessary labor, they were often protected against repression that went too far. For these and other reasons, free Blacks often had a clear social sphere, sharply distinguished from that of slaves. This was perhaps most clearly true in South Carolina, where the treatment of the small number of free Blacks was frequently mitigated by the large degree to which many were related by blood to powerful slaveholders (Joyner 1984:59–65).

Southern slave owners, of course, had great influence over the policies of the federal government. In the northern states, there were also numerous economic interests that were tied to the cotton plantation economy. Abolitionists pointed to the coalition of the northern textile manufacturers, the "lords of the loom," with the "lords of the lash." The port of New York City, which accounted for over two-thirds of all imports and one-third of all exports in the country as a whole, was notorious in its economic ties to the slavocracy and the sympathies of its capitalists for slavery (Bruchey 1967:Tables 3M and 3N). As Miller points out, look how difficult it is today to win victories over the tobacco industry, whose role in the economy is minuscule compared with that of the pre-Civil War cotton growers (Miller 1996:11), and one begins to see the scope of the problem. Because free Blacks were the least protected part of the labor force, they were often the easiest for employers to hire cheaply. For those who competed with them direct-ly, as the Irish workers did in certain venues, Blacks were the easiest to exclude from the job market because they had few recourses and their self-defense was the most unacceptable. Such was the case in the port of New York City, where by the 1850s the Irish had succeeded in driving Black water-front workers from their jobs (Ignatiev 1995:120).

On one level, discrimination against Blacks in the North does not need any sophisticated psychological, cultural, or identity-formation theory in order to be understood. Frederick Douglass, for example, gives a relatively simple and quite plausible explanation. He argues,

> Properly speaking, *prejudice against color* does not exist in this coun-try.... While we are servants, we are never offensive to the whites, or marks of popular displeasure.... On the very day we were bru-tally assaulted in New York for riding down Broadway in company with ladies, we saw several ladies riding with *black servants*.... If the feeling which persecutes us were prejudice against color, the col-ored servant would be as obnoxious as the colored gentlemen, for the color is the same in both cases; and being the *same* in both cases, it would produce the *same* result in both cases.... We are then a per-secuted people; not because we are *colored*, but simply because that color has for a series of years been coupled in the public mind with the degradation of slavery and servitude." (Douglass 1975:II:128–29) [June 1850]

One might add that since over 90 percent of African Americans during the pre–Civil War period were in the South, these associations would pre-dominate.

Yet, despite the commonalities in attitudes and policies in the North and the South and the strong interests in making these uniform, an irrec-oncilable conflict over the institution of racial slavery developed that led to the Civil War. Why this happened is central to understanding both how social development takes place and why racial questions have been at the center of U.S. political life from the beginning to the present. There are several aspects to a full answer. We need not dwell on the differences over federal government policies that had enormous economic ramifications, from the question of tariffs to the building of infrastructure to facilitate commerce to issues of banking and finance. These issues obviously played a central role in the growing antagonisms between the plantation capitalists of the South and the manufacturing and commercial capitalists of the North. There are, however, a more diffuse, yet equally important set of ideological issues conducive to rapid capitalist development that need to be understood. For the laws, ideology, and public policy that supported slavery both hindered unfettered capitalist development and ran counter to the bourgeois value system that justified it.

The first such issue in this system is that of free labor. For workers, free labor meant the dignity of work, the ability to have access to the labor market, to be able to live decently and get ahead. All these were undermined and threatened by the widening use of slave labor and to a lesser extent low-paid immigrant labor. For capitalists, labor, as Marx has pointed out, needed to be free in a double sense if it was to be exploited most fully, flexibly, and profitably: First, workers had to be free of property, especially ties to the land that would enable them to survive without working for wages. They had to be "free" from encumbrances so that they were forced to work if they did not want their families and themselves to starve. Second, they had to be free to choose, to respond to labor market demand, to go wherever and whenever their work was needed. The more restrictions on labor flow, the more difficult it was to utilize labor. Thus, capitalists have often opposed immigration restrictions, as many important spokesmen for capitalist interests, including the *Wall Street Journal,* do today. Slavery, which placed restrictions primarily on the utilization of Black labor but also on the use and mobility of white labor, restricted the "freedom" of labor both for northern capitalists and for white workers (E. Foner 1970:38–39; Sellers 1991:passim).

The second issue was that the system of slavery undermined precisely those values that served to legitimize capitalism to the majority of those on the bottom. How, especially in a respresentative democracy, can one justify the immense inequalities of wealth and income, particularly in an increasingly affluent society? The only answer that capitalism can give is that everyone is equal in the marketplace. The only color that counts, so to speak, is the color of one's money. Buyers and sellers of labor power or other commodities, as Lincoln pointed out, must have abstract rights that are equal. The argument is laid out most fully and brilliantly in Hegel's *Philosophy of Right* (Hegel 1962, or for the most consistent version, Hegel 1983). Nothing must inhibit exchange relations, property ownership, or the recognition of these rights. Only one's merit, hard work, skill, intelligence, perseverance count. As Sellers notes, successful businessmen in the North became highly committed to this liberal ideology, not the least of reasons because it justified their beneficent conditions (Sellers 1991:17–8). Such an ideology, of course, is merely an ideal. Capitalism has often been able to function quite well with great exceptions, although in the most dynamic, especially early, periods of capitalist development, there is often strong pressure to reconcile the ideology with reality. Thus, both white supremacy and male supremacy, while they may support certain aspects of bourgeois rule, functioned at other times to undermine its legitimacy.

On certain key issues, North and South clashed over ideology. A number of these issues served to let people in the North know that the claim by southern elites that they merely wanted states' rights (i.e., local control) was a hypocritical lie, as in fact it always has been and continues to be to this day in American politics. It was for the South only the first line of defense in protecting racial subordination. Or, as Lincoln made clear, the nation could not remain half free and half slave; one system or the other would have to dominate. Several issues made this clear.

The first was the question of free speech. In 1834 and 1835, hostility to abolitionists was virtually as strong in the North as in the South. Abolitionist speakers had their meetings broken up, were the subject of threats, rocks, and sometimes more violent behavior. William Lloyd Garrison was led through the streets of Boston by a mob with a rope around his neck, and the preacher-editor Elijah Lovejoy was murdered by a mob in Alton, Illinois, in 1837. Most of these mobs were led by and included the most eminent and affluent citizens in the communities. Nevertheless, repression was far more severe in the South, as opponents of slavery were forced to flee the region. Further, the initial repression in the North was quite specific, directed at abolitionist speakers and leaders. In the South, it was draconian and pervasive. Permanent Committees of Viligance or Committees of Public Safety, made up of eminent citizens, were established throughout the whole South; these groups searched out and attacked those who might deviate in the slightest from the rigid defense of white supremacy. These organizations, the precursors of the later Ku Klux Klan, even went so far as to tar and feather suspicious northern traveling book salesmen (Miller 1996:76). Southern representatives argued from the floor of Congress "that it would be an offense against heaven not to kill any available abolitionist" (Miller 1995:39); they raised money and put prices on the heads of the most prominent of them.

Southern postmasters began searching the mails and destroying abolitionist literature, making sure that no one in the South would read the *Liberator* or the *Slave's Friend*. Yet, even northern establishment newspapers whose commitment to white supremacy was not sufficiently doctrinaire were often destroyed. These latter violations of the rights of free press and the mails for bourgeois elements, as opposed to the violations of the rights of the abolitionists, generated a storm of protests. Although the South defended these outrageous violations of the civil liberties that most whites in the country felt were guaranteed by the constitution as within the sphere of states' rights, southern elites then went even further. Southern representatives in Congress showed that they cared not a whit for states' rights. With the help of their northern allies, they instituted a gag rule that prohibited the discussion of slavery in areas outside the South, including in the nation's capital.

Such undemocratic, brutal, uncivilized, and oppressive behavior was—contrary to the claims often made about the "gentility" of slave society—as Frederick Douglass argues, the norm for the pre–Civil War slavocracy. He cites the "mobocratic demonstrations against the right of free speech" in Congress, the display there "of pistols, bludgeons, and plantation manners" (Douglass 1962:292). These and other actions shocked the not-so-genteel people from the North:

> No one act did more to rouse the North to a comprehension of the infernal and barbarous spirit of slavery and its determination to "rule or ruin," than the cowardly and brutal assault made in the American senate upon Charles Sumner by Preston S. Brooks, a member of Congress from South Carolina. Shocking and scandalous as was this attack, the spirit in which the deed was received and commended by the community was still more disgraceful. Southern ladies even applauded the armed bully for his murderous assault upon an unarmed northern Senator, because of words spoken in debate! This more than all else told the thoughtful people of the North the kind of civilization to which they were linked and how plainly it foreshadowed a conflict on a larger scale. (Douglass 1962:294)

As one prominent abolitionist explained, "We commenced the present struggle to obtain freedom of the slave; we are compelled to continue it to preserve our own" (Tyler 1944:511).

The second issue which suggested that the "rights" of slave owners took precedence over the rights of sovereign northern states was the struggle over fugitive slaves. The claims that southern slave catchers had a right to seize suspected runaways who were living in northern states, that northern and federal authorities had the legal obligation to assist them, that the laws of the northern states about slaves and fugitives were irrelevant, and that the supposed fugitives had no right to a hearing by the communities and states in which they resided were a direct affront to large numbers of northern citizens. It put the lie to the argument that the South held the rights of states—other than, of course, its own—to be sacred. Battles and rescues involving

real people—peaceful, often married, productive members of the community—often took place on a grand scale and elicited widespread sympathy among northern whites. These flesh-and-blood fugitives led large
numbers of white northerners to become abolititionists. As Du Bois argues,
"The fugitives presented themselves before the eyes of the North and the
world as living specimens of the real meaning of slavery. What was the system that could enslave a Frederick Douglass?" (Du Bois 1969:82).

Finally the most overwhelming proof that states' rights was a sham was
the nature of the Confederate state itself. With the exception perhaps of Nazi
Germany, the South during the Civil War developed one of the most draconian, centralized, authoritarian states in world history. They seized property and crops, redistributing them to war widows and their children; they
told farmers what to grow; they let no individual, local, or state's right stand
in the way of winning the war (see Bensel 1990).

Into this vortex of growing conflict between northern and southern capital—over economic policy (which included banking and financial policy,
railroads, canals, and infrastructure, and tariffs), over ideology and culture,
over the laws concerning the use of labor, over the political character and
control of the new territories, and over the use of western land and its availability for white homesteaders—stepped the abolitionists. There exist many
disagreements over their importance and character, some of which I will
touch on in order to place the role of the abolitionists in perspective. Two
issues, which can be stated stenographically and without the necessary subtlety, are central: First, how important were they in winning northerners to
anti-slavery and abolitionism, in sharpening the sectional conflict, in shaping the Republican Party, and in bringing on the Civil War? Second, how pure
were they; or rather, were they really anti-racist, and what class interests did
they ultimately represent? These questions are, to be sure, intertwined.

There have been several cycles of abolitionist interpretations (see E. Foner
1970:2–4 and 1980:16 for useful analysis and references). An earlier view
saw them as marginal, largely religious fanatics, perhaps kooks, with little
or no influence (see, e.g., Hofstadter 1989:177–80 for a summary). A subsequent view saw them as having been idealists who were the nation's con-
science, winning the North to anti-slavery. More recently, there have been
those who argue that despite their important role, they were defective. Many
were racially paternalistic, if not out-and-out racist. They were often anti-
labor union; and in the argument of some, they served as the stalking hors-
es for the northern bourgeoisie. Finally, at least two important authors argue
that the abolitionists were proletarian internationists, implicitly or explicitly anti-capitalist, having views similar to Marx (see Aptheker 1989:32–34;
Ignatiev 1995:205).

We can begin with a brief critique and dismissal of the older view that the abolitionists were not central to the events that led to the Civil War by discussing what they did and the impact they had on American politics. The abolitionist movement that developed in the late 1820s and early 1830s marked a new departure in anti-slavery agitation. The new abolitionism not only said that slavery was wrong—that had been argued by Quakers and others for decades—but that it was the most heinous of wrongs, that it should be *the* political priority of all those who opposed it, and that all one's energies should be devoted to ending it. Further, it was so wrong that it should be ended immediately (not gradually, as some had hitherto argued) and that those individuals who perpetrated it were evil, deserving no compensation for the loss of their property that abolition would entail. Here was a new departure.

In 1829, David Walker, a free Black, issued *Walker's Appeal...to the Colored Citizens of the World*, calling for violence and revolt to address the wrongs Blacks had suffered. In 1830, a white anti-slavery colonialist William Lloyd Garrison, believing that slavery should be ended by shipping U.S. Blacks "back" to Africa, was converted to immediatism. The first issue of Garrison's paper, the *Liberator*, came out on January 1, 1831. That issue threw down the gauntlet, Garrison stating in his editorial not merely the case for immediatism with no compensation but that "I am in earnest. I will not equivocate; I will not excuse; I will not retreat a single inch; and I will be heard." Initially, the *Liberator* had only fifty white subscribers. It was largely supported by its overwhelmingly Black subscribers and several wealthy followers, Black and white (Filler 1986:80). In 1833, the United Kingdom abolished slavery in the West Indies; the American Anti-Slavery Society was formed in Philadelphia in December of that year.

At first, abolitionists were denounced throughout the country, especially in New England. They were stoned, had their meetings broken up, were arrested, and were threatened with death. Yet, they persevered. By 1838, abolitionist societies existed throughout the North, with as many as 1,350 local groups and almost a quarter of a million members (see Aptheker 1989:56 for a discussion of figures). By the late 1830s, the daily talks of Garrison and dozens of other abolitionist leaders were drawing thousands. In 1854, the entire text of Garrison's remarks in New York City to a larger meeting was reprinted the next day in the *New York Times*. Pamphlets and books by leading abolitionists sold in the hundreds of thousands, and Harriet Beecher Stowe's antislavery novel *Uncle Tom's Cabin* sold millions of copies in the United States and tens of millions of copies abroad (Aptheker 1989:55). Certain sections of the country, such as the Western Reserve area of northern Ohio, became abolitionist strongholds, not only sending numerous petitions to

Congress and electing antislavery representatives, but also sheltering fugitive slaves and wanted abolitionists (Miller 1996:80).

Although not necessarily agreeing with the racial egalitarianism espoused by abolitionists, millions of white people in the North treated them with great sympathy and respect, which is the only explanation for the northern reaction to the hanging of John Brown. Perhaps that reaction had something to do with an observation made by Brown in 1851: "Nothing so charms the American people as personal bravery" (Aptheker 1989:126). How else can we explain the following extraordinary situation. In 1858, Brown and his men had gone into Missouri, freed eleven slaves, killed the master, and successfully fled with them into Canada. There was a warrant for his arrest. President James Buchanan personally offered a $250 reward for his capture. Yet, later that year, during the trial in Cleveland, Ohio, of the Oberlin-Wellington rescuers, thirty-seven people who had forcibly freed a fugitive slave from four southern slave catchers, John Brown walked the streets of Cleveland openly for a month, spoke at meetings in defense of the rescuers, and even visited them in jail (Aptheker 1989:128–30). The reader may draw his or her own conclusion about what this event and others like it meant for the distance the abolitionists had traveled in two decades, the degree of moral authority they commanded among ordinary people (none of whom saw fit to attempt to obtain the reward), and what it meant for the power of civil authority to enforce the law of the land in the North when it came to slavery. Thus, Eric Foner's subtle analysis of the role of abolitionism within the emerging anti-slavery Republican coalition in the late 1850s needs to be amplified. Foner argues that the abolitionists, although a minority, were defended by those who disagreed with them because of common anti-slavery views and belief in the right of free speech. Yet, something deeper and more powerful was also involved. People who disagreed with immediate, uncompensated abolition also often admired and supported abolitionists and had great respect for them, deferring at times to their recognized moral authority, a powerful, even if contradictory type of support.

The activities and agitation of the abolitionists were the key ingredients in exacerbating the conflict that led to the Civil War. They exposed the system of slavery in its full inhumanity to all of northern and western opinion, leaving it open to moral condemnation, showing its inconsistencies with the principles of the Republic, the emerging values of modern society, and all of modern, democratic thought.

They inspired and goaded southern leaders to display the whole irrationality and untenability of their situation, these leaders denying civil rights and civil liberties first to the citizens of their own region and eventually making claims on the federal government and even the citizens of the North.

The moral conversion of hundreds of thousands into committed abolitionists, the giving of open support for slave rebellions, and the eventual winning of the sympathy, if not the outright agreement, of much of the North
made the conflict irreversible and inevitable. Without the abolitionists, the
economic and political differences between northern and southern capitalists might have been compromised, as both Barrington Moore and Eric Foner
suggest. The activities and arguments of the abolitionists made a revolution
from above inevitable.

Let us now turn to the abolitionist movement itself. Earlier historians
have tended to dwell almost exclusively on the activities of the white abolitionists, either neglecting or relegating to secondary importance the role
of African-Americans. Even recent writings, in more subtle ways to be sure,
continue to undervalue their contributions. Miller, for example, argues that
"the very structures and attitudes against which they fought left black persons too far from any levers of power and too far from the central stream
of the society to become key leaders, and hence symbols, to the entire nation,
the way King could in the next century" (Miller 1996:82). Some smaller number of other scholars, on the other hand, have attempted to emphasize the
role of Blacks. Herbert Aptheker makes this argument quite powerfully: "In
general, when considering the history of antislavery, primary weight should
always be given to the activities of black people, slave and free, for they were
the catalysts and indispensable components of the movement to end slavery" (Aptheker 1989:75–76). Or,

> Although a salient feature of the Abolitionist movement was its
> black-white character, it is important to emphasize the over-
> whelming consequence of its black component. Slavery was the
> unique experience of black people in the United States....They alone
> endured it, survived it, and combated it. They were the first and
> most lasting Abolitionists. Their conspiracies and insurrections,
> individual struggles, systematic flights, maroon communities,
> efforts to buy freedom, cultural solidity, creation of antislavery orga-
> nizations and publications—all preceded the black-white united
> efforts....Without the initiative of Afro-American people, without
> their illumination of the nature of slavery, without their persistent
> struggle to be free, there would have been no national Abolitionist
> movement. And when the movement did appear, the participation
> of black people in every aspect was indispensable to its function-
> ing and its eventual success. (Aptheker 1989:xiii)

Let us try to give some plausibility to this claim. I have already noted the
importance of plots and rebellions for earlier abolitionist activity during the

revolutionary period. It is also claimed that the Nat Turner rebellion gave a major impetus to northern abolitionist activities in the 1830s. Likewise, the issues raised by mutinies on two slave-transport ships, the *Creole* and the *Amistad,* accelerated the debate over slavery. And it was the specter of northern-supported slave rebellion explicit in the raid John Brown led on the Harpers Ferry arsenal that deepened the gulf between North and South. Eugene Genovese, who attempts to universalize his thesis about the submissiveness of Blacks under slavery, belittles the degree of resistance of Blacks by arguing that most chose to run away during the Civil War rather than fight their masters (Genovese 1984:139). Potter, in his vendetta against John Brown, gives an even more one-dimensional account, quoting Genovese out of context and losing what subtlety existed in the latter's analysis (Potter 1976:374). Slave revolts were difficult enough in Haiti, where Blacks outnumbered both whites and mulattoes by seven to one (Jordan 1977:385) and only the events of the French Revolution in the motherland provided a suitable context for successful revolt. When opportunity presented itself, slaves often availed themselves of it, whether on transport ships or by running away. During the war itself, there were numerous instances of assertions of power by slaves that further belie the conclusions of Genovese and Potter. (Saville 1994, for example, notes numerous such cases in South Carolina as the Civil War proceeded).

Spectacular escapes of slaves captivated the attention of the nation, bringing home the degree to which Blacks would risk death to sever their chains. In 1843, one couple, the woman almost white, traveling in the guise of a sick young male, the man as her servant, made their way North, emerging there to tell their story to fascinated multitudes. When slave catchers attempted to recapture them, abolitionists sent them to England, where they spoke to tens of thousands about U.S. slavery. Another man—appropriately named Henry "Box" Brown—emerged from a small shipping box in Philadelphia that had been sent from Richmond by a white shoe merchant. Brown's escape engrossed huge numbers of people who turned out across the North to hear his story (Aptheker 1989:72–73).

Free Blacks played a central role in initiating and sustaining the abolitionist movement. The Walker Manifesto and the first Black convention, which initiated the Negro Convention Movement, both took place in 1830, before the first issue of the *Liberator.* The Black church also played an important role in supporting abolitionism. Both the Underground Railroad, which helped Black slaves escape to the North and to Canada, and the Vigilance Committees that warned northern Blacks about slave catchers and helped rescue fugitives were overwhelmingly Black (see Quarles 1964 and Pease and Pease 1965 for additional details). Black males, including Frederick Douglass, Charles

Remond, and Robert Purvis, played leadership roles in the anti-slavery movement. Black women organized female anti-slavery societies, beginning a year before the organization of the American Anti-Slavery Society. Two African-American women, Sojourner Truth and Frances Ellen Watkins, were among those who played leading roles in the general abolitionist movement.

The leading white abolitionists were in important ways dependent on the northern free Black community for sustenance and support. Garrison, of course, was converted from colonization to abolitionism by Black colleagues. The early *Liberator* and his initial trips were financed by Blacks (Aptheker 1989:67). Many other brave white abolitionists were kept afloat and given strength by their support from the Black community. This undoubtedly included the educator Prudence Randall, who set up a Black school when the parents of her white students tried to force her not to enroll a Black student (A. Davis 1983:34–35). Theodore Weld and his religious followers, who formed the initial cadre of abolitionist lecturers, gained strength by living and working in Cincinnati's "Little Africa" (Miller 1996:90). And for those who might doubt the commitment of free northern Blacks to abolition, the reactions to John Brown's raid in Baltimore are instructive. "When Baltimore police broke into the annual caulker's ball, they discovered the hall bedecked with pictures of Brown and a bust inscribed 'The martyr— God bless him.' Chalked on the floor was an outline of Governor Henry Wise straddled by 'a huge Ethiopian,' surrounded by 'inscriptions unfit for publication,'" (Berlin 1974:374–75).

So how do we characterize the abolitionist movement, perhaps the most important, as well as the most radical, social movement ever in American history? Let us look first at their strongest opponents. Leonard Richards has analyzed anti-abolitionist mobs in Cincinnati, Ohio, and Utica, New York, concluding that the rank-and-file overwhelming consisted of commercial and property men (L. Richards 1970:136-40), in stark contrast with the composition of abolitionist ranks in both cities. Aptheker argues that "the most avid opponents of Abolitionism were the rich—slaveowners and their lackeys, the merchants and their servitors, the dominant figures in politics, the press, the churches, and the schools," at least until the late 1840s, when alignments changed (Aptheker 1989:41, 46). These arguments are important, although they neglect the significant working-class component of anti-abolitionism, most notably a segment of the Irish workers (see, for example, Ignatiev 1995: passim and Foner 1980:26).

The abolitionist movement seems to have had its base of white support in three venues. The first, correctly emphasized by most historians—although often to the exclusion of other forces—were the revivalist, religious adherents to the Second Awakening, whose strongholds were in New England, upstate New York, western Pennsylvania, northern Ohio, and other areas where Protestant New Englanders and Quakers had migrated. These reformers, disproportionately female, similar in their perspectives to today's adherents in Latin America of "liberation theology," were involved in virtually every reform movement of the day, including women's rights, racial equality, temperance, as well as free love, spiritualism, Fourierism, and vegetarianism (Messer-Kruse 1994:15). They provided much of the energy and base for abolitionist activity. In addition, there was the developing middle class of professionals and merchants whose self-justifying values conflicted most sharply with slavery. Finally, there was the important artisan base, noted by a large number of recent scholars, representing in many places a majority of the signers of anti-slavery petitions, although less represented among the leadership (Foner 1980:61; Richards 1970; Dawley 1976:65; Magdol 1986:65, passim).

What also distinguished the abolitionist movement as a social movement was the unusually large involvement of women in the leadership, as well as in the rank-and-file, and the important attention given to the question of equality for women. The early signers of abolitionist petitions were disproportionately women, as were many of the volunteers who circulated them (Miller, 1996:65, 108). The large numbers of women who spoke and took leadership roles were a significant change from previous social movements. Among these women were Sojourner Truth; Lucretia Mott; the daughters of a prominent Charleston slave-owning family, Sarah and Angelina Grimke; and a host of others. The abolitionist movement was far more advanced on the question of women's rights than previous movements had been, although even here, many male abolitionist leaders opposed the mere participation of women in the movement, largely on the male-supremacist grounds that women belonged in the home. Yet, on this issue, when the American Anti-Slavery Society split in 1840, the majority voted to allow women to participate (Filler 1986:169–71). The issues of full female equality were pushed by female abolitionists, supported by Wendell Philips, Weld, Garrison, and Douglass. Except for Philips (and later Weld, who was converted by the Grimke sisters before his eventual marriage to Angelina), the others occasionally had specific objections to the full and equal participation of women (Aptheker 1989:8). Yet, at the 1840 World Anti-Slavery Convention in London, when women delegates were denied seating, they were joined in the spectators' gallery by several American male delegates, including Garrison, Charles Remond, and Nathaniel Rogers (A. Davis 1983:47–48). It was from these roots that the nineteenth century women's movement emerged.

In attempting to evaluate the abolitionist movement, one must assess the degree to which the movement, in particular its white leaders and members, was racially egalitarian. Since the 1960s, there have been many attempts to cast doubt on their racial practices. Pease and Pease (1965), for example, argue that the "antislavery crusaders were beset by a fundamental ambivalence in their attitude toward the Negro himself," although they hardly give much concrete evidence aside from "the middle class values to which almost all abolitionists subscribed." They do, nevertheless, admit that "despite concepts of racial inferiority,...abolitionists in fact did demand just and equitable civil liberties for colored persons" (Pease and Pease 1965:682, 688). Examples of overt racism may be found, to be sure, especially among more moderate abolitionists. At a Michigan convention of the abolitionist Liberty Party, two Black delegates were denied credentials because they were not legal voters. In 1844, the party nominated for vice president ex-Senator Thomas Morris, an opponent of Black voting. Yet, "throughout the North, the party was an ardent opponent of political and social discrimination against the free Negro" (Foner 1980:78). Early abolitionist groups often debated the wisdom of accepting Black members (Litwack 1961:216–18). The debates over the degrees to which abolitionists should advocate complete interracial social relations (thus incurring the wrath of mobs who accused them of being racial amalgamationists) are often difficult for one to evaluate, in particular, the degree to which arguments were based on real concerns versus the degree to which they sometimes expressed racial prejudice. Yet, even among the more radical abolitionists, one can find patonizing attitudes, often in abolitionist writings, Harriet Beecher Stowe's *Uncle Tom's Cabin* being only the most obvious. The advice given to the recently escaped Frederick Douglass by leading abolitionists smacks of such attitudes. John A. Collins told him, "People won't believe you ever were a slave.... Better have a little of the plantation speech than not...it is not best that you seem too learned." Douglass, of course, did not follow such advice and was soon denounced by antiabolitionists as an impostor who had never been South (Douglass 1962:217–18).

Yet, to dwell on these exceptions and complexities is to miss the intensity with which both Black and white abolitionists detested and fought the system of white supremacy in virtually all its manifestations. Even by today's standards, their record is impressive. Together, they fought discrimination in schools, housing, and restaurants, physically sitting in at racist hotels, boats, stages, and railroads. They fought antimiscegenation laws that prohibited intermarriage. There was a high degree of intermingling at the personal, social, and political levels, reflected in the accounts of many of the leading Black as well as white abolitionists. Although it is important to be aware of the blemishes, it is well that we draw a bottom line in describing the full picture: The abolitionists displayed a greater commitment to racial egalitarianism than any other interracial movement in the United States has, before or since.

Yet, there are more complex issues that have been raised by scholars about the abolitionists, and their relation to the rising capitalist system in the North and those who were oppressed by it, as well as their relation to the nascent labor movement that attempted to defend the victims of early American industrialization. To what degree, it has been asked, did the abolitionists represent a capitalist opposition to the northern labor movement. Conversely, there has been a long-standing debate over the degree to which the labor movement supported or rejected abolitionism. Finally, there are many questions about how abolitionists and northern labor organizations did and did not coalesce in the period leading up to the Civil War.

These questions are central to our investigation for a number of reasons. If the system of white racial domination is in good part rooted in socio-economic or class relations, as I have argued, then the ability of anti-racists to successfully combat the system of white supremacy will depend in part on the degree to which they are able to confront its socio-economic roots. And if the problems of effective labor organization are largely dependent on their ability to overcome racial divisions, develop broad solidaristic activities, and lead a staunch fight against racial domination, then their relation to the movements that are leading these battles is crucial. Further, if the possibilities for success of popular movements are magnified during decisive historical turning points, then an understanding of these issues during perhaps the most decisive such moment may prove illuminating.

The argument that all, or virtually all, the early and most radical abolitionists were anti-labor is long-standing. Herman Schlüter, for example, argued this case quite strongly in 1913. In discussing the appeal of Fourierist Albert Brisbane in the *Liberator* in 1845 that abolitionists should "include in their movement a reform of the present wretched organization of labor, called the wage system," Schlüter writes:

> It is surely needless to note especially the fact that Brisbane's appeal to the Abolitionists was in vain. They were unable to understand him and the aspirations of the workingmen, and to some extent probably did not want to understand. (Schlüter 1965:49–51).

A similar stance is taken by Bernard Mandel, who argues:

> ...they had almost without exception, a blind spot for the ills that beset the working men, except as the abolition of slavery would benefit them....Scarcely an issue of any of their papers lacked an article or poem demonstrating the nobility of free labor, refuting the arguments of labor leaders and reformers that the wages system was

a disguised form of slavery, and presenting evidence of the constant improvement in the condition of the proletariat. (Mandel 1955:89)

Even Angela Davis, far more sympathetic to the abolitionists than Schlüter or Mandel, makes a similar argument, quoting several lines from William Lloyd Garrison in the first issue of the *Liberator*, where he says that "it is in the highest degree criminal...to inflame the minds of our working classes against the more opulent, and to persuade them that they are contemned and oppressed by a wealthy aristocracy" (A. Davis 1983:65; See also Mandel 1955:91; *Liberator*, January 1, 1933; and for a more complex argument that in the end takes the same position, see Kraditor 1969:244–53).[3] One can, on the other hand, find some historians noting contrary information, particularly for the 1850s and 1860s. David Montgomery, for example, notes the large number of abolitionists, including Garrison, who endorsed the eight-hour campaign in the 1860s, concluding that "in short, the widely accepted notion that among the antislavery men of the Bay State Wendell Phillips alone was sympathetic to labor's cause is pure myth" (Montgomery 1967:123–24).[4] A more nuanced, commonly accepted view argues that anti-labor stances among many abolitionists may be traced to two factors: First, many (particularly the religiously motivated ones) held the belief that freely acting individuals received their just deserts in a democratic, capitalist society. Slaves were kept from controlling their own destinies, denied individual rights. Workers (especially whites, but sometimes including free blacks) had the freedom to move, refuse work, compete in the marketplace, and thus through hard work and ability got their due; when they did not, they had only themselves to blame. Fredrickson states this position especially incisively, arguing that "most of the abolitionists believed that the capitalist free-labor system of the North was healthy to the core" (Fredrickson 1971:38, 33; see also Williams 1969:254; Glickstein 1979:206.) Second, in their polemical stance against slavery's ideologues, who often argued that southern slaves lived better than northern and British workers, abolitionists were often tempted to defend the existing conditions in the North. As Foner argues, the abolitionists "served to justify the emerging capitalist order of the North...by isolating slavery as an unacceptable form of labor exploitation, while refusing to condemn the exploitative aspects of 'free' labor relations" (Foner 1980:24). And in by far the most subtle form of this argument, David Brion Davis argues that abolitionist arguments which separated them from concern for working-class oppression helped to reinforce the legitimacy of the emerging capitalist order in both the United Kingdom and the United States (D. Davis 1975:347–61, 364, 373–74).

A good chunk of this argument is cast into doubt by the compelling analysis of Timothy Messer-Kruse (1994). He argues that few of the critics look at the evolution of abolitionist views over time or the contexts in which the most extreme anti-labor remarks were made. The abolitionists, according to Messer-Kruse, evolved over time, coming eventually by the late 1840s and early 1850s to link the problems of northern labor, racial egalitarianism, and abolition. Many of their number, including possibly Garrison, Phillips, and Sumner, had by the 1870s joined the First International led by Karl Marx. Several other scholars have noted in passing changes in abolitionists' attitudes toward labor, but Messer-Kruse gives by far the most in-depth analysis (see Foner 1980:67–69; Aptheker 1989:40; Montgomery 1967:123–24). Messer-Kruse argues that the early abolitionists did indeed have the views attributed to them. Yet, even Garrison freely criticized northern and British society by the late 1840s, when he was removed from the polemical context of the debate with slavery's defenders. In 1845, Garrison, Phillips, and other leading abolitionists attended the convention of the New England Workingmen's Association (Messer-Kruse 1994:43). Their evolution during this time was not unequivocal, and few had developed as radical a critique of the emerging industrial system as they had of slavery; yet, the change was dramatic. One sign is that the increasing strength of the coalition between abolitionists and labor reformists led southern ideologues to change their stance toward northern labor, denouncing labor leaders along with abolitionists as dangerous subversives. In 1858, at a radical labor meeting in Boston whose purpose was to express broad working-class solidarity and to honor the memories of several European revolutionary martyrs, a letter of strong support was read. It was signed, "Yours to break every yoke, Wm. Lloyd Garrison" (Messer-Kruse 1994:64–65). Despite their individualist presuppositions and religious beginnings, many abolitionists had traveled a great distance since the early 1830s. In addition to their concerns for universal reform, they were attacking one of the most central features of American society, and their perspective was indeed revolutionary. Whatever their limitations, and I am far from arguing that they had none, every radical movement from the Civil War on was to be leavened by the yeast of abolitionist cadres, their commitments, their experience, and their radical concerns for freedom for all peoples. Their harvest was reaped by the women's movement, the Haymarket martyrs (one of whose central figures, Albert Parsons, had become committed to racial egalitarianism by his participation in the Reconstruction movement), and as Foner notes, the National Labor Union, the Knights of Labor, and "even the Irish-American Land League" (Foner 1980:76).

What, then, of the other side of the equation? To what degree did the northern white labor movement support abolition? In 1847, Garrison submitted the following resolution to the Massachusetts Anti-Slavery Society:

Resolved, That of all classes in this country, to whom the three millions of our enslaved and chattelized countrymen have a right confidently to look for sympathy, aid, and complete deliverance from their horrible servitude, THE WORKING-MEN of the North constitute that class; and so long as they stand aloof from the Anti-Slavery enterprise, they will not only be guilty of manufacturing yokes for the necks, and fetters for the limbs, of the Southern Slave population, but will fail in all their efforts to remove those burdens and monopolies, under which they themselves are groaning. (Kraditor 1969:267)

What, then, were the interests of white workers in the North, South, or West in this escalating class conflict between northern and southern capitalists? With the development of industrial capitalism in the North, workers there were faced with the standard brutal features of early industrialization in capitalist societies: low wages, insecure livelihoods, child labor, disease, accidents, injuries, disfigurement and crippling, early death, and repression of their attempts at organization. These, of course, are the same types of conditions that one sees in many Third World countries today that are attempting to industrialize: child labor in Pakistan, repression in Mexico, alleged use of prison labor in China, similar conditions in Thailand and Indonesia. The question of whether white workers suffering under these conditions of early industrial development had an interest in the abolition of slavery in the South has been a matter of dispute. Now, it is agreed by many who are sympathetic to organized labor that the long-term interests of workers are best served by broad solidarity and mutual support of wide strata of laborers. Those fighting their battles alone often become isolated and defeated, particularly in the long run. Yet, many have argued recently (as did most white labor leaders at the time) that the abolition of slavery was not in the immediate interests of white workers. Abolition would supposedly unleash a huge number of potential competitors into the labor force. This view, however, only looks at part of the picture. First, slave labor is always cheaper to maintain than free labor. In many parts of the South, it was already successfully driving free white labor off the market. This was most clear in agriculture, where poor whites often lived a marginal existence. Further, skilled labor on the large plantations was almost exclusively done by slaves. In large southern cities, the majority of skilled work by midcentury was being done by Black slaves, many of whom were rented out by their masters or even at times allowed to work for wages. Abolition was surely in the immediate interests of poor southern whites, whose best chance to live well was in the freeing and subsequent raising of the living standards of their slave competitors. Slave labor was also beginning to compete successfully with free white labor in many ports, in canal digging, and even in some places in mining and other traditional industries (Starobin 1970). The continuation of slavery (inseparable from its expansion) was bound to bring more of the same, with slave labor and its white competitors competing more and more within those venues in which northern white workers held dominance. Many of the immediate interests of white workers should have led them to side with the abolitionist movement.

There were, in fact, important labor components of the abolitionist movement. I have already mentioned the large numbers of artisans who had signed abolitionist petitions in the 1830s and 1840s, not merely in New England but in New York City as well. Montgomery has argued that native American workingmen in New England were often very involved in abolitionism in the spirit of millenialist, religious reform. According to one source, they were the heart of the antislavery movement, "which was not strongest in the educated class, but was predominantly a people's movement" (Montgomery 1967:118). In New York, a Workingman's Party newspaper was the only publication to defend the Nat Turner uprising. The radical artisans who met each year on Tom Paine's birthday usually included a toast to the liberators of Haiti (Foner 1980:61). The most numerous immigrant group among workers and among the population at large as well during the nineteenth century was the Germans. Among them, there was sometimes strong support for abolition, particularly among the 48ers, those Germans who were refugees from the failed 1848 uprising in their homeland; such was certainly the opinion of Frederick Douglass (Levine 1992:9). There were small organized Marxist groups that called for abolition during the 1850s not only in New England, New York, and Pennsylvania but in parts of the South, including Maryland, Virginia, Kentucky, Missouri, Louisiana, and Texas (Aptheker 1989:40). Most of these radical groups were secular. Those that were not Marxist tended to have views rooted in the republican ideals described so extensively by many labor historians, or in rationalist viewpoints based in the Enlightenment. Even the non-Marxists were often vehemently opposed to the evangelicism of many of the religious abolitionists.

Yet, despite the abolitionist activities of many workers and working-class organizations, these were not the dominant tendencies in the labor movement and among working people. There were many contradictory and inconsistent responses, as the reaction to John Brown's hanging surely indicates. The 1830s and 1840s, however, saw numerous riots and pogroms against free Blacks in northern cities; five of these took place in Philadelphia, the city of "brotherly love." Key causes of one such riot were given as the hiring of Blacks while whites were unemployed and the activities of the Black community to protect fugitive slaves. One meeting dominated by workers agreed to boycott merchants who hired Blacks (Litwack 1961:100–02, 159–61). Noel Ignatiev cites the particular frequency of Irish working-class mobs in attacking Blacks. In 1842, one Philadelphia riot, "a distinctively Irish affair," was a response to a Black parade on the anniversary of the British emancipation of slavery in the West Indies. Many striking Irish coal miners also participated in the racist atrocities (Ignatiev 1995:136–37). Ignatiev gives a compelling analysis:

> We begin with the knowledge that some Irish had reasons to hate and fear people of black skin. We also assume that not all Irish felt that way, at any rate not strongly enough to join a white suprema- cist mob…[which] numbered hundreds in a community of many thousands. Yet that organized force of hundreds was able to batter those who opposed it, or even those who held back, into silence and submission, so that in time it came to speak for the entire com- munity. Rioters do not merely reflect public opinion; they shape it. (Ignatiev 1995:130)

Finally, we have the prevalence in the North and West of the most popular form of mass entertainment in the 1840s and 1850s, racist, slavery-defend- ing, blackface minstrelsy even as it was racially contradictory and subver- sive at times, analyzed with great sensitivity and perspicuity by Alexander Saxton (1990:165–182), David Roediger (1991:115–31), and Eric Lott (1993). Black minstrelsy, with its white working-class appeal, ridicule of upper-class pretensions, and strident attacks on abolitionists "propagandized metaphor- ically the alliance of urban working people with the planter interest in the South," under Democratic Party leadership (Saxton 1990:165).

One can, of course, as Sellers forcefully argues, note the role of north- ern capitalists, establishment preachers, and politicians in "stirring plebian racism and nativism to virulence…diverting cresting plebian anger from a frightened bourgeoisie." The divide-and-conquer approach by elites to fomenting race hatred has always been an important component of class rule in this country. One can also see the scapegoating of Blacks by urban whites faced with job insecurity and the "psychological pain of white fail- ure" (Sellers 1991:386). Labor market competition has often led to violent conflicts between competing groups, even when, as Ignatiev, shows they were sometimes Irishmen from different parts of the homeland. Although these are important parts of the full explanation, we must search for the fuller fabric of which these are important threads.

Pre–Civil War labor unions failed the most minimal test of racial egal- itarianism in virtually every instance. As scholars have noted, there was hard- ly a trade to be found, whether organized nationally, locally, or at one work- place, where white workers, whether by constitutional provision or by custom, did not exclude their Black brethren (see Wolfe 1912; Du Bois and

Granville 1912; Spero and Harris 1968). Thus, one must in the end have a harsh assessment of those such as Schlüter (1965) and Mandel (1955) who describe labor unions as anti-slavery and racially egalitarian, placing the blame for conflicts between the white labor movement and abolitionists exclusively on the shoulders of the latter. In a certain sense, even the cautiously optimistic assessments of Eric Foner, Herbert Aptheker (1989:xiii–xv; 39), and Timothy Messer-Kruse (1994) would appear to be too positive. To paraphrase Mark Twain, the death of racist practices in the labor movement prior to the Civil War seems to have been greatly exaggerated.

Although anti-slavery sentiment among the lower classes grew during the 1840s and 1850s, much of it, as Eric Foner (1970) so persuasively demonstrates, was racist and anti-egalitarian. The racism of much of anti-slavery and its explicit conservatism on racial issues may be gleaned from the pride with which one New York City Republican noted that of the 32,000 who had voted for Lincoln in 1860, only 1,600 had supported the state's Black suffrage amendment (Litwack 1961:271). New York City, it should be noted, was at the time the most proletarianized city in the Union.

The northern workers' movement, and this included the bulk of its radical left wing, was peculiarly obtuse about the plight of their darker brethren in the South as well as in the North. Thus, the pre–Civil War abolitionist movement, with its Black and white supporters, and the pre–Civil War white workers movement had hardly a point of intersection. As Du Bois describes it:

> Here then, were two labor movements: the movement to give the black worker a minimum legal status which would enable him to sell his own labor, and another movement which proposed to increase the wage and better the condition of the working class in America, now largely composed of foreign immigrants, and dispute with the new American capitalism the basis upon which the new wealth was to be divided. Broad philanthropy and a wide knowledge of the elements of human progress would have led these two movements to unite and in their union to become irresistible. It was difficult, almost impossible, for this to be clear to the white labor leaders of the thirties. They had their own particularistic grievances and one of these was the competition of free Negro labor. Beyond this they could easily envision a new and tremendous competition of black workers after all the slaves became free. What they did not see nor understand was that this competition was present and would continue and would be emphasized if the Negro continued as a slave worker. On the other hand, the Abolitionists did not realize the plight of the white laborer, especially the semi-skilled and unskilled worker. (Du Bois 1964:20–21)

White labor leaders suffered from a blind spot. They preached the doctrine of Free Soilism, an illusory, escapist solution to the plight of labor that had a "whites only" tag on it. Until the early 1850s, when Joseph Wedemeyer and other radical followers of Karl Marx who understood the importance of abolition for white workers gained some small influence in the northern workers, movement, labor leaders as a whole were more interested in freedom from African-Americans than in freedom for white workers. The rallying cry of white-worker–supported Free Soilism in 1845 was the Wilmot Proviso, which not only barred slavery from the new territories but also suggested that land rights should be reserved for whites only. Such an approach was counterposed against the more radical and more realistic approach offered by Frederick Douglass for Kansas in 1854. Douglass argued that 1,000 free Black homesteading families settling in Kansas would put a "wall of living fire" through which slavery could not pass (Douglass 1950:II:311–14). He argued that this action would provide a more certain and more peaceful approach to stopping the spread of slavery.

The history of social movements has made clear that there are often great difficulties and barriers placed in the way of oppressed groups uniting with their natural allies. In the South, loss of livelihood, terror, and lynching were among the likely social costs to poor whites following their class interests. Although the strictures were not so harsh in the North, the connections were less obvious as well. No broad struggle or unity is foreordained. Among the factors missing in the North from the 1830s to the 1850s was a determined labor or radical organization whose leaders and members saw the connection between the struggle for freedom for African-American slaves and that of "free" labor in the North. Yet, we are not merely dealing with two different ruling classes fighting over who would get the biggest piece of the pie. The northern manufacturing-based capitalist system not only had different economic needs from the southern slave-based agricultural capitalist system. Each had vastly different legal, social, and ideological needs as well. And in these spheres, only one class would gain hegemony/dominance. Would the legal, social, and ideological environment of the country as a whole be designed to promote free labor (and hence unrestrained capitalist development) or slave labor? Would the country as a whole become one whose function was to protect and enhance the rights of slave owners wherever they and their chattel resided? This, of course, was the demand of the Confederacy, as Karl Marx clearly saw at the time (Marx and Engels 1969:4,61,72–83,280). Eric Foner (1970) sees a similar confluence of issues but tends to stress "ideology" and worldview over economic interests.

1. There is, of course, a long-standing, intense debate over whether slavery was capitalist or not. For a work that argues that it was a precapitalist economic form, see Genovese (1967); for one that takes the opposite view, see Oakes (1982); for Marx's views, see Lawrence (1976).

2. Even the fabled size of the nation's geographically largest state is a direct product of the slave issue. The Texas territory was conceivably entitled to be divided into as many as five states. Yet, this could potentially have given slave owners a majority in Congress, tipping the political balance decisively toward the southern slave states. Karl Marx argues, however, that slave owners were cautious in pressing for this advantage because there was so much free labor, anti-slavery sentiment in parts of Texas, particularly among the large German population (Marx and Engels 1969:78 [*Die Presse,* November 7, 1861]).

3. For a guide to the literature on this question, see Messer-Kruse 1994:6–8, footnote 1.

4. Such empirically false claims may be found, among other places, in the assertions of Hofstadter, who claims that Phillips "was the only major figure who combined in one career the abolitionist ferment of the prewar period with the labor movement of the postwar industrial epoch" (Hofstadter 1989:180).

CHAPTER 4

The Civil War and Reconstruction

> The South, after the war, presented the greatest opportunity for a real national labor movement which the nation ever saw or is likely to see for many decades. Yet the labor movement, with but few exceptions, never realized the situation. It never had the intelligence or knowledge, as a whole, to see in black slavery and Reconstruction, the kernel and meaning of the labor movement in the United States. Du Bois 1964:353

> The War had been over four or five years then, but nobody white or black seemed to know it. Odd clusters and strays of Negroes wandered the back roads and cowpaths from Schenectady to Jackson. Dazed but insistent, they searched each other out for word of a cousin, an aunt, a friend...Some of them were running from family that could not support them, some to family; some were running from dead crops, dead kin, life threats, and took-over land. Toni Morrison 1987:52

THE CIVIL WAR

Despite often contradictory attitudes toward the recognition of Black Americans as human beings entitled to equal rights in this country, the conflict between the North and the South over slavery was inevitable with the election of Abraham Lincoln, the northern anti-slavery Republican presidential candidate. According to Frederick Douglass, the crisis was brought to a head by the increasingly truculent actions of the slaveholders themselves. He cites the annexation of Texas "for the avowed purpose of increasing the number of slave states and thus increasing the power of slavery in the Union," "the perfidious repeal of the Missouri Compromise when all its advantages to the South had been gained and appropriated, and when nothing had been gained by the North—the armed and bloody attempt to force slavery upon the virgin soil of Kansas," the attempts to drive from public life those hostile to slavery, including William H. Seward and Charles Summer, and the growing brazenness of many southern leaders in demanding that slavery be spread to every state in the Union (Douglass 1962:292–95). Interestingly, in a careful analysis of southern statements and actions, Marx argued that the real purpose of the Civil War on the part of the South was to make slave labor the norm, the dominant form of labor in all the country (Marx and Engels 1969:4, 61, 72–83, 280). He concluded that the "slaveholders' rebellion was to sound the tocsin for a general holy crusade of property against labor" (Marx and Engels 1969:280). We can see the previously described social chasm between the two systems; southern capitalists understood that their economic interests could not be protected unless their social system dominated. Contrary to the Beards, it was the aggressive defense by southern slave owners of their way of life that brought about the Civil War. The Civil War was to have an enormous impact on all of U.S. political, economic, and social life, with its influence still felt to a strong degree today.

Perhaps most important of all was the abolition of slavery, taking place in the form of a series of revolutionary governmental measures, unprecedented in modern societies in which slavery was ended: immediate emancipation, no compensation to the slave owners, followed closely by a declaration of full citizenship for the former bondsmen. The war had begun over slavery, but not over abolition. As Marx noted:

> The whole movement was and is based, as one sees, on the *slave question:* Not in the sense of whether the slaves within the existing slave states should be emancipated or not, but whether the twenty million free men of the North should subordinate themselves any longer to an oligarchy of three hundred thousand slaveholders (Marx and Engels 1969:71)

Yet, as the most prescient observers knew from the beginning, abolition would be the result. Du Bois notes, it was the first shot fired by southern troops at Fort Sumter that freed the slaves (Du Bois 1964:55; see also Douglass 1962:33; Marx and Engels 1969:82–83). The logic of the struggle, a fight to the death for one social system or the other, would necessitate revolutionary measures. In order to save the Union, just as Bacon had offerred freedom to his many enslaved and bonded followers, the North was inexorably led to abolition.

Emancipation solved numerous problems for the North that allowed it to win a war that it might have otherwise lost. First, there was the question of the southern economy, a large part of which was held together during the early stages of the war by the work of Black slaves, thus allowing a large percentage of white males to fight in the army. What better way to undermine the home base of the Confederacy than to offer freedom to the South's shackled labor? Second, although both sides had large-scale desertions from their armies and increasing difficulties drafting recruits as the war progressed, the North's problems were perhaps more complex. The growing opposition to the continuation of the war was being led by

Democrats who were gaining political strength. Resistance from northern white recruits grew during 1862. Volunteers declined and public anger at the draft intensified, as the 1863 New York City draft riots made clear. Reluctantly, although inevitably, the North turned to Blacks, who were eventually to make up almost one half of the northern army—a strategy abolitionists had been advocating since the beginning. How better to motivate them than to link the war to emancipation? In those areas of the country where abolitionist sentiment was strong (for example, New England, the strongholds in the upper Northeast and Midwest, and parts of the Northwest) the impact of emancipation was also inspirational for many whites. Finally, the North had an international problem far more serious than during the American Revolution. The strong economic ties of the United Kingdom and France to the South (which supplied the raw materials to the British textile industry), left open the strong possibility that these countries would recognize the Confederacy, break the northern blockade, and even intervene militarily on the side of the secessionists. (See the interesting analysis on this problem by the Beards 1944:273-5.) In the United Kingdom and other countries, claims were made that there were no principled differences between the two sides. The Emancipation Proclamation of 1863 aroused public opinion in Europe to side with the North. It thereby lessened the chances that Great Britain would intervene on the side of the Confederacy. With abolition, "Slowly but surely an economic dispute and a political test of strength took on the aspects of a great moral crusade" (Du Bois 1964:80). This would not be the first or the last time that the oppression of African-Americans within the United States would figure prominently in the country's international relations.

By freeing the slaves and recruiting them into the Union army, the North gained hundreds of thousands of Black volunteers, who were literally fighting for their own freedom. And it was the African-American troops of the North that turned the tide in the war. As Du Bois notes with considerable irony, when African-Americans labored for the nation's wealth or engaged in acts of kindness or generosity, or when their cause was pleaded by Frederick Douglass, few recognized their humanity. "But when he rose and fought and killed, the whole nation with one voice proclaimed him a man and brother. Nothing else made emancipation possible in the United States. Nothing else made Negro citizenship conceivable, but the record of the Negro soldier as a fighter" (Du Bois 1964:104). Thus, quite literally, newly freed Blacks saved the Union. By this chain of circumstances which included first and foremost the actions as well as the presence of the African-American slaves themselves did Jubilee Day arrive.

As is well known, even with the passage of the Thirteenth, Fourteenth, and Fifteenth Amendments, which not only abolished slavery but also assured formal equality, citizenship, and full voting rights, freedom for Blacks was far from realized. There is, thus, an attempt by some to downgrade the importance of these world historical events. Even such perceptive writers as Eric Foner and Harold Baron fail at times to strike the right note.[1] Short of being on a prison farm like Mississippi's Parchman Penitentiary, which may well have been "worse than slavery" (Oshinsky 1996), the status of being a free, even if highly circumscribed, Black laborer in the South was indeed a great advance over enslavement. As Du Bois notes,

> But there was in 1863 a real meaning to slavery different from that we may apply to the laborer today. It was in part psychological, the enforced personal feeling of inferiority, the calling of another Master; the standing with hat in hand. It was the helplessness. It was the defenselessness of family life. It was the submergence below the arbitrary will of any sort of individual. (Du Bois 1964:9)

The overthrow of this condition of "social death," (to use Orlando Patterson's poignant phrase), was a tremendous advance, no matter how circumscribed the result.

The second revolutionary result of the Civil War, part and parcel of emancipation, was the destruction of the slave-owning class as a major contender for national power. It was "the uncompensated liquidation of the nation's largest concentration of private property" (Foner 1988:2).

Third, the Civil War led to vast changes in public policy in Washington. Unencumbered by southern congressional representation, import tariffs were substantially raised to protect domestic industry, including not only such items as pig iron but also wool grown by western herders. A national banking system was established, centered in the Treasury Department, with one national currency, eliminating the power of individual states to issue their own. The Homestead Act of 1862 met the demands of Free Soilers by allowing any homesteader 160 acres of public land for a ten-dollar registration fee. The biggest winners were the railroad companies, which were given almost 200 million acres of free land and hundreds of millions of dollars in loans, tax concessions, and payments for their security bonds. The governments of Haiti and Liberia were recognized in June 1862. Slavery was abolished in the District of Columbia and in the territories, even before general emancipation. And at the state level, ever so slowly, discriminatory laws were repealed. In early 1865, the issue of whites-only transportation became a national embarrassment. In Philadelphia, Black war hero Robert Smalls was removed from a segregated streetcar and had to walk several miles to the navy yard, where the southern ship that he had stolen from the

Charleston harbor was being fixed (Foner 1988:28).

The Civil War provided a tremendous stimulus to the northern economy, which grew tremendously. Although the economy as a whole expanded, those industries with ties to military supply, grew most rapidly. Railroads
expanded, textile mills supplying clothing to the Union army increased their
output, pig iron production multiplied. Hogs slaughtered in Chicago (the
center of the industry in the North) rose from 231,000 just before the war
to over 900,000 in 1864, and also trippled in St. Louis (Halpern 1989:22).
Production workers increased 50 percent between 1859 and 1869 (Historical
Statistics 1975:I:666; see also Foner 1988:18–19, for general information and
quotes from industrialists).

Finally, the social impact of the Civil War on race relations was enormous. The rigid system of white racial identities and separateness of white
labor was shaken, although not destroyed. In the next chapter, I will probe
the contradictory character of this development for the whole last third of
the nineteenth century. Let us begin this examination by looking at Marx's
famous assertion about race and the Civil War:

> In the United States of North America, every independent move-
> ment of the workers was paralysed so long as slavery disfigured a
> part of the Republic. Labour cannot emancipate itself in the white
> skin where in the black it is branded. But out of the death of slav-
> ery new life at once arose. The first fruit of the Civil War was the
> eight hours agitation, that ran with the seven-leagued boots of the
> locomotive from the Atlantic to the Pacific, from New England to
> California. (Marx 1967:301)

We have seen how the issue of slavery compromised the northern white
workers' movement before the Civil War. Marx, writing in 1867, clearly did
not realize the convoluted form that the death of slavery would take, continuing to brand those with black skin. Yet, in order to tally the balance sheet
correctly, it is incumbent to look at both sides of the ledger, neither dismissing the radical changes as many have done (in order to highlight the
unfulfilled promises to Blacks) nor seeing the upsurge of the later labor
movement as without blemishes and unrelated to the issues of emancipation and racial subordination (as numerous others have).

Radicalization of many whites over racial issues did take place during
the war. As I have noted, with the large increase in Black troops in the last
two years of the war, many northern whites were stirred (overawed) by black
fighting mettle. Yet, for those in the Union army itself, the interracial com-
raderie of death was even more intense. Abolitionists were disproportionately represented among lower-ranking officers from the beginning. Radical

pro-abolitionist Fenians organized among the Irish. The large numbers of German Marxist officers gave revolutionary lectures and classes to their troops. Union soldiers debated the political issues of the day, including emancipation. And as the army eventually drove into the Deep South, "and encountered the full reality of plantation slavery, soldiers became imbued with abolitionist sentiment," including many who had been Democrats and were previously racially obtuse (Foner 1988:9). Thus, the Civil War led not merely to a greater consciousness of racial issues, but to an increase in abolitionist support in the North.

Yet, this was not the only trend. Polarization was intense, as northern Democrats and others spewed forth racist filth, tying it to popular resentment against the war effort. Democratic women in Indiana marched with signs saying "Fathers, save us from nigger husbands" (Foner 1988:32), while largely Irish antidraft rioters in New York City in 1863 began a murderous racial pogrom in which even the Colored Orphan Asylum was burned to the ground (Iver Bernstein 1990). We shall try to keep this contradictory racial legacy in mind as we continue to explore the course of race relations and American political development after the war.

While northern labor held back, failing to appreciate the momentous worldwide significance of the war to free the slaves, the South itself was not monolithic in its support of slavery. Few secession conventions had obtained real, noncoerced majorities.[2] Even during the Civil War, a surprising number of southern whites were loyalists. Theodore Allen estimates that one out of twenty white Southern soldiers fought for the North. This fact was largely ignored until recently because most Civil War historians were well-known to be sympathetic to the Confederacy. There was even a largely white county in Mississippi, Jones County, which seceded from the Confederacy and engaged in guerrilla warfare against the Confederate rebel armies (V.O.Key 1984:328). Northern labor in general missed its chance to support and gain strength from abolitionism before the war, during it, and in its aftermath. And this failure of white workers to recognize their closest potential allies is a central theme of Du Bois's 1935 book, Black Reconstruction.

Reconstruction

The odyssey of Reconstruction, its violent overthrow by planter-led voting fraud and extralegal violence, and its ultimate abandonment by the North and the federal government have been one of the most hotly disputed subjects in U.S. history. Certain of the older interpretations have, of course, been put to rest. The view that dominated for almost a century, first in popular and political discourse, eventually codified by William Dunning and his followers, was a racial apology for southern white supremacy. The Dunning school argued that Reconstruction from 1867 to 1877 was an attempt by anti-southern northern radicals to install by force southern state governments led by ignorant Blacks and their unscrupulous white allies from the North (carpetbaggers) as well as the South (scalawags). These governments were so corrupt and oppressive, that Reconstruction represents one of the most sordid chapters in the country's history. They were eventually overthrown by the "civilized" (i.e., white) people of the South. Though intellectually demolished in W.E.B. Du Bois's magisterial *Black Reconstruction*, which includes a special chapter on Dunning and other historians entitled "The Progaganda of History," only in the last several decades has the Dunning school inter- pretation been recognized as based on lies and distortions (See Foner 1988:xix–xxiv for an informative historiographic overview).

Although much of Du Bois's facts, criticisms, and even analysis are gen- erally accepted among historians, his alternative views are often considered overdrawn and romantic. For Du Bois saw Reconstruction not merely as a "splendid failure" (Du Bois 1964:708) but also as perhaps the most radical, democratic, and hopeful chapter of American history. Reconstruction, in Du Bois's opinion, was "the story of a normal working class movement, suc- cessful to an unusual degree" (Du Bois 1964:383), a radical, interracial labor movement that democratically installed labor governments in southern states and carried out not merely broad social reforms but also social rev- olution, anti-property in thrust, with socialist implications. Many have taken issue with Du Bois's arguments both about the radicalism of Reconstruction and its potential for change, including C. Vann Woodward, who considers the period not only nonradical but conservative (Woodward 1966:125–47). There is also disagreement on a related issue. Du Bois argues that the defeat of Reconstruction marked not only the complete resubordination of Blacks in the South but also the destruction of the possibilities for democracy in the country as a whole. The defeat of Reconstruction was for him the cen- tral turning point in American political development. Du Bois's views are sharply, if implicitly, criticized by those who view the 1890s and the early twentieth century as more decisive. Not only C. Vann Woodward but also Morgan Kausser and Lawrence Goodwyn (who sees the defeat of the Populist movement in the 1890s as the most critical episode in U.S. history) take this stance. All these issues are central to our investigation of the centrality of race in American political development, and will be addressed here, although the coda to the last argument can be presented only during my discussion of the next critical period—the 1890s.

The story of Reconstruction can be traced simply, because the facts (if not the analysis) are generally agreed upon, largely synthesized in Eric Foner's comprehesive *Reconstruction* (1988). By the war's end, with the surrender of Confederate General Robert E. Lee to Union General Ulysses S. Grant at Appomattox, the southern economy had been devastated. The South's main source of income and means of foreign exchange was largely eliminated by the war and the completeness of the northern blockade. The figures tell the story. Cotton production, over five million bales in 1860, had been reduced to only 299,000 by 1864, and some of that was in Union-aligned border states; cotton exports, 1,768 million pounds in 1860, were only nine million pounds in 1865 (*Historical Statistics* 1975:I:517-18, 898–99). 260,000 men, one fifth of all adult white southern males, had died in battle; many who survived were maimed. In 1865, Mississippi spent 20 percent of its state budget on artificial limbs. Not only was the Black labor force free and insubordinate but land and plantations were largely destroyed, many by General Sherman's army, some by fleeing slave owners, others by newly freed slaves (Foner 1988:125, 70–71).

Nevertheless, the planters and Confederate leaders acted as if they had been the victors in the Civil War. By late 1865, Deep South states began instituting Black Codes that required Blacks to have year-long labor contracts to plantation masters; leaving their jobs before the contractual obligation was done meant forfeiture of all wages. Failure to have written proof of current contracts left them liable to arrest by any white person (as in slavery times). They were limited in renting land, from engaging in any occupation besides farm laborer or servant, from promulgating "mischief," and even preaching without a license. The Mississippi law had the catchall clause that all previous penal codes specifying crimes for slaves and free Blacks were still in force. And so it went, with slight variations by state. The whole system was everywhere administered by all-white courts and officials. Although many northern capitalists hoped for a return of labor discipline and the speedy resumption of cotton production in the South, the Black codes, which greatly restricted the rights of Black labor in the marketplace, caused serious problems for overwhelming numbers of persons in the North. After all the blood shed in defense of the Union by northerners, the South's actions spelled treason, a refusal to accept defeat and the end of slavery. Further, they were an extension of mistreatment not only to Blacks but also loyal white southern Unionists and northerners in general. The South's institution of the Black Codes created an uproar (Foner 1988:200, 220, 225).

The southern elite's insolence went even further. They demanded more extensive representation in Congress based on the newly emancipated, but still disenfranchised Black freemen. They elected former Confederates to Congress in December 1865, who appeared and demanded to be seated. The newly elected included the vice president of the Confederacy, four Confederate generals, five colonels, six cabinet officers, and fifty-eight

Confederate congressmen. These new representatives threatened to revise the tariffs, repudiate the national debt, lower taxes, eliminate the national bank, create strict regulation of industry, and even gain compensation for their former slaves (Du Bois 1964:35, 185). At this point, even the northern business class had had enough. The intransigence of even the upper South soon converted initially reluctant southern unionists to support Black equality and enfranchisement. As one wrote, he was not "afraid of negro equality," if the alternative was "rebel superiority" (Foner 1988:271).

And so a revolution from above began. An outraged public in the North joined abolitionists who wanted to ensure full freedom for Blacks, and northern capitalists who saw disenfranchisement of rebels and enfranchisement of freemen as the only way to secure the victory won by arms. To accomplish this task, northern troops were sent back to the South, military districts were established, and new state conventions were mandated to be chosen by Blacks and loyal whites.

Let us try to assess how radical Reconstruction really was with respect to changing the system of racial domination in the South and the class relations on which the system was based. First, in all states there was a vast social, political, and economic mobilization of African-Americans. Across the South a dense web of social organizations developed. Black-initiated schools, many begun before the end of the Civil War, many only later aided by northern philanthropists and the Freedman's Bureau, proliferated. Independent Black churches, precursors of the all-important churches that exist throughout Black communities in the United States today, sprang into existence. Burial societies, debating clubs, lodges, fire companies, trade associations by the thousands sprang up in every part of the South. As Peter Rachleff documents for post-Civil War Richmond, Virginia, these organizations were to be both the training grounds and the backbone for broad political and labor organizing within southern Black communities (Foner 1988:97, 95, 162; Rachleff 1989).

Although previously largely uneducated and isolated on plantations, African-Americans mobilized politically to a degree rarely seen in the United States by any group at any time in history. Voting turnouts for Blacks especially in the early years of Reconstruction, and when violence did not prevent them from casting ballots, sometimes reached as high as 90 percent (Foner 1988:291, 314). Huge political rallies and meetings often involving thousands of Blacks were common. When important issues were debated in the Virginia constitutional convention, African-Americans overflowed the galleries, causing heavy absenteeism in local tobacco factories and a lack of servants in white households (Foner 1988:316). The major political organization for African-Americans was the Union League, originally founded by white loyalists. Blacks flocked to these local groups, often displacing the initial white organizers with Black leaders and taking on defense, land, and labor issues in response to their members. Although engaging in many places in extensive self-defense training, including the organization of armed militias, this activity was most often discouraged by white Republican leadership at the state and national levels (Fitzgerald 1989 gives the fullest account of the league). Economically, Black urban and rural workers engaged in numerous strikes and agricultural workers were so adamant in their refusal to work in plantation-style labor gangs that sharecropping, renting, and tenancy were the long-term result.

Charles Fourier, seconded by Marx, argued that the treatment of women was a good indicator of the progressiveness of movements and societies. During Reconstruction, women participated heavily in social organizations, especially in education, the church, and fraternal societies; they went to rallies in large numbers, played supportive roles in the Union Leagues, whose membership, like the vote, was limited to men. Reconstruction legislation established the rights of women in many spheres, especially with respect to property ownership and divorce. Although a dramatic change from the rigid antebellum male supremacy of southern society, the degree to which such activities and measures led to full equality for women should not be exaggerated. Likewise, there was a large degree of interracial political activity, particularly in the early years of Reconstruction, most pronounced in many Union League organizations. There are records of a chapter in East Tennessee composed largely of white loyalists, who chose a number of Black officers and successfully elected a Black justice of the peace and four Black city councilmen in an area that was only one-tenth Black (Foner 1988:284).

These phenomena indicate deep-rooted mass political mobilization of Blacks and poor whites throughout the South. Given the previous rigid control of every aspect of southern life by a small oligarchy of large slave owners, this democratization and turnaround in class relations had immense import. To the extent, however, that there existed events displaying social revolutionary potential, it was in the Deep South, especially the plantation areas. If anything, mobilization there was even more intense and extensive than elsewhere. In the 1867 constitutional referendum in South Carolina, there were numerous plantation counties in which every single Black male was registered to vote (Seville 1994:167). In Mississippi, the turnout for elections was often 90 percent (Foner 1988:291). Thousands of Blacks, men and women, young and old, might attend political meetings, sometimes guarded by women with muskets (Seville 1994:167–69). Although scalawags and carpetbaggers almost always maintained control at the highest levels of government, 600 Blacks served as legislators, almost all (except in

Louisiana and South Carolina) former slaves, virtually all from plantation counties in the Deep South. "The spectacle of former slaves representing the lowcountry rice kingdom or the domain of Natchez cotton nabobs epitomized the political revolution wrought by Reconstruction" (Foner 1988:355). Nashville's city council was one-third Black, Little Rock's council occasionally had a Black majority. In Black Belt counties, nineteen black sheriffs were elected in Louisiana and fifteen in Mississippi in counties representing one-third of all African-Americans in the Magnolia state. Tallahassee and Little Rock had Black police chiefs; half of the police forces in Memphis and Vicksburg, over one-fourth in New Orleans, Mobile, and Petersburg were Black. In Louisiana, Blacks and Chinese as well as whites were employed to repair the levees and all now received equal wages (Foner 1988:356, 362). Black militia organizations were especially prolific in the Deep South, although military authorities and Reconstruction governments did their best to disarm and demobilize them, wrongly believing that by doing so they would deter violence by not offending the planters and pro-Confederate whites.

It was, however, both the racial and class aspects of many Deep South convention meetings and legislative sessions that suggested, in the words of a British observer, "the mighty revolution that had taken place in America." Most delegates, for example, possessed little or no property (Foner 1988:316). The South Carolina 1867 constitutional convention had a Black majority. An indication of its class composition is given by the taxes that delegates paid. The forty-seven white delegates paid a total of $761, $508 being paid by one conservative. The seventy-four Black delegates paid $117, of which $85 was paid by one Charleston Black. Twenty-three whites and fifty-seven Blacks paid no taxes. Du Bois argues that this representation of the impoverished "showed certain tendencies toward the dictatorship of the proletariat" (Du Bois 1964:389–91). Nevertheless, the distances between situations with revolutionary implications, with class programs that threaten existing elites, with stimulating imagery and colorful psychodrama, and those situations where one class actually overthrows the rule of another can sometimes be quite large.

Aside from the level of lower-class and Black political participation (so much in contrast to the situation today in the United States), several substantive issues are especially important. First, these Reconstruction legislatures had a strong class notion of the role of an activist government. They built public schools, hospitals, penitentiaries, insane asylums, and orphanages. South Carolina provided free medical care for the poor and Alabama not only provided legal counsel for poor defendants but also protected minors from child abuse (Foner 1988:364). Second, and perhaps even more radical, was the degree to which large numbers of freemen and their representatives were committed to the confiscation and redistribution of the land of the former rebel plantation owners.3 It is instructive to examine the reasons for the widespread holding of these revolutionary beliefs; why, in contrast to other postslave societies, U.S. freedmen believed these positions were not merely desirable possibilities, but that the government would also support them; and what these beliefs meant in practice. First, there were a number of actions by the federal government that led the freedmen to their beliefs that land confiscation and redistribution were likely. During the war, a number of such widely publicized activities did take place, largely in the Deep South. When the U.S. Navy seized Port Royal, South Carolina, in November 1861, virtually the whole white population fled to the mainland. The remaining 10,000 Blacks on the Sea Islands sacked the plantation houses, divided the land, and began growing crops for their own use. Davis Bend, Mississippi, the former site of the large plantations of Confederate President Jefferson Davis and his brother, was collectively run by Blacks after the Civil War. The Davis Bend freedmen grew cotton, earned large profits, and had their own government with elected officials (Foner 1988:51, 58–59). As Sherman's troops approached the rice plantations along the South Carolina coast in 1865, slaves and nonslave-owning whites drove off overseers, confiscated property, and divided the land among themselves. In some cases, these confiscations were sanctified by the newly arrived armies (Seville 1994:12–13). And, after the end of the Civil War, when some planters refused to pay adequately those freemen who had worked their crops, plantation workers simply seized the harvest that they deemed to be rightfully theirs (Seville 1994:69). Most of the initial seizures, however, were wartime measures; further actions tended to be scotched after the war.

Yet, the notion of confiscation and redistribution did not disappear. The initial Freedmen's Bureau endorsed full civil and political equality for Blacks; one of its three members James MacKaye urged that this could only be assured by confiscation and redistribution of planter land and the "social reconstruction of the southern states." At the beginning of Reconstruction, the Freedman's Bureau had large amounts of abandoned land under its control, most of it in the Deep South. With the cooperation of Union military commanders, they began redistributing this land to freedmen and their families until they were tragically forced to return it to its former owners by orders from President Andrew Johnson. But this issue was not left there. In Pennsylvania's Republican convention in the fall of 1865, Thaddeus Stevens called for the seizure and redistribution of 400 million acres belonging to the richest 10 percent of southerners, which would break the power of the southern ruling class, laying the basis for a successful southern Republican

Party based on Black and white farmers. George Julian in Congress and Benjamin Butler, Wendell Phillips, and Charles Sumner were among the radical Republicans who voiced similar concerns. Although those radical Republicans advocating confiscation were in the minority in the North, they kept the issue and promise of land to the freedmen alive. It was the subject of continuous agitation in the Deep South and "animated grass-roots black politics in 1867." In Savannah, Georgia, an armed mass meeting of freedmen listened to Aaron Bradley demand division of lands belonging to wealthy whites. The call for confiscation was also strong in many white loyalist areas, although in most cases they were more concerned with gaining compensation and retribution for themselves than with benefiting poor freemen. Yet, in some cases they included Black families in their demands for homesteads. While these demands were more often than not a "marriage of convenience," they nevertheless led to the defending of equal rights for Blacks. Although racist attitudes had hardly disappeared, these many Black-white alliances of the rural poor "underscored the extent of the political revolution that swept across the South in 1867." In most cases these demands were supported by free Blacks; however, in Louisiana they vehemently opposed them, undercutting the more radical rural freedmen. In other places the demands were opposed by many whites, and in numerous legislature sessions the demands were simply shelved for fear that they would lead to vehement opposition from northern Republicans (Foner 1988:68–69, 158–61, 235, 309–11, 290, 302–3, 306, 329).

In the Deep South especially, there were other ways in which confiscation could work besides dramatic seizures. In South Carolina, for example, taxes on the impoverished planters were quite high in order to support the broad social programs, and the penalties for failure to pay were so severe that the taxes themselves were in fact a program for land seizure. This, argues Du Bois, was actually the intention of the Black and white laborers whose votes had elected the legislators (Du Bois 1964:419–20, 591). Tax assessment, which had relied on the benign judgments of the planters themselves in the antebellum era, were now sometimes done by their less charitable former slaves. At one time in Mississippi, one-fifth of the state's land— six million acres—was in state possession for failure to pay taxes. Although most lands were eventually returned to their original owners, the specter of confiscation was not merely a figment of planter imagination (Foner 1988:375–74). In other places, bankrupt planters sold their lands to Blacks or state land commissions. In Colleton County, South Carolina, several large plantations in the 1870s were being run collectively by a Black laborers' society, which one newspaper labeled "a sort of communism." Around Charleston and Savanah, "a unique combination of circumstance," including early government policies, the lengthy period of Black political power, and the intense mobilization of the Black population, as well as a lack of Northern investment, led to extensive Black land ownership (Foner 1988:403).

Thus, in the Deep South in particular, especially in the former plantation areas, one can see the beginnings of small pockets of revolutionary, alternative bases of power that threatened to transform completely the economic structure, politics, and social power of the region. Yet, the history of revolutionary struggles suggests strongly that dual power bases can only last so long. They must spread and gather strength or be crushed. In the South, they were ruthlessly destroyed, especially in those areas where they were most deeply rooted and their programs most radical.

Reconstruction was formally ended in 1877 with the withdrawal of federal troops from the South. As C. Vann Woodward (1966) convincingly argues, however, the 1877 compromise was merely the capstone of the demise of Reconstruction that had been underway several years at different times to differing degrees in different states. It is important for us to understand how and why Reconstruction was overturned, what it all had to do with race, and how complete a reversal it represented, especially with respect to the resulting system of racial subordination that was established.

The simplest answer to the first question is that Reconstruction was overthrown by voting fraud, economic intimidation, violence, and widespread political murder on a scale never before or since approached in American society; these efforts were led and largely organized by the Black Belt planters of the Deep South. I have already noted the failed attempt at counterrevolution immediately following the Civil War, which Reconstruction was meant to, and did for a time, block. A continuing thread through the post-Civil War period in the South was the lack of punishment for white men who murdered Blacks. In Texas, for example, of 500 who were indicted for the murder of Blacks in 1865 and 1866, not one was convicted (Foner 1988:204). During the 1868 election campaign, Democrats organized merchants to eliminate credits to Blacks going to Republican election meetings and landlords attempted to evict their activist Black tenants. The Ku Klux Klan at the same time assassinated both Black and white Republican leaders during the campaign, including legislators, convention delegates, and at least one congressman; meanwhile, in many places white mobs destroyed Republican newspapers, shot at election parades, and massacred Blacks indiscriminately. Eleven Georgia counties with Black majorities recorded no votes for any Republicans during 1868. There was little done by federal or state authorities to counteract this violence or punish the perpetrators. The violence, however, was not universal throughout the South and did not at this time penetrate many overwhelmingly Black strongholds, particularly in South Carolina (Foner 1988:340–43).

The violence continued to escalate for the next several years. Although the Democrats, and later scholars, tended to blame the prejudices of poor whites, this position bears little relation to the facts. The violence was led and organized by leading members of the white southern ruling class (Foner 1988:431–33), including leaders of the Democratic Party. In some places white Republicans as well as Blacks engaged in armed self-defense, yet these efforts were generally discouraged not only by national Republicans but also by both Black and white local officials. Even where militias were organized and led by Black war veterans, they were usually outgunned and slaughtered, as in the Colfax massacre where 280 Blacks died (Foner 1988:434–37). In most places state and national Republican officials vacillated, trying to conciliate those who were behind the violence. By 1874 and 1875, the violence had become most extensive in the Deep South Black Belts. In Mississippi, Democratic rifle clubs openly paraded, violently eliminating Black political activity. In Vicksburg, armed white supremacists intimidated enough Black voters to oust the Republican city government in 1874; in the countryside outside the city almost 300 Blacks were murdered (Foner 1988:557–58). The result of this extreme degree of repression was felt in all spheres of life, not merely in the destruction of the Black franchise. Collective action by rural laborers became impossible. An 1887 strike on a Louisiana sugar plantation led to the massacre of over 100 Black workers. In 1891, fifteen leaders of a cotton pickers' strike in Arkansas were killed, nine being lynched after arrest (Foner 1988:595).

This violence, however, was not unstoppable or uncontrollable. In two states, decisive action by Republican governors virtually ended all the white supremacist violence. Governor Powell Clayton of Arkansas declared marshall law in 1868, mobilized a militia made up of Blacks and scalawags, arrested numerous suspects, trying and executing three. Many Klan members fled the state and the violence largely ended. In Texas, the 200-member state police (40 percent of whom were Black) made 6,000 arrests and suppressed the Klan (Foner 1968:440).

Thus, it is clear that the federal government and northern Republicans could have ended the violence and ensured the continuation of Reconstruction if they had had the desire or will. Why they did not is complicated, emitting no easy answer. In my opinion, no scholars have yet presented a satisfactory analysis. I will discuss some of the candidates and evaluate them.

First, let us look at northern opinion, to the extent that one can determine it. In the 1866 congressional mid-term elections, for the first time in

American politics, Black equality was a central issue. Contrary to the usual pattern in which the presidential party loses seats, Republican militants swept the elections, gaining more than a two-thirds majority in both Houses over Democrats and conservative Republicans. In the 1867 elections, the much more controversial issue of Black suffrage was at center stage. Republicans were united in support of the issue, while Democrats throughout the country ran one of the most virulently racist campaigns ever, pledging in Ohio to save voters from "the thralldom of niggerism." In California, Democrats added anti-Chinese stances. Republican strength increased in the South; their previous margins in many parts of the North, however, were eliminated particularly in a number of state legislatures, encouraging moderates in the party to back off on their commitments to full equality for Blacks. Yet, northern voters were growing more committed to Black equality. In 1868, for the first time two Northern states, Iowa and Minnesota, voted to give Blacks the vote. By 1872, Republicans swept the elections in both the North and the South, largely based on their stands on Black rights and protection of southern Blacks against violence (Foner 1988:267, 313–15, 343, 509). As Du Bois concludes: "For a brief period—for the seven mystic years that stretched between Johnson's 'Swing around the Circle' to the Panic of 1873, the majority of thinking Americans of the North believed in the equal manhood of Negroes" (Du Bois 1964:319–20). Thus, we can conclude that it was not northern public opinion or white voter backlash that forced northern Republicans to withdraw their support from Reconstruction in the South before 1873.

Much has been made of the sundering of the alliance between northern radical Republicans and northern capitalists. As northern capitalist became more secure in their national power and more apprehensive about the results of Reconstruction, they drew back, sometimes aiding in the electoral defeat of congressional radicals. Their concerns, overwhelmingly economic, had important racial implications.

Those capitalists with strong economic links to the South, eastern merchants, financiers, and textile manufactures, who had originally supported the concilliatory policies of President Johnson, had grave misgivings about Black empowerment. These capitalists wanted cotton production resumed as quickly as possible; yet, Black freedom often meant a rejection of rigid labor discipline and long-term work commitments, while Black land ownership, with the exception of highly organized ventures like Davis Bend, often led to more subsistence farming and less cash crops. There was also a vast transformation of the capitalist class after the war. Conservative seaboard merchants, whose antebellum wealth had depended on Atlantic trade (and low tariffs) and cotton investments, had opposed antislavery and supported the Democrats. After the war, many shifted their investments to railroads and western investments. The House of Cook, Lehman Brothers, J.P. Morgan, and many others, readjusted their interests in line with the new tariffs, railway subsidies, and the new arrangement of political power, adding their conservative, sympathetic orientation to the South and to dominant Republican ruling-class circles (for a penetrating analysis, see Berk 1994:27–37). Northern capitalists as a whole became increasingly uneasy over the demands to confiscate land. Capitalist-supported moderate Republicans were not willing to be "run over by the car of Revolution," and attacked Thaddeus Stevens's confiscation and distribution proposals. As anti-capitalist radicals like Congressmen Ben Wade and Ben Butler extended their demands for confiscation to northern capital, it was felt that the precedents proposed, according to the *New York Times* "would not be confined to the South" (Foner 1988:309). In addition, northern business, including major northern newspapers, who had initially allied with the radicals to help blunt planter dominance, began to feel that their marriage of convenience was no longer necessary. One of their fears in 1866 was that a resurgent South would ally with Western agrarians and defeat pro-northern economic development policies. By 1869, the Union Pacific and Central Pacific were joined by the golden spike at Promonatary Point, Utah. Before long, cattle were heading from Texas and the West to Chicago. Coupled with the enormous northern industrial development in the years after the war and the immense resources and power this conferred, capitalists no longer felt quite so threatened by southern planters. There was even an alternative southern strategy put forward by moderate Republicans, not all that dissimilar from the one of a century later. They would abandon their emphasis on Black support and appeal to moderate pro-business whites to gain Republican dominance in much of the South. This strategy, however, was based on a gross miscalculation. Southern whites largely remained Democrats. Although most southern state elections were competitive until the 1890s, with only two brief exceptions, they were all won by Democrats. Nationally, the end of Reconstruction meant the loss of secure control of the federal government, as Republicans and Democrats most often split control of Congress and the Presidency in almost every election.

Yet, the missing ingredient in the North, as Du Bois argues so persuasively, was strong support for Reconstruction by northern organized labor. The large-scale industrial growth and development during the Civil War gave a strong impetus both to the formation of national trade unions and to the first national labor federation, the National Labor Union (NLU), founded in August 1866 in Baltimore, Maryland. As Messer-Kruse (1994) shows convincingly, former abolitionists after the Civil War flocked to the support of labor reform, especially the eight-hour movement. Abolitionists were occasionally cheered by the principled defense of the rights of Blacks by fellow white workers, as when white workers in a Harrisburg, Pennsylvania, iron works forced their employer to integrate the tables at a company dinner (Messer-Kruse 1994:101). Such instances, however, were few and far between. Virtually all national labor unions excluded African-Americans and were "unwilling to expand their membership beyond the ranks of white men" (Foner 1988:479).

Numerous instances of local opposition to African-American workers can be found. For example, in Washington, D.C., the bricklayers union forbade its members to work with Blacks. When four white union members were found to be working with some African-Americans on a government project, the union voted unanimously to expel them (Commons 1946:II:135). One worker publicly disagreed with the union, but he was the exception (Foner 1962:I:395). Perhaps the most celebrated case was that of Lewis Douglass, the son of the Black leader Frederick Douglass. Lewis Douglass was denied admission into the Washington branch of the Typographical Union, even though the union had no clause forbidding Black members. An appeal to the national union eventually failed.

Much of the contradictions of the period can be seen through the medium of the NLU, a national political labor umbrella with little influence over its affiliates. The NLU was characterized by its positive attitude toward women workers, including a position of equal pay for equal work for women workers. This position, of course, did not come naturally for many male workers and their organizations. Although women were among the first factory workers in America—the earliest New England textile mills largely used children and young single women working long hours in abominable conditions—the skilled trades had historically been almost exclusively occupied by men. The Civil War, however, had drawn large numbers of women into many formerly all-male occupations. Most trade unionists and their organizations, however, excluded women, preferring to drive them out of their jobs to prevent competition, rather than trying to organize them. Women were forced to form their own organizations, including unions of women cigar makers, collar workers, tailoresses and seamstresses, umbrella sewers, cap makers, textile workers, printers, furnishers, laundresses, and shoemakers (Foner 1962:I:382–83). A few working men and their organizations began to cooperate with the women unionists. The Cigar Makers' International Union altered its constitution in 1867 to allow women into their union. At the September 1868 meeting of the NLU in New York City, delegates from women's organizations appeared. While many top leaders endorsed women's rights, there was much resistance among many male trade unionists and individual unions. Nevertheless, as a symbol of its commitment to these issues, President William Sylvis appointed Miss Kate Mullaney, the chief directrix of the Collar Laundry Workingwomen's Association of Troy, New York, as assistant secretary of the NLU (Commons 1946:II:128).

The NLU was more obtuse, however, when it came to recognition of the rights and special problems of Black workers. Although they called for the organization of all workers, skilled and unskilled, they took no position on the organization of African-American workers. This was not fortuitous since the overwhelming majority of trade unions completely excluded Black workers in their trade, occupation, or industry from membership. Though the top leaders of the NLU called for the admission of African-Americans into trade unions, this stance had little effect. The opposition to Blacks was reflected in the debates at the 1867 convention of the NLU. The *Boston Daily Evening Voice* on August 7, 1867, wrote specifically about this issue in its discussion of the convention: "The debate on the question of Negro labor was also very discreditable to a body of American labor reformers.... it is a disgrace to the Labor Congress that several members of that body were so much under the influence of the silliest and wickedest of all prejudices as to hesitate to recognize the Negro" (Foner 1962:I:377).

Yet attitudes toward African-Americans were often contradictory, as they are today. Four African-American delegates first appeared at the 1868 meeting of the NLU. More (9 out of 142) appeared at the 1869 convention in Philadelphia. Horace Day of New York introduced a resolution which said: "The National Labor Union knows no North, no South, no East, no West, neither color nor sex on the question of the rights of labor, and urges our colored fellow members to form organizations in all the legitimate ways, and send their delegates from every state in the Union to the next congress" (Foner 1962:I:399). Despite the mixed policies of various unions and the contradictory attitudes described above, much evidence suggests that the Black delegates were treated warmly at these meetings. A *New York Times* article reported the following:

> When a native Mississippian and an ex-confederate officer, in addressing a convention, refers to a colored delegate who has preceded him as 'the gentleman from Georgia,'...when an ardent and Democratic partisan (from New York at that) declares with a 'rich Irish brogue' that he asks for himself no privilege as a mechanic or as a citizen that he is not willing to concede to every other man, white or black...Who shall say now, that prejudices, no matter how strongly they may have been implanted in the human breast, may not be rooted out? (Foner 1962:I:400).

Yet, northern labor remained obtuse to the critical struggle that was taking place in the South. This obtuseness, neglect, ignorance, this blindspot was even evident in William Sylvis, the leader of the NLU, so revered in much radical historiography. Du Bois contrasts Sylvis's stance unfavorably with that of his contemporary Karl Marx, who had a lucid understanding of the importance of the plight of the former slaves to the white workers of the North (Du Bois 1964:357–58). Though Sylvis was among the white leaders who spoke in favor of admission of Blacks to labor unions and supported equal pay for equal work, he was especially obtuse about the importance of the struggles of southern freedmen. He never indicated any sympathy for their demands in the South for land, education, and the vote. He denounced the Freedmen's Bureau as "a huge swindle" and called for its closing (Todes 1942:75). He even called for the immediate restoration of the southern economy, which would not only have squashed attempts at African-American homesteading but also have necessitated aid and support to the former plantation owners. Sylvis was one of the foremost proponents of international workers' organization and had taken the lead in affiliating the NLU with the International Working-Men's Association. A letter was sent to Sylvis in 1869 from the International's General Council, signed by Karl Marx, which talked of the importance of the "liberation of the slaves and the impulse which it thereby gave your own class movement." Sylvis acknowledged the letter, but mentioned nothing about slavery, only attacking the monied aristocracy (DuBois 1964:357). Like other white labor leaders Sylvis was caught up in the Greenback controversy, believing that cheap money would be a panacea for the problems of U.S. workers.

But even on the question of interracial union organizing in the North, fair words and good feelings were not enough. Because of their total exclusion from the overwhelming majority of white trade unions, African-American workers decided to form their own national organization, separate from the NLU. The National Colored Labor Union (NCLU) first met on December 6, 1869, where it elected a Baltimore caulker Isaac Myers as president. The organization had as a primary purpose the protection of the rights of African-American workers. It made no mention of Greenbackism and other monetary plans, but emphasized instead land in the South and education. It did, however, agree with the NLU on the need to exclude Chinese contract labor, about which I will have more to say later (Commons 1946:II:136–37; Foner 1962:I:403–6). Myers and other working-class leaders were eventually pushed into the background in the NCLU, which became more oriented toward gathering votes for the Republican Party than in supporting the struggles and aiding in the organization of Black workers (Foner 1962:I:407).

Although both the leaders of the NLU and leading African-American labor leaders wished for greater cooperation and solidarity between Black and white workers, none understood the issues at stake. White leaders failed to understand the importance of the labor struggle around Reconstruction in the South and the degree to which the Democratic Party was the party of racism and reaction. Black leaders failed to see that the Republican Party, the party of abolition and Black freedom in the South for a brief period, was also the party of big business and had no long-term commitment to either the rights of labor or even freedom and equality for African-Americans. Both labor organizations rapidly waned in size and influence during the 1870s, never realizing their potential.

Railway workers employed in the leading industry of the United States from the 1870s on were equally obtuse with respect to racial matters. In 1877, a year that historian Robert Bruce calls the "year of violence," rail centers throughout the country were aflame, as repeated wage cuts made life for railway workers intolerable. Workers, their families, and whole communities battled troops. In many cases these were the same military units that had just been withdrawn from the South, insuring the defeat of Reconstruction at the hands of the Ku Klux Klan and other planter-supported vigilantes. The armories which disfigure the many cities of our country were first built in 1877 in order to have ready arms to defeat working-class insurgencies in railroad towns.

As Du Bois argues:

> Thus labor went into the great war of 1877 against Northern capital unsupported by the black man, and the black man went his way in the South to strengthen and consolidate his power, unsupported by Northern labor. Suppose for a moment that Northern labor had stopped the bargain of 1876 and maintained the power of the labor vote in the South; and suppose that the Negro with new and dawning consciousness of the demands of labor as differentiated from the demands of capitalists, had used his vote more specifically for the benefit of white labor, South and North? (Du Bois 1964:367)

For Du Bois, the period of Reconstruction represented a missed opportunity for changing the face of U.S. politics, for erasing the exceptional nature of American society. It was not American individualism that blocked this alternative, but racism and the white blindspot.

> The South, after the war, presented the greatest opportunity for a real national labor movement which the nation ever saw or is likely to see for many decades. Yet the labor movement, with but few exceptions, never realized the situation. It never had the intelligence or knowledge, as a whole, to see in black slavery and Reconstruction,

the kernel and meaning of the labor movement in the United States.
(Du Bois 1964:353)

This opportunity for a unified labor movement, North and South, Black and
white, was missed. The southern labor movement, led by the forces of
Reconstruction was crushed by planter-led extralegal violence. The withdrawal of federal troops in 1876 with the Hayes-Tilden compromise sealed
its fate. Northern white workers, by failing to oppose the crushing of
Reconstruction, thus went into their battles in 1877 totally isolated. They
not only lost a valuable ally in southern labor but also strengthened immea-
surably the southern opponents of labor, thus assuring that they would have
the implacable hostility of the federal government in their struggles. Even
most revolutionary socialists failed to realize in the early 1870s, according
to Du Bois, that the greatest potential for their "successful rooting" in the
working class lay with the southern worker (Du Bois 1964:360).

The immediate post–Civil War period was a particularly propitious one
for the empowerment of labor because of the sharp divisions between northern and southern capital. Although northern capitalists had reasons to
oppose the widening of the social revolution in the South, northern workers did not. The interests of northern capital provided no valid excuse for
the blindness of northern labor, whose interest in the fate of their potential allies in the South were different.

What then was the impact of the defeat of Reconstruction and the
Compromise of 1877? The main proponents of the view that the effect of
the period has been exaggerated and that the 1890s were at least as significant argue their positions with great nuance and qualification. They certainly recognize many of the factors argued by those who see the end of
Reconstruction as an historic turning point. Their case is based on two phenomena, which were not largely eliminated until the 1890s: (1) lack of discrimination in the public arena and (2) the many integrated social relations
involving lower-class Black and white southerners. Woodward makes this
case most sharply, arguing that even some abolitionists found the degree of
tolerance and acceptance of Blacks across the South greater than in New
England (Woodward 1955:17; 17–48 passim). Accounts of urban areas, especially New Orleans, are sometimes even more glowing (Bennetts
1972:194–208; Blassingame 1973:210). Reconstruction, as Foner notes, greatly accelerated interracial social contact among the lower classes in urban
areas. Though these contacts continued, a more reserved behavior on Blacks
began to replace their assertiveness during Reconstruction (Foner 1988:371,
592–93). Still, rigid Jim Crow laws, affecting public facilites, transportation,
mortuaries, bars, restaurants, and vacation spots were not to become the
rule until two decades later.

Morgan Kousser likewise argues that disenfranchisement and the elimination of major opposition to southern Democratic and planter rule in the South were not accomplished until century's end. He argues against historians who try to read the characteristics of twentieth-century southern politics into the post–Reconstruction decades. These historians, among whom he includes the political scientist V.O. Key, "too easily dismiss the national Republican party's post–1877 commitment to protecting the political rights of its Southern followers, underestimate the residual power of the Southern GOP in the late nineteenth century, and disregard the transformation of Southern politics that took place about the turn of the century" (Kousser 1974:2–3). Kousser cites the lack of solidarity among southern whites in support of the Democrats, the majority Black turnout rates in all southern states except Mississippi and Georgia (Kousser 1974:15, 27–28), the commitment of northern Republicans to defending the rights of Blacks from 1880 to 1896, and their recognition that the Compromise of 1877 had been a failure (Kousser 1974:18–23, 24). He argues that the decline of Black political influence and even the effectiveness of violence and intimidation have been "exaggerated" (Kousser 1974:11, 14).

Some might think that this dispute is largely a matter of an argument over whether the glass was half full or half empty, but there is much more involved. It is certainly true that the decades after 1877 were to a large extent transitional and contradictory with regard to race relations in the South and the country as a whole. It is also true that the changes at the turn of the century were overwhelming. Yet, to focus merely on some of the levels of interracial contact and voting turnout is to slight the drastic changes that took place in the underlying social reality. The crushing of Reconstruction destroyed in the Deep South, most decisively in the overwhelmingly Black majority Black Belt areas, the most radical, militant, arenas of Black power. As Kousser recognizes, it was in these areas where the affluent whites had the most to lose and where the counterrevolution was most complete. These areas would lead the continued counterrevolution of the 1890s and would control the politics of the South well into the next century. The defeat of Reconstruction also reduced Black agricultural labor to the semifeudal condition in which it would remain for three-quarters of a century. While overwhelming disenfranchisement and rigid segregation had to wait several decades, the rigid enforcement of labor discipline through laws on vagrancy and contracts as well as the harsh repression of attempts by agricultural Black labor to organize followed swiftly in planter-controlled areas. However competitive oppositions to conservative Democrats were on paper, the two victories against them (in Virginia in 1879 by the Readjusters and a decade later in North Carolina by the Republican-Populist alliance) were short-lived.

Democrats, racist to the core, allowed little influence by the remaining Black local officeholders or their constituents.

Those who downplay the defeat of Reconstruction miss the central changes, especially the importance of the crushing of the social movements, which empowered Blacks throughout the country. Thus, in the end one must agree with the assessments of Foner and Du Bois:

> Reconstruction's demise and the emergence of blacks as a disenfranchised class of dependent laborers greatly facilitated racism's further spread...[and] shifted the center of American politics to the right. (Foner 1988:604)

For Du Bois, the defeat of Reconstruction is the secret to American exceptionalism. In answer to the question of "Why no socialism?" in the country as a whole, he counters, "Why no liberalism?" in the South.

> No liberal movement in the United States or the world has been able to make advance among southerners. They are militaristic and will have nothing to do with the peace movement....It has no sympathy with the oppressed of Africa or Asia....there can be no real labor movement in the South; their laboring class is cut in two. (Du Bois 1964:704)

And, on the world level, "reinforced by the increased political power of the South based on the disenfranchisement of black voters...[the U.S. has] degraded colored labor the world over" (Du Bois 1964:630).

Just as Alfred North Whitehead once argued that all western philosophy was but a footnote to Plato, it is even more arguable that all subsequent U.S. political history, if not a footnote, has largely been the working out of those contradictions bequeathed by the Civil War and Reconstruction.

1. Foner argues that "the continued existence of second-class status" after emancipation "changes the terms but not the essence" (Foner 1985:21) and Baron states that "Abolition of slavery did not mean substantive freedom to the black worker" (Baron 1971:13).
2. Marx was one of the first to assemble the data for this assertion and analyze its significance (Marx and Engels 1969:228–32).

3. While many have historically seen such programs—as many also saw it at the time—as explicitly anti-capitalist, both Marx and Lenin argued that such demands were revolutionary bourgeois democratic demands, not necessarily anti-capitalist. Post-World War II land reform in Taiwan among other places suggests that their perspective is the more reasonable one.

CHAPTER 5

The Creation of the System of 1896

> We would like...to tell our visitors...that two hundred and sixty years of progress and enlightenment have banished barbarism and race hatred from the United States...that here Negroes are not tortured, shot, hanged, or burned to death, merely on suspicion of crime...that the American Government...will send its men-of-war to chastise the murder of its citizens in New Orleans or in any part of the south, as readily as for the same purpose it will send them to Chile, Haiti, or San Domingo...But unhappily, nothing of all this can be said, without qualification, and with[out] flagrant disregard of the truth. Douglass 1975:4, 470–71.

> In view of the number of vote frauds in the 1870's and 1880's that had been directed against white candidates who received black votes, it would also seem that the equanimity with which Northerners accepted traditional Southern concern about "misrule" revealed rather more about the deepening climate of white supremacy throughout the nation than it did about the fine points of black capabilities. Goodwyn 1976:277–78.

> ...it is not to be denied that American conditions involve great and peculiar difficulties for a steady development of a workers' party. ...First, the Constitution...Then, and more especially, immigration ...And then the Negroes. To form a single party out of these requires quite unusually powerful incentives. Often there is a sudden violent *élan*, but the bourgeois need only wait passively, and the dissimilar elements of the working class fall apart again. Engels in Marx and Engels 1953:258

The Civil War unleashed tremendous economic, social, and political forces throughout the whole country. Economically, the war called forth unparalleled growth. The main beneficiaries were northern industrialists and bankers. Yet, their dominance was challenged in almost every arena. Electoral politics at the national, state, and sometimes even at the local level was characterized by high rates of political participation, the competitiveness of elections, the volatility of political struggle, and the fragility of party dominance.

Socially, as well as politically, the period was defined by the power, militance, and large number of mass struggles. Some of these popular activities were interracial; others were limited by racial shortsightedness on the part of whites. These disparate tendencies were a heritage of the Civil War and Reconstruction eras.

The 1870s through the 1890s are best viewed as a contradictory transition period shaped by both the successes and failures of the Civil War and Reconstruction. The transition period ended with the establishment of the System of 1896.[1] It involved the crushing of mass movements; the decline of popular politics; the end of competitive party politics in virtually all states; the stable, long-term national dominance of the northern capitalist-supported Republican Party; and the complete abandonment of the rights of Blacks by Republicans, including the ceding of full independent control of the South to the Dixiecrat politicians and planters. The establishment of the System of 1896 also paralleled—and was closely related to—the expansion of U.S. imperial interests, with the accompanying national chauvinist ideology that taking up "the white man's burden" entailed. Race, it turns out, was at the center of all this.

Let us begin with the accelerated economic development that emerged from the Civil War. The new policies of the Union government during the war, including the high protective tariff, the national banking system, and the unequivocal support for infrastructure development (particularly railroads), spurred the rapid growth of northern industry and commerce. In addition, the Civil War, as a continuation of the bourgeois revolution begun during the Revolution/founding period, swept away those obstacles to pure market relations in the North and West and established the dominance of the cash nexus in social relations, making this perhaps the most purely bourgeois of all countries. Even today, the comparisons with other modern countries that continue to have many small precapitalist remnants, regulations, and intrusions into the market are striking. In Germany, for example, the degree of licensing for common activities (including windsurfing), regulations about which names are acceptable to give newborn children, and laws requiring state registration of radios and televisions as well as changes in residence are in stark contrast to the more consistently bourgeois relations in the United States. It was the Civil War that solidified unencumbered market relations and swept away virtually all obstacles to rapid capitalist development in the non-southern parts of the country.

There is some disagreement, however, over when the rapid increase in economic growth actually began, whether it started during the Civil War or later. Thomas Cochran (1967), for example, argues that the Civil War actually retarded economic growth in the North. In my reading of the data,

Cochran is only able to make his argument by an improper aggregation of statistics on pig iron production, which increased enormously from 1861 to 1864 but suffered a large decrease in 1865. Since the war ended in April 1865, Cochran's argument can only be made by his use of figures for the whole of 1865, which includes a significant but temporary dropoff in production after the Civil War and a benchmarking of this lull to the unusually high peak in the prewar year of 1860 (See *Historical Statistics* 1975:I:600). Whatever one's final assessment of the starting point, the enormous economic growth in the wake of the Civil War is indisputable. (For further discussions, see North 1961; Engerman 1967; and Scheiber 1965.) Pig iron shipments were over 50 percent higher in 1866 than in 1860, with a price that more than doubled. Shipments more than doubled again by 1872, almost doubled anew by 1885, more than doubled once more by 1890, and continued a phenomenal growth through 1900, even as it was being in part replaced by the rapid increase in the use of steel (*Historical Statistics* 1975:I:599–600; Hughes 1990:329). Pig iron and later steel were absorbed to a great degree by the largest, most highly capitalized, most industrially advanced, and most national of all industries—railroads. Aided by huge subsidies and investments, railroads bound together the whole country and created a national market for domestic goods. One indication of this is the growth in the miles of track: 35,000 miles in 1865, 53,000 in 1870, 74,000 in 1875, 167,000 by 1890, 207,000 in 1900 (Hughes 1990:268) Similar swift rates of growth may be seen in hog slaughtering, rising from 166,000 in 1860 to 750,147 in 1865 and to 4 million in 1878 (Halpern 1989:22); farm implement and machinery manufacture (Andreano 1967:77); wheat production (*Historical Statistics* 1975:I:512); and wool. Perhaps the most meteoric rise was in the use of bituminous coal, with 9 million tons mined in 1860, 12 million in 1865, 50 million by 1880, 111 million in 1890, and 212 million tons by the turn of the century. This rapid economic development supported the growth of the mass politics, social protest, and class struggles of the post–Civil War era. On the surface, of course, the mass electoral politics and campaigns were a continuation of the popular politics that had begun during the Jacksonian period. National levels of voter turnout for presidential elections hovered around the 80 percent mark from 1876 to 1900. Figures for the North are slightly above the average, while those for the South tend to be 10 to 15 percent lower, in good part a consequence of the crushing of Reconstruction (Piven and Cloward 1988:30; for alternative figures that are lower, although they tell the same story, see Kousser 1974:12). And in most places voting was far from a passive activity.

From the Jacksonian period until the 1890s, political campaigns had mass participation and exhibited "spectacular displays of exuberant partisanship," involving torchlight parades, mass rallies, marching companies, stump speeches, and original campaign songs. Campaign clubs and marching companies represented school, township, ward, and election districts. In the cities, there were ethnic clubs, Black clubs, workplace clubs, and clubs based on "every constituency imaginable," including veterans, old men, even deaf mutes. In New York City, as many as 50,000 might turn out for a parade. In New Haven, with 62,000 inhabitants in 1880, there were forty-two clubs and sixty-eight companies, with 5,000 of the 16,000 eligible voters belonging to one or the other. New Haven was rather typical, since it is estimated that more than 20 percent of northern voters were active in campaigns (McGerr 1986:22, 24, 26–27).

Yet, the activities during the postwar period had a different character from those in the antebellum era, largely because they were shaped by very different social forces. Farmers, in particular, were in a new, often insecure position. The rapid increase in farm and livestock production for the market, a trend that had been developing since the beginning of the century, placed formerly independent farmers throughout the country at the increasing mercy of market forces and middle men (see Post 1996, Reidy 1992, and Sellers 1991 for the earlier period). As a consequence farmers were to be key actors in the class politics of the country for decades.

Workers were also to emerge as an important social force. The number of production workers rose steadily from 1.3 million before the Civil War to over 5 million by the turn of the century, by which time a million worked on the railroads and over 700,000 in the coal mines (*Historical Statistics* 1975:I:516, 138). Enormous social dislocations and tensions were created by this rapid economic development, forces that ended the earlier republican dream of independence for small farmers and artisans. Let us examine the consequences of this social development by glancing at the electoral activities of these two groups.

Among farmers, organizational and electoral gains were especially extensive. From the end of the Civil War until the turn of the century, farmers in the West, parts of the Midwest, and throughout the South mobilized on a large scale. As Sundquist notes, "In the newer states in the west, in particular, tens of thousands of farmers were developing an intense class consciousness and an acute hostility toward the powerful class of financiers and entrepreneurs that appeared to control not only the economy but the polity as well.... The farmers found neither major party responsive to their interests...." (Sundquist 1983:107). All of which suggests that notions of class consciousness and class struggle—contrary to the views of consensus historians and the strident modern conservatives who unabashedly claim that such ideas are alien to the United States of America and were only recently invented by anti-American countercultural, political correctness elites (whoever they might be)—are as American as apple pie and absolutely central to understanding the dynamics of American political development.

In response to declining grain prices and the exploitation of their labor by grain elevator operators, railroads, and money lenders, farmers began to organize. In 1873, Illinois farmers overwhelmed both major parties, electing independent slates of judges and legislators committed to tightly regulating the railroads. At the same time, farmers made important electoral inroads in Wisconsin, Minnesota, Kansas, Indiana, and California. By 1876, this phase of the largely sectoral revolt of the farmers had run its course (Sundquist 1983:112).

These early electoral protests, however, served merely as the background for the more extensive and more radical organization of farmers in the 1880s and the 1890s. The Farmers' Alliance, founded in Texas in 1878, spread throughout the South, Midwest, West, and Northwest, becoming an influential, challenging force in politics. Eventually, members of the Farmers' Alliance formed their own political party, the People's (Populist) Party. Southern populism was especially strong in the 1880s. Its white leaders and members in many of the more radical Populist strongholds realized early that they could not succeed, especially in the South, without their African-American brethren (for a broad overview, see Goodwyn 1976). Thus, questions of race were to become integral to the development of this country's most militant agrarian revolt.

Workers in the North and the Midwest at times also had an important impact on electoral politics. In Pennsylvania, Greenback-Labor candidates were elected to offices, including the future Grand Master Workman of the Knights of Labor, Terrence V. Powderly, who was elected mayor of Scranton. Labor candidates also did well in Wisconsin, Iowa, and Toledo, Ohio. The highpoint of labor electoral success was in 1886 when local Knights of Labor assemblies ran slates of candidates. Labor candidates were successfully elected to office in Milwaukee; Fort Worth; Richmond; Lynn, Massachusetts; Leadville, Colorado; and Key West, Florida. In the 1894 elections, workers in the urban North and Midwest turned against Democratic president Grover Cleveland, leading to a large Democratic defeat. Cleveland had been at the helm during the 1893 depression and had also repulsed organized labor and its sympathizers by using troops and court injunctions to break the Pullman strike and jail its leaders, including Eugene V. Debs. Attorney General Richard Olney, a railroad lawyer and executive before assuming office, declared that his objective was to "make it a failure everywhere." He appointed as special U.S. attorney in Chicago the general counsel of the railroad General Managers' Association and together the government and the association devised the legal measures to crush the union. And for this the Democrats were eventually made to pay by outraged workers (Sundquist 1983:113, 121, 148–49).

The mass electoral politics of the era, however, cannot be understood except as a pale reflection of deeper militant currents. This is especially true with respect to the labor movement, whose renewal and invigorated reemergence was both inspired and constrained by the contradictory impulses of the Civil War and Reconstruction.

The economic development during and after the Civil War helped revitalize a trade union movement that had been relatively moribund since the 1857 depression. Labor shortages during the Civil War, caused by the expansion of wartime production and the large amount of manpower drawn into the Union army, created a classic tight labor market, giving workers increased leverage. On the other hand, the rapid wartime inflation which easily outpaced the more limited wage increases, coupled with the amassing of numerous great fortunes (including that of J.P. Morgan, whose sale of defective rifles to the Union army was denounced by a Congressional committee but left Morgan unpunished and far richer) and the highly discriminatory draft, increased workers' resentments, stimulated worker militancy and a rapid growth of trade unions during 1863 and 1864 (Roediger and Foner 1989:83). The new trade union movement, however, was qualitatively different from that before the Civil War. Aside from standard trade union issues like wages and conditions, it had a broad class focus on the eight-hour day, an increased rhetoric about the need for wide solidarity, especially among Blacks and white workers, some occasional openness to actual interracial organization, and a few dramatic changes in interracial activity. This changed character cannot be adequately explained merely by the rapid economic developments.

In talking about these important changes, especially the liberating effects of the Civil War and Reconstruction on the northern white workers' movement, it is important to strike the right note, to avoid certain oversimplified tendencies quite common in the labor history literature of the period. First, one wants to avoid the uncritical glorification of the eight-hour movement and the massive railway strikes, being cognizant of certain weaknesses, especially with respect to racial issues. On the other hand, there is a tendency among other commentators to expound on the weaknesses, to note correctly the extreme limits of the incipient interracialism, and then to dismiss these movements as foreshadowing a rather inevitable racist future, especially that expressed by the American Federation of Labor by the end of the century. Both of these approaches, while sometimes yielding important information, are inadequate as analysis; they tend to be one-dimensional scholarship that miss the complexities of social development, including the possibilities and limits in the post–Civil War social world.

Marx claimed that the eight-hours agitation was "the first fruit of the Civil War" that "ran with seven-league boots of the locomotive from the Atlantic to the Pacific, from New England to California." Eight-hour leagues and supporting groups sprang up across the country; the demand seemed to have universal support among workers (Montgomery 1967:236). As opposed to the extremely narrowly focused, pre–Civil War labor movement, the eight-hour movement had a broader perspective. First, its proponents argued that the reduction of work to eight hours not only would be beneficial to the health of the affected workers but also, because of increased leisure, would encourage their democratic participation in politics and the raising of their cultural levels. Such liberty would allow workers to be human beings and not be enslaved to their employers. The extension of the logic of such arguments on the part of the more radical eight-hour advocates frequently drew its proponents into challenging private property itself, because it was the desire for greater profits by those who owned the means of production that led to the degradation of labor in the first place. As one labor editorial asserted, *"property is a tyrant, and the people are its slaves...the penal-* ty for resistance to its orders is starvation" (Montgomery 1967:238–39). The eight-hour movement continued to grow in the 1870s and 1880s and led to the widespread eight-hour strikes of 1886, which established May 1 as international labor day and culminated in the bloody Haymarket affair.

The breadth of the eight-hour movement is also suggested by the extent of participation and leadership of the movement by leading antebellum abolitionists, who were often the most sought after speakers at workers' meetings. Wendell Phillips, perhaps the most extreme case, was the most popular labor-reform speaker after the Civil War—just as he had been the most popular white abolitionist speaker before the war—especially sought by Irish workers. Other abolitionist leaders who supported the eight-hour movement included William Garrison, William Channing, Josiah Abbott, Rufus Wyman, Ezra Heywood, and Benjamim Butler (Montgomery 1967:123). The abolitionist preacher Henry Ward Beecher, who was vehemently antiunion before the war, in 1872 threw his support to the eight-hour movement, calling it "one of the most promising signs of the times," arguing further that "I thank God for any power to overthrow the union of capital, which has produced nothing but corruption and intolerance." New York bricklayers expressed their appreciation for the abolitionist preacher by passing a resolution thanking him for his sermon (Messer-Kruse 1994:98–99). Perhaps the most interesting joining of abolitionism and labor reform was in the person of Ira Steward, the leading labor exponent of the eight-hours movement, himself an antislavery activist before the war who may have fought with John Brown in Kansas (for discussions of Steward, see Montgomery 1967:249–60;

Messer-Kruse 1994:79–100; and Roediger 1986).

In the immediate post–Civil War period, the rhetoric (if not the practice) of interracial unity was proclaimed with growing frequency by labor leaders. Aside from Wendell Phillips, Ira Steward, and William Sylvis who we have already met, George McNeill and Richard Trevellick held interracialism as a central tenet. Trevellick was the leader of the Detroit Trades Assembly and was to become the head of the National Labor Union (NLU) after Sylvis's death. However little this incipient egalitarianism was embodied in actual union organizations, the rhetoric itself and its growing receptivity was something new (Montgomery 1967:221–29; Messer-Kruse 1994:94).

Yet, in addition to the rhetoric, there were some small beginnings in actual interracialism. In 1869, the New York section of the International Workingmen's Association (the Marx-led First International), set up a special committee to organize unions among Black workers. Within weeks they not only had organized several groupings of African-American workers but also had gained the admission of these Black unions into the Workingmen's Union, the central labor center for New York City (Foner 1962:I:416). During the 1877 railway strikes, there were numerous instances of initial acceptance of African-American workers by whites. In Keyser, West Virginia, Black and white railroad workers met together and voted to join the growing strike. At a mass meeting in New York City to support the strikers, sponsored by many of the city's main unions, the main speaker was J.P. McConnell, the Marxist editor of the *Labor Standard*. McConnell received "tremendous applause" when he proclaimed "It was a grand sight to see in West Virginia, white and colored men standing together, men of all nationalities in one supreme contest for the common rights of workingmen" (P.Foner 1977:37, 122). Interracialism emerged in other places, including Galveston, Texas, and St. Louis. A meeting of thousands in Cincinnati, Ohio, was addressed by Peter H. Clark, a Black member of the First International (P.Foner 1977:130). These small examples of interracial labor activity in the North were, of course, fitful starts, both contradictory in themselves and counterposed to much more frequent instances of hostility to blacks and exclusionary racial policies. But they were something new and a decided departure from antebellum labor struggles.

There were also some surpising examples of previously antagonistic groups of workers becoming more sympathetic after the war to the claims of blacks for equality. Perhaps the most dramatic change was on the part of Irish workers. Before the war, segments of the Irish working class were among the most hostile not only to abolitionism but also to antislavery. Yet, when Wendell Phillips died in 1884, Irish-Americans memoralized the "golden trumpet" of abolitionism in meetings and tributes, with one group praising his commitment to "universal liberty and equal rights of all men." The central figure representing this changed orientation was Patrick Ford, the editor of the *Irish World*, the hegemomic paper among Irish workers. Ford, an abolitionist printer who had worked before the war on Garrison's *Liberator* and fought in the Irish army, saw as one of his main tasks the fighting of racial prejudice within the Irish community. He also tied the struggle of land for Blacks in the South with the land question in Ireland. Ford's most concentrated constituency lay in the high percentage Irish mining districts in northeastern Pennsylvania. Out of this tradition of Irish interracialism was to come Terrence Powderly, the future leader of the interracial Knights of Labor, and many other Irish Knights leaders. In the 1880s, the Irish and Irish-Americans looked back in pride at those small number of antebellum Irish abolitionists. This changed orientation was so influential that even Tammany Hall, no leader in progressive causes, was by this time extolling the support that the great Irish nationalist leader Daniel O'Connell had given to abolitionism before the war, at a time when his stance was almost universally opposed within the Irish American community (this account is taken from E.Foner 1980:150–200).

One of the most intriguing cases of conversion is that of Albert Parsons. As a youth, he fought for the South in the Civil War as a scout in the calvalry of the brigade of his brother William, a Confederate general. After the war, he began school at Waco University (now Baylor) and soon became a Radical Republican, advocating complete equality for Blacks. When the Democrats took control of Texas in 1873, Parsons and his wife Lucy moved to Chicago, where they were to become leaders of that city's labor movement, helping to infuse it with the racial egalitarianism they had preached in Texas. Albert Parsons, of course, is the most famous of the Haymarket martyrs, framed and hanged for the 1886 Haymarket bomb explosion in which several policemen were killed. Lucy Parsons was active in the labor and radical movements until her death in 1942, in 1941 playing a role in helping the racially egalitarian left-led Congress of Industrial Organizations (CIO) Farm Equipment union to organize the International Harvester plants in Chicago (Avrich 1984:3–25, *passim;* Ashbaugh 1976).

Both the broadened class perspective of the northern workers movement and the fitful motion toward interracialism were in part a consequence of the Civil War. Such relations are, of course, denied by many people. Alan Dawley, for example, sees the Civil War as undermining the growth of anticapitalist class consciousness among northern workers. These workers were "sidetracked in the 1860s because of the Civil War," seeing the class enemy as the slaveholders and their employers as their allies (Dawley 1976:238). This interpretation is implausible and fails to see the degree to which the existence of slavery and racist attitudes among white workers limited the breadth and solidarity of the pre-war labor movement. For it was the revolutionary implications of emancipation and the threats to seize slaveowners' property that helped open broad radical vistas. Labor organizations began to see Black liberation as a model and precursor for the general liberation of labor, something applauded in labor publications after the war. David Roediger, in one of the more astute analyses of this question, argues that these new attitudes are reflected in the changing lyrics of minstrel verses which began to extol John Brown and the ability of Blacks to fight (Roediger 1991:174–75) while Lott (1993) notes the potential for such attitudes in an earlier period. The freeing of Blacks from the stigma of slavery, their new-found respect as fighting men, and the growing abolitionism of many Union army veterans were all a legacy of the war which helped redirect the labor movement to a broader direction. Dawley's remarks thus must be added to the pantheon of white labor apologies.

While the Civil War and Reconstruction had its liberating effects, it also had its constraining effects. The end of this historic turning point was, as I have argued, not the gaining of equality by Blacks but a contradictory state of both freedom and nonfreedom, which also placed difficult roadblocks in the path of the post–Civil War labor movement in generating a more consistent, broad solidarity. The failure of northern white labor to support the gaining of land by the freedmen in the South and to defend the radical Reconstruction governments was a fatal shortcoming. Despite the frequent rhetoric of equality and the occasional interracialism exhibited during struggles, white trade union organizations and worker militance extolled by many social historians remained by and large racially exclusionary. Some have argued that the extreme racism of many unions during this period emanates from the narrow craft basis of many unions. There is undoubtedly much truth in this claim. The attempts to gain better wages and working conditions were based on their union's ability to control the labor market by limiting entry of newcomers to their trades, a form of exclusion that lent itself naturally to racial discrimination. While this arena of racism is undeniably important, it does not help us explain other forms of racism that seem tied to broader forms of white working-class mobilization. In this context it is helpful to look at the anti-Chinese racism that swept the continent in the late nineteenth century, which some writers have argued played a role in creating a white "class" consciousness.

Anti-Chinese Exclusionism

The obtuseness and chauvinism of Northern workers and their leaders reached perhaps its highest level in the West Coast-initiated anti-Chinese agi-

tation of the late nineteenth and early twentieth centuries. The Chinese, like
the earlier indentured servants, African slaves, the Irish, and later millions of
Southern and Eastern European immigrants, were brought to North America
by employers and their agents for their labor. Chinese workers were employed
as miners beginning with the 1848 California gold rush and were used extensively in the arduous and dangerous work of building the western leg of the
transcontinental railroad. As many as 10,000 Chinese laborers worked between
1867 and 1869 for the Central Pacific Railroad (Saxton 1971:62).

When jobs were plentiful and the labor market was tight, no one object-
ed to the presence of Chinese labor, especially because they were generally
kept out of skilled jobs. No whites were known to complain when Central
Pacific head Leland Stanford used thousands of Chinese to tunnel through
the Sierra Nevada range in the winter of 1866, killing untold numbers in
snow drifts and cave-ins. When the economy soured and competition for
available work became intense, the Chinese served as scapegoats for the difficulties faced by white workers, becoming the objects of violence, expul-
sions from jobs and from whole towns, and even the victims of mass murder. Such violence, of course, against recent immigrants was nothing new
in America. Native Philadelphians had burned down Catholic churches and
blocks of homes in Irish neighborhoods in the 1840s, and the 1850s saw
Germans as the targets throughout much of the Midwest (Saxton 1971:12).
When times were bad, white workers often complained that jobs were
reserved for Chinese workers and that the latter were the recipients of
favoritism and even received better assignments, although the reverse was
almost always the case. How the echoes of the misinformation put forth by
those opposed to affirmative action today span across the century.

Whites in California engaged in mass campaigns for the exclusion of
Chinese immigrants, until no politician in the state could survive without
a strong anti-Chinese stance. At the time of the adoption of the state constitution in 1879, a state referendum was held in which total exclusion was
favored by a vote of 150,000 to 900. At various times, pogroms took place
up and down the West Coast, from Seattle, Washington, to San Diego, where
whole Asian populations were driven out of town; occasionally, large numbers were murdered. In Rock Springs, Wyoming, a fistfight between a
Chinese and white coal miner triggered the burning of the Chinese section
of town in 1885 by a mob of white workers. The official body count was
twenty-eight, with the rest of the Chinese driven out of town (Saxton
1971:201–2). The Knights of Labor, an otherwise relatively progressive labor
organization, defended the white miners (Black 1963:68). In another incident in Los Angeles, "a mob shot and hanged 20 Chinese, pillaged homes
and stores and tortured Orientals" (Hill 1973:48).

Unions and working people, although not the only participants, often played a major role in the development of the anti-Chinese movement. As the cigar-making industry became mechanized, skilled cigar makers were replaced by cheaper, less skilled labor. By 1870, the overwhelming majority of this labor was Chinese. Rather than organize this new workforce into their union, attempting to raise the living and working standards of Asian and white workers alike, the Cigar Makers International Union (CMIU), led by Adolph Strasser and Samuel Gompers, devised a plan to drive them out of the industry. In 1874, they had developed a white label to indicate that white men had made the cigars. The union then went about demanding the eviction of all Chinese workers from cigar establishments, boycotting those manufacturers who did not comply. The campaign was totally successful; in an early case of extreme affirmative action, thousands of Chinese cigar workers were deprived of their jobs in order to provide work for supposedly more needy white workers (Hill 1973:48–49; Mink 1986:79). Few complained of *this* preferential hiring and firing, for white workers were merely getting the jobs they deserved, the ones to which they were entitled. The famous union label had its origins in this campaign. Anti-Chinese activity eventually went national, even in areas where there was absolutely no job competition from Chinese labor. As Herbert Hill notes, there were only 368 Chinese outside the West in 1870 and "even the most insistent labor politician could not factually argue that the depressed conditions of white workers were the result of competition from Chinese labor" (Hill 1973:45; Majka and Majka 1982:22, 30).

Given the actions of the CMIU, it should come as no surprise that the American Federation of Labor (AFL) under Samuel Gompers' presidency supported Chinese exclusionism, but the aggressiveness of his stance takes one aback. In 1902, Gompers coauthored an AFL pamphlet entitled "Some Reasons for Chinese Exclusionism: Meat vs. Rice: American Manhood vs. Asiatic Coolieism—Which Shall Survive?" (Mink 1986:96; Hill 1973:52). And here it is perhaps appropriate to note the slanders and myths that invariably accompany such stances. Gompers denounces the Chinese for bringing to the United States "nothing but filth, vice and disease" (Mink 1986:96). He also paints a picture of the Chinese luring white boys and girls into opium dens. "What other crimes were committed in those dark fetid places...are almost too horrible to imagine" (Hill 1973:52).

Gompers' racism seemed to have no limits. In 1903, Japanese and Mexican workers in Oxnard, California, organized the Sugar Beet and Farm Laborer's union and successfully struck in the beet fields. This activity opened the eyes of the Los Angeles Council of Labor, who in a moment of solidaristic sentiment, passed a resolution to organize all Asian workers in the state. The union applied for a charter to the AFL. Gompers, however, was not fooled and issued a charter only to the Mexican workers, specifically excluding Japanese or Chinese workers from membership. The Mexican section of the union returned the charter, refusing to exclude their Asian brethren. They were supported by the Los Angeles Council and by the Chicago-based *American Labor Union Journal* (see Black 1963:71-2; Hill 1973:53).

The racial stance of Samuel Gompers and the AFL is reflected in the dominant school of U.S. labor history by its founder John Commons (a labor reformer revered by many liberals), who writes:

> The anti-Chinese agitation in California, culiminating as it did in the Exclusion Act of 1882, was doubtless the most important single factor in the history of American labour, for without it the entire Country might have been overrun by Mongolian labour, and the labour movement might have become a conflict of races instead of one of classes. (John R. Commons and Associates, *History of Labour in the United States*, 1946:II:252–53)

A modern version of Commons' orientation may be seen in historian Nick Salvatore's introduction to Gompers' writings in which Salvatore fails to mention Gompers' bigotry (Salvatore 1984).

But anti-Chinese attitudes were not limited to those who were also racist against Blacks, as with Commons and Gompers. The attitudes were so deep-seated that they often appeared among those who championed the rights of African-Americans. Hinton Helper, a chief antebellum Republican polemicist against slavery, considered the Chinese "semi-barbarians" (Saxton 1971:19; Majka and Majka 1982:35). The Knights of Labor, who often played a progressive role in organizing and defending the rights of Blacks, was many times also a leader in the anti-Chinese campaigns in the West. At a time when southern Populists were attempting to forge unity between Black and white farmers, the California Populists 1894 platform, which suppported female suffrage, an eight-hour day, public jobs for the unemployed, and state inspection of all workplaces, called for the total exclusion of Asian immigrants (Saxton 1971:237). The Socialist Party supported anti-Chinese legislation and the United Mineworkers, perhaps the most racially egalitarian union in the AFL, had anti-Chinese material in its paper. And as we saw earlier, even the National Colored Labor Union had Chinese exclusion in its platform.

There were, to be sure, a small number of exceptions, people who opposed the anti-Chinese movement. For a time, California industrialists who used Chinese contract labor did not want their cheap labor source cut off. Nationally, there were industrialists who feared that the anti-Chinese politics would lead to general restrictions on immigration and eliminate their own source of wage slaves. There were also diplomats and those concerned with foreign policy who hesitated to offend foreign states. Though these people contributed to the initial hesitancy of the Republican Party in joining the anti-Chinese bandwagon, their resistance was not long lived. More principled opposition existed among various old-line abolitionists and religious leaders, who exerted some influence within the Republican Party in the years immediately after the Civil War. Finally, there were a small number of left-wing socialists, perhaps typified by Eugene Debs. In 1910, Debs denounced the exclusionist position of his own party calling it "utterly unsocialistic, reactionary and, in truth, outrageous," having "no place in a proletarian gathering under the auspices of an international movement that is calling on the oppressed and exploited workers of all the world to unite for their emancipation" (Black 1963:71).

The real reason for the prominence and viability of the anti-Chinese movement in American politics, however, is that it served as an important "wedge issue" for the Democratic Party in the way that race has played that role since 1964 for the Republicans. And it provided the vehicle for many nineteenth-century Republicans to abandon the civil rights tradition of its party, just as Democrats are doing today.

At the end of the Civil War, Democrats had a dilemma. As a largely southern party that had defended slavery, their patriotism was suspect. Hostility toward the rights of African-Americans had connotations of secession. Yet, California before the Civil War had been majority Democratic. The party needed a vehicle to win back their former constituency, especially among manual laborers, and regain majority status. They found that they could make racist appeals and take a stand in favor of the supposed interests of white workers with anti-coolieism. In addition, they had found an issue that drove a wedge into the divisions among Republicans.

For Republicans, the Chinese issue itself was especially divisive; steamship companies and railroads had stakes in Chinese immigration; abolitionists and radical Republicans believed correctly that at the core of anti-Chinese nativism was race prejudice (Mink 1986:89). Other Republicans, including as we have seen some abolitionists, opposed further Chinese immigration. Second, however, many Republican supporters were ambivalent over key aspects of the party's program, including the need for extensive southern reconstruction, how far to grant rights to former Black slaves, and what to offer labor. For them, Chinese exclusion served as an excuse to abandon their party. Thus, the Chinese issue was both divisive in itself and a perfect surrogate issue for separating ambivalent Republicans from their party.

The Democrats played the issue to the hilt in the 1867 California elections. "During the 1867 campaign, Democratic candidates passionately denounced the Chinese, demanded immediate restrictions on Chinese immigration and immediate deportation of resident Chinese, and advocated changes in the Burlingame Treaty" (Mink 1986:80). The party platform stated that it was "impractical to maintain republican institutions based upon the suffrage of negroes, Chinese and Indians" and asserted that the regulation of voting was a state prerogative (Saxton 1971:89), underscoring once again that states' rights was then, is now, and has always been a racist, anti-popular demand. As California and other states are doing today, Democrats in California greatly exaggerated the effects of immigration and continually demanded relief from Congress. The Democrats, who had used the anti-Chinese campaign to develop an alliance with the trade unions, had also made promises to shorten the legal working day to eight hours, to raise the standard of living of workers, to take action against the monopolies, and to curb the influence of special business interests. Yet, they came through on none of these class demands; only in opposing Chinese immigration did they keep their promises (Saxton 1971:111).

For many Republicans, anti-Chinese arguments provided the first opportunity to break their "now burdensome alliance with abolitionism" (Saxton 1971:105). And their refusal to oppose exclusionism foreshadowed their willingness to abandon Black Reconstruction. By 1876, the Republicans had followed the Democrats in placing anti-Chinese positions in their national platform. It is perhaps appropriate to note that politicians and unions were not the only groups carrying the cross of anti-coolieism, academics also did their share. In the spring of 1900, a special California convention was held against the Japanese. An important speaker was Professor Edward A. Ross of Stanford, a leading U.S. sociologist. His remarks reached Mrs. Leland Stanford, the widow of Leland Stanford, the former senator, Republican governor, founder of Stanford University, and first president of the Central Pacific Railroad, as well as the importer of thousands of contract Chinese laborers in the 1860s. Mrs. Stanford successfully demanded that Ross be fired. A distinguished committee of professors reported to the American Economic Association and condemned the university. Thus, perhaps the first defense of academic freedom on the West Coast was done not to defend unpopular views but to protect the right to preach racial exclusion (Saxton 1971:248).

How are we to look at the racial blindness—or rather such acts of white chauvinism—on the part of white workers and their organizations? Could it be that it all really is rooted deep and indelibly in human nature, or that such passions and activities stem from the unshakeable heritage of Anglo-American culture? It is, of course, easy to answer unequivocally in the affirmative. To what degree were white workers in California limited by social forces and structures much larger than themselves, including the defeat of

Reconstruction, the reemergence of degrading conditions of life and labor for African-Americans, and the consequent degrading attitudes toward all people of color? In probing these questions, it is instructive to compare certain aspects of the labor movement in Chicago with the movement in San Francisco during the late nineteenth century. Especially illuminating is the different orientations with respect to race and ethnicity in the two cities and the degree of success attained with respect to education issues, which played an important part in the political life in both metropolises during this period.

In contrast to Europe, late nineteenth-century workers and their organizations in the United States exhibited strong support for common public schools, including overwhelming votes in favor of tax increases to finance them. (My discussion of these issues follows Katznelson and Weir 1985.) Typically, labor movements sought common schools open to all groups and classes. They preferred broad educational programs so that working-class children might have some possibility for the opportunities enjoyed by children of the higher classes. With respect to manual education, in contrast to employers who generally desired specific job-oriented training, workers wanted broader training for their children so they might be prepared for a variety of future occupations. Finally, they did not want to see vocational training in public schools used to undermine the control of union jobs and union working and living standards.

In San Francisco—one will not be surprised to learn—the school struggles were fragmented by race and ethnicity. Workers tended to unite with other members of their ethnic and racial groups across class lines. Teachers usually identified with higher-ranking educational professionals and did not form labor organizations for themselves. Few demands sought by labor unions in San Francisco were won; schools were exclusionary, with many Asians, not surprisingly, kept out of white schools. Reformers and those battling business interests were easily divided by race and ethnicity and hence conquered. Chicago, while no racial utopia, was quite different. There, the labor movement was not sharply divided by ethnicity or race and presented a united front in their demands. Teachers successfully unionized and were an integral part of the labor movement. As a result of the unified class positions, schools in Chicago were highly diverse, "open to virtually all children, irrespective of their class, neighborhood, race, ethnicity, or sex" (Katznelson and Weir 1985:96). The Chicago Teachers Federation, whose leaders were women representing an almost exclusively female constituency, defended the interests of its members both as women and teachers. The relatively unified labor movement won many important demands in addition to open common schools, including broad manual training, and higher wages not only for teachers but also for janitors and other service workers (Katznelson and Weir 1985:106–9). At a time of increasing white chauvinism nationally, the Chicago labor movement was not poisoned and divided by racism to the degree that the San Francisco working-class was. Thus, the anti-Chinese movement in California and nationally, although giving us important insights into the racial dynamics of late nineteenth-century America, especially the racial attitudes of white workers, is insufficient in itself to understand either the complexities or the full range of options open to labor organizations and their leaders.

I have, to be sure, argued that the greatest possibilities for changes in the system of racial domination and its potential overthrow—as well as the greatest possibilities for social change in general—take place during those critical turning points when large numbers of people are politically mobilized, those "moments of madness" when all things appear possible. Yet, even within the more structured and limited periods, including the transition period from the 1870s to the 1890s, a wide range of racial practices can be observed, some of them based on different social and economic conditions, some of them based on different types of leadership. We must keep the full range of racial experiences in mind before jumping to hasty conclusions from one or another set of circumstances.

The South

To fill out our picture, let us turn our attention briefly to the South. The South's economy was devastated by the war, its currency worthless, and its ruling class defeated and impoverished; the war had placed the South in a far different situation than the northern and western sections of the country. Although large amounts of federal revenues were directed toward public projects in the country as a whole, less than 15 percent were allocated to the South. The previous system of agricultural labor was destroyed and a new one slowly developed. Sharecropping and tenant farming replaced gang labor by slaves as the dominant form of cotton production. A new southern ruling class emerged composed of a combination of the landlord and merchant classes, which came to dominate both the commerce and agriculture of the cotton economy. There remains a good deal of debate over the degree to which this class was made up of members of the former planter class and the degree to which they were supplanted by newer elites. (See, e.g., Wiener 1978:3–34, for a sharp presentation of the issues.) This new class dominated cotton production, keeping not only Black and white tenants and sharecroppers under control but also upcountry white yeoman farmers in a state of dependency. In the Deep South Black Belt areas, the labor force remained overwhelmingly Black. There, the defeat of Reconstruction not only created widespread disenfranchisement but also semifeudal labor relations with harsh legal punishments for vagrancy, indebtedness, and contract violations, as well as extralegal retribution when it was deemed necessary.

Even before the new labor system completely dominated agriculture, cotton production was rebounding quickly from its wartime destruction. From its low point of 300,000 bales in 1864, it had reached 2 million bales a year by 1865 and 4.3 by 1870. By 1880 the 6.6 million bales were well above the prewar 5 million bale figure; in 1890, production was at 8.6 million bales, 1900 at 10.1 million, and 1905 at 13.2 million (*Historical Statistics* 1975:I:517–18). Exports followed a similar pattern, exceeding the prewar value in both weight and value by 1880. Yet, prices never reached their prewar levels and continued a steady decline through the 1890s, keeping most who labored on the crop in permanent poverty (Rostow 1980:132–33; *Historical Statistics* 1975:II:898–99).

Although it generally dominated the Democratic Party and state governments throughout this post–Reconstruction period in all the southern states, the new planter and commercial class did not have uncontested political control. In the 1880s and through the 1890s, opposition party candidates in southern gubernatorial elections were highly competitive before the enactment of extensive disenfranchisement laws. And in most of these states, with the exception of Georgia and Mississippi, Blacks played an important role in the opposition (Kousser 1974:27, 41). Agrarian labor protest in the South was a central component of the political turmoil of the transition period. Its bases, however, were uneven. As we have already seen, protest became increasingly difficult in certain areas, especially the Black Belt regions of the Deep South after the end of Reconstruction.

Agricultural labor militancy began among Blacks before the end of the Civil War. In South Carolina, Blacks drove off overseers, while in Georgia they did this as the war ended. In the sea islands of South Carolina, Black laborers, engaged in slowdowns and strikes during 1863 and by the spring of 1864, were demanding higher wages (Saville 1994:13, 60–63; Foner 1988:281). By 1866, there were numerous work stoppages over rates of pay, the speed of work, and the methods and timing of payments (Saville 1994:140). Events in the South Carolina low country in 1876 showed the dependency of rural popular struggles in the Black Belt areas on political power. In May of that year, hundreds of day laborers walked off their jobs, demanding both higher pay and payment in cash rather than script only redeemable at the plantation store. They marched through the fields getting more workers to join them. Armed strikers were confronted by a Democratic rifle club; political leaders defused the confrontation. Ten strikers were initially arrested, but a Black judge eventually dismissed all charges. The planters finally granted the strikers' demands. This, however, was to be one of the last hurrahs of Black plantation workers. Post-Reconstruction Black rural Deep South labor strikes were more likely to end as did the 1887 Louisiana Black sugar workers' strike in which over 100 were massacred by the state militia and vigilantes (Foner 1988:573, 595). Reconstruction also witnessed the birth of an urban labor movement among Black workers. Struggles for higher wages took place early among Richmond, Virginia, factory workers; Jackson, Mississippi, washerwomen; and mechanics in Columbus, Georgia (Foner 1988:107). The vanguard of the Black southern labor movement, however, were the longshoremen in southern ports, who at the very beginning of Reconstruction were already striking in Charleston, South Carolina; Savannah, Georgia; Mobile, Alabama; and the union stronghold of New Orleans, the South's largest and the nation's second most important port. Striking longshoremen in Florida along with striking timber workers prodded Black lawmakers to successfully champion several pro-labor measures in the state legislature in 1874 and 1875 (Foner 1988:281, 539). Unlike the organizing among Black rural laborers, Black industrial labor was to have many highpoints of successful struggle throughout the transition period. Even after the defeat of Reconstruction, the isolated strength of Black and interracial unionism is rather remarkable. Recent scholarship, for example, has uncovered extensive organization of Black and white workers in the South by the Knights of Labor during the 1880s and 1890s. Melton McLaurin (1978) describes not only joint organization but also integrated struggles against segregation and successful political activities. Peter Rachleff's (1989) study of Richmond in the 1880s and 1890s shows the strength of solidaristic interracial unions and the rise of Black political power and influence, as well as the occasional forthright stands of the Knights on racial issues. For example, at the 1886 Knights convention in Richmond, the capital of the old Confederacy, national leaders successfully insisted that Richmond theaters and hotels accept African-American delegates, which caused a stir throughout the whole South. In 1886, in the 4th congressional district of North Carolina, made up of the eight counties centered in the Raleigh-Durham area, state master workman John Nichols, a pro-Union printer (i.e., he defended the North during the Civil War because he was an abolitionist) and outspoken supporter of the Knights' liberal racial policies, was elected to Congress (McLaurin 1978:82–84). The policies of the Knights were, to be sure, highly contradictory, but their activities in Richmond and elsewhere—especially their commitment to integrated unions—often necessitated a frontal challenge to white supremacy.

Varying degrees of interracial unity were also achieved by New Orleans waterfront workers from the end of the Civil War in 1865 until the crushing of union organization in the Crescent City in the 1920s (Bennetts 1972, Rosenberg 1988, Shugg 1938, Arnesen 1991). And the mine workers were committed to interracial organizing in the Deep South from the 1890s on. These cases were, of course, atypical, although it is unclear to what extent more was possible had there been additional energy and commitment directed toward such attempts.[2]

The Crushing of the Popular Movements

Despite the undermining of broad class unity over wide sectors of the laboring population, popular protest and struggle challenged elites throughout the land. From the 1870s on—for over two full decades—insurgencies, strikes, and mass political action took place across the country, involving workers and farmers, and peaked in the late 1880s and early 1890s. It was only the crushing of these militant class struggles which ended the transition period and allowed the establishment of the System of 1896; this critical turning point instituted a more rigid system of white supremacy that both characterized class rule and affected social relations in the whole country. The contours of these struggles and their destruction are instructive for us.

The first series of struggles to peak and be destroyed were those under the aegis of the Knights of Labor. The Knights, a broad-based, highly solidaristic yet diffuse labor organization, whose growth did not take off until the early 1880s, was to be the vehicle of a new, broad-based national labor insurgency. In early 1885, Knights of Labor railway workers won a startling victory over the Southwest System, one of the largest railroads in the country. The owner, Jay Gould, was a Wall Street financier, perhaps the most hated of the "robber barons" of the period. Gould was forced by a system-wide strike to rescind a wage cut and to agree to the union's other demands. Workers flocked into the Knights of Labor, with membership rising within one year (1885–86) from just over 100,000 to well over 700,000. A much smaller labor organization, the Federation of Organized Trades and Labor Unions, called a strike for May 1, 1886. During May of 1886, hundreds of thousands of workers struck for an eight-hour day. May Day, which was to become an international workers holiday and was attacked during the McCarthy period as a foreign communist holiday, owes its origin to the 1886 strikes in the United States.

Chicago was the center of the eight-hour movement. On May 4, 1886, at a rally protesting police brutality against striking workers, a bomb was thrown and seven policemen and an undetermined number of participants were fatally wounded. The identity of the perpetrator is unknown to this day. Commonly known as the Haymarket affair, after the site of the bomb blast, the incident was used as an excuse to bring repression down on the whole labor movement. Eight Chicago labor leaders, including the previously mentioned Albert Parsons, many of whom were not even at the rally at the time of the blast, were arrested and charged with murder. The incident put the Knights of Labor and other labor organizations on the defensive, divided leaders and membership, lost labor virtually all public sympathy, and legitimized the unleashing of a reign of terror against all labor activists. Police raids were made on known radical and labor leader hangouts, arrests were made without warrants, rallies and speeches were prohibited, and newspapers were seized and shut down (P. Foner 1955:II:248). These activities took place across the country, representing another incident in the periodic denial of civil liberties and the crushing of radical and labor dissent when it had become too threatening to corporate America. This repression of the Left—an almost continuous, if cyclical feature of American society—usually denied by conservatives and seen often by many liberals as small aberrations, has never been systematically directed against organizations of the Right, who have never presented a serious challenge to the increased profit margins of major capitalists. The far deadlier blast in Oklahoma in 1995 has had little repressive impact on the broader Right, except for some mild exposés of the militia movement. The repression against radicals and the labor movement in the late 1880s effectively destroyed the Knights of Labor, but not surprisingly in the South, which was still enough of a national backwater as to be insulated from the immediate impact of many national events.[3]

Another high point of labor struggle that was destroyed by state power was the 1892 strike of iron and steel workers against the Carnegie Steel Company at Homestead, Pennsylvania. The strike was provoked by the company's attempt to break the union, reduce wages by as much as 20 percent, and undermine union-enforced working conditions. Though led by the skilled Amalgamated Association of Iron and Steel Workers, who represented only a tiny portion of the labor force, the strike was actively supported by the unskilled, recent immigrants, and Black workers. Communities around Homestead mobilized with arms to support the strikers. In perhaps the most famous incident, strikers and their armed supporters engaged in a victorious gun battle with more than 300 armed Pinkerton guards. The Pennsylvania governor then sent in 8,000 troops, arresting hundreds of strike leaders and other workers and aiding in the defeat of the strike (for a brief summary, see Foner 1955:II:206–18). Unionism was stifled in the steel industry for decades, but it is not clear whether it need to have been. The union, as Philip Foner argues, would have been in a far better position to recover from its defeat if it had attempted to build on the unity displayed during the strike. Yet, the union reverted to its former position of rejecting the organization of unskilled workers and excluding Blacks from membership, dooming it to impotence in its abilities to challenge the power of the steel companies (Foner 1955:II:218). Racial discrimination gave certain privileges and identity to elite white workers but it did so at a cost. The balance sheet was not nearly so clear as those who argue for the benefits from labor market discrimination received by white workers assert in their theories.

Integrated struggles of coal miners took place in the 1890s in Tennessee and Alabama. Western miners also organized successfully, eventually forming the Western Federation of Miners under the legendary leadership of William D. (Big Bill) Haywood. Though some of these struggles were initially victorious, most were eventually defeated, if not by force, then by the loss of economic leverage brought about by the 1893 depression.

Two struggles during this period are significant and in certain ways stand counterposed to each other with respect to racial issues. The vanguard of the southern labor movement was in New Orleans. There, workers engaged in numerous interracial alliances, expressing at times an impressive degree of solidarity given the degree of white supremacist violence that existed in post–Reconstruction Louisiana. Despite tensions, Black and white skilled screwmen (who packed cotton into ships' holds) struck together in 1883, refusing attempts by management to divide them by race. By 1887, three of the five elected officials of the city-wide union Cotton Council were African-American. In late 1892, a general strike was called in the city, demanding an eight-hour day and other benefits for the city's workers. The strike involved forty-nine unions and 25,000 workers. Attempts to divide the workers by race notwithstanding (and even to settle with some of the white unions but refusing to give in to the Black ones), were unsuccessful; workers and their organizations held firm for eleven days. The strike was violently crushed by state militia sent by the governor, a legacy of the defeat of Reconstruction in the state (see, e.g., Bennetts 1972:319).

The most dramatic and publicized strike of the 1890s, however, was the 1894 Pullman strike under the leadership of Eugene Debs' American Railway Union (ARU). Wage cutting had grown severe with the 1893 depression. Safety conditions were nonexistent, as over 2,000 railway workers were killed in industrial accidents each year from 1888 to 1893. To defeat the strike, Democratic President Grover Cleveland mobilized federal troops. The focal point of the strike was Chicago, the nation's rail center. Troops were sent to Chicago to reopen the rail lines, despite the explicit statement of Illinois Governor John Peter Altgeld that the strikers were nonviolent and that he did not want federal troops. No defender of states' rights—least of all those from the South—rose to denounce federal intrusion into the sanctified realm of state jurisdiction and against the democratic wishes of the people of

Illinois and their elected governor—another piece of evidence that the cry of states' rights is hypocritical and based not on principle but on the freedom of local and state governments to practice racial discrimination and bigotry without being hindered by national standards and guidelines.

Yet, as several historians have argued, the strike might have been won. It was not a local strike such as the New Orleans general strike or Homestead. Rather, it was national in scope and had broad support. When Debs and other strike leaders were arrested and the ARU Chicago headquarters was ransacked, Chicago workers launched a city-wide general strike. But Debs and Gompers flinched, disassociated themselves from the Chicago support, and soon called the whole strike off. At least as important, the ARU had a fatal flaw. Its own solidarity had been undermined from the start at its 1892 founding convention. Against the pleas of Debs, delegates had voted 113-102 to exclude women and African-Americans from membership (Foner 1955:II:255). This vote was not only a severe moral handicap, undermining any broad class claims, it was also a crucial tactical problem. Across the country many porters and laborers were Black. In the South, large numbers of Blacks still maintained positions as firemen and brakemen that Blacks had occupied under slavery. Eric Arnesen claims that they held a majority of such positions on the Gulf Coast Line, southern portions of the Illinois Central, the Louisville and Nashville line, and more than 90 percent on the Seaboard Air Line (Arnesen 1994:1609). The short-sighted railroad craft unions had trouble organizing in the South because of their unwillingness to organize Blacks. As a result, management used this situation to break strikes, maintain dangerous working conditions, and to keep wages low (Arnesen 1994:1621–22). This fatal flaw in the railway union was to hinder substantially its ability to wage a solidaristic united national struggle against the companies.

There is a temptation to conclude this discussion with merely an epitaph that the racial blindness of white workers and their unions represents the final nail in the coffin of the successful building of a broad solidaristic labor movement during this period. Yet, it might be argued that some of the previously discussed struggles had very little to do with race. Even in those situations where racial discrimination and exclusion weakened the struggles, it could be argued that they would most likely have been defeated in the late nineteenth century with even the fullest and most farsighted degrees of racial egalitarianism. Such an argument, I maintain, would be shortsighted.

Intense class struggles in individual locales or in single industrial sectors are often overwhelmed by unified corporate and state oppositions. In the end, the only hope for decisive working-class victories lies in broad solidarity across skill, occupation, region, ethnicity, gender, and race, and even eventually across country. What determines whether struggles ultimately obtain widespread support, whether supporters are willing to go to the greatest extent for a battle other than their own? The key issue in the United States on both sides of the equation is the commitment to racial solidarity on the part of whites. Although the connections are most often not direct, the historical lessons are clear. The achilles heel of the labor movement and its greatest potential for broad unity revolve around issues of race. In the United States, this has always been the key to moral legitimacy and strength. Although one can cite gains and even setbacks here and there, because of racial egalitarianism on the part of particular labor organizations, it is only the changed racial orientation of the movement as a whole that can decisively alter the terrain and obtain widespread support for broad class struggles. We have seen such solidaristic changes and support elsewhere in embryonic form at key historic junctures, including the interracial universalistic pre-Revolutionary mobs to the high moral authority and acknowledged leadership of the abolitionists.

In this context it is useful to compare the aftermath of various struggles. In those situations where unionism was not able to base itself on even the most elementary forms of interracial organization (as in steel and railroads), unions lingered on at best, in a limited manner, usually unsuccessfully for decades. On the other hand, in the coal and New Orleans longshore sectors, when unionism was defeated while exhibiting impressive degrees of solidarity, especially for the South, the unions were able to rebound quickly.

At least as important for the critical turning point of the 1890s was the complete destruction of the Populists, especially in the South. During the 1880s and 1890s, under the leadership of the Colored Farmers' Alliance, the Farmers' Alliance, and the People's (Populist) Party, when crops were selling well below their cost of production, Black and white farmers briefly joined hands to fight against banks, railroad magnates, and trusts. Even the Populists for a time understood and practiced an impressive degree of solidarity during the 1890s. As C. Vann Woodward reports in his biography of the Populist leader Tom Watson:

> At a time when Georgia led all states in lynching, Watson announced that it was the object of his party to "make lynch law odious to the people." And in 1896 the Populist platform of Georgia contained a plank denouncing lynch law. In the campaign of 1892 a Negro Populist who had made sixty-three separate speeches for Watson was threatened with lynching and fled to him for protection. Two thousand armed white farmers, some of whom rode all night, responded to Watson's call for aid and remained on guard for two nights at his home to avert the threat of violence. (Woodward 1938:44)

Consensus historians in the 1950s had written off the Populists, describing them in highly unflattering terms. Recent historians, however, have portrayed Populism as a vast democratic movement in rural America (for several representative, excellent accounts, see Goodwyn 1976, Schwartz 1976, McMath 1975, and Hahn 1983).

Repression against the Populists in the South was even more draconian than that directed against the labor movement in the North. Populism in the South was destroyed by electoral fraud, terror, especially in the planter-dominated Black Belt areas with the largest percentages of African-Americans, and by open appeals to white racism. Numerous pivotal election victories in the South were denied to Populist candidates by massive levels of ballot-box stuffing and the physical intimidation of voters, a clear legacy of the defeat of Reconstruction.

The violence, lynching, murder, corruption, and electoral fraud that had been permitted in the 1870s in the South proved too overwhelming to dislodge. This level of violence and extreme disregard for human life was embedded in the fabric of southern social and political life during this period and is certainly not unrelated to the present violent nature of U.S. society, from levels of personal violence and murder to police brutality and capital punishment.

The violent attacks against the Populists were led by the southern planters and their allies. The planters feared that their ability forcibly to exploit white and African-American labor was being threatened by the united struggle of Black and white farmers. While many white Populist farmers were willing to reach out to African-American farmers to support their joint demands, they did not understand that the struggle for African-American political equality was the key to their joint successes. Populism in the South was, thus, forcibly split along racial lines under the battle cry of white supremacy. The crushing of Southern Populism by the late 1890s allowed the establishment of a new social system based on a more rigid system of white supremacy, whose Jim Crow laws and vigilante violence, although having roots in the prewar slave system, had important differences (see Woodward 1964, Haywood 1948, Perlo 1953). The defeat of Populism opened the way for a determined group of plantation owners and their entourage of Black Belt whites to dominate not only the African-Americans of their region but also the rest of the whites in the South, too. Poor whites as well as Blacks were disenfranchised and controlled.[4] Although Black-white wage differentials remained the highest in the country (indicating the privileged position of poor whites), the wages of whites remained the lowest in the nation.[5] As in colonial and antebellum times, white-supremacist planters and their allies (including many southern industrialists) forced their racial policies on the rest of the nation until at least the early post–World War II period. The violent, repressive nature of Dixiecrat dominance made virtually any oppositional politics, liberal or socialist, precarious and dangerous in the South. Thus, national movements were invariably weakened from the start by their exclusion from a major region of the country.

In a variety of ways the Black Belt planters maintained their influence on national political life, American culture, the legal system, and, above all, the standards and mores of race relations. The bedrock, of course, was their control of the cotton economy through land ownership on the one hand, and through their control of Black and white labor on the other, via the crop-lien system, disenfranchisement, and, in the case of African-Americans, legal and extra-legal terror. The southern veto over the national Democratic Party in Congress (through control of key committees and the filibuster) and over presidential nominations prior to 1936 (through the two-thirds rule) is well known, particularly when questions of race were involved. From the 1896 *Plessy v. Ferguson* Supreme Court decision, sanctifying "separate but equal" railway cars, to the unwillingness of Franklin Delano Roosevelt to support federal antilynching legislation in the 1930s and 1940s, Black Belt planters' preferences were felt and heeded. The shadow of the plantation covered the whole of the United States with hardly an exception.

The Defanging of Populism

In a broad, illuminating work on the Populist movement, Lawrence Goodwyn argues that there was a shadow movement of opportunist politicians who appealed to Populist supporters but were neither committed to their main demands nor bona fide members of the movement. These opportunists, according to Goodwyn, included some of the best-known "Populists," among whom were William Jennings Bryan and "Pitchfork" Ben Tillman of South Carolina. These politicians helped to undermine the independence and radicalism of the movement. Through demagoguery they used the anger and political involvement of the Populist constituency to fight for and obtain positions of influence within the Democratic Party (Goodwyn 1976:387–423, passim).

It was these opportunist politicians, not the real Populists, who led the masses of Populist supporters back into the Democratic Party. At the 1896 convention, they defeated the forces loyal to the regular wing of the party, adopted a free-silver platform, and refused overwhelmingly to commend the administration of Democratic President Grover Cleveland. They then nominated William Jennings Bryan as the party's presidential candidate. Bryan successfully split and undermined the Populist movement, rhetorically appealing to a coalition he called the "toiling masses"—farmers and

urban workers, organized as a class party against the interests that exploited them. As Sundquist notes, however, Bryan's program was "hardly radical." He dropped the more far-reaching demands of the Populists and the
Farmers' Alliance, including government ownership of the railroads
(Sundquist 1983:151, 155). Further, he abandoned the emerging non-racial
egalitarianism of some important segments of the southern Populists,
upholding the party's standard racism. He was at times an open racist. In
later years, at the 1924 Democratic National Convention, he helped narrowly
defeat a resolution denouncing the Ku Klux Klan.

The Destruction of the Democratic Party in the North

Despite his lack of radicalism, Bryan and his modest program were met by
elites in the country by "something akin to terror." Theodore Roosevelt fore-
saw "a red government of lawlessness and dishonesty as phantastic and
vicious as the Paris Commune itself." As Sundquist argues,

> And if it was not the immediate platform that terrified the conser-
> vatives, it was the prospect of what might happen if the 'toiling
> masses' really did succeed in organizing against them, of what might
> follow a shift of control of the government in the polarized coun-
> try, to the opposite pole. If Bryan was no extremist, Altgeld, Watson,
> Debs, and the prairie Populists were (or appeared to be), and Bryan
> would be beholden to his radical supporters. Such a prospect war-
> ranted a massive and crushing counterattack. As it happened, the
> genius to organize the counterattack was on the scene, in the per-
> son of Marcus A. Hanna, manager of the Republican candidate,
> William McKinney." (Sundquist 1983:155–56)

In the North the strategy was to eliminate and destroy the Democrats as a
meaningful alternative party. "Hanna raised unprecedented sums by the simple expedient of assessing major corporations…Hanna matched his sys-
tematic money-raising with the most thorough and methodical political
organization the country had yet seen." Employers threatened their employees; coercion was bold, unashamed, and effective. Republicans spent five to
fifteen times as much as Bryan, according to Sundquist (1983:157). The press
and clergy mobilized overwhelmingly against Bryan. A concerted, highly
successful attempt was made by the Republicans to win the northern urban
labor vote.

The Democratic Party's demise in the urban North was sealed by the
adoption of much of the progressive program at the state and local level.
According to Walter Dean Burnham, the progressive good-government
campaigns were in good part designed to eliminate the high participation

rates of the lower classes, especially those in ethnic immigrant communities. Personal registration laws were instituted, often applying only to large cities. In New York State, for example, the initial laws applied only to New York City. Attacks were made on patronage. City politics was depoliticized in many places with the widspread adoption of the city manager system. The institution of party primaries undermined opposition parties by channeling opposition into the dominant party. Burnham even argues that part of the impetus behind support for the suffrage movement was its desire to enfranchise white Protestant native-born women, who were more likely to vote in large numbers than the more sheltered immigrant women (Burnham 1970; see also Piven and Cloward 1988).

The consequences of one-party rule and the new electoral arrangements were a dramatic decline in voting participation in the country. The distinctive and exceptionally low voter participation rates and the class skew in voting that have been a characteristic of twentieth-century American politics date from this period.

The South to a certain extent was merely a more extreme version of the North, according to Burnham. The Populists, however, were not defeated by being outorganized by southern elites. In a claim about Virginia, which could easily be extended to much of the rest of the South, Burnham argues that

> In view of the spectacularly radical proclivities of its white rural electorate as revealed in the traumatic Readjuster episode of the 1880's, its economically colonial status after the Civil War, and its ever-present "Negro problem"—progressivism and "good government" could only come about in Virginia through the substantial liquidation of political democracy....the elite impulse to convert democracy into oligarchy was not only specifically Virginian but specifically progressive as well....For it may well be argued that Virginia, in dismantling political parties and erecting high legal and customary barriers to political participation at the mass base after 1890, only carried to a local extreme an impulse which profoundly influenced American politics as a whole during those years. (Burnham 1970:79)

Elimination of lower-class influence in politics was consolidated in the South by taking progressivism to its logical extreme. Blacks were completely and systematically disenfranchised. A majority of poor whites were also disenfranchised by a variety of inhibitors, including poll taxes and literacy tests. The two wings of the working class were kept separate by the development of a rigid system of white supremacy that pervaded all aspects of society and was enforced by law. A description of the consolidation of the System of 1896 by the political scientist E.E. Schattschneider is worth quoting at length:

The 1896 party cleavage resulted from the tremendous reaction of conservatives of both major parties to the Populist movement, a radical agrarian agitation that alarmed people of substance all over the country....One of the most important consequences of the creation of the Solid South was that it severed permanently the connection between the western and southern wings of the Populist movement. ...the conservative reaction to Bryanism in the North was almost as spectacular as the conservative reaction to Populism in the South. As a result the Democratic Party in large areas of the Northeast and Middle West was wiped out, or decimated, while the Republican Party consolidated its supremacy in all of the most populous areas of the country. The resulting party lineup was one of the most sharply sectional divisions in American history. In effect, the new party division turned the country over to two powerful sectional minorities: (1) the northern business-Republican minority and (2) its southern conservative Democratic counterpart.

The new alignment became possible when the southern conservative Democrats decided they they were willing to abandon their ambitions to win power nationally in return for undisputed control of the South. The Solid South was one of the foundation stones of the Republican system because it weakened the Democratic party disastrously and virtually destroyed for a generation the possibility of an effective national opposition party....The result was that organized party alternatives disappeared in large areas of the country in the North as well as the South. Both sections became more conservative because *one party politics tends strongly to vest political power in the hands of people who already have economic power.* (Schattschneider 1960:78–80)

The acceptance of this Faustian bargain by the North, in what Schattschneider describes as an "under-the-table alliance," was prefigured by a number of events in the 1890s meant to reassure southern conservatives that there would be no northern interference with their states' rights to maintain the system of white supremacy. In 1891, the final attempt to reconstruct the South with respect to voting rights for African-Americans, the Lodge Force Bill, failed. It was clear that the question would not be raised again. In 1894, the last piece of congressional Reconstruction legislation was repealed. Finally in 1896, in a decision that would not be overturned until the 1954 *Brown v. Board of Education* case, the Supreme Court upheld *Plessy v. Ferguson*, accepting as legal "separate but equal" facilities for Blacks.

The rapid economic expansion from the Civil War through the 1890s led to an increased need for new markets and raw materials for large corporations. The end of unlimited domestic expansion was underscored by the final elimination of Native American resistance at the 1890 Battle of Wounded Knee and the claim by Frederick Jackson Turner in 1893 that the U.S. frontier had finally been eliminated. U.S. business and the national government turned their attention to foreign soils, often justifying oppressive intrusions there on explicitly racist bases. In 1893, the United States passed up the opportunity formally to annex Hawaii; the explanation given by Republican President Theodore Roosevelt was that it would be "a crime against white civilization" to incorporate an area that was overwhelmingly nonwhite. The war against Spain in 1898 allowed the United States to take control of Cuba, Puerto Rico, Guam, and the Phillipines; U.S. businesses soon dominated the economies, resources, and agricultural land of their new acquisitions. Intervention followed intervention, as the marines landed in virtually every Latin American country over the next few decades, many being blessed with multiple occupations. The long and sordid history of U.S. imperial domination of nonwhite peoples played a key role in the final abandonment of southern Blacks by the Republican Party and the ease with which whites in the country as a whole accepted the more rigid system of white supremacy that was the hallmark of the System of 1896.

Without highlighting these underlying socio-economic features, one's possibilities for understanding the period are diminished. Thus, most historians do not give plausible explanations for the abandonment by the Republicans of many of their token commitments to civil rights for African-Americans after 1896. Though the Republican Party platforms after 1896 continued "in ritual fashion" to condemn lynching and disenfranchisement and continued to call for civil rights action by Congress, its "appeal was illusory" (Katznelson 1976:46). Yet, many only look at the deaths and retreat from politics of Republican leaders from the Civil War generation, rather than at the deeper changes in the system of racial domination and control.

What status then shall we assign to this critical turning point, and what was its relation to the Civil War/Reconstruction era? On one level, I have maintained, the System of 1896 was merely the final coda to the defeat of Reconstruction, as both W. E. B. Du Bois and Eric Foner have argued. Yet, Morgan Kousser and C. Vann Woodward, although they may be in error in downplaying the importance of the defeat of Reconstruction, are not completely wrong to emphasize the dramatic differences between the period before the 1890s and that which followed it. This critical turning point in American history which set up the System of 1896 was, it must be emphasized, centered on race. Although the defeat of Reconstruction undermined the self-confident, assertive attitudes acquired by Blacks after the Civil War, the rigid white supremacy and racial domination that extended throughout the whole country after the turn of the century was in sharp contrast to the fluid and uneven system of racial subordination that existed during the transition period. Disenfranchisement of African-Americans, previously widespread only in Deep South Black Belt areas, covered the whole South. Poor whites in the South were also overwhelmingly disenfranchised and large voter turnouts in the country as a whole, as well as the decades-long tradition of mass political involvement, became a thing of the past. Class struggle, especially among southern farmers and industrial workers, diminished greatly, while direct control of the national and state governments by ruling-class groups became more secure. All this, as I have argued, was tied to the rise of U.S. imperialism. Much of the present character of U.S. politics may, of course, be traced to events in this period. What ties this turning point so closely to that of the Civil War and Reconstruction era—and here it is Du Bois and Foner rather than Woodward and Kousser who have their finger on the pulse —is that it was largely made possible by the failure of northern white workers in the 1860s and 1870s to support Reconstruction and the social revolutionary African-American vanguard in the Black Belts of the Deep South.

Early Twentieth-Century Politics
In general, the period after 1896 brought forth an intensification of racism and the establishment of greater discriminatory practices throughout the country as a whole. Although not always as rigid as in the South, racial discrimination was established in many arenas in the North and in the country as a whole. Segregation existed extensively in the armed forces and in government employment. Schools were segregated throughout the North. In those skilled trades where Blacks had traditionally been highly represented (e.g., on railroads and in construction trades), they were mostly driven out (Spero and Harris 1968). Blacks were confined in employment to the most menial positions, with few existing in skilled trades, clerical work, or sales positions where whites were customers (e.g., bus drivers and train operators) and even in most semi-skilled work, not to mention doctors, lawyers, managers, professors, and other high-level occupations. In addition, many public places in the North, as well as in the South, first became segregated during this period, including movie theaters, swimming pools, golf courses, hotels, and de facto many stores. Intense discrimination existed in buying housing, obtaining loans, insurance, and health care. The shadow of the plantation in the North was long and dark.

When he took over as president in 1901, Theodore Roosevelt did continue the traditional Republican practice of appointing blacks to minor patronage positions in the federal government. Both Republican Presidents Roosevelt and Taft, however, despite their political dealings with African-Americans through their relationship with BookerT.Washington, thought Blacks as a racial group were inferior, and "became enchanted with the possibility of wooing the white South away from the Democrats" (Katznelson 1976:47, Woodward 1971:462). At this point, visions of the modern Republican southern strategy were merely a dream that would have to be deferred.

In the 1912 presidential elections, important Black leaders, disheartened by the backsliding of the Republicans, urged other Blacks to vote for the Democrat Woodrow Wilson. Even the National Association for the Advancement of Colored People (NAACP) radicals announced support for Wilson after he made a play for African-American votes. Such hopes, however, were sorely misplaced. As the head of Princeton University, Wilson had prevented Blacks from enrolling and opposed social relationships between the races, in contrast to the less rigid practices at Harvard and Yale universities. In 1913, Postmaster General Burleson, with Wilson's support, moved to eliminate Blacks supervising whites in federal employment and to segregate Black and white railway clerks from working together in the same railway cars. "Though Wilson never issued any executive orders on the subject, by the end of 1913 segregation had quietly been introduced in the Post Office, the Treasury Department, the Bureau of Engraving and Printing, and in other Federal offices. In 1914, applicants for civil-service positions were directed to submit photographs.The President's correspondence makes clear that he favoured these developments." By September 1913, the NAACP had broken with Wilson and was attacking him, correctly calling him the most racist of all presidents (Katznelson 1976:50–51, 53, 54, 55).

Early Twentieth-Century Labor and Radicalism
The heightened, more rigid system of racial domination instituted by the System of 1896 made interracial labor organizing far more difficult and unlikely. At the turn of the century, few, even including radical groups, comprehended the significance of white supremacy and how the development of a unified class struggle and an independent labor movement required a frontal assault on it. Du Bois, who wrote in *The Souls of Black Folk* in 1903 that "the problem of the 20th Century is the problem of the color line," was one of those few. Labor groups varied from the racist craft unions that echoed or capitulated to white chauvinism to the mineworkers who recognized the importance of organizing Black and white miners together, but not the strategic importance for labor of fighting the whole system of white supremacy.

The racial domination of and discrimination against African-Americans, I have argued, does not originate in the modern workplace. Its origin and

roots can be traced to the economic needs and desires of southern plantation owners, both during slavery and after the Civil War, to maintain cheap,
exploitable agricultural labor. Yet, this system of white supremacy had a
tremendous impact on the work situations of white and nonwhite workers, their interests in interracial class unity, and their potential or capacities
for achieving it.

It is important to get beyond the simple-minded macrolevel formula-
tions of those who conclude that it is in the interests of white workers generally to support the racial subordination of nonwhite workers in order to
gain more leverage for themselves in the labor market. Rather, one must
ask, in what occupations, industries, situations is it in the interests (or not)
of white workers to express interracial solidarity and when is it possible or
likely (or not) that they do so.[6]

There exist certain skilled privileged sectors of the racially dominant
workforce where white workers maintain their positions by excluding
other workers from entry into their trade. Because their skills are not readily replaceable by employers, these workers maintain control of their jobs
by excluding other workers, by licencing, by limiting apprenticeships, by
limiting entry into apprenticeships through tests, by requiring recommendations, and so on, the latter often implying nepotism, certainly ethnic and
racial "understandings." Such unions attach little importance to expanding
their membership. The reverse is more often the case. Their craft interests
are best served by keeping the pool of certified workers as small as possible. It may be that workers in these trades have an immediate interest in
discriminating against non-whites, both in denying them entry into their
trade and to a lesser degree in the society at large. To the extent that their
work environments are relatively stable and not damaged by the technological undermining of their trade or the economic demise of their industry, such workers often take the route of exclusionary, racially discriminatory unionism, although even here one occasionally sees exceptions. The
qualifications usually occur when other workers have already obtained the
necessary skills (be it the skilled screwmen on the New Orleans docks in
the late nineteenth and early twentieth centuries; workers in the trowel trades
in many areas). In these situations, it is often necessary and possible for
skilled white workers to reach a working relation with racially subordinate
workers, so that the whites will not be undermined in the labor market and
themselves excluded from work. One might stretch things a bit and also
argue that skilled white construction workers in the post–world War II period, who gained job control and high wages in good part on the basis of
racially exclusive practices, sealed their later fates; when their industry contracted, unions were driven out; conditions and wages disintegrated in the

late 1960s and early 1970s (although one might argue here that the first generation to benefit was not necessarily the same as the final group to suffer).
Their previously exclusive practices made it impossible for them to gener-
ate broad support when they needed it the most. But here we begin to verge
on an argument that broad inclusive organization and alliances with other
workers are always the best long-term strategy.

Most workers, however, are not able to obtain significant job control.
Their labor is less skilled and more easily replaced by employers with that
of the unemployed. Workers in these work situations have interests in forming alliances and often inclusive organizations. White workers are often led
to form some type of interracial organization, although the range of possibilities, from broad solidaristic class organization to various types of discrimination, are large. In describing this tendency, Greenberg argues:

> It is a plausible scenario. And certainly in industries where subor-
> dinate workers are present in large numbers, where they are
> employed in positions alongside dominant workers, and where
> there is little skill differentiation, unions would be hard pressed to
> organize on any other basis. Nonetheless, we should not underes-
> timate the difficulty of open industrial unionism in a racial order
> and the likely costs. Multiracial industrial unions are organized
> against the tenor of society: often against the inclinations of the
> dominant workers directly involved, and almost always against the
> prevailing sentiments in the dominant section and the general
> direction of state policy. (Greenberg 1980:284–85)

Thus, interracial unions in industrial settings often face and respond to contradictory pressures. Even the most conservatively led unions (such as the
United Steel Workers in Alabama during the 1950s) are often forced to engage
in some solidaristic behavior; conversely, the most radically led solidaristic
unions (e.g., the Mine Mill and Smelter Workers in Alabama during the
1930s) are sometimes forced to make certain concessions to the prevailing
racial environment. Among the factors that determine which end of the spectrum the unions veer toward is the leadership of the union. With this extended preface, we turn to an examination of the practices of certain characteristic labor organizations during the early twentieth century.

From shortly after the time of its founding in the 1880s until the 1940s,
most of the craft unions in the American Federation of Labor (and most of
the independent unions like those in railroad) had racially discriminatory
policies of one form or another. The major exception to this general trend
was the United Mine Workers (UMW). From the turn of the century on,
with varying degrees of success, this organization attempted to organize both

Black and white workers throughout the southern and northern coal districts. Very early they had constitutional clauses with penalities for discrimination. In 1924, with the rise of the Klan, they added a clause outlawing
KKK membership. The UMW had many Black officials, including local presidents in areas of low African-American concentration. Black officials were,
of course, also prominent in those areas of high African-American concentration in the mines of Alabama and parts of West Virginia.7

During the early part of the twentieth century, the Industrial Workers
of the World (IWW), with their program for organizing all oppressed labor,
organized Black and white workers together, both North and South. In
Philadelphia, between 1913 and the early 1920s, they maintained their organization of dock workers, approximately 50 percent of whom were African-
American and 50 percent of whom were white, in the face of racist appeals
from both employers and American Federation of Labor (AFL) unions.
Between 1910 and 1913, tens of thousands of African-American and white
woodworkers in Louisiana and Texas, organized by the IWW-affiliated
Brotherhood of Timberworkers, also achieved impressive solidarity and
organization from 1910 to 1913.8 The timber workers, with a membership
evenly divided between Black and white, often defied Jim Crow barriers in
the Deep South to maintain their organization and provide integrated democratic meetings. Even the IWW, which challenged Jim Crow practices in the
South in their organizing in a courageous manner, did so not because they
understood the importance of the issue but because they doggedly refused
to let local customs and mores separate them from organizing the most
downtrodden workers.

During the pre–World War I period, the Socialist Party emerged as the
dominant organization of U.S. radicalism. As both a leader and reflection of
opposition to the government, the Socialist Party, with its extensive press
and elected government officials, rolled up large presidential votes in 1912
and 1920; with Eugene Debs as the candidate, its total in the former year
reached over 700,000, or 6 percent of the vote, and in the latter year almost
a million. Its positions on the role of white supremacy and of the importance of the struggle against racial discrimination were, however, much less
forthright than that of the IWW. Many of its leaders, including the Socialist
congressman from Milwaukee Victor Berger, aped the racism of Samuel
Gompers and the AFL.9 The more radical, progressive leaders, epitomized
by Eugene Debs offered at best benign neglect. Debs asserted "We have nothing special to offer the Negro, and we cannot make separate appeals to all
the races" (Spero and Harris 1968:405). The Socialist Party, barely finding
time to organize immigrant industrial workers during the pre–World War
I period, certainly could not be troubled by reflecting seriously on the plight

of African-Americans, no less the socially and politically excluded Asian and Mexican workers on the West Coast. And this lack of concern for the situation of immigrants and non-whites is a major reason why the socialists were not more successful in organizing industrial workers.

U.S. labor and popular history, of course, is replete with examples of narrowness, national chauvinism in the guise of patriotism, male supremacy, and most of all, white racism, even polluting some of the broadest upheavals, staining some of the finest examples of militant, solidaristic multiracial, ethnic, and gender struggles and organization (Saxton 1971; Spero and Harris 1968). Now, I have suggested that racism and ethnic chauvinism —or, at the very least, obtuseness to the importance of solidarity in the fight against white supremacy—have been instrumental in the defeat or failure of many of these movements. But that is not the only strand. What presents us with an enigma or contradiction is that U.S. labor and social history is also filled with inspiring examples of African-American and white working-class solidarity. It is certainly not merely a history of race hatred and a lack of solidarity by white workers. And it is these cases whose existence and occasional success must be explained.

These numerous, often complex and contradictory, sometimes solidaristic interracial struggles were rarely the result of concerted leadership, organization, and policy at the national level. And as our earlier discussion indicates, many of the examples of interracial solidarity, often in the face of strong racist public opinion, come from local labor movements. Widespread interracial struggles, based on the strategic importance of white workers joining with non-whites workers in the fight against white supremacy, would have to wait until the next historical turning point of the 1930s.

1. I have taken large liberties in the appropriatation of this phrase. Political scientists tend to use it to describe the new system of party dominance that existed after the 1896 national elections, looking only implicitly at the new power relations that the electoral shift represented (see, e.g., Schattschneider 1960:78–80; Burnham 1970; McCormick 1986). I have expanded the term to include explicitly not only the new arrangements of political power but also the hardened system of racial domination that emerged in the 1890s.
2. Dubofsky even suggests that much more organization was possible for those who were audacious enough to try (Dubofsky 1969:209).

3. For a detailed history of political repression in the United States, see Goldstein (1978).
4. Populism of sorts did re-emerge later among southern whites, no longer challenging the right of southern planters to maintain forced control over African-American labor. Tom Watson, the militant Populist defender of African-American rights in the 1880s and 1890s, was reborn after the turn of the century as a racist "populist" demagogue (Woodward 1938).
5. In a broad historical view it seems clear that the existence of racial privileges and high racial wage differentials have limited the wages of white workers as well as hurt those of nonwhites. The lower

wages of white southern workers in the
racially exclusive southern textile industry
(from the late nineteenth century to the
mid-twentieth century compared with
their unionized Northern counterparts
is a definitive case in point. Although there
are clearly some situations where racial
exclusion is in the immediate interest of
some white workers, I would argue along
with Reich that this is generally not the
case. For counter arguments, however,
one should see Bonacich, Shulman,
and Williams.

6. In the discussion that follows, I rely
heavily on the seminal analysis of
Greenberg (1980).

7. For widely differing perspectives on the
depths of egalitarianism in the UMW, see
Gutman (1968), chapter 10 of Spero and
Harris (1968), and Hill (1988). For a fuller
discussion and extensive references, see
Goldfield (1993).

8. See Green 1973, Dubofsky, 1969:209–20,
and Foner 1965:233–57.

9. For a compelling analysis of the racist
policies of the AFL, see Mink (1986).

PART II

Twentieth-Century Politics

CHAPTER 6

The Depression / New Deal Era

No one ever considered Carnegie libraries steeped in the blood of the Homestead steel workers, but they are. We do not remember that the Rockefeller Foundation is founded on the dead miners of the Colorado Fuel and Iron Co. and a dozen other similar performances. We worship mammon...

It is a pity that Wall Street, with its ability to control all the wealth of nations and to hire the best law brains in the country has not produced some financial statesmen, some men who could see the dangers of bigness and of the concentration of the control of wealth... they are still employing the best brains to serve greed and selfish interest. People can stand only so much, and one of these days there will be a settlement...

Senator Harry Truman in his first major Senate speech after his 1934 election victory. (Alonzo Hamby 1973:44)

We won't organize any black man to be a Democrat or a Republican because both of them have sold us out. Both of them have sold us out; both parties have sold us out. Both parties are racist, and the Democratic Party is more racist than the Republican Party.

Malcolm X, Organization of Afro-American Unity Founding Rally, New York, June 28, 1964.

Virtually all serious commentators on the 1930s argue that this period was the greatest political upheaval of the twentieth century, representing in the words of Carl Degler "The Third American Revolution," comparable in scope to that of the American Revolution and the Civil War (Degler 1959:379). Let us begin then by trying to find out what is considered so important about this historic turning point.

The Great Depression provided the context for the events of the 1930s. It was the deepest depression in the nation's history, when the country suffered a complete economic collapse, enormous rates of unemployment, and the disruption of life for the whole nation. The 1930s began with the largest electoral shift from one party's control to the other in U.S. history to this date, ending three-and-a-half decades of Republican dominance. As a consequence, it is highly studied by political scientists and political historians, especially those interested in critical election theory. The 1930s was also a time of widespread mass popular movements, broad radical politics, and the entry of new constituencies into the center of U.S. politics, including labor union members and Blacks. Finally, there were substantial changes in government that remain with us to this day: the rise to power of the executive branch of the federal government; the transfer of responsibility in many venues from local and state control to the national government, a change that both Republicans and Democrats are presently trying to reverse; the inauguration of public policies that have been described as "radical" and even "revolutionary," (Leuchtenberg 1963:336; Brandeis 1957:195, 198), including Social Security (involving pensions and social welfare), the National Labor Relations Act, banking reform, minimum wages, federal power and development projects such as the Tennessee Valley Authority and Hoover Dam, unemployment insurance, work relief, anti-discrimination initiatives, public housing, and a host of others. Like all important historical periods there are a number of issues central to our concerns that are disputed among scholars. First, there have been differences about whether the changes in government policies were really as momentous as some suggest.

Some historians argue that the achievements of the New Deal were rather limited (B. Bernstein 1968:263–88 C. Gordon 1994:4). So perhaps if there were anything radical about the period, it would be best not to look at the changes in public policy and the growing role of the national government. Second, there are the now familiar debates about the motive forces, the importance of the elites—their ideas or their interests—the role of underlying economic and social forces and of governmental structures, and above all there is debate about the role of the mass movements (see Goldfield 1989 and 1990 for further discussion of these issues; see also Piven and Cloward 1979 who argue for the importance of popular insurgencies). Were they central or really secondary to the events of the 1930s? Were they a main determinant of the political outcomes of the era or merely a colorful sidelight, a reflection rather than a generator of events (Dubofsky 1969; C. Gordon 1994:202, 237). And one surely has the right to ask of me what race has to do with any of this. Unlike the turning points of the Civil War or the 1890s, few commentators argue that questions of race were central to the period. The standard interpretations suggest that racial issues were either largely irrelevant to the events of the 1930s or at most were a secondary consequence of the New Deal, whereby Blacks, along with a number of other groups, were incorporated into the politics of the era and were the beneficiaries of many federal programs, to the extent that they were race neutral. It will come as no surprise to the reader that I will be disputing this interpretation. We will, thus, want to know how important race was to this critical historical turning point. What role did it play in the mass movements and the politics of the period? Further, we will want to determine how racially egalitarian the various forces and movements were, especially President Franklin Roosevelt and the New Dealers and the new industrial union movement confederation, the Congress of Industrial Organizations (CIO). Finally, as the 1930s recede further into the past, the left-wing politics and social movements seem to many today as more and more atypical occurrences in the United States. At century's end, we therefore wish to know whether the 1930s were a period of unrealized potential where there existed possibilities for creating a solidaristic class labor movement that might have totally transformed U.S. politics and society, putting an end in fact to the question of American exceptionalism—as some on the left have argued. Or were the 1930s merely a mild, social-democratic deviation (as Hofstadter 1955:308, for example, argues), a blip on the historical screen of a basically conservative America, which only took place because of the severity of the Great Depression—as some conservatives assert?

It is to these questions that I now turn. By way of preview, I wish to alert the reader to the perspective that I will be elaborating. It will be my argument here that the transformations in public policy and government were largely a result of pressure from the mass movements. The policy changes themselves, although seemingly large-scale departures from previous government activities, were not as extensive as one might have expected, given the degree of social protest. The mass movements were at the center of the events of the 1930s. They drew their strength and potential from three linked forces: (1) the power of the upsurge of the Black population, especially the Black working class; (2) the solidaristic thrust of the interracial labor organizations; (3) the actual strength and seeming potential of left-wing organizations. The movements lost much of their strength and moral authority when key sections of it, and eventually the mainstream of the CIO, abandoned the Black working class and the earlier interracialism that had seemed to be the CIO's hallmark. Nevertheless, the forces set in motion by the assaults on the system of racial domination and subordination (themselves the legacy of the Civil War and the 1890s turning points), the tasks and unfinished business that remained from the 1930s, the change in the approach to these issues, and the resistance to the completion of these tasks are the factors that define and structure political life in the United States today. Thus, issues of race and the agency of African-Americans, especially the Black working class, are the key to understanding the critical turning point of the 1930s and its legacy for today. In order to lay bare the actual importance of racial issues, their contours, and their centrality to the New Deal, we must take a multi-layered approach and probe a number of issues that at first may seem unrelated to our main topic. Thus, I shall begin with the dramatic shift in political ascendancy from the Republicans to the Democrats.

THE ELECTORAL SHIFT

The elections of the 1930s constituted an electoral reversal even larger than that which established the System of 1896, itself the most substantial numerical change to that date. Republicans, who gained the presidency in 1896, only lost it in 1912 to the Democrat Woodrow Wilson because their party was split. They gained 120 congressional seats in 1894, going from a 220 to 126 minority to a 246 to 104 majority. They maintained modest majorities except when they lost control briefly in the 1910 to 1916 period. Beginning in 1930, they suffered a series of electoral defeats from which it is not clear that they have so far recovered. In 1930, they lost 49 seats and maintained a bare 218 to 216 congressional majority. In 1932, they lost the presidency and another 101 seats giving Democrats a 313 to 117 majority. By 1936, they were down to 89 seats (to 333 for the Democrats) in Congress and 17 (to 75 for the Democrats) in the Senate. Republicans only regained control briefly in 1946 and 1952. Until the turnabout in 1994 (whose long-term effects are not yet clear), Republicans did not have a majority in the House for four decades.

Mere numbers for Congress and the Senate do not begin to tell the story. Numerous congressmen and senators were elected as third-party candidates to the left of President Franklin Roosevelt. A number of Republicans were also radical or "progressive" Republicans, well to the left of mainstream Democrats, representatives of the long-standing tradition of prairie radicalism that existed from the late nineteenth century. Also, although Democrats in 1930 and 1932 were replacing Republican incumbents, in 1934 and 1936 many left-wing Democrats were replacing more conservative members of their own party. And one could convincingly argue that what was happening in the Congress and Senate was itself but a pale reflection of the attitudes and activities of American citizens throughout the country.

Not only had the two parties realigned in terms of their respective strength, but there was a class realignment in terms of constituency support. Workers and the lower classes lined up solidly behind the Democrats, while the affluent were more likely to be Republican. Perhaps the most dramatic switch took place among African-American voters, whose traditional Republican allegiances gave way to overwhelming Democratic Party support. Jews, Catholics, and a variety of ethnic working-class constituencies (including Poles, Italians, Germans, Yugoslavs, Czechs, Lithuanians, and Swedes) switched to the party of Roosevelt (Sundquist 1983:217–19).

The politics of the country had moved far to the left, and both the president and Congress were responding to the mood of the country rather than leading reluctant constituents. In his now classic work *The Dynamics of the Party System*, James Sundquist summarizes the situation:

> But if by any chance the Democratic party had halted the leftward movement that was so apparent in Congress in 1932 and chosen instead to share the conservative side of the political spectrum with Hoover, then the insurgents in both parties would have had to unite behind someone...who would have caught the spirit of the times. The forces of protest were too powerful to be denied political expression (Sundquist 1983:211)

CAUSES OF THE UPHEAVAL
Depression

The events of the 1930s, of course, cannot be understood outside the context of the Great Depression. Although officially recorded unemployment figures for the 1920s are relatively low, the roaring twenties were not so prosperous for many workers and farmers. There are many parallels to the situation in this country in the 1980s and 1990s. There were large increases in productivity and industrial output in good part because of automation and other technological breakthroughs (unlike the present period). There was little increase in real wages for the majority of wage earners (similar to today). Small farmers were being driven off the land, unable to earn a livelihood with falling prices and competition from large-scale farmers and agribusiness. Like the 1980s and 1990s, the 1920s prosperity benefited only the more affluent. According to estimates by David Weintraub, real unemployment in the 1920s was 13 percent in 1924, 1925, and 1928, and 10 percent in 1929. (David Weintraub, "Unemployment and Increasing Productivity," in National Resources Committee, *Technological Trends and National Policy* (Washingon, DC: 1937), cited in Irving Bernstein 1969:523). The much lower official estimates appear in Table 7.1. Well before the onset of the depression, unemployment was recognized as a serious problem. For example, on December 17, 1928, President Daniel Willard of the Baltimore and Ohio railroad made the following statement before a Senate subcommittee:

> It is a dangerous thing to have a large number of unemployed men and women—dangerous to society as a whole—dangerous to the individuals who constitute society. When men who are willing and able to work are unable to obtain work, we need not be surprised if they steal before they starve. (cited in Irving Bernstein 1960:60)

As in the 1980s and 1990s, however, growing income disparities and low-ered standards of living for many people did not lead to broad social protest. All this was to change with the 1929 stock market crash. Between September 3, 1929, and November 13, 1929, the Dow Jones average dropped from 452 to 224, with the biggest drops taking place on Black Thursday, October 24, and Black Tuesday, October 29. In the ensuing months, the economy ground to a halt, with many industries, including automobile, mining, and textile, virtually collapsing. Gross business investment dropped from $16.2 billion in 1929 to $.8 billion in 1932 (McElvaine 1984:73) Official jobless estimates went from 492,000 in October of 1929 to 4,065,000 in January of 1930. The country was devastated. In cities across the land, bread lines, soup kitchens, street beggars, and apple sellers appeared in large numbers. In major trans-portation hubs, most pronounced in Chicago (the nation's transportation center), large makeshift shantytowns, dubbed Hoovervilles, appeared. Both private and municipal resources broke down, unable to provide relief. Millions of people left their homes in search of more promising places to find jobs, many becoming hobos, riding the railroads.

TABLE 7.1

Estimates of Unemployment

Year	Labor Force (millions)	Unemployment BLS estimate (millions)	%	Unemployment Darby estimate (millions)	%
1929	47.6	1.55	3.2	1.55	3.2
1930	45.5	4.34	8.7	4.32	8.7
1931	42.7	8.02	16.0	7.72	15.3
1932	39.5	12.06	23.6	11.47	22.5
1933	41.0	12.83	24.9	10.64	20.6
1934	43.9	11.34	21.7	8.35	16.0
1935	45.3	10.61	20.1	7.5	14.2
1938	47.8	10.39	19.0	6.8	12.5
1941	52.5	5.56	9.9	3.35	6.0
1943	54.6	1.07	1.9	.99	1.8

Note: Figures from Darby (1976)

The social environment, values, and attitudes of the vast majority of peo-ple in the country changed abruptly and decisively. Business and business-men, who had been the heroes and demigods of the 1920s, were totally dis-credited. Journalist Elmer Davis wrote in 1933 that businessmen were "about as thoroughly discredited as any set of false prophets in history" (McElvaine 1984:16). Fear by the rich of a revolution by the dispossessed was common in 1932 and 1933. A large percentage of the country's population believed that capitalism had failed and needed to be replaced. Over 20 percent responded to polls that socialism was the best alternative (Lipset 1983). These sentiments made themselves felt in Congress even before the 1932 land-slide. As tax revenues declined, political leaders at the time, like both Republicans and Democrats today, believed that balancing the budget was their top priority. To this end, the leaders of both parties decided to pass a federal sales tax. A spontaneous groundswell of protest was directed at con-gressmen by their constituents, including an unprecedented quantity of mail. Responding to this outcry, both Democrat and Republican Congress members, rebelled against their leaders by defeating the sales tax and vot-ing to increase income taxes, surtaxes, and estate taxes. Shouts of "soak the rich!" and "conscript wealth!" rang from the House floor, apparently with-out prompting from the 1960s anti-private property counterculture. Democratic leader Henry Rainey complained: "We have made a longer step in the direction of communism than any country in the world ever made except Russia," suggesting perhaps that idiotic statements and obtuseness to the needs of ordinary citizens have a long, venerable historical tradition among both Republican and Democratic national leaders in this country (McElvaine 1984:86–87). What is most clear, however, is that the roots of the political changes of the 1930s lay in the economic depression that had enveloped the country.

Mass Upheaval and State Crisis
Although the devastation brought by the Great Depression covered the whole land, the initial response was uneven. Many people were demoralized and unsure. In particular, massive layoffs demobilized workers and did not ini-tially lead to increased workplace activity or union growth. Thus, it is worth tracing the development of the early New Deal social movements, their impact on, and eventual support for the more slowly emerging labor movement.

Unemployment and Relief
Unemployment quickly became the dominant political focus at the begin-ning of the depression; the early protests of the unemployed were the ini-tial vanguard of the mass politics of the depression.[1] Millions of people roamed the country looking for work. State governments aproached bank-ruptcy with relief efforts that scarcely scratched the surface of the problem (see Irving Bernstein 1960:287–311, 416–36, 456–74 for detailed descrip-tions).[2] Protests of the unemployed in the beginning of the depression were often massive and militant. With the exception of the less confrontational self-help groups, nearly all of the protest was radical led. The largest orga-nization for the unemployed during the early 1930s was the Communist

Party (CP)-led Unemployed Councils, which was concentrated in large cities throughout the country. Also significant were the Socialist Party-led Workers Alliance and A.J. Muste's Conference for Progressive Labor Action-inspired Unemployed Leagues.

Unemployed protests began immediately with the onset of the depression. On March 6, 1930, well before the impact of the depression was to be felt on local, state, or national politics, over one million people demonstrated across the country under CP leadership (Klehr 1984:32–3). Contrary to uninformed claims by some that this protest was concentrated in a small number of large cities (New York, Detroit, and Chicago are sometimes mentioned), concerted unemployed activity seems to have touched virtually every part of the land. The South and the West, as well as the Northeast and Midwest, were all affected. In large cities, including Seattle, Milwaukee, Toledo, Pittsburgh, Baltimore, San Francisco, Minneapolis, Atlanta, and many more, much evidence exists to suggest large-scale unemployed activity and organizations. Records show small- and medium-town activity in such places as Fairmont and Charlestown, West Virginia; Camden, New Jersey; Indianapolis and Terra Haute, Indiana; Lewiston, Maine; Racine, Wisconsin; Warren and Ashtabula, Ohio; and even in small towns in Mississippi.

Some of the activities of the unemployed organizations were large in scale. In New York City, for example, in late January 1930, 50,000 attended the funeral for a Communist Party activist killed by the police. A similar funeral in Detroit in 1932 for four party activists killed by the police at a protest march on Ford's River Rouge plant was attended by 20,000 to 40,000 people: "Above the coffin was a large red banner with Lenin's picture" (Klehr 1984:33, 59; Sugar 1980:64–71). Perhaps the high point of such activity was in Chicago. In one incident in 1931, 500 people in a Chicago southside African-American neighborhood brought back furniture to the home of a recently evicted widow. The police returned and opened fire; three people lay dead. The coffins were viewed, again under an enormous portrait of Lenin. The funeral procession with 60,000 participants and 50,000 cheering onlookers was led by workers carrying Communist banners: "Within days, 2,500 applications for the Unemployed Councils and 500 for the Party were filled out" (Klehr 1984:322–23). The impact of these activities on relief and the public policy process was often immediate. In 1935, the Pennsylvania Unemployed League in Pittsburgh successfully forced the city council to allocate funds for school children who were not attending school because they had no shoes. Mass agitation finally pushed the recalcitrant mayor into releasing the funds. Later, the Unemployed League occupied and operated the Pittsburgh Lawrenceville district relief station for fifty-nine days. In Ohio, the Franklin County Unemployed League "convinced" a reluctant Governor

White to hold a public hearing by massing 7,000 to 10,000 unemployed outside his office (Feeley 1983:37–38). Even in cities in the Deep South, including Atlanta, Birmingham, and New Orleans, racially integrated unemployed
mobilizations took place. These protests, sometimes making the front page
news but more often remaining unpublicized, did not fail to leave deep
impressions on people in power, as well as on the more disadvantaged members of the population (see also Piven and Cloward 1979:41–95).[3]

The early unemployed protests have many parallels to the political
mobs that were at the center of the movement leading to the American
Revolution. Both had an anarchic participatory, nonexclusionary quality to
them. Both were fully interracial and multi-ethnic, made up of large numbers of women as well as men. Each movement stimulated large-scale government responses, as well as encouraging, inspiring, and coming to the
aid of other embattled constituencies. There were, however, certain crucial
differences that are noteworthy. First, the unemployed movements did not
merely exist in the more militant urban centers, as was the case with the
pre-Revolutionary mobs, but seem to have sprung up in virtually every cor-
ner of the land. Second, unlike the pre–Revolutionary mobs, their leadership was never from the "better" classes, but from radical left-wing groups
who usually had deep roots among workers. Third, African-Americans were
not just secondary participants—as they were in the pre-Revolutionary
urban mobs—but more fully, even disproportionately, represented and
more active, especially in the more radical working-class urban centers.

Much unemployed activity, of course, took place in ethnically homoge-
nous neighborhoods in both small towns and big cities. It should not be at
all surprising, therefore, that African-Americans, especially in large industrial cities, were so active in unemployed protests, given the higher degree to
which they were unemployed. What is especially striking, however, are the
large numbers of militant interracial unemployed organizations that seemed
to have operated in a powerful manner. In Warren, Ohio, for example, the
Unemployed League, made up largely of Black and white laid-off steel workers, had a Black chairperson. The Peoples' Unemployed League of Baltimore
had an active membership between 7,000 and 12,000 in twenty different locals;
between 2,000 and 3,000 of the organization's members were Black. In 1935,
the head of that city's Urban League noted, "The history of this group of white
and colored workers in a Southern city is unique" (Feeley 1983:27).
Unemployed League leader Louis Budenz pointed with pride to a committee in Austintown, Ohio, which had twelve men and eight women, noting
that most unemployed organizations began with only men (Feeley 1983:30).

Here was something quite different from earlier twentieth-century mass
movements. If not totally new in U.S. history, the unemployed struggles

harkened back to the interracial struggles of Bacon's Rebellion, the pre–Revolutionary mobs, the mass politics of early Reconstruction, the best racial practices of the Knights of Labor and the Populists, in certain respects exceeding them all with respect to their solidarity. And it was the early unemployed movements that defined the political context for all other mass movements, especially the industrial union movement, which would eventually come to lead and influence the whole social protest environment. Before developing these themes further, however, additional aspects of the mass movements, some with at most indirect bearing, involving other active, aggrieved constituencies need to be noted.

Farmers

Farmers too developed widespread militancy in the early years of the depression. Many sectors of the farm economy had been in crisis throughout the 1920s. By 1932, an economist for the Farmers Union estimated that the cost of producing a bushel of Iowa corn was 92 cents, at a time when farmers were getting 25 cents on the market. In the same year, Iowa dairy farmers claimed that it cost $2.17 to produce a hundredweight of milk, at a time when they were only getting a dollar (Dyson 1982:72,75). The economic impact on small farmers was apparent everywhere. Farm income had dropped from $15.4 billion in 1920 to less than $5 billion in 1932. Farmers either lost their lands because of foreclosure by mortgage holders (often banks or insurance companies) or were forced to become tenants on land that they had previously owned. Between 1925 and 1935, approximately 40 percent of all farms in the country went through a forced sale (Feeley 1983:68).

As in previous eras, farmers responded to these worsening conditions with large-scale protests and increasing political radicalism. They engaged in numerous producers' strikes, blockading major distribution centers. In August 1932, the Farm Holiday Association set up "picket camps" around every road leading to Sioux City, Iowa, a major distribution center, convincing trucks carrying produce to turn around. When persuasion failed steel cables across the road, railroad ties and large spikes were used. Similar actions were carried out in Omaha, Nebraska, with strong labor union support. Auctions of foreclosed properties were frequently stopped by armed "penny sales," where potential bidders were discouraged from bidding by armed farmers, while sympathizers bid small amounts (often literally only pennies), returning the property to the original owners (Dyson 1982:102). Although communist and other radical influence in the farmer movement was not nearly as extensive as among the unemployed, it was far from negligible (Klehr 1984:139–46; Dyson 1982). Even established farm leaders such as John A. Simpson, head of the National Farmers Union, declared: "I feel the capitalistic system is doomed. It has as its foundation the principles of brutality, dishonesty, and avarice," suggesting that the adherence to the free enterprise system that conservatives feel is so central to the American experience was not always thought to be so important by many citizens. Edward O'Neal of the American Farm Bureau Federation, a conservative, told Congress in the winter of 1992, "Unless something is done for the American farmer we will have revolution in the countryside in less than twelve months" (McElvaine 1984: 91–92). In the early stages of the depression, when virtually all farmers were desperate, militant farm organizations were sympathetic and supportive to both unemployed and union struggles (Shover 1965; Valelly 1989).

Equally militant and radical organizations of tenants and farm laborers also emerged during the 1930s; they were less successful than the farmer organizations and far more aggressively suppressed. This was especially true in the South, where the legacy of the crushing of Reconstruction and the Populists still resonated in the region. In the South, the Sharecroppers' Union (communist-led) and the Southern Tenant Farmers Union (socialist-led) organized thousands of sharecroppers and farm laborers, white as well as Black, to demand equity and livable conditions from violently repressive planters. On the West Coast, the Communist-led United Cannery, Agricultural, Packing, and Allied Workers of America (UCAPAWA) mobilized tens of thousands of migrant workers in demanding some small measure of justice from California's agribusiness. The wealthy landowners and their allies in local government responded with a murderous brutality that, however shocking to much of the rest of the nation, ultimately broke the union. From these activities the disinterested observer might reasonably infer that protection of democracy and citizen rights is not necessarily best served by reliance merely on local government, which is many times more easily controlled directly by powerful business groups (see Daniel 1981 for an in-depth account of California farm workers). This chapter in American history also suggests that the patterns of violent repression of peaceful, democratic movements, combining legal and extralegal terror, were not solely confined to the Deep South.

Numerous other constituencies took part in protest activities. Large-scale protests by students, often under the influence of the CP or other radical groups, began in the early 1930s (Klehr 1984:307–23). At the same time, thousands of intellectuals and artists, including a number of the nation's most prominent, publicly declared their allegiance to communism. In some instances, these intellectuals formed support committees and widely publicized working-class grievances (Cochran 1977:54–57; Klehr 1984:70–84).

This atmosphere of social protest and radicalism was nourished and gained recruits from the broader milieau of unorthodox movements. Adding to the atmosphere of insurgency was the retirees movement. The center of this movement was the Townsend Clubs, organized by retired doctor Francis E. Townsend. The Townsend Plan proposed that the government would pay every citizen over sixty years old $200 a month. By 1936, the Townsend Clubs claimed 3.5 million members. In three months time, they collected over 20 million signatures on their petitions, one-fifth of the adults in the United States at that time, more than any other cause before or since. Old-age pensions had broad public support. In December 1935, 89 percent polled, favored them for needy persons. The constituency of the Townsend movement tended to be middle class, respectable, and old (McElvaine 1984:2). Nevertheless, this movement added to the general social turmoil of the 1930s and was one more factor placing significant pressure on politicians.

There were also two contradictory movements, each of which during the early years of the Great Depression helped to capture and focus some of the anger against capitalists, the rich in general, and various establishment elites. Father Coughlin, the radio priest from Royal Oak, Michigan, was initially pro-union, anti-capitalist, and occasionally supportive of the New Deal, for a while seeming to have a home in the broad progressive movement. At the height of his influence he appeared to have millions of faithful listeners. By the late 1930s, however, he had become a reactionary, anti-Semitic racist and an extreme anti-communist, sympathetic to fascism.

Somewhat different was Louisiana's Huey Long who claimed to speak for the downtrodden and gained national support with his Share-the-Wealth campaign. Although hardly an anti-racist battler, the common people for him included African-Americans, a sharp break from the dominant racist politics of the Deep South during this period. He was distinguished from many other populist southern politicians of his era by his general refusal to engage in race baiting, and his threat to the Ku Klux Klan not to set up shop in Louisiana. As governor of Louisiana, Long had hospitals, roads, bridges, and a major university constructed. He provided free textbooks for all school children, and also made sure that Blacks were represented in public employment. His support in Louisiana was strongest in those hill-country counties that had opposed secession from the Union, supported Reconstruction, had given their votes to the Populists in the 1890s, and supported Socialist Party candidate Eugene Debs' 1912 presidential campaign. The "enduring radicalism" of Long's own Winn parish typifies his popular base (see, e.g., Foner 1988:606). Long's movement seemed to have millions of supporters throughout the country who identified with his attacks on the New Deal from the left (for a well-balanced discussion of both Coughlin and Long, see Brinkley 1983; for a standard biography of Long, see Williams 1969). The radical threat from Long is credited by some commmentators with having reinvigorated the New Deal in 1935, leading Roosevelt to say that he was "stealing Long's thunder" (Sundquist 1983:211–12).

Finally, one must mention the wide array of state-level third parties and left-wing insurgencies within state Democratic parties. There were also hundreds, if not thousands, of local labor parties during the early 1930s which had varying degrees of success (Davin and Lynd 1979-80). It is within this environment that the labor movement in the early 1930s began to assert itself in the nation's workplaces.

THE LABOR MOVEMENT

During the 1920s, groups of Communists had organized themselves in industrial plants throughout the country. In many nonunionized industries they were the only organizers, occasionally having the broad sympathies of their fellow workers on the basis of clandestinely published shop papers (Cochran 1977:43–81, esp. 63–64; Keeran 1980:39–44; Marquart 1975:33–35). In the fur and leather industries, centered primarily in New York City, the union was openly led by communists (P. Foner 1950). In a number of other industries (including mining, textile, and some maritime sectors), they led and participated in large-scale, though generally unsuccessful, strikes. In early 1933, however, months before the passage of the National Industrial Recovery Act (NIRA), the CP, along with members of the Industrial Workers of the World and independent radicals, led a series of successful strikes at Briggs in Detroit that were to help them establish early hegemony and respect in the auto industry (Keeran 1980:77–95).

The long, continuous decline in union membership from 1920 to 1933, was reversed in 1934, as union membership increased by 20 percent, rising by over 600,000 members from roughly 2.9 to 3.5 million members (Wolman 1936:16). Strike statistics took an extraordinary leap.[4]

But these are merely incidental statistics, which fail to convey the depth of the explosion. One does not even have to rely on enthusiastic radical accounts, accurate as they may be. Irving Bernstein, for instance, writes over three decades later of 1934:

> A handful of years bears a special quality in American labor history. There occurred at these times strikes and social upheavals of extraordinary importance, drama, and violence which ripped the cloak of civilized decorum from society, leaving exposed naked class conflict. Such a year was 1886, with the great strikes of the Knights of Labor and the Haymarket Riot. Another was 1894, with the shattering conflict of Eugene Debs' American Railway Union against the Pullman Company and the government of the United States. Nineteen thirty-four must be added to this roster.

In the summer of that year Eric Sevareid, who covered the great
trucking strikes for the *Minneapolis Star,* returned home to find his
father on the screened porch. The elder, a Minneapolis businessman,
was reading the headlines and his face was pale. "This," he said, "this
—is *revolution!*" (Bernstein 1969:217).

Three labor struggles, if not revolutionary, were certainly deep social
upheavals: in the 1934 conflicts in Toledo, Minneapolis, and San Francisco,
highly organized workers were victorious. All three struggles were led by
avowedly revolutionary groups and linked previously mobilized separate
constituencies. In Toledo, the working class and organizations of the unemployed formed a major alliance, with tens of thousands of radical-led unemployed workers battling scabs and National Guardsmen to a standstill, res-
cuing a defeated strike. In San Francisco, even the conservative AFL unions
were drawn into the general strike. And in Minneapolis—a previously
open-shop, low-wage citadel—not only the unemployed, AFL unions, and
Farmer-Labor Party organizations joined in the struggles of the Minneapolis
working class, but also militant farmers under the banner of the Farm
Holiday Association (Dobbs 1972:68). To these conflicts, one should add the
1934 textile general strike in which over half a million workers struck. In
the South, where the strike was the largest ever to date, almost 200,000 workers struck, engaging in major demonstrations and battles with company
thugs, vigilantes, and local law enforcement officials (see Janet Irons 1988
for the definitive account).

These conflicts stimulated and encouraged workers throughout the
country, both directly and indirectly, well after the strikes had ended. After
the 1934 San Francisco general strike, the longshore and maritime industries
along the whole West Coast remained aflame with militancy, largely under
communist leadership. The Trotskyist-led triumph in Minneapolis laid the
future basis for the successful organization of tens of thousands of over-the-
road truck drivers throughout the Midwest. And in auto, organizing outside
of Detroit by communist-led shop groups and in Detroit by the radical
Mechanics Education Society of America was greatly accelerated (Keeran
1980:103–7, 121–37; Preis 1964:19–33). As happened in General Motors after
the 1936–37 Flint strike, workers engaged in numerous unofficially sanctioned
(and undoubtedly officially *unrecorded*) job actions, gaining working conditions that employers never would have conceded in the previous bargaining. Most likely, these strikes increased the fear of revolution among the rich.
In all probability, they made politicians committed to capitalism somewhat
apprehensive. For AFL leaders, however, these strikes had the appearance of
the grim reaper. They signified the existence of an emerging mass-based labor
movement led by radicals, completely outside their control. The movement

threatened to overwhelm them even inside the confines of their own organizations (M.Davis 1986:56–57).

Thus, it was the upsurge of mass movements, eventually centered on the
labor movement, that drove the politics of the period and was the underlying cause for the electoral shift noted in the beginning. Conversely, it was the
divisions and hesitancies at times that allowed conservative politics to regain
its foothold. Few commentators have noted any relation between the mass
protest of the 1930s and questions of racial equality or the struggles of African-
Americans. I shall now attempt to argue that this oversight is misplaced.

AFRICAN-AMERICANS

By the early 1930s, political protest in African-American urban areas in the
North already had a rich history. This initial context is important for understanding the central role that African-Americans, especially Black workers,
played in the politics of the 1930s. On the one hand was the National
Association for the Advancement of Colored People (NAACP), founded in
1909 as a militant alternative to the accomodationist politics of Booker T.
Washington, who advocated industrial education along with an acceptance
of social and political inequality for Blacks. The NAACP stood for challenging racial discrimination, legally as well as socially accepted forms. It did
this by political agitation, lobbying, and the filing of legal suits, appealing
largely to more educated affluent Blacks. The NAACP must be credited with
a number of impressive achievements during the 1920s. It lobbied extensively for antilynching legislation; in part as a result of its efforts, the Dyer
Antilynching Bill passed the House on January 26, 1922, before dying in the
Senate. It defended victims of race riots, sometimes succeeding in prevent-
ing convictions against innocent Blacks. One of its most famous cases was
the successful defense of Dr. Ossian Sweet of Detroit. The Sweet family had
moved into a previously all-white neighborhood. When the family was
attacked at home by a deadly racist mob, they defended themselves with
arms. In the conflict, one of the attackers died, and Dr. Sweet was indicted
for murder. The NAACP secured Clarence Darrow; the Sweets were eventually acquitted. The NAACP also litigated over numerous Fourteenth and
Fifteenth Amendment cases, including many involving voting and school
segregation (see Meier and Rudwick 1976:243–45 for a summary).

The largest group counterposed to the NAACP during the 1920s was the
United Negro Improvement Association (UNIA) led by the West Indian
Marcus Garvey. Although having strong support from small ghetto businessmen and Black professionals and intellectuals, Garvey's largest base of
support was from the urban African-American lower classes. Counterposing
his organization to the NAACP, Garvey attacked racial wage inequality, Black

exclusion from unions, restrictions on Black businesses, the failure of white businesses in Black areas to hire Blacks, discrimination in the military services, and Jim Crow laws in general. The UNIA called for Black control of the ghettos, putting forward a nationalist perspective that emphasized pride, dignity, and self-reliance, using a myriad of cultural and organizational vehicles (including Black nurses' and veterans' groups) to inspire its followers. Coupled with his concern for the social and economic problems of the lower classes was his incongruent, utopian goal of going back to Africa, the rhetorical solution of the most extreme white racists in America. Thus, at times, the Garvey movement sought alliances or offered praise to such virulent racists as the KKK and Mississippi's Senator Theodore Bilbo, the latter introducing a bill in the Senate to deport the entire Black population of the United States (for an incisive analysis, see Haywood 1978:103–12).

In addition to the UNIA and the NAACP and other less influential groups during the 1920s, the rapid increase of the Black population in northern and midwestern cities led to the growth and strength of the Black church. Although hardly militant in most places and in certain cities tied to the most conservative white elites, the church was to change during the 1930s and at times provide support for the developing movement in the African-American community.

During the 1920s and early 1930s, various strains of Black radicalism developed, which were to play a role in the 1930s upsurge of Black workers. Important groupings of Black socialists gathered around two African-American newspapers in the wake of World War I: West Indian Cyril V. Briggs' *Crusader* and A. Philip Randolph's *Messenger*. Although initially close, the two groups split over a variety of issues, the most central of which was support for the October 1918 Bolshevik Revolution in Russia. Randolph emerged as the leading African-American figure in the Socialist Party; in 1925, he became the head of the Brotherhood of Sleeping Car Porters, a union which was to play a significant, if secondary, role in the 1930s upsurge in the Black community. In 1919, Briggs went on to form a revolutionary nationalist organization, the African Black Brotherhood, which at its peak claimed several thousand members in chapters across the country; the Brotherhood eventually merged into the U.S. Communist Party, supplying its most important initial Black leaders and activists. In addition, there were a wide range of independent Black radicals. Some like Du Bois and Abram Harris inhabited more conservative organizations like the NAACP, while others, including John P. Davis and Ralph Bunche, were tied to a radical group of Black Harvard graduate students, later connected with Howard University (see Griffler 1995 for an incisive, albeit unsympathetic analysis; see also Haywood 1978:122–31; Robinson 1983; Turner 1988:45–68; Ralphe Bunche's book-length memorandum on "Negro Betterment and Interracial Organizations," prepared for Myrdal's study, June 7, 1940, in Schomburg Library archives; and Kelley 1992, especially 45–46, which gives extensive references).

Although all these groupings were important to the social movements of the 1930s, the most central were the Blacks who joined the Communist Party. Even in its early period the CP was far more committed to anti-racism than was the Socialist Party (SP), as is suggested when CP members who joined the SP-initiated Auto Workers Union in the early 1920s convinced the leaders to end the practice of allowing racist jokes in the union's newspaper (Keeran 1980:54). Nevertheless, their overall stance and approach did not differ in substance until the late 1920s. Yet, the mechanisms for change existed in the CP but not in the SP. Black CP members played an aggressive role in raising criticisms of the U.S. party to the Communist International (CI). In 1928 and 1930, the CI passed resolutions that placed the "Negro Question" at the center of U.S. CP work. With its thesis that African-Americans in the United States constituted an oppressed nation whose roots lay in the Black Belt South, the CP in the late 1920s and early 1930s put a special emphasis on the fight against white supremacy and highlighted political activity among African-Americans in the South. The intensity and missionary zeal with which the CP pushed forward its political stance left even other radicals aghast. In 1929, during a major strike at the all-white Gastonia, North Carolina, textile mills, the CP raised the fight against racial oppression as a central demand, even including African-American organizers in their organizing group. Its agitation was not without its impressive moments; at one point white textile workers mobilized to save Black CP organizer Otto Hall from a lynch mob.

In 1931, the CP took initiative in a case that was to gain it major political leadership among African-Americans throughout the country. The case was that of the Scottsboro Boys, nine African-American youth seized from a freight train in rural Alabama, accused of raping two young white women who had been riding with them on the same train. The case not only became a focal point of mass activity in this country, but also received worldwide attention. African-American communist agitators emerged in major cities around the country, while the intransigent commitment of white CP activists to fighting racial discrimination earned grudging admiration from even conservative African-American newspapers. As historian Mark Naison notes, "Not only Jews felt moved by the Party's position: Finnish, Polish, Hungarian, Irish, Italian, and Slavic Communists became passionate exponents of the Party's position on the Negro question" (Naison 1983:49). Communist commitment to the fight against racism was so impressive that they even recruited members of the secondary leadership of Garvey's nationalist UNIA during 1929 and 1930.[5]

The Scottsboro defense laid the basis for large-scale influence and recruitment of African-Americans of every stratum throughout the United States. Defense activities involving significant numbers of whites as well as many Blacks were numerous, widely attended, broadly supported, and well publicized (See Du Bois 1940:298).

The communists extended their activities to the organization of Black sharecroppers in the heart of the Black belt South. They successfully organized large concentrations of African-American workers into the Mine Mill and Smelter Workers in the Birmingham area, the Food and Tobacco Workers, and the packinghouse and maritime workers' unions. It was almost a *sine qua non* during the 1930s: where militant, interracial unionism with strong stances and willingness to struggle for the equality of Black workers existed, one would almost invariably find the CP. So dominant and uncompromising was its orientation that even liberals and moderates within the CIO industrial union movement were forced to adopt the CP rhetoric, while often complaining about CP "disruptions" over issues of Black equality.[6]

These activities and the reputation gained by the CP as a reliable defender of Black people gave it entrée and influence among highly concentrated African-American industrial workers, including in such places as the Birmingham steel mills, the Briggs automobile plants in Detroit, and the Ford River Rouge plant, then the largest manufacturing plant in the United States (Goldfield 1980, 1985; Haywood 1978; Honey 1986; Hudson 1972; Huntley 1977; Keeran 1980; Meier and Rudwick 1979, 1982; Naison 1983).

Black workers had, of course, been central to labor union-organizing struggles before the 1930s and without the CP: the Knights of Labor in the South in the late nineteenth century; Alabama and West Virginia coal miner organizing from the late nineteenth to the first part of the twentieth century; the dock workers in New Orleans and other Gulf Coast ports; the International Workers of the World (IWW) organizing of southern timber and the Philadelphia docks. The 1930s, however, were the first time in the United States that African-American workers were seen as central to labor organizing nationally and the gaining of their equal rights was viewed as one of the defining characteristics of the movement by both friends and foes. There exists, to be sure, much debate over whether the CIO actually was racially egalitarian—a vehicle for Black freedom—or in the end merely another version of the racially discriminatory AFL, ultimately a means for maintaining white privileges and holding back Black advancement (See Goldfield 1993 and 1994 for discussion and references). The issue is complex and worthy of a detailed discussion. Nevertheless, Black workers and their grievances emerged as central to a wide range of industrial union organizing.

Not all of this important organizing was under the auspices of the CP or even the CIO (albeit much of it was), although one could easily argue that left-wing activity was crucial to the existence and success of organizing in other arenas. In most organizing campaigns, Black workers—once their initial doubts about white-dominated unions had been overcome—especially in the South, were the first to join, were the most steadfast of members, and were the most militant and radical. This was true in the longshore organizing along the Mississippi River, the Gulf of Mexico ports, and the Eastern Atlantic Coast, which took place under the auspices of the AFL's International Longshoremen's Association (ILA). This was also true in the high-percentage Black mining areas of Alabama and West Virginia, which was organized by the United Mine Workers before they broke with the AFL to form the bedrock of the new CIO in the post-1935 period. In numerous other key industries, however, the role of the communists—often Black Communists—was central: the National Maritime Union, whose Secretary-Treasurer Ferdinand Smith was the highest-ranking Black official in any national union; the early steel organizing where left-wing Black organizers played a pivotal role in mobilizing workers in many of the heavily African-American steel centers. Left-led Black workers at the center of the meat-packing industry in Chicago played the key role in not only energizing the union but also making it among the most racially egalitarian of any within the new CIO. In the South, Black workers were in the vanguard in the tobacco industry and metal mining, as well as in many industrialized cities, including Memphis, Tennessee. In the West, male Chicano miners and their wives—immortalized in the McCarthy-era film *Salt of the Earth*—organized by the Mine Mill and Smelter Workers, played a similar role. In auto, one finds the exception that proved the rule. Black workers were the largest percentage of the workforce in the heart of the Ford empire at the massive River Rouge complex; although initially hesitant about the union, when they did join they quickly became not only staunch members but overwhelming supporters of the left.

When CIO unions did not deal well with racial issues, they sometimes lost out, as was the case in eastern and Gulf Coast longshore where they failed to dislodge the AFL. It was also the case in southern wood working, where a racially blind conservative leadership based in the Northwest failed to exploit the many possibilities that existed in an industry whose work force was one half African-American.

As I have argued elsewhere, despite the egalitarian rhetoric espoused by the CIO as a whole, the racial policies of CIO unions varied greatly. Nevertheless, the role of Black workers, and the claims to support their grievances by CIO unions, were central to the whole upsurge of the 1930s for a number of reasons.

First, and most obviously, many industries could not have been organized without the strong support of African-American workers. Such was
clearly the case in steel, coal and metal mining, longshore, parts of auto,
meatpacking, tobacco, maritime, and much of food processing. In many
places, however, especially in the South, Black workers were not merely a
necessary addition but the bedrock of union support, a fact recognized clearly by even the most conservative of CIO organizers. In many thousands of
CIO reports on labor board elections and organizing campaigns, most
notably in the South, one sees a divided white workforce and a near unanimity with which African-American workers supported the CIO. In numerous key arenas, and contrary to numerous legends and images, it was Black
workers who played the vanguard role.

Second, the moral authority that its espousal of racial egalitarianism gave
to the CIO (whatever the varying degrees of substance) cannot be overes-
timated. It was symbolic of a concern for broader class concerns beyond
the particular economic- and job-related interests of individual members.
As we shall see, the issue of racial equality was to serve this function for
many urban ethnics at times, even when they did not always support the
rights of Blacks in situations that were close to them. The importance of the
issue of freedom and equality for the country's African-Americans and many
of the complexities and contradictions that the issue raised in American politics are by now familiar to us: The struggle over the definitions of freedom
and citizenship at the time of the American Revolution and the Constitution
period; the incredible moral authority of the abolitionists in the North, even
among those who did not agree with them; the brief periods of partial interracial solidarity under Reconstruction and the Populist Era.

The high points of racial egalitarianism among certain CIO unions are
indeed impressive: The early organizing in steel, with its numerous leftist
organizers, many of whom were Black, emphasized the importance of racial
equality for the building of a unified union. In some situations, white workers instinctively recognized that antiracist demands were at the root of strong
solidaristic unions. White steelworkers joined with their Black comrades in
their own "civil rights revolution" in the late 1930s in newly organized steel
towns lining the Allegheny, Monongahela, and Ohio rivers, desegregating
everything in sight, from restaurants and department stores to movie theaters and swimming pools (Davin 1989:30–31). In the Birmingham, Alabama,
industrial region, the left-wing Mine, Mill and Smelter Workers (known as
Mine Mill) aggressively organized the majority Black workforce in the metal
mines. They not only fought in the workplace for better working conditions
and for racial equality, they campaigned actively in the community. Along
with Alabama coal miners and steelworkers, Mine Mill members engaged

extensively in voter registration and in campaigns against the poll tax and lynching, giving these unions the character of broad-based social movements as well as workplace organizations. Robin D.G. Kelley claims that "more Blacks were elected to leadership positions within Mine Mill than any other CIO union, and its policy of racial egalitarianism remained unmatched" (Kelley 1990:145–51).

The racial practices of the United Packinghouse Workers of America (UPWA) are especially inspiring. The center of the industry and much early organizing took place in Chicago. From the beginning, union committees and executive boards were racially and ethnically integrated. In 1938, a key to the organization of the large Armour plant, with its high percentage of Black workers, was the successful union demand to remove the stars on the time cards of Blacks, which easily identified them as the first to be laid off. The union had a broad range of fully integrated social activities in Chicago, including baseball, basketball, and bowling leagues; child care and recreation facilities; dances and picnics. Along Ashland Avenue, in the heart of the meatpacking district, groups of white and Black workers desegregated all the formerly whites-only taverns. The first contracts in Chicago contained language guaranteeing that Black workers be hired at least in proportion to their percentage in the Chicago population. The 1944 UPWA convention gave up the air-conditioned comfort of an Omaha hotel, which refused to house Black members, to meet in a sweltering union hall. During the war, the union led successful job actions to integrate formerly all-white departments; after the war it forced the hiring of Blacks in sales and supervisory positions. By 1952, the UPWA had obtained the desegregation of facilities in all its southern plants (Halpern 1989:338, 365, 383, 507, 509, 534; Brody 1964:176; Horowitz 1990:642).

Of special interest for our purposes are the racial practices of several left-led unions with small percentages of Black members. The National Maritime Union (NMU), for example, was a communist-led union with no more than 10 percent Black membership. The union was formed in 1937 as militant workers broke from the segregated International Seaman's Union (ISU). The unified Black and white sit-downs that formed the union, according to Donald Critchlow (1976), became a part of the union's tradition. The union elected a Black secretary-treasurer and had large numbers of Black delegates at conventions. The NMU cautiously but steadfastly struggled for the full rights of Blacks on ships. It did this even in the face of racist appeals to white workers by the Sailor's International Union–Sailor's Union of the Pacific (SIU-SUP), a syndicalist union supported by the third-camp Workers Party, whose aggressive anticommunism led them to support an overtly racist union against the communist-led NMU. The NMU conducted educational campaigns on the role of Blacks in the industry and reported extensively on civil rights activities. Its education department, headed by Leo Huberman, widely publicized successful struggles for integration and carried on a steady stream of educational activities through its newspapers, pamphlets, books, organized discussions on ships, and in-port lectures. The communist-led Inland Boat division of the NMU, representing a 100 percent white constituency on the southern Mississippi River, not only agitated around civil rights issues but also successfully mobilized its membership to support the struggles of overwhelmingly Black longshoremen in Memphis and other southern river ports. The inland boat workers opposed the poll tax and lynchings and even expelled a member for stirring up racial prejudice. During this period, however, they did not attempt to change the racist hiring practices of the inland boat companies. The NMU began to break down the racial division of labor on ocean vessels during the war and in the Deep South on river vessels after the war, but this activity came to a complete halt when anticommunists gained control of the NMU and purged the communists in the late 1940s (Critchlow 1976:238; Honey 1988:244, 292, 343).

Equally impressive were the activities during the late 1940s and the early 1950s of the left-led Farm Equipment Union (FE) at the Louisville, Kentucky, International Harvester plant. The story is told in great detail by Toni Gilpin (1992). FE Local 236 represented all production and maintenance workers except those in the foundry. The plant, which opened in 1946, had 6,000 workers by 1949, approximately 14 percent of whom were African-American. Local 236 was characterized by a large steward system, frequent well-attended meetings, an active militant membership, and many work stoppages. From the beginning, its leaders and members, white as well as Black, displayed an unusual aggressiveness around the issues of racial equality, both within the plant and in the community at large. The local was unusual, especially in the South. It was a largely white local with many African-American leaders as local officers and even as stewards in overwhelmingly white departments. The main in-plant organizer in the initial campaign to organize the plant was Frederick Marrero, a left-wing Black man brought in from outside Louisville. In addition to its aggressive stance in defending the rights of Black plant workers and refusing to countenance segregated locker room, washroom, and cafeteria facilities, Local 236 mobilized its white and Black members to fight for the integration of parks and hotels in Louisville. Finally, there was a great deal of socializing, often involving wives and families, of Black and white workers outside the plant, something unheard of in Louisville in the late 1940s and early 1950s.

The left-wing of the CIO supported a wide range of issues that expressed its sense of solidarity with the causes of people around the globe. Opposition

to the successful attempt of fascist Italy to conquer Ethiopia, the only independent nation in Africa at the time, was widespread among U.S. Blacks.
Support for the popular front loyalist government in Spain against the Nazi
and Italian fascist-aided forces of Spanish fascism was extensive as well,
drawing numerous Blacks among the 3,000 American volunteers, a large
number of whom gave their lives in the fight (See Collum and Berch 1992).

Thus, in certain bastions of CIO and left-wing strength, one can see the
beginnings of an alternative, more solidaristic culture being built, a culture
that included not only union and political activities but also songs, social
and sports events, education, newspapers, children's camps, and vacation
places. This alternative culture competed for a while with the dominant culture, which emphasized individualism, racial domination, and the sanctity
of private property rights and wealth over all other values. In this context,
it is worth making some comments on questions of culture and the role of
racism within it. It is always a mistake to view culture as some autonomous
cloud or an unchangeable residue from the past, whose role in the formation of individual identities is unrelated to presently existing social structures. Although there may be some important degrees of disjunctions and
semiautonomous existence, in the end the dominant culture serves to justify the prevailing arrangement in society, the structure of wealth and poverty, the existing inequalities, including the system of racial domination and
subordination. In addition, the dominant culture gives individuals a framework not only for interpreting the world but for understanding their place
within it. The framework is dependent on maintaining the existing order,
which the public may at various times in a variety of ways be called on to
defend. Alternative cultures that challenge this hegemony by their nature
lead a difficult, tenuous existence, although they may persevere for long periods of time.

With all this said, it is important to know the impact of the struggles
of Blacks and other constituencies on New Deal racial policy. In particular,
one must look at the differing forces that were pressuring the government
in order to understand the highly contradictory racial policy results. Thus,
for the next piece of our mosaic, we must turn to the Roosevelt presidency and the New Deal itself.

RACE AND THE NEW DEAL

On the surface, and in most standard accounts, race was a secondary issue
for the New Deal and the Roosevelt presidency. Even the small minority of
civil rights activists within the Roosevelt administration tended to push race-
neutral programs that they believed would have the side effect of benefiting African-Americans (Kirby 1980:32–35). Conventional wisdom asserts that

New Deal Democrats emphasized class-based issues—relief, minimum wages, public employment, old age and survivors' assistance, social security, union rights—and the development of a lower-class electoral coalition. This program and electoral perspective supposedly helped incorporate African-Americans as workers and citizens. Although there is some surface truth to this argument, it is, in general, misleading. Not the least of its errors is the convenient overlooking of the continuing control and influence that racist southern Dixiecrats and their sympathizers in the North had over the Democratic Party, especially its racial policies, a legacy of both the Civil War and the System of 1896. Second, the racial discrimination and exclusion of the labor market meant that so-called race-neutral policies, even when they were implemented in a nondiscriminatory way, often only served to strengthen the system of racial domination as it already existed. Thus, race and class considerations were the central determinants of the scope and limits of virtually all New Deal social policies.

To understand the New Deal and Franklin Delano Roosevelt's often contradictory policies, one must begin with the traditional Democratic Party and its evolution during the 1920s and 1930s. One must further distinguish between the interests that the party served and its base of support.

WHO THE DEMOCRATIC PARTY SERVED

On one level the Democrats and Republicans have historically served the same general interests—large capitalists. Debs' Socialist Party, which coined the phrase "not a dimes' worth of difference," and the radical farmers in the Northwest who saw both parties as the parties of Wall Street, were always clear on these matters. As Gore Vidal has written, "There is only one party in the United States, the Property party...and it has two wings" (Vidal 1977:268). James Reston, a senior editor of the *New York Times* has more recently argued that there are no substantive differences between the two major parties.[7] Yet, although these facile characterizations express a good deal of truth, there have always been significant differences between the two capitalist-dominated parties. At least since the end of Reconstruction and until after the New Deal period, the Democratic Party has historically been the party of the South and of the large plantation owners. It has also served their allies, those with ties to large cotton planters and those in export industries who, like the planters, opposed the high tariffs supported by northern manufacturers. This coalition included people in certain port cities, most notably New York City, whose profits depended on the export trade.

By the 1932 presidential campaign, however, the Democratic Party had gained much broader business support, reflected in the stances of its successful northern leaders. Roosevelt was typical of this new breed of Democrats who, like the New Democrats today, had incorporated certain of the key business-oriented policies of the Republicans. As Theodore J. Lowi has noted, "even as late as 1932, Roosevelt was running as a Republican," berating "Hoover for spending and deficits," promising to balance the budget (Lowi 1995:35; Burns 1956:143). Colin Gordon (1994) has convincingly argued that Roosevelt's main concern throughout the New Deal period was the maintenance of business confidence. By 1935, FDR was being attacked convincingly, not as being too liberal but as too conservative and too subordinate to business. Because of his limited responsiveness to mass protests, he seemed to be in political trouble. The probusiness tilt of the Roosevelt administration was being assailed from many quarters. John Davis, a member of the intellectual circle at Howard University centered in the Joint Economic Committee, argued that "there must be an immediate change in emphasis from protection of private property to protection of human beings from misery and poverty" (Davis 1936:12). And there were many others who were not members of radical groups who were prepared to go much farther. For example, a report from the New York East Methodist Episcopal Church said: "The twenty-five months of strenuous effort under the New Deal to reform the system has only proved that it is beyond reform. The conviction grows, therefore, that capitalism must be discarded. The tenderness with which the sacred cow of private profits has been protected while suffering has been indescribably inhuman, indicts both the intelligence and character of our nation" (Davis 1936:12). So much again for the supposed sanctity of free enterprise throughout American history.

DEMOCRATIC BASE OF SUPPORT

To fully understand the dynamics of the Democratic Party, however, it is insufficient only to understand who the party served. One must also look at its base of support, and the pressures that its constituents often put on it. In order to serve various vested interests, the party had to be elected. Sometimes a party can get away with lip service and flimflam and other times it must produce something for its constituents. Ronald Reagan, for example, was able by skill and circumstance to achieve the former. He promised many constituents that he would balance the budget and produce on social issues such as school prayer and banning abortion. On the one hand, he ran up huge budget deficits by cutting taxes for corporations and the affluent while greatly accelerating defense spending. The social issues have been a problem for Republicans, because those who are more affluent tend to be socially liberal, especially on issues like abortion. Reagan solved this problem by talking socially conservative, yet doing little. Roosevelt was in a more difficult position and for a time had to produce more or greatly weaken his support.

Let us therefore look at the Democrat's disparate base of support. Historically, they were first and foremost the party of white supremacy and southern-generated racial prejudices. The Democratic Party was reforged as a highly conservative party after waging battle with the Populists in the 1890s, although it occasionally displayed neo-populist rhetoric in the South. In the North (as well as in some places in the South), it was pro-craft union and had an ethnic working-class base in some urban areas. It occasionally appealed to these latter constituencies with anti-northern-capitalist rhetoric. Nationally, the Democrats from 1896 to 1932 were clearly the minority party, with a stable if contradictory base of support.

Some of its appeal began to change in the 1920s. It started to develop greater urban, immigrant working-class support, gaining increased strength among unskilled Catholic workers, especially after 1928. In 1928, during the campaign of Democratic Al Smith for President, who was attacked by the KKK and other nativist groups because of his Catholicism, the Democrats began to attract greater support among African-Americans, particularly in northern cities. The Democratic Party thus developed two broad bases of support—its traditional Southern base and a rising multi-ethnic, multi-racial working-class base in the North. Or as one pundit has stated, they had become the party of both the lynchers and the lynchees.

Such a mixture was potentially volatile, causing two types of contradictory pressures on the Democratic Party. First, the growing, increasingly militant, politically demanding and influential working-class base, with many of its newer representatives to the left of FDR, was insisting that the party should serve them, not big business or southern planters. The urban working-class coalition was supplemented by rural, midwestern and western radical constituents, whose representatives in Congress, although often nominally Republican or third party, were frequently allies of the left-wing Democrats. These urban/labor/left/civil rights/rural radical forces were also desirous of greater action on civil rights demands, much to the consternation of the southern political and economic elites.

THE ROOSEVELT COALITION

Roosevelt dealt with these contradictions masterfully (if occasionally duplicitously), holding the various components of his coalition together. On class issues, he supported or gave tacit consent to a whole series of moderate reform measures, while undermining a large number of more far-reaching measures. He did not nationalize any industries or banks, despite strong popular pressure. He pushed the passage of the probusiness National Recovery Act as a replacement for the more radical Black Bill, which would have mandated a 30-hour week with no loss in pay. He supported the Agricultural

Adjustment Act, which helped the richest farmers and did nothing for the poorest sharecroppers and renters. He got a contributory retirement act passed (in Social Security) in contrast to the more radical and universalist Lundeen Bill. Rather than supporting national entitlement programs for relief and unemployment, he successfully pushed for them to be local programs, continually weakened by local budget pressures and local prejudices. And he often cut back his programs in the name of a balanced budget and greater efficiency, which at least one sympathizer argues was the cause of the 1937–38 "Roosevelt recession" (McElvaine 1984:297–98, 143). The administration's policies on civil rights issues and the effect of these policies on African-Americans are, however, more complicated and must be viewed in the broader context of the situation of the African-American community during the depression and the racially stratified labor market in which they attempted to find work, and the effect of public policy on them.

AFRICAN-AMERICANS DURING THE DEPRESSION

The impact of the depression on African-Americans was even more devastating than on whites. First, Blacks were concentrated in those areas that were hit the hardest, large urban manufacturing centers in the Northeast and Midwest and in agriculture. Second, wherever they were, blacks were the first laid off. Even in those industries where they were well established, they disproportionately lost their jobs. Third, in many cases they were displaced from their traditional areas of employment (including restaurant, hotel work, personal services, and even as elevator operators and doormen) in order to make room for the employment of unemployed white males. (A parallel trend can be seen today, as African-Americans are being partially replaced in high-paying foundry and blast furnace jobs, which were once overwhelmingly consigned to Blacks.) As a consequence, the discriminatory nature of the labor market left African-Americans as a group with more severe problems than most whites. Thus, it is not sufficient to look only at the racial slant of various government policies. One must also examine their interaction with a highly discriminatory labor market (see the forthcoming book by Michael Brown for a penetrating analysis).

Traditional analysts have described the beneficial effects of New Deal policy on African-Americans. Although an overall positive assessment of New Deal policy would be shortsighted, it is useful to indicate some of the measures that formed the basis for the strong African-American support for Roosevelt. As Michael Brown notes, "Roosevelt's was the first federal administration since Lincoln's to actively minister to the needs of black Americans" (Brown 1992:37). By October 1933, it was estimated that 17.8 percent of African-American families were receiving relief. A year and a half later, in

January 1935, the conservative Federal Employment Relief Agency (FERA) estimate was up to 30 percent. And in 1935, 20 percent of the total number of families on relief were African-American, at a time when Blacks represented less than 10 percent of the population (Davis 1936:4). Despite extensive discrimination, with Blacks often getting far less than their conditions or numbers entitled them, the benefits were extensive and recognized. Blacks also were participants in public works projects, public housing, and federal youth programs. As Gunnar Myrdal notes: "For almost the first time in the history of the nation the state has done something substantial in a social way without excluding the Negro" (Myrdal 1944:74). These benefits had two divergent consequences. On the one hand, they led to growing support of African-Americans for the Democratic Party. On the other, they tended to stigmatize relief and those benefits that were received disproportionately by African-Americans, a feature that is still with us today, most pronounced in the now-defunct AFDC and public housing policies.

Appointments of African-Americans to federal jobs above the lowest rank were rare. Still, there were a number of dramatically publicized, high-level appointments. In good part symbolic, they were not without their importance. Among those African-Americans highly placed in New Deal agencies were Robert Weaver, Mary McLeod Bethune, E.K. Jones, William H. Hastie, and Ira DeA. Reid. Along with others, they became known as the Black cabinet. Pro-civil rights white southernors, including Will Alexander, Clark Foreman, Aubrey Williams, and Beanie Baldwin, were also given high administration positions. The head of the Department of the Interior, Harold Ickes, had himself been president of the Chicago branch of the NAACP and was openly promoting equality for Black Americans. Perhaps the most important asset of the administration was the president's wife Eleanor. She was constantly active in civil rights causes. In one dramatic incident, Mrs. Roosevelt publicly resigned her membership in the Daughters of the American Revolution (DAR) when that organization refused to allow Black singer Marian Anderson to use Constitution Hall for a concert. Eleanor arranged for the Department of the Interior to allow an outdoor concert in front of the Lincoln Memorial, MC'd by Ickes. Later, at the 1940 NAACP conference, Eleanor Roosevelt herself presented Anderson the NAACP's prestigious Spingarn medal.

Still, there was little substantive movement on civil rights in Washington or elsewhere compared with the 1860s or the 1960s. Almost every federal policy had its downside for African-Americans. Even though the number of Blacks on relief nationally was high, in parts of the South, particularly in rural areas, many were arbitrarily excluded from aid to which they were entitled. In numerous southern counties with large African-American populations, they were underrepresented on relief rolls (despite their worse economic situation compared with whites) and given substandard benefits; many local southern officials asserted that Blacks could live on less than whites. The most extreme case was not surprisingly rural Mississippi, where in 1933 only 8 percent of all Blacks and 14 percent of all whites were on relief (Kifer 1961:212–13). Sterner, looking at disaggregate income data, based on the Consumer Purchases Study of 1935–36, found in the rural South that relief rates were "consistently lower for Negroes than for whites in spite of the fact that the proportion of families with very low incomes were far higher among the Negro than white farm families" (Sterner 1943:219). He also found large disparities with relief rates in some rural counties quite high for African-Americans, while in others they were minisculely low (Sterner 1943:223; in general see 219–38). African-Americans were also often excluded from relief rolls in the North by methods that were not necessarily overtly discriminatory. One way of limiting relief to needy persons generally was strict state residency requirements. By late 1939, sixteen states had three-year residency requirements. Even the most liberal states required a year. And in some States, including California, New Jersey, Rhode Island, and Massachusetts, five years was required (Howard 1943:59–60). Because many of the most poverty-stricken Americans during the depression were moving around looking for work, state-level relief, in contrast to broad national programs, did not provide an adequate safety net for those who were worst off. This historical precedent is undoubtedly a harbinger of things to come in this country, as much of our social welfare programs are being moved from the federal to the state level.

Perhaps the biggest fiasco for Blacks was the Civilian Conservation Corps (CCC), an outdoor work relief program for males between the ages of seventeen and twenty-three and a half. The director was an old friend of FDR's, an officer of the racially discriminatory International Association of Machinists. Numerous state officials were also racist. Despite the anti-discriminatory mandate of the CCC, discriminatory local officials in the South and elsewhere often excluded Black youth almost entirely from the program, discouraging applicants, finding those that applied unqualified, and giving a litany of varied excuses. In Texas recruiters were more open than in most places, stating "this work is for whites only" (Kifer 1961:12; passim for a penetrating discussion). By June 1933, when over a quarter million males had been accepted, less than 3 percent were Black. For those who got in, racist CCC officials provided harsher discipline, more demeaning work and requirements, and more ready expulsion from the program.

Discrimination in all the New Deal work relief programs was rampant. In Georgia, for example, it was found that while males were getting 90 cents

an hour for work on roads and school buildings while Blacks doing the
same work were getting 40 cents. Unemployed domestic servants were in
some cases being farmed out and receiving only board instead of cash from
the Federal Emergency Relief Agency (FERA). As usual the worst cases
seemed to come from Mississippi. In Jackson, the mayor refused all requests
to build parks, pave roads, and install sewer lines in the Black parts of town.
When a school in an African-American neighborhood was finally repaired,
only white construction labor was used. Robert Weaver, an assistant in the
Department of the Interior, was convinced that the exclusion of Blacks from
jobs, particularly when skilled, and discriminatory pay rates were common
not only in the South but also in "almost every state" and the District of
Columbia (Kifer 1961:216–17). Reliance on local administration in America
almost always equals racial discrimination.

Discrimination was most extreme in the more skilled trades, where
racially discriminatory craft unions successfully pressured hardly reluctant
government officials to reserve the jobs for unemployed whites, even when
the latter were totally inexperienced in the trade. Urban League officals found
sidewalk projects employing over a hundred men where African-Americans
were not permitted to work. In New York City, Works Project Administration
(WPA) subcontractors refused to hire Blacks (Brown 1992:44–45). But discrimination was hardly the province of the craft unions. A survey of the
Cleveland area by the African-American press found "Not a single Negro
has a job on the state WPA staff. Not a single Negro…has an executive position on the WPA county staff. Out of the hundreds of clerks employed by
the WPA headquarters not one is a Negro. Of the hundreds of foremen on
the scores of projects that are being operated by the WPA here there are
only two Negroes" (quoted from the Cleveland *Call and Post*, by Wye
1972:636). And much larger percentages of Black than white skilled and
white-collar workers, when they were hired, were placed in unskilled positions (Wye 1972:636; Brown 1992:45).

Housing Policy
One of the areas where government policies actually made things worse was
housing. The high degree of segregation in many U.S. cities in the present
period can, at least in part, be traced to federal housing policy under FDR.
In many cases, government officials accentuated or made worse already existing segregated housing patterns. Blacks were refused admission to all-white
publicly subsidized housing, even when it was completely under federal government control, as in the lily-white town of Norris, Tennessee, which was
"owned and controlled by the federal government under the auspices of
the TVA" (Davis 1936:11). In Cleveland, some federal housing projects were

kept segregated, even though they were built in formerly integrated neighborhoods! (Wye 1972:623). Many of these segregationist policies were the
result of discriminatory realtors who had been appointed as local officials.
Yet, they had been appointed by the federal government and little was done
to insure that they followed federal policies that supposedly forbid discrimination. Although overly optimistic about the ability and willingness of top
white officials to fight such local discrimination, it is definitely true, as Gunnar
Myrdal notes, that Blacks got a large share of the public housing administered by the U.S. Housing Authority (Myrdal 1944:350).

While African-Americans got a significant share of "housing project"
dwellings in inner-city neighborhoods, they received little of the subsidies
for more "middle class" housing. They were heavily discriminated against in
the granting of Federal Housing Authority (FHA) and Veterans Administration
(VA) loan guarantees and subsidies. In Miami, only one Black family received
FHA backing between 1934 and 1949, and it appears that they were not recognized as African-American (Judd, forthcoming). Federal administrators
had no problem working with discriminatory realtors, builders, and banks,
even underwriting the huge Levittown development outside Philadelphia,
whose restrictive covenants kept its 82,000 residents all-white until at least
1960. FHA and VA policies, supported by Republicans and Democrats, liberals as well as conservatives, not only encouraged suburban building to the
exclusion of that in central cities, but also "sealed the suburbs off to blacks
for decades" (see Judd's forthcoming seminal analysis).

The Military and Defense Industry

The administration's responsiveness to southern racist sensibilities continued throughout the decade. Initial policies in the defense industry in 1940
led many companies to hire only white workers, few if any even considering Black workers for skilled jobs. Typical of the policies of American corporations was the 1941 statement of the president of North American
Aviation Company:

> While we are in complete sympathy with the Negro, it is against
> company policy to employ them as aircraft workers or mechanics
> …regardless of their training.…There will be some jobs as janitors
> for Negroes. (cited in Garfinkel 1959:17).

These corporate policies, unchallenged by the administration in
Washington, did little to alleviate the situation of Blacks, even as the early
wartime hiring began dramatically to lower white male unemployment. As
a result of the decline in overall unemployment, the administration began
to scale back relief to the extreme detriment of the Black unemployed.

In the U.S. military itself, racial exclusion and second-class citizenship were the officially stated poliicy. Undersecretary of War Patterson publicly defended segregation in the military. When this policy was challenged, a 1940 White House statement replied that "the policy of the War Department is not to intermingle colored and enlisted personnel in the same regimental organization" (Garfinkel 1959:26, 34).

Anti-Lynching Legislation

Little advance was made on even the most minimal of civil rights legislation, that of anti-lynching. Less progress was made in Congress than in the 1920s, when the Dyer Antilynching bill passed the House but was held up by southern filibuster in the Senate. FDR, who allegedly sympathized with the bill, refused publicly to endorse it for fear of alienating southern Democrats.

Exclusion from Domestic Legislation

Finally it is important to emphasize that a number of bills to protect workers, in particular the National Labor Relations Act and the Fair Labor Standards Act, failed to cover a large percentage of the Black working population by their exclusion of agricultural labor and domestic servants.

We may thus provisionally give a succinct summary of the New Deal approach to social policy: In response to the massive protest movement, the Roosevelt administration instituted a large number of minimal social programs. Although implementing numerous minor anti-discrimination policies and some small number of symbolic gestures—with a high variance by program—Roosevelt moved cautiously in order to maintain the support of southern Dixiecrats. Yet, the pressures of the mass movements and the general turn of events would eventually allow these small cracks in the dikes to become a flood, despite the continuing limited nature of the social policies and the renewal of intense discrimination in urban and industrial labor markets.

HOW DID RACIST HEGEMONY CHANGE?

From the late 1890s until well into the 1920s, white supremacist doctrines exerted a virtual monopoly over American life. Biological theories of Black racial inferiority dominated all the social sciences, allegedly verified by the differences in average IQ test results between the races, differing cranium sizes in brain measurements, a thriving eugenics movement that preached a hierarchy of racial types, and the supposedly authoritative statements of the leaders of virtually all academic disciplines; these latter included the warnings against loosening discrimination by Pratt Fairchild, the president of the American Sociological Association and the 1907 assertion by the country's leading labor historian and liberal reformer John Commons, who argued that the degraded position of Blacks had nothing to do with white attitudes and discrimination, because they had been given not only equal opportunities to advance, but "preference over whites" (Sitkoff 1978:29, 14–15). As Speaker Gingrich notes, studying American history can indeed be instructive. We can see that racist arguments in the 1990s have changed little from the past, giving the lie to conservative arguments that they would have supported civil rights initiatives in the past when opportunities for African-Americans were *indeed* restricted.

More popular manifestations of anti-Black culture included the ever popular, explicitly racist *Amos 'n' Andy* radio show of the 1920s or the earlier Thomas Edison movies such as *Colored Boy Eating Watermelons,* or the more incendiary Woodrow Wilson-era film by D.W. Griffith, *Birth of a Nation,* which was used as a major recruiting tool in the 1920s revival of the KKK. The South, ever the pacesetter, segregated its phone booths in Oklahoma, and mandated Jim Crow bibles in its Atlanta courtrooms. In 1911, white citizens of Livermore, Kentucky, bought tickets to participate in a lynching of a Black person at a local theater. In 1916, in Waco, Texas, of all places, over 10,000 watched the "stabbing, mutilation, and burning alive of a young Negro defective." The victim's parts were sold as souvenirs. In these and other cases, the federal and state governments refused to intervene (Sitkoff 1978:27,7,21,9,18). As previously noted, Republican presidents attempted to outdo the Democrats in wooing racist opinion. When the memorial to Abraham Lincoln, the Great Liberator, was dedicated in Washington during the mid-twenties, Blacks were segregated far from the statue. Liberal Democrat William Jennings Bryan, not to be outdone, passionately defended disenfranchisement of Blacks. These attitudes were fully reflected in the court decisions of the land.

The Culture Wars (that most conservatives and some liberals decry today) were in full swing during the 1920s and 1930s. Then as today, they revolved around issues of race and class. Studies that "proved" that Blacks had smaller craniums were shown to be based on fraudulent research (See Myrdal 1944:91; Gould 1981, chapter three). A seminal work by the social psychologist Otto Klineberg convincingly demonstrated that IQ was closely related to education and environment; he showed that northern Blacks had higher average IQs than southern whites, a piece of disaggregated data that was somehow overlooked by those who had "proven" the inferiority of Blacks by noting the higher IQ's of white army recruits (the majority of whom were northern) over Black army recruits (most of whom were southern). In the 1930s, several leading proponents of Black inferiority publicly recanted, admitting that their previous work had been defective.[8]

The pendulum began to swing the other way. The Harlem Renaissance made visible to the world a highly vibrant African-American artistic culture.

Media reporting and articles began to change. Alongside *Amos 'n' Andy* was the striking figure of Paul Robeson, dominating over whites with his deep bass voice in Eugene O'Neill's play *The Emperor Jones*. By the 1936 elections, both parties were competing with each other in their efforts to solicit African-American votes. Unlike today's conservative Republican history buffs, the GOP then lauded the legacy of John Brown and Frederick Douglass, even claiming at one point credit for saving the Scottsboro Boys. National Democrats offended southern Dixiecrats not only by having the first African-American delegates to their nominating convention, but also by choosing a Black minister to give the opening prayer. When the rabid racist South Carolina Senator "Cotton Ed" Smith walked out over these affronts to his principles of white supremacy, the Democratic National Committee supplied Black newspapers with details of the incident (Sitkoff 1978:92–94). Finally, the entry of the United States into World War II against the Axis powers gave racism a bad name. Government and media wartime propaganda emphasized that this was a war against Nazi theories of racial inferiority.

Though much was still the same, the climate of racism had dramatically changed. The Culture Wars were not over, but one side seemed to be winning. This new cultural climate was important and clearly influenced deeper societal forces. Yet, the changed ideas about racism were themselves the product of those deeper societal forces with which they interacted. So, it is to those fundamental material causes that we must now turn.

CHANGING DEMOGRAPHICS

To understand the new racial situation in the 1930s, one must begin with the dramatically altered demographics. Before 1910, African-Americans were overwhelmingly located in the South (over 90 percent before 1900) and overwhelmingly rural. To the world and the country as a whole, they were largely invisible. This situation was to change between 1910 and 1940, accelerating again with the beginning of World War II. A look at the figures is instructive.

The main growth of the African American population was in the largest industrial states of the Northeast and Midwest. As Tables 7.2 and 7.3 suggest, this growth was overwhelmingly urban. By 1940, over 6 million African-Americans, almost 48 percent of the total Black population, was classified as urban. New York City, with a Black population of almost 92,000 in 1910, 1.9 per cent of the total population had 477,494 (or 6.4 percent) in 1940. Chicago had a Black population of 282,244, 8.3 percent of its total in 1940, while Detroit, with only 5,000 Blacks in 1910, had over 150,000 by 1940, nearly 10 percent of its population. Philadelphia had 252,757 in 1940, over 13 percent of its population, while Baltimore and Washington, DC, had 165,843 and 187,266, respectively. St. Louis, Kansas City, Newark, Indianapolis, Cincinnati, Pittsburgh, Cleveland, and Los Angeles also gained significant numbers and percentages of African-Americans during this same period (Sitkoff 1978:89–92).

TABLE 7.2

U.S. Population by Race and Region (in thousands)

NORTHEAST:

Year	Population Total	Black	Urban Total	Black
1900	21,047	385	13,911	312
1910	25,869	484	18,563	410
1920	29,662	679	22,404	607
1930	34,427	1,147	26,707	1,055
1940	35,977	1,370	27,568	1,265
1950	39,478	2,018	31,373	1,946

NORTH CENTRAL:

Year	Population Total	Black	Urban Total	Black
1900	26,333	496	10,165	324
1910	29,889	543	13,487	403
1920	34,020	793	17,776	674
1930	38,594	1,262	22,351	1,203
1940	40,143	1,420	23,437	1,278
1950	44,461	2,228	28,491	2,137

WEST:

Year	Total Black Population
1900	30
1910	51
1920	79
1930	120
1940	171
1950	571

TABLE 7.3 *Urban Population in South*

Year	Total Black Population
1900	1,369
1910	1,862
1920	2,261
1930	3,310
1940	3,631
1950	4,922

CAUSES

The causes of the Great Migration of African-Americans were mixed. Some are obvious, yet others are a matter of dispute. The most initial important cause was the demand for labor in the North, becoming especially intense during World War I. The start of hostilities in Europe created a large market for U.S. manufactured goods, with gross national product (GNP) increasing by 12.3 percent between 1917 and 1918 (U.S. Bureau of the Census 1976:226). The war also cut off the flow of immigrants. Between 1905 and 1914, foreign immigration averaged close to one million a year, with six of the years topping the one million mark. In 1914, there were 1,218,000 immigrants. In 1915, the number dropped to 326,700, and by 1918, there were barely 110,000; From 1931 to 1945, there were never over 100,000 immigrants in any one year. The boom in northern manufacturing and the lack of immigrants sent thousands of labor recruiters South, bringing hundreds of thousands of African-Americans to the promised land. Once established African-American communities existed in northern cities, the flow of southern migrants continued for decades (Lemann 1991). There is, to be sure, some dispute over the degree to which conditions in the South pushed African-Americans away from the South—these conditions being the decline of the cotton economy, mechanization, boll weevils, the AAA policies of the 1930s, and the general suppression of African-American rights—and the degree to which it was mostly a product of the pull caused by the calculated potential gains from the higher-paying northern labor market.[9]

For our purposes here, the matters under dispute are of secondary importance. What is crucial to understand about this period is that the African-American population in the North increased immensely. Most importantly, it became highly concentrated in the largest industrial states and in the biggest, most economically and politically important cities. In industrial areas around the country, an African-American working class developed, with its own culture, permanence, and tremendous leverage. Black workers became a significant part of the industrial workforce in steel (especially in Pennsylvania, Chicago and Northern Indiana, and Cleveland), in auto in Detroit, in meatpacking in Chicago and other northern locales, in tobacco manufacture in the South in North Carolina, in Birmingham metal mining, in woodworking and longshore across the whole South, in coal mining in West Virginia and Alabama, and in large numbers of other industries and places.

From the turn of the century to the 1930s and beyond, African-Americans had relocated from a part of the country where they had little economic and political influence to places where their potential for exerting leverage was enormous. Thus, changing demographics of the African-American population and their critical location in the modern economy provided the key to understanding the new racial situation during the 1930s and provided the material—that is, socioeconomic—basis for the dramatic cultural and political changes that have already been discussed. The new demographics were to make the Black vote central to national politics.

THE BLACK VOTE

From the time of Abraham Lincoln through the 1920s, the African-American vote in the North as well as in the South (tiny as it became after 1900) was overwhelmingly Republican. The GOP, taking this vote for granted, did little for its Black constituents. Frederick Douglass had noted this "degeneracy in the Republican Party" in 1890 (Moon 1948:87). During the early part of the twentieth century, Republicans sacrificed the interests of their Black constituents in an attempt to appeal to the southern white racist vote. Still, Blacks continued to be loyal to the party of Lincoln, electing the first northern Black congressman, Oscar DePriest, as a Republican, from Chicago's Southside in 1928. Yet, by this time the Black vote was already becoming increasingly independent.

The 1928 presidential election marked a watershed, as large numbers of African-Americans abandoned Republican Herbert Hoover to vote for the Catholic Democratic candidate Al Smith, the object of vicious anti-papist attacks by the KKK. African-Americans and the NAACP played a small role in conjunction with labor unions in 1930 in pressuring the Senate to defeat Judge John J. Parker, Hoover's nominee for the Supreme Court. Parker had publicly opposed African-American voting in his 1920 North Carolina campaign for governor. More significant, from organized labor's standpoint, Parker had issued the famous "Yellow Jacket" decision, in which the mine workers union was enjoined, under threat of prison, from soliciting members among miners who had signed yellow-dog contracts—promises made when hired that they were not members of unions and would not join so long as they remained employees of the company. Although these hiring contracts were clearly coercive, Judge Parker felt that this was an attempt to get organizing workers who had signed them to breech their contracts, a heinous violation of the law in his opinion. The *New York Times*, conservative and status quo-oriented then as it is today—contrary to the claims of today's conservatives—saw "no principle...at stake" in the battle over Parker's confirmation (Moon 1948:110). Nevertheless, on May 7, 1930, the Senate denied confirmation 41-39, the first Senate rejection of a Supreme Court nominee in the twentieth century. In the 1930 elections, African-Americans played a role in helping to defeat pro-Parker Republican senators in Kansas and Ohio, overwhelmingly switching their votes to Democrats, while in New Jersey they helped defeat a pro-Parker Republican Senator running for governor. In 1932, they successfully opposed other Republican senators. To what degree these Republican defeats were a product of the policies of the Hoover administration and the developing depression, and to what degree they were a result of the wrath of African-American voters is not always easy to tell, although Republican Arthur Capper, running for Senate reelection in Kansas in 1930 with strong NAACP support, won easily against his opposition (Sitkoff 1978:86). What did emerge clearly, however, aside from the NAACP claims that the Black vote was in Henry Lee Moon's words "The Balance of Power," was that the African-American vote could not be taken for granted and would switch parties, depending on the issues, in overwhelming numbers and percentages. More importantly, African-American voters were strategically located. The argument is made most incisively by Moon, who noted in 1948 that Black voters were "Already recognized as an important and sometimes decisive factor in a dozen northern States and in at least seventy-five non-southern congressional districts" (Moon 1948:9). Their importance was that they existed in large numbers in numerous large, closely contested states and districts. As Moon argued, "The Negro's political influence in national elections derives not so much from its numerical strength as from its strategic diffusion in balance-of-power and marginal states whose electoral votes are generally considered vital to the winning candidate" (Moon 1948:198). This point was to be underscored in Clark Clifford's all-important 1948 campaign strategy memo to President Harry Truman (Clifford 1947:11).

In Chicago, New York City, and Philadelphia, as well as other places, Democrats began making more vigorous efforts to attract African-American voters. In 1934, DePriest was defeated for Congress by Arthur Mitchell, an African-American Democrat, in a southside district that has remained Democratic to this day. In some places, the CP blocked with African-American politicians. Adam Clayton Powell first won an at-large seat on the New York City Council with support from Harlem constituents centered in his large Abyssinian Baptist Church and lower-Eastside radical Jewish workers loyal to the CP. In 1944, he used the labor and communist-supported American Labor Party as the vehicle to become Harlem's first Black congressman.

Alliances with labor and the left bore fruit in numerous places around the country. Support for civil rights became a litmus-test issue for the whole urban/labor/left/civil rights coalition. The CIO's political action committee (CIO-PAC) played an important role in the 1944 elections in eliminating from Congress many anti-labor, anti-Black conservatives, including Senator "Cotton Ed" Smith of South Carolina, Joe Starnes of Alabama, and Congressmen Hamilton Fish of New York, John Costello of California, and Martin Dies of Texas. In the Democratic Party primaries in 1946, Blacks and the CIO-PAC united to defeat Roger C. Slaughter of Kansas City, Missouri, who as a member of the House Rules Committee had helped quash the attempt to establish a permanent Fair Employment Practices Commission (FEPC). In the same year, the communist-led Food and Tobacco Workers Union (FTA) in Winston-Salem, North Carolina, mobilized its largely Black membership to elect two members to the city council. The coalition nearly succeeded in electing a Black person from Richmond to the Virginia House of Delegates in 1947 (Moon 1948:140,51,143,156–65). In 1944, the Supreme Court held that the white primary was unconstitutional. In part as a consequence, between 1944 and 1946, Black voting registration tripled in the South (going from 250,000 to 750,000).

THE ROLE OF BLACK LABOR

Most analysts who look at the increased importance of the Black vote during the 1930s tend to do so in isolation from deeper social forces. Some, of course, highlight the demographic factors and the growth of established African-American organizations. Few, however, root the heightened political consciousness and influence of the Black community in the proper place: the growth, organization, and militancy of the Black working class; the role of left-wing (especially Communist Party) influence; and the impact of both on more established African-American organizations.

As we have already seen, the militant unemployed activities early in the depression gave African-American communists an important foothold and organizational base in Black communities around the country. Its leadership of the Scottsboro defense gave it support, entrée, and close working relations with relatively conservative organizations, including the Black church as well as some nationalist groups. Its dispute with the NAACP over the Scottsboro case tended to isolate the NAACP, rather than the radicals, from activists in the community. In the end, it was the NAACP and the Urban League that were forced to change their orientation in order to retain influence among Black workers and to keep up with the growing radicalism among African-Americans.

The NAACP had not wanted such an inflammatory case as Scottsboro publicized. They wanted to deal with it, if at all, with purely legal tactics and in relative obscurity. Even Du Bois, highly critical of the communist approach at the time, shared this unrealistic perspective: "With quiet and careful methods, the Scottsboro victims would have been freed in a couple of years without fanfare or much publicity" (Du Bois 1940:298). The left approach—mobilizing the whole African-American community and taking the case to the court of world opinion as well as national public opinion—"struck a chord with a population the NAACP had not been able to reach" (Bates 1996:3). Unemployed organizing, support for Black strikers,

"Don't Buy Where You Can't Work" campaigns, were shunned by the national NAACP throughout most of the 1930s. The NAACP continued to lose major influence within the African-American community as the vast majority of 1930s activists and local organizations (including many grassroots NAACP activists and local chapters) broke ranks with the national leadership and joined with the newly formed left-wing National Negro Congress (NNC). The new civil rights organization was initiated by John P. Davis, Ralphe Bunche, and A. Philip Randolph, in association with communist activists, and an important segment of the rapidly growing industrial union movement, as well as activists and supporters from Randolph's Brotherhood of Sleeping Car Porters. It was the NNC that worked closely with and supplied Black organizers to many of the emerging CIO unions. Within the Black community, the NNC was often considered independent of white control in a way that the NAACP—dependent on wealthy white donors like the Rosenwald family which owned Sears—was not (see Bates 1997 for details, especially with respect to the activities and relations of both organizations in Chicago).

It was only in the early 1940s that the NAACP was able to regain its position of major influence. First, the national organization changed its orientation, symbolized by the role of Walter White in supporting the 1941 Ford strike. Second, splits within the NNC itself diminished its influence and provided the opening for the reemergence of the NAACP.

Thus, the importance of the Black vote, the leading role of the Black community in the protest movement, the overwhelming support given by virtually all segments of the Black community to the industrial union movement can only be understood in terms of the organization and mobilization of the Black working class and the role of communists among them. Let us now try to pull some of the pieces described so far together. First, the transformation of American politics during the 1930s was powered by the social protest movements. The early vanguard of the movement was the interracial, radical-led unemployed struggles, whose broad constituents had striking parallels with the pre–Revolutionary mobs of the late eighteenth century. One important difference was the central role of African-American workers and their demands within the unemployed movement. Second, Black protest, whether among the unemployed, over Scottsboro, for southern sharecroppers, or as part of the CIO, was central not only to the success of many of the movements but also to the moral legitimacy, style, and support. This is most clearly seen with respect to the CIO, whose interracialism built tactical unity and broad solidarity and gave it a claim to represent broad societal interests well beyond the particular concerns of its members for higher wages and better working conditions. Yet, even the CIO was not all of one mind with respect to racial issues.

WARTS IN THE PICTURE

The preceding discussion, of course, is not meant to suggest that racist attitudes, practices, politics, and the whole system of white supremacy were not alive and well. Some examples from the supposedly racially liberal North will help balance the picture.

Most significant were the large number of hate strikes during World War II, walkouts by white workers in opposition to the hiring or upgrading of African-American workers to jobs to which they were entitled based on their workplace seniority and qualifications, but which had previously been reserved for whites. Although many took place in nonunion enterprises, the most prominent were in workplaces represented by the seemingly racially progressive United Auto Workers (UAW).

Immense pressure from the African-American community, organized labor, and the left, along with the logic of events, had forced the federal government to insist on the hiring and upgrading of African-American workers in war-related factories. The companies that were considered cooperative hardly complied with the spirit of fair practices, instead merely giving token positions to Black workers. Others, however, rejected even these overtures and stalled completely. In response, African-American workers concentrated in foundries and janitorial services often protested and stopped work. Most often the resulting upgrading took place peacefully with strong union support. At other times, white workers, fearful that they were about to be displaced and open to racial scare tactics—occasionally started by company officials—stopped work or walked out at the first appearance of Black workers in the new departments. The largest such walkout took place at the Packard plant in Detroit in 1943, when 25,000 white workers engaged in a wildcat strike. Though the racism of many white workers was undeniable, the vacillation of the local union and the existence of an openly racist management were contributing factors. The strike was only ended when the federal government took decisive action by threatening to fire the white workers for obstructing the war effort, while the UAW national leadership vowed to support the firings of those who continued the walkout.[10] Soon after the settlement of the Packard strike, white protest in Detroit was to become even more violent over the newly built Sojourner Truth Housing Project. Federal government reversals over whether the housing would be for Blacks or whites (integration being out of the question because the Federal Public Housing Authority "generally demanded jim crow arrangements") helped inflame the situation, first eliciting denunciations from Black and labor groups (initially including even the Wayne County AFL), then providing encouragement for white racist mobilization. The struggle was replete with racial clashes and KKK-led cross burnings. Although the AFL became more withdrawn as the battle heated up, the UAW, with unanimous international executive board support, threw itself into the fray in support of the prospective African-American tenants, using integrated groups of white and Black workers for defense and picketing with much of the leadership and cadre coming from left-wing African-American workers from Ford's River Rouge UAW Local 600 (for important background material, see Capeci 1984).

As Martin Glaberman convincingly argues, the attitudes of white workers in the hate strikes were often contradictory. This is suggested by the events surrounding the 1944 Philadelphia transit strike. The Philadelphia Transportation Company had refused to upgrade any Blacks to platform or operating jobs, despite persistent pressure from the federal FEPC. In the 1944 union certification elections, the AFL Amalgamated union and the independent Philadelphia Rapid Transit Employees Union both campaigned on an explicitly racist basis, opposing the upgrading of Black employees. The Communist-led Transportation Workers Union (TWU) was forthright in its position of ending all job discrimination and was supported in the campaign by the national CIO office. The TWU was red-baited and race-baited extensively in the campaign. Nevertheless, the TWU won the election with large majorities in all units and among all whites, as well as winning virtually all the votes from the 500 or so Black employees. Soon after, eight Black employees were upgraded to operators. The leaders of the defeated unions then organized a hate strike involving the majority of white workers. As Herbert Hill makes plain, the hate strike was clearly supported by the company, and one might add parenthetically, by labor priests associated with the virulently anti-communist Association of Catholic Trade Unionists (Rosswurm, 1992:129). The strike was only ended by a threat of government seizure, the firing of the strike leaders, and resolute opposition by the TWU. In the next union election, held later in the year, the TWU actually increased its support.[11] The contradictions are subtlely analyzed by Glaberman who concludes that "a majority of white workers had shown by their vote for the TWU that they were ready to accept the upgrading of Black workers, but they were not ready to do battle with their extreme racist fellow workers on the issue and they stayed home" (Glaberman 1988:117).

Although the racism of white workers and their willingness to support racist actions at times were central features of the hate strikes, the role of management in opposing anti-discrimination measures and in supporting the most extreme racists in many of the situations was also significant. The hate strikes and other racist activities were ominous signs, but any reasonable balance sheet must give them a secondary place. For the period contrasts sharply with those times when white racist mobilization was the dominant political activity, for example, during the massive resistance in the Deep

South during the late 1950s or the "white backlash" to Black civil rights during the late 1960s. For a wide range of commentators, perhaps the most striking feature of working-class people during the 1930s and 1940s was their broad class consciousness and strong solidarity across ethnic, religious, and racial lines differences. This period represented important potential for a broad working-class movement, inclusive of women, racial and ethnic minorities, people of differing religions, independent of the two business-dominated parties.

According to political commentator Samuel Lubell, the demographic basis for this movement was located in the cities. First, there were the children of the 13 million immigrants who came to the United States between 1900 and 1914, who came of age during the 1930s (Lubell 1955:29). Second, between 1920 and 1930 6.5 million people left the farms and hills for the cities, 4.5 million arriving in New York, Chicago, Detroit, and Los Angeles alone. Here was the human material for a "revolutionary political change." Lubell argues, "The formation of the CIO marked the fusing of the interests of the immigrant and native-stock workers. That I believe is perhaps the most telling accomplishment of the CIO." He speaks of "the rise of a common class consciousness among all workers. The depression, in making all workers more aware of their economic interests, suppressed their racial and religious antagonisms. Put crudely, the hatred of bankers among the native American workers had become greater than their hatred of the Pope or even of the Negro. …This rise in class consciousness…was a nation-wide phenomenon." Lubell, like Sundquist, saw this strong class consciousness expressed in the high class vote in the 1936 elections. Lubell argues that the battle for equality for African-Americans came to symbolize for many working-class people, especially the children of immigrants, the fight for equal treatment for all Americans. And contrary to our perceptions today, Lubell found that the militantly antiracist campaign of Henry Wallace in 1948 got its strongest support in integrated neighborhoods that had only recently become a significant percentage African-American (Lubell 1955:29, 32, 48, 49, 91–96).

LABOR PARTY SUPPORT

This broad solidaristic class orientation was reflected in the strong degree of working-class support for independent labor party politics in the first half of the 1930s and continuing to lesser degrees until the late 1940s. Eric Leif Davin cites an August 1937 Gallup Poll that reported that 21 percent of the population at large supported the formation of a labor party (Davin 1995:8); even among city-level elected CIO officials in 1950 (long after the time had passed and the left-wing unions had already been expelled), 31 percent still favored the formation of such a national labor party. But it was not mere attitudes and sentiments as reported to pollsters that suggest the readiness of many American workers to abandon the two major parties. Distrust of both political parties, especially the Democrats, was overwhelming in many unions, particularly in 1934 and 1935. At the 1935 AFL convention at which John L. Lewis was able to muster a little over a third of the delegate votes for industrial union organizing, the formation of a labor party just missed passage. The vote was 108 against to 104 in favor, with the latter including a majority of delegates from state federations of labor and urban centers (Davin forthcoming:18). Major unions were on record supporting a labor party, and advocates of the idea attracted huge audiences around the country. Local labor parties with widespread support existed in virtually every industrial center and city in the country. Newspapers and other publications fully expected the formation of a labor party before the 1936 elections. At the April 1936 UAW convention, delegates voted unanimously to form a national farmer-labor party, even voting down a resolution to endorse FDR for reelection. With a direct appeal from John L. Lewis and threats to the UAW leadership from CIO hatchetman Adolph Germer that Lewis would withdraw financial support for the UAW organizing campaign, the convention narrowly adopted a pro-Roosevelt resolution while refusing to change its support for a labor party.

How the mass labor party support, particularly among CIO members, was steered toward FDR and the Democrats in the 1936 election is a long and complicated story. FDR's dramatic move to the left during the 1936 campaign is, of course, a crucial element. The national leadership of the CIO, however, played a more critical role. Unanimous in its desire to see Roosevelt reelected, the CIO created a number of vehicles that would allow people to express third-party sentiment, yet still vote for FDR. Nationally, it created Labor's Non-partisan League to support Roosevelt. In a number of places, the CIO brokered arrangements where people could vote for local and statewide third parties (as in Minnesota with the Farmer-Labor Party) and still support FDR for president. In New York State, many people found voting for the Democrats and Republicans so distasteful, that CIO leaders created the American Labor Party ticket so that hundreds of thousands of left-wing working-class people could vote for Roosevelt without voting Democrat. A number of CIO leaders even asserted that these efforts would be redirected to the formation of a labor party after Roosevelt's reelection. Much of these claims turned out to be hypocritical, as both strong initiatives by local labor parties and broader labor party efforts within CIO unions were undermined by top-level CIO operatives. Still, important moves to launch labor parties continued throughout the 1930s and 1940s. Davin believes that the destruction of the 1936 efforts was the "last hurrah." James

Cannon, the leader of the Trotskyist Socialist Workers Party, convincingly argues that the attempts to gain working-class support for Roosevelt and the destruction of third-party efforts could not have been successful without the blessing and active encouragement, of not only the mainstream CIO leaders but also the Communist Party, whose prestige and support among class-conscious militants enabled it to divert them away from an independent labor perspective.[12] Whatever the case may be, strong rank and file support, and even lower and intermediate leadership, for an independent labor party was undercut by top CIO leaders as well as the communists.

CONTRADICTORY NATURE OF CIO

In a large variety of spheres and venues, broad class, insurgent, solidaristic perspectives existed simultaneously and often competed with narrow, cautious, racially divisive, sectoral approaches. This was true not only in the middle and late 1940s but also from the very beginning of the CIO. Much has been written about the innovative tactics in auto in organizing GM and Ford. More recently, new research has documented successful militancy and solidarity in a variety of left-wing unions, including packinghouse, food and tobacco, farm equipment, metal mining, maritime, transport, and longshore. These unions, their programs, and their militant campaigns often had support and resources from the national CIO. Simultaneously, however, numerous backward steps were being taken in other venues which seriously weakened the long-term strength of the CIO. In virtually all of these, where it was not the pivotal issue, race was an important subtext. In this respect, it is clear that tendencies toward business unionism and racial exclusion existed in the CIO, along with more solidaristic approaches, from the very beginning of the federation's existence. And it was the growing domination of this conservative thrust that was to undermine the power of the labor movement and stall the potential for a more thorough racial transformation.

Racism and Business Unionism — The Downside of the CIO

In 1937, the CIO launched the Textile Workers Organizing Committee (TWOC). The TWOC was headed by Sidney Hillman, whose Amalgamated Clothing Workers seemed to require the organization of the textile industry for the long-term stability of their union. And the key to the textile industry lay in the South, where the heart of cotton textile was located. Fresh on the heels of the CIO victory over GM and a new wave of massive working-class insurgency, Hillman opted for a corporatist strategy, rather than a mass mobilizing and organizing campaign, similar to that which had been successful in auto, steel, and rubber. Although he utilized socialists and planned to work closely with United Mine Workers of America (UMWA) militants and Steel Workers' Organizing Committee (SWOC) organizers, Hillman's was a cautious strategy. He excluded communists, whose legendary skills and mobilizing abilities had given them an historic place in the industry. Most of those chosen were southern born, so as not to offend southern "sensibilities." Even more significant, Hillman made every effort to cultivate numerous southern politicians and to convince manufacturers that "textile unionism means profits," as his article in Barron's argued (Fraser 1991:388). He arranged meetings with mill owners, arguing that the TWOC would prevent strikes. He also placed major reliance on help from the federal government, especially the National Labor Relations Board (NLRB). And Hillman hoped that the passage of the Fair Labor Standards Act would undermine textile employer resistance. Virtually all of Hillman's wishful thoughts failed to bear fruit. Intense violent resistance by textile owners and their refusal to obey government directives defeated numerous organizing campaigns. Hillman's corporatist strategy helped disarm workers and kept the organizing campaign from being more successful. It also slowed the development of the overall campaign, postponing much organizing until the corporate strategy could unfold; this delay was ultimately to prove fatal.

Despite these limitations, the TWOC campaign, when it was finally begun, evoked a tremendous response, especially among southern mill workers. As Paul Richards writes, "Again and again, mill hands voted in favor of TWOC only to be suppressed by mill owners and local governments" (Richards 1978:57). Still, the TWOC campaign seemed full of promise and had large numbers of successes. Yet, Hillman's corporatist strategy took too long to get off the ground. By the time it was in high gear in the fall of 1937, economic collapse had come, destroying all momentum in not only textile but the labor movement as a whole. The strategy of the CIO right wing to depend on the national Democratic Party, curry favor with businessmen and local politicians, have a respectable image, and in return guarantee labor peace and responsibility, had been a clear loser. But hope springs eternal and it was a lesson that was never to be learned, a scenario repeated over and over again with similar results, a strategy that was eventually to replace completely the more successful organizing and mobilization model.

The campaign to organize steel in the 1930s was initially subsidized by the UMWA. UMWA and CIO President John L. Lewis saw the organization of steel as critical to the stability of the miners' union; thus, he gave it the highest priority within the CIO, assigning hundreds of organizers, numerous high-ranking UMWA officials, and a large budget; Lewis and his lieutenants also assumed day-to-day, hands-on control. The initial activities of the SWOC seemed infused with the same racial idealism as that associated with the UMWA.[13]

Steel had higher wages and more strong occupational differentials than coal; job hierarchies were stratified ethnically, but even more so racially. Still, the multi-ethnic, multi-racial nature of the workforce, especially in the steel centers of Pittsburgh, Chicago, and Birmingham, seemed to require both an interracial and egalitarian approach. To facilitate such a campaign and the building of racially egalitarian unionism, the SWOC developed an alliance with the NNC, which made special appeals to African-American workers (Cayton and Mitchell 1939:205). Lewis directly enlisted the support of the CP, which, according to CP leader William Z. Foster, contributed 60 of the initial 200 organizers, a number of whom were Black. Without these alliances and the many African-American organizers, most with left-wing affiliations, it is doubtful that the SWOC campaign would have been successful. As a conscious part of its interracial strategy, there were many racially egalitarian activities that characterized the initial SWOC organizing in many places, including those previously discussed in the Pittsburgh area.

Unlike the UMWA, however, this racially egalitarian thrust was to disappear quickly as a defining characteristic of the union once organization was completed. Here and there, battles against discrimination burst forward after the steel industry had been organized. Invariably led by Black workers, these struggles usually received at best only minimal, reluctant support from the leadership and had little resonance within the union.[14] The reasons for this outcome are only partly explained by the racial hierarchy of wages and jobs and the associated, entrenched racial privileges of an important segment of white workers. Equally important was the stifling of rank-and-file organization, militancy, and democratic control of the union by the highly bureaucratic Murray leadership. The establishment of the first contract with U.S. Steel without the types of struggles that took place in auto, longshore, meatpacking, and other industries, allowed CIO-appointed Steelworkers President Philip Murray to assert top-down control, appointing all initial officials and stifling opportunities for democratic rank-and-file influence. This too was an important legacy of the UMWA as nonelected former Lewis supporters controlled all the top positions in the new steelworkers union. Communist and other leftist organizers, their services now unnecessary, were quickly removed. No longer having a need to mobilize all segments of the workforce to engage in successful struggle against the company, demands which were designed specifically to enlist the support of African-American workers dropped in priority. Privileges of white workers were frozen and highly discriminatory job classification systems were strengthened with the acceptance of departmental rather than plant-wide seniority. These discriminatory provisions, contractually codified by the union, were successfully challenged in court during the 1970s, one of the most important cases being the consent decree at the Sparrows Point, Maryland, Bethlehem steel plant that forced the union and the company to pay aggrieved Black workers millions of dollars in pay equity.

The union congealed along its nonegalitarian path in 1949 and 1950 with its destruction of the Mine Mill and Smelter Workers, largely Black Birmingham locals. The successful attempt of the steelworkers in 1949 and 1950 to take over Alabama Mine Mill locals relied on overtly racist appeals to white workers. The racism of the leaders of the secession and their support from the top ranks of the CIO leadership are described by Vernon Jensen, an ardent supporter of the CIO right wing and a vehement, unequivocal anti-communist. Jensen describes the case of Homer Wilson, a right-winger in Mine Mill, who was defeated for the vice presidency in that union in 1947. After his defeat, Wilson conferred with CIO President Philip Murray, Organization Director Alan Haywood, and Operation Dixie head Van Bittner. Wilson was eventually sent to Alabama to urge iron-ore miners to leave Mine Mill and join the steelworkers.

> When he arrived in Besember, only whites were in attendance at the meeting that had been called. *The most conservative and reactionary union men in the district were leading the movement, with no intention of including the Negroes as they had long been included in the Mine Mill locals.* Wilson then told them they had to have the Negroes if they were going to win for the Steelworkers and advised bringing them in and explaining to them that the Communists were not the only effective grievance machinery—that the Steelworkers would be very effective along these lines. The local conservative leaders would not listen. They did not wish to have Wilson around, and so informed Haywood, whereupon Haywood promptly telephoned Wilson and discharged him. Instead, Van Jones was hired and the white men among the iron-ore miners were approached on the ground that they were going to have a white union." (Jensen 1954:234)

Just before the 1949 Tennessee Iron and Coal Company (TCI) election between the steelworkers and Mine Mill, the KKK staged a large rally in support of the steelworkers. Despite the early anti-racism of the SWOC, the leadership of the union, led by CIO president Murray, barely complained. In demogogic fashion the steelworkers attempted to hide their activities by accusing Mine Mill of fomenting racism and further claiming that this overwhelming Black local union with its Black leadership was itself allied with the KKK. The steelworkers, in tactics reminiscent of the KKK during Reconstruction and in the counterattack on the Populist movement, attempted to isolate Black workers by physically attacking the small number of whites who remained loyal to

Mine Mill. In at least one instance, at the Muscoda Local 123 in Besemer, Black Mine Mill members rallied armed contingents from the Black community to defend successfully their white union brothers from Steelworker-led assaults (Huntley 1977:162, 189, 208–9). These racist activities and assaults by the steel-workers were among many things that moved the CIO as a whole from an incipient anti-racism to acquiescence if not open support for discrimination against Black workers.[15]

The International Woodworkers of America (IWA) was formed in 1937 when a militant faction of lumber and sawmill workers in the U.S. Northwest and Canada broke from the AFL to join the CIO. Left-wing forces were dominant, controlling the main offices and the majority of the exec-utive board, although from the beginning there was conflict between the left and a right-wing faction. Although the latter group was not without its brand of militance, it had little propensity for new organizing. Its nar-row job-control rhetoric also often had racial overtones, expecially in its rejection of the left-wing's call to organize the Black and white southern woodworkers, whose low wages undercut union conditions in the Northwest but whose oppressive working conditions represented a fertile environment for organizing.

When the IWA called on the CIO national office to assist them finan-cially with their new organizing, the union may have made a fatal mistake. John L. Lewis, who was not at the time adverse to working with Communists or Communist-led unions and groups, sent in Adolph Germer to intervene in the union, under the guise of assistance. Germer, a highly skilled though ruthless, factional, antidemocratic, highly bureacratic ex-Socialist, saw the removal of left-wing influence in the union as his most important task (Lembcke and Tattam 1984:80–81). He surrounded himself with a group of organizers who were largely roving goon squads, undermining left-wing locals and building up the right-wing ones (Lembcke and Tatum 1984:92). When the International leaders complained, he turned all their criticisms around for an all-out attack, raising the conflict within the union to truly destructive levels. With Germer's aid, the right-wing gained control of the union at the 1941 convention.

The control of the IWA by Germer and his following of right-wing fac-tionalists was to have disastrous effects for the creation of class-wide inter-racial solidarity, particularly in the South. By the late 1940s, when the CIO was trying to organize the South, even right-wing southern CIO leaders com-plained about IWA unwillingness to organize. Other unions that had orga-nized woodworker locals in the South for them then found the IWA even to be unwilling to engage in minimal efforts to maintain and service their new units.[16]

Although the right wing castigated the left wing for its undemocratic stance and its ties to forces outside the union and the working class, key CIO officials engaged in activities that were far more consequential in undermining the independence of the unions. Most pernicious were their secret ties to government agencies that helped destroy democracy in many unions. The most serious of these ties were to the House Un-American Activities Committee and the Federal Bureau of Investigation (FBI). The best documented activities are those of James Carey, secretary-treasurer of the CIO, and of the Association of Catholic Trade Unionists. In Sigmund Diamond's important study, he asks to what degree interference in ostensibly membership-controlled organizations by the political police of the government (in this case the FBI) undermined not only the democracy of various unions but also their effectiveness as independent organizations representing their members. While claiming the mantle of righteousness for themselves, attacking CP secret meetings and caucuses, Carey and other right-wing leaders engaged in actions that they kept absolutely secret. The reason for this had nothing to do with national security, but rather that it would have discredited them among precisely those to whom they were trying to appeal.

Carey and his cohorts, supposedly carrying on an ideological struggle with left-wing opponents, conspired with the FBI and other government agencies to deny passports for their opponents who were to travel abroad, gained extensive background information for use in attacks, and coordinated public congressional hearings, smear campaigns, and even arrests to coincide with union elections and conflicts. The government was used to undermine left-wing unions, including the longshoremen, food and tobacco workers, and the electrical workers. Government attacks and hearings at critical times were claimed to be coincidental and further evidence of the unpatriotric nature of their left-wing opponents. The relationships permeated large numbers of unions, including the electrical workers and the autoworkers. As Diamond argues, "the consequence was the *de facto* assimilating of autonomous organizations like labor unions into the government's intelligence apparatus" (Diamond 1986:319).

Thus, it turns out that the portrayal of many of the opponents of the left in the unions as sincere, even democratic oppositionists by anticommunist historians, turns out to be a falsehood. Much former scholarship on the role of the Catholic Church, the CIO right, and the Association of Catholic Trade Unionists (ACTU) still needs to be revised to accord with the facts. Anti-communist historians who have praised the anti-communist ACTU (including Philip Taft and Michael Harrington) have judged this organization by its democratic pretenses, not by its anti-democratic actions (Diamond

1986:322; see also Rosswurm 1992:131).These activities were to cast a long-term pall over the effectiveness of the union movement.

Although solidaristic, mass mobilizing strategies were to dominate the CIO in the 1930s, by the end of World War II they were no longer the main tenor of CIO organizational activity.

A NOTE ON THE COMMUNISTS

It would, of course, be remiss to suggest that the right-wingers were the only ones responsible for the undermining of class solidarity in the CIO. During World War II, the CP joined the CIO right in opposing strikes and protests, no matter how justified the grievances.The official position was that it was more important not to disrupt the war effort. In some instances, the CP even outdid the right, as when CP General Secretary Earl Browder in 1942 began advocating the adoption of incentive pay and piecework in order to increase wartime productivity; the CP-led electrical workers were the first to adopt this position. In 1943, the CP lost major influence in the UAW when it tried to push this position, which was historically opposed by virtually all industrial unionists as a company vehicle to divide and more deeply exploit workers (Cochran 1977:211–18). The low point in CP activity, ostensibly in support of the war effort, came with the Montgomery Ward strike in Chicago in 1944. During that year, in defiance of the National War Labor Board, Ward chair Sewell Avery cut wages, fired and transferred employees, and attempted to break the union, the United Retail, Wholesale, and Department Store Employees (URWDSE). The strike was reluctantly endorsed by the CIO national office, while the CP denounced it as irresponsible. Harry Bridges, president of the International Longshoremen's and Warehousemen's Union (ILWU), who was in the CP orbit, even ordered the ILWU-represented war distribution center local in St. Paul, Minnesota, to work overtime during the strike to handle orders unable to be filled in Chicago. (Lichtenstein 1982:213). So much for solidarity.

The CP's stance during World War II was complicated and defies simple description. Officially, they did not support work stoppages of African-American workers against discrimination and balked at large-scale antidiscrimination campaigns in aircraft on the West Coast. They also rejected the "Double V" slogan pushed by Black newspapers (victory against fascism abroad, victory against Jim Crow at home). On the other hand, labor historians have documented extensive evidence of CP activists supporting and leading job actions in maritime, packinghouse, and in FTA-represented plants in Memphis.[17] It is perhaps appropriate to make some additional comments on the Communist Party, whose many efforts in challenging racial domination and in building interracial protest and organizations I have described in positive terms. Its role during the 1930s was complex. How one draws the balance sheet, the nature of one's criticisms and praise, both identifies one's position on the political spectrum, and sometimes even determines, as we have seen, whether one supports or is opposed to racial bigotry, discrimination, and oppression.

There is, of course, a right-wing critique of the CP: that it was a subversive fifth column in American society, anathema to all that is held dear about the American way of life. No tactic in destroying the communists was beyond the pale, whether it was working with the FBI, sabotaging democratic decisions in favor of communists by workers, aligning with racists, supporting repressive dictatorships abroad, and aiding frame-ups and repression. This position, held by some within the labor movement, dovetailed all too well with that of the racist Dixiecrats and extreme opponents of labor. That is why even Walter Reuther when he was a militant trade unionist denounced anti-communism as a tactic of the bosses.

Even leftist opponents of the Communists tended to exaggerate the anti-democratic aspects of CP tactics and organizations, which historical hindsight suggests hardly look worse than the repressive organizations built by non-communists in the mineworkers, steelworkers, or the autoworkers unions after the Reuther group took control. The Trotskyist Socialist Workers Party, usually to the left of the Communists on major class and political issues, was occasionally led astray, while the more unconditionally anti-communist Workers Party did so more often. The support of both groups for the racist SIU is a case in point.

Yet, the CP was a highly contradictory party, difficult many decades later but more so at the time, to place in a balanced perspective. On the one hand, it was the authentic heir of American radicalism, drawing into its orbit many of the dynamic activists from the Socialist Party, the old IWW, the Black socialist milieu, and the left-wing trade union oppositions. Its stance on fighting against racial oppression, whatever its inconsistencies and defects, was far more forthright than any other multi-ethnic, multi-racial grouping.

On the other hand, the Communists were the U.S. outpost and uncritical apologists for the brutal Stalinist regime, often adjusting their policies, even if it meant at times undermining the mass movements, to serve as what Leon Trotsky called "border guards" for Soviet Russia's sometimes narrow foreign policy objectives. At times there was little conflict between these two standpoints. At other times, as during World War II, the conflict was great. At times their moral capital was high, especially in their struggles for racial equality. At other times, it was bankrupt, as when they were fingering opponents for the FBI and "cheering for the imprisonment of the leaders of the Socialist Workers Party," prosecuted as enemy agents under the Smith Act, which would eventually be used against the Communist Party leadership itself in the late 1940s (Cannon 1973:129). James Cannon argues that the rapid decline of the CP when the witch-hunts began was a result of its long history of moral bankruptcy which eventually caught up with them. Perhaps the most intriguing argument about the CP and the potential of the mass movements during the 1930s is the one put forward by Cannon. He argues that the contradictory nature and behaviour of the CP allowed them not only to get important influence and a huge following among the more radical militant workers, but also to use this influence ultimately to undermine, demoralize, and destroy a movement that had much greater revolutionary potential. Cannon's assessment, at such variance with most standard interpretations, is worth quoting at length:

> The chief victim of Stalinism in this country was the magnificent left-wing movement, which arose on the yeast of the economic crisis in the early Thirties and eventually took form in the CIO through a series of veritable labor uprisings. Such a movement, instinctively aimed at American capitalism, was bound to find political leadership. Conditioned by their frightful experiences, the workers in the vanguard of the great mass movement were ready for the most radical solutions. The Stalinists, who appeared to represent the Russian Revolution and the Soviet Union, almost automatically gained the dominating position in the movement.

Yet, the CP betrayed the confidence of the tens of thousands of militants it attracted.

> By their whole policy and conduct; by their unprincipled opportunism, their unscrupulous demogoguery, systematic lying and calculated treachery—the Stalinists demoralized the left-wing labor movement. They squandered its militancy and robbed it of the moral resources to resist the reactionary witch-hunt instituted in the unions with the beginning of the 'cold war.' Murray and Reuther only appear to be the conquerors of the left-wing workers. It was really the Stalinists who beat them. (Cannon 1973b:295–96).

I have written about the CP at greater length elsewhere (see in particular my 1985 article). What is quite clear, however, is that if not for the limitations of the CP as a radical organization, its strategic and often tactical subordination to the dictates of Moscow, the possibilities for interracial, racially egalitarianism would have been immensely greater, potentially transforming the politics and the balance of power in the country as a whole. On the other hand, the high points of its activities, especially in mobilizing workers, white as well as Black, to fight against racial subordination, suggest the possibilities that forthright activities might achieve during those historic turning points that have shaped the United States' whole history.

In sum, the 1930s and the 1940s changed dramatically the role of the national government, creating numerous national social programs and policies. The period brought the question of the rights of African-Americans and their role in society to center stage in a way that had not existed since the Civil War and Reconstruction. African-Americans themselves, led by Black workers and their struggles, emerged as both the most militant, solidaristic component of the working class, as well as the leading force demanding equality for Blacks and a fulfillment of the promises of the Declaration of Independence. The question of Black rights and its rhetorically unquestioned moral necessity was once more a staple of national politics.

Yet, although some New Deal policies were to open opportunities for African-Americans, others were to close them (like housing) or stigmatize them (as with much of social welfare). Importantly, the increased narrowness and bureacratization of union organizations, as well as its retreat from racial egalitarian policies, would shape the changing definition of what constituted civil rights and the changing alliance of forces that would be pushing civil rights issues.

1. Much of the material for this section I have gleaned from a superb unpublished manuscript by Diane Feeley (1983).

2. Roosevelt's Secretary of Labor Frances Perkins notes the dominance of unemployment over all national political life in 1933 (Perkins 1946:182–83).

3. Even those largely hostile to the role of radicals in the mass movements generally recognized these connections:

Literally tens and maybe hundreds of thousands of American workers who might not otherwise ever have heard of radical political parties and programs, became sympathizers of these programs. Having found that the left-wing leadership of their unemployed organization fought militantly for their benefit on a day-to-day basis and in a great number of places and instances won real measures of success, workers certainly must have been less suspicious or even enthusiastic supporters, of left-wing leadership if they found it in local unions which

they subsequently joined (Karsh and Garman 1957:96).

4. Those who try to diminish the significance of these strikes and the importance of the reversal of the previous fourteen-year stagnation in the labor movement are, in my opinion, inattentive to the most important aspects of social reality. For a recent attempt to downgrade their importance, see Colin Gordon (1994:212).

5. Although the CP as an organization composed largely of immigrant ethnic unemployed and employed white workers was itself not devoid of racism, it moved resolutely during the early 1930s to control and eradicate much of it. For further discussion and detailed references see Goldfield 1980.

6. For more detailed information and references, see Goldfield 1980 and 1985. An interesting strain of argument may be found in Lembcke (1988) and the pathbreaking work of Regensburger (1987). Both argue that CP organizers made an important difference in the South. Regensburger writes that the broad class perspective and militant interracialism of the CP was the key variable in those industries where unions succeeded in the South during the 1930s and 1940s. The main characteristic, according to Regensburger, of those industries that were not successfully organized was the absense or exclusion of the CP from the organizing campaigns and obtuseness or caution on the race question.

7. Reston states that it is a "clear fact that both parties in the last half-century have adjusted their policies and prejudices to a changing political and economic world, and have actually come closer to one another on major domestic and foreign policies than any two major parties in any other modern nation in the world" (New York Times, 10-26-88).

8. For a dated, but still highly useful collection of materials, see Block and Dworkin's *The IQ Controversy* (1976).

9. For differing opinions and summaries of arguments, see Higgs 1976; Kirby 1983, 1984; and Fligstein 1981.

10. See Meier and Rudwick 1979:162–74, for a detailed account; see also Martin Glaberman 1988 for a critique of their interpretation of the Packard strike.

11. For detailed descriptions, see Herbert Hill 1985:274–308; and Winkler 1972; for a more critical perspective on the TWU leadership, see Meier and Rudwick 1982.

12. For detailed references on Cannon's remarks, see Goldfield 1985.

13. Note, for example, the highly positive early evaluation by Cayton and Mitchell (1939:224).

14. For opposite evaluations of the progress of the union and its commitment to racial egalitarianism in Birmingham during the 1940s and 1950s, see Norrell 1991 and Stein 1991b.

15. For a more detailed analysis and references on the degeneration of the steelworkers, see my two articles in *ILWCH*, 1993 and 1994.

16. Numerous documents in the papers of the Southern Organizing Committee of the CIO make this clear. See, e.g., the letter from Van Bittner, national director of the committee, to James E. Fadling, right-wing president of the IWA, July 31, 1946; also the report of Bittner's state director for Virginia, himself a conservative CIO official, dated May 31, 1949, complaining about the IWA.

17. See my 1993 for references.

CHAPTER 7

The Post–World War II Period

> The struggles of the American workers and soldiers became inter-
> linked and confronted the American capitalist ruling class with an
> invincible power....In the twelve months following V-J Day more than
> 5,000,000 workers engaged in strikes. For the number of strikers, their
> weight in industry and the duration of the struggle, the 1945-46 strike
> wave in the U.S. surpassed anything of its kind in any capitalist coun-
> try, including the British General Strike of 1926....It is clear, in ret-
> rospect, that the American monopolies stood helpless before this awe-
> some display of labor power. Art Preis 1964:275–76

> The consequences of C.I.O. success will benefit the whole country
> politically....On the day that the South is finally organized, the death
> knell will sound for the elective restrictions which deprive the poor
> white and the Negro of their votes. More information and better edu-
> cation will follow in the wake of unionization. The combination spells
> the beginning of the end of the long domination by prejudice—it
> means a happy goodby to the Bilbos and the Rankins. A.G. Mezerik
> in *The Nation*

There exist numerous opposing interpretations of the immediate
post–World War II period. For many conservatives, it was the return
to normalcy after the 1930s upheavals, a golden age that was to last through
the 1950s, of prosperity, conformity, suburbanization, adherence to religious,
family, and patriotic values—before the 1960s upheaval that brought irre-
sponsibility and a decline in respect for both hard work and established
authority, sexual liberation, long hair and beards, rebellious Blacks and
women, who no longer knew their place, flag burning, draft dodging, and
riots. For many liberals and social democrats, the period was a time of lost
opportunity, when the possibilities for extending the New Deal and increasing the strength of the putative labor/liberal/civil rights coalition seem to
have slipped away. Both popular interpretations, I will argue, are wistful
and fail to take into account broader and underlying features of social reality, including the evolution of industrial unions, the course of race relations, and the development of the world economy. The lens of race will
again prove central, especially as the implications of the 1930s turning point

played themselves out. In exploring these issues and highlighting the centrality of race, my approach will again be a bit roundabout. I will begin with a brief examination of the world economy and the role of the United States within it. Although international politics and economics have arguably always been essential to understanding domestic politics, from World War II on they are the indispensable context. I will then explore three Congress of Industrial Organizations (CIO) campaigns during 1946 which suggest the diminishing capacities of the labor movement to appeal to broad sectors of the population, the decline in its moral hegemony, and the consequent failure to extend unionization to additional segments of the population. Finally, I will be examining the 1948 presidential election campaign and the role that racial issues played both in Harry Truman's upset victory and the bolt of the Deep South Democrats in the Dixiecrat movement from the Democratic Party.

THE 1946 CONJUNCTURE

Let us begin with the world economy. Although the United States was already edging out the United Kingdom as the strongest capitalist economy during the interwar period, after World War II it assumed a new position of dominance. The magnitude and degree of U.S. supremacy is instructive.

First, all other economically developed economies besides the United States had been drastically disrupted by the war. Although it was undoubtedly true, contrary to wartime propaganda, that productive capacities were largely intact in both Europe and Japan, economic life in most economically developed countries was in shambles. In Japan, half the housing in the major cities was destroyed, while Tokyo, Osaka, and Kobe had been largely evacuated. In Europe as well, starvation and its accompanying diseases (tuberculosis, dysentery, typhoid, rickets, and infant mortality) were widespread. The transportation system, including bridges and railroads, were immobilized, and food and fuel were in short supply. Japanese and European shipping had been virtually eliminated. Although only 296,000 Americans had died, the allies had lost 40 million lives, including 15 million civilians (Armstrong and Glyn 1991:22–23; F. Greene 1970:96; Hobsbawm 1994:50–51).

In contrast, the U.S. economy had grown immensely. Gross National Product (GNP), which had fallen from $100 billion in 1929 to $56 billion in 1933 and was still only at $91 billion in 1939, climbed to $210 billion in 1944 (*Economic Report of the President* 1984:220). Shipping capacity had tripled and the United States gained unchallenged global naval supremacy (Armstrong and Glyn 1991:29). Having 5.7 percent of the world's population, the United States had almost half of the world's wealth, harvested one-third of the world's wheat, picked half of its cotton, smelted 55 percent of its steel and other basic metals, pumped 70 percent of world oil, used 50 percent of the rubber, generated 45 percent of the electrical energy, produced 60 percent of the world's manufactured goods, possessed 81 percent of the automobiles, flew 83 percent of the world's civilian aircraft, and enjoyed 45 percent of the world's annual income (F. Greene 1970:95). The world's dominant military power had over 400 U.S. military bases around the globe (Lotta 1984:220–21) and was the only one with the atomic bomb. U.S. technology and productivity of labor was far ahead of that of its competitors (Bowles, Gordon, Weisskopf 1983:69; Mandel 1975:202). With the collapse of the pound sterling, the U.S. dollar became the dominant world currency, backed by U.S. gold in Fort Knox which represented two-thirds of the world's reserves (Armstrong and Glyn 1991:23; Wolfe 1981:14) up from one-third in 1934 (Lotta 1984:221). With the Europeans and Japanese dependent on U.S. imports and their recovery dependent on American policies, the U.S. dictated the terms of the Bretton Woods currency stabilization and the set up of the International Monetary Fund (IMF) and the World Bank, overriding objections by the world's former bankers in London (Armstrong and Glyn 1991:28–29; Bowles, Gordon, Weisskopf 1983:65). The new headquarters quite naturally set up shop in New York City.

Preaching open markets and independence for Europe's colonies, U.S. business replaced Britain and other imperialist powers around the world. The U.S. share of Middle Eastern oil output rose from 16 percent in 1939 to 31 percent in 1946 and 60 percent in 1953, at a time when little of it was needed for domestic consumption (Armstrong and Glyn 1991:30). U.S. corporations likewise penetrated markets and gained control of raw material production in Africa and Asia (Lotta 1984:221–22). Even Latin America, commonly thought of as a U.S. satellite, had seen more European than North American investment as late as 1938, with Argentina being a special British concentration point. After World War II, U.S. companies gained unchallenged sway (Lotta 1984:191, 194, 217). These new prerogatives were jealously protected and backed up by military force when occasion arose (e.g., Bowles, Gordon, Weisskopf 1984:66–67).

The war and the role of the United States in the world economy and world affairs had important domestic implications, which I shall attempt to highlight over the course of this and succeeding chapters. The relation of class forces at the end of World War II, though quite complex, was decidedly different than it was before hostilities had begun. Business in particular emerged from the war immensely stronger than it had been in the 1930s. First, it was more concentrated and much wealthier. For example, the fifty-six largest arms manufacturers secured 75 percent of all defense contracts, while corporate profits skyrocketed from $6.3 billion in 1939 to

$23.8 billion in 1944 (*Historical Statistics* 1975:I:236; Preis 1964:157–58, 203–4, 301). Second, business's image had improved. By the war's end, corporate America was largely politically rehabilitated. Discredited during the Great Depression in the eyes of the vast majority of the population, they were now viewed by many much more positively. During the 1930s, they were seen as people and institutions whose selfishness had caused suffering and economic collapse; now they were seen in part as those that had helped win the war against fascism. The fact that thousands of business officials had worked in the war apparatus with no pay from the government did not hurt their new personae (Wolfe 1981:16). They had not only seemingly worked selflessly but also successfully organized the war economy, providing sufficient military supplies for the troops as well as full employment at home. Third, during the 1930s, strong antibusiness and antimilitary sentiment among the general population had meant that close relations between politicians and business had a political price.[1] During the war, businessmen and their priorities soon came to dominate virtually every aspect of policy making, giving business much greater leverage and more direct influence than it had enjoyed previously. Labor unions became completely isolated. Reformers were soon replaced with conservative business types.

Workers, however, were not without their own resources. Labor unions had stabilized their presence in basic industry across the country during the war, growing from 10 million to 14 million members. In their unions, workers had mass organizations that were capable of powerfully affecting all levels of society. Unions were also viewed positively by the overwhelming majority of the population, not the least of which involved the large percentage of military veterans among their ranks (Goldfield 1987:10, 35). The end of the war found resentment of the upper class amongst virtually all segments of the working-class population. In addition, as George Lipsitz (1994) notes in several perceptive chapters, the upsurges of the 1930s and the increased influence of unions had brought working-class cultural issues to the fore in a way that had not previously existed in the United States. Wartime workers, whose factory experience had a continuing influence on their art, included Marilyn Monroe, Hank Williams, Chester Himes, and Robert Mitchum. The war led to an increase in the popularity of working-class music, both from the African-American blues and jazz traditions and from white southern country music. Thus, it is no accident that the recently departed Bill Monroe, the founder of bluegrass music, was launched into national prominence and popularity during this period. In the current period of high levels of racial hostility, it is often hard to comprehend the degree to which race relations had changed during World War II. The growth of integrated industrial workforces and the saliency of issues of racial equality during the war, including the militant stances of certain left-wing CIO unions, had encouraged a tremendous cross-fertilization among white and black musicians. As Lipsitz argues, it was this context that not only would lead to the cultural emergence and eventual dominance of rock and roll music in the 1950s, but expressed and made relevant many of the experiences, contradictions, problems, and aspirations of working-class life (Lipsitz 1994).

Perhaps the most important of those changes that emerged from the struggles in the 1930s and the wartime experience was the changed situation of African-American workers. Strengthened by their own organizations (by the late 1940s, approximately 1.5 million Black workers had joined organized labor unions) the importance of the Black vote in the North, and the critical importance African-American workers had in the CIO, Black demands had a more central role in U.S. social and political life (Wynn 1975:173). The antiracist ideology that was a key feature of wartime antifascist propaganda at home and the existence of large numbers of African-American veterans gave Black issues an increased saliency.

Capitalists and workers thus battled for advantage on numerous fronts. Three CIO campaigns, however, represented critical turning points for labor —one campaign an ostensible success, one a nonstarter, and another a clear failure. Much of the narrowness and class collaborationist policies of the CIO, which had hardened during the war, came to a head in 1946, undermining its class solidarity and its independence of the government and corporations, foreclosing the possibilities for a fundamental transformation of American politics, and setting the terms for the failure to resolve the racial dilemmas that remain with us today.

THE 1946 STRIKE WAVE

During World War II, unions had forsworn strikes, placing themselves at the mercy of federal government labor boards for wage increases and the settlement of grievances. Large corporations made huge profits (corporate profits averaged between 20 and 40 percent during the war), further gaining government-subsidized facilities and huge tax write-offs. Workers, on the other hand, subservient to business-controlled labor boards, were left with loss of hourly earnings due to inflation, long hours, rationed and limited goods, and with many unsettled grievances (Preis 1964:157).

As the war ended, economic pressures on workers mounted. Hours worked dropped substantially. Average hours worked went from 45.2 a week in January 1945 to 40.3 in January 1946 mostly due to decreases in overtime in war-related industries (Armstrong and Glyn 1991:73–74; *Historical Statistics* 1975:I:169). This process was especially pronounced among male manufacturing workers whose average weekly hours declined from 46.9 to 40.4, which resulted, even with extensive inflation, in a reduction of average week-ly income from $54.65 in 1944 to $50.72 in 1946 (*Historical Statistics* 1975: I:172). V-J Day in mid-August led to the overnight cancelling of some $24 billion in war contracts. The result was a wave of layoffs and downgrading. Unemployment, which had fallen to 800,000 in August 1945, jumped to 2.7 million by March 1946. Despite steady wage gains throughout the war (the average manufacturing wage increased from 86 cents an hour in 1939 to $1.03 an hour in 1945), the elimination of overtime and a dramatic upsurge in prices (the Consumer Price Index rose from 52.7 in 1944 to 66.9 in 1946) resulted in a 15 percent decline in real income in the first three months fol-lowing the war's end (*Historical Statistics* 1975:I:210; Finklestein 1992:41; Lichtenstein 1982:221, footnote 48; Lipsitz 1994:99).

By the end of the war, the cutback in hours of work, rise in prices (for example, the cost of chuck roast and round steak doubled after price con-trols were lifted), and producer-induced shortages where prices had been frozen led to a deterioration of living standards. Returning veterans faced these same conditions when they were lucky enough to find jobs; when they were not, they joined the ranks of the unemployed (*Historical Statistics* 1975:I:213).

In reaction to these conditions and under immense pressure from their members, unions across the country launched a broad wage offensive. As many analysts have noted, the 1946 strike wave was, in terms of number of strikes (4,985), numbers of strikers (4.6 million), and number of days of work lost (116 million), the largest that this country has ever seen (*Handbook of Labor Statistics* 1978:508). There was tremendous union solidarity, exten-sive community support, and in those rare cases where strike breakers were brought in or unions were threatened, general strikes sometimes took place. Ostensibly, the 1946 strike wave was a huge success for unions. Most sig-nificant was the 18.5 cent increase granted by GM that set the bargaining pattern for the rest of the industrial sector and pushed manufacturing wages upward throughout the country—the average manufacturing wage increased from $1.01 an hour in 1945 to $1.22 and hour by 1947 (*Handbook of Labor Statistics* 1978:313). There were no killings and little violence as in past large-scale labor disputes. There were no large-scale firings or replaced workers. No union organizations were broken. Finally, unions had made strong showings and proved that they were a unified force with which to be reck-oned (Lichtenstein 1982:229–30; Brecher 1972:228–30)

Still, the glorification of this massive strike wave, by many who are impressed by its breadth and potential (including Art Preis and George Lipsitz) is, I argue, greatly misplaced. For large-scale strikes involve not only ready and militant workers but also demands, strategies, and leadership. In these latter aspects, the 1946 strike wave was grossly inferior to the big strike waves of the 1930s, helping to isolate and weaken workers and their unions rather than to strengthen their organizations, especially politically, and laying the basis for retreat on issues of racial solidarity.

The strikes of the 1930s, beginning with the 1934 strikes, helped to temporarily unify a variety of aggrieved constituencies, including the unemployed, farmers, African Americans, and non-union workers, along with urban ethnics and newly unionizing workers. A far-sighted leadership in 1946 would have similarly developed a broadened appeal to working-class constituencies throughout the population, including unemployed veterans, African-Americans, and women workers. With exceptions here and there, little attempt was made to do this. Except in occasional rhetoric, organized labor's postwar agenda never included broad class demands, such as universal healthcare and pensions, the extension of the Fair Labor Standards Act (including minimum wages, overtime provisions, and so on) and the National Labor Relations Board (NLRB) to agricultural workers in the South and West (many of whom were Black and Latino) and to domestic workers (many of whom were African-American women), the universalization of social welfare programs, the rebuilding of cities including adequate mass transportation systems, the ending of racial discrimination and anticity biases in federal housing programs, and the need for full employment. With the exception of a small number of left-wing unions, little prominence was given to the special demands of African-American workers, although the symbolic and detached manner in which these demands were pushed by liberals often served to heighten the fears of working-class whites. And except for the electrical workers and one or two other left-wing unions, women workers were totally abandoned as they were laid off out of seniority and found by management to be incompetent to work at jobs they had successfully performed throughout the war. This phenomenon took place in industries across the country and few unions made it a major issue. At one International Harvester plant in Chicago, represented by the racially progressive Communist Party (CP)-led Farm Equipment Workers Union that had a large percentage of women workers during the war, women workers were given tests that few men would have passed—including climbing up multistory ladders carrying heavy objects—and fired for incompetence. When the bloodletting ended, only a handful of women workers were left in this plant (L. Cohen 1990; Faue 1991).

Contrary to the claims of many, spontaneous working-class activity, however solidaristic and joyous, only carries workers so far without broad social demands and farsighted leadership. Despite his occasional rhetoric to the contrary, the epitome of this narrow perspective was perhaps Walter Reuther, elected president of the United Auto Workers (UAW) in 1946. Blinded by the intensity of their anticommunism and not especially sensitive to the importance of issues of racial discrimination, certain left groups that had played an important role in the UAW opposing the no-strike pledge during World War II mistakenly gave full support to Reuther at a critical juncture in his struggle for leadership in the union. Although soon to regret their decision, the Trotskyist Socialist Workers Party supported Reuther in 1946, while the more anticommunist Workers Party continued to do so in 1947, when the corporatist and undemocratic direction of Reuther's caucus was even more clear.

INFLATION AND PRICE CONTROLS

The narrow agenda of the 1946 strike wave was mirrored in other important social struggles. Especially noteworthy were the protests over price gauging, price control, and food shortages. In 1946, inflation and consumer product shortages were considered by two-thirds of the population as the country's number-one problem. In April 1946, 82 percent favored a continuation of the wartime price controls, despite the unanimous opposition of business and the Republican Party. As producers withheld goods, restaurants and grocery stores experienced major food shortages, with meat almost disappearing. When price controls expired on June 30, 1946, goods suddenly reappeared, with meat in New York City rising in price an average of 30 percent. When a new price-control bill was passed, meat disappeared again. The unwillingness of Congress to deal with the issues of inflation and shortages caused a large backlash against the Democrats and was a major factor in their defeat in the 1946 national elections. Here was an issue with wide class appeal, an issue that labor unions could have seized, made a national issue, and set forth a strategy of militant action. The CIO, however, was long on rhetoric and short on action, calling on consumers to engage in a buyers' strike to hold down prices. Although the Democratic-controlled New York City Council, in response to heavy public pressure from its constituents, voted 19 to 2 in October 1946 to call on President Truman to seize all meat in the country from ranchers and distribute it fairly to the public, the CIO shied away from such proposals. Reuther, as usual, helped demobilize workers by denouncing the government and corporations in quite radical language, warning of the danger of fascism and threatening a national strike; this was all mere rhetoric, no action being planned or taken. The only strategy offered by top CIO leaders was to reelect an even more Democratic Congress. As Steven Ashby notes, "On July 16, 100,000 workers demonstrated in Detroit's Cadillac Square, demanding the government return to wartime price controls. Reuther spoke to the crowd, but despite his fiery language and calls for class warfare against the wealthy elite, he offered little in the way of a strategy to combat the business-induced inflation and shortages" (Ashby 1993:275, 277, 281, 285, 288, 289, 292).

Workers became disillusioned. "Particularly within the auto workers union, a segment of militant workers were disgusted with the meek strategy of the CIO leadership and its focus on telling workers to write letters to their congressional representatives in support of price controls, to give a dollar to the CIO Political Action Committee, to turn out and vote in the November elections and defeat Republican congressional representatives, and to boycott overpriced consumer goods" (Ashby 1993:292). The CIO leadership strategy was a dismal failure, because workers in the meantime had to buy food, overpriced or not, so that they could eat. This important chapter is surprisingly missing from Nelson Lichtenstein's recent book which tends to gloss over these aspects of Walter Reuther's career (Lichtenstein 1995; for a critical review, see Goldfield 1997).

The overall CIO strategy helped to isolate it from the population at large including nonunion workers and played an important role in demoralizing rank-and-file union members, leaving them far more inclined to rely heavily on more narrow, self-protective strategies, both at work and in the community, even when such an approach for whites would lead them to act in a divisive racist manner. Early in 1946, CIO unions had led massive, disruptive strikes for their own members, but doing little on broader class issues. In this context, the enormous business and media assault on unions began to take its toll, as "many non-unionists began to believe the business leaders and newspaper editorials that blamed the Democrats, the CIO, and striking unions for inflicting economic chaos upon the country" (Ashby 1993:294). Thus, during the course of 1946, unions not only failed to build broad support for their own economic or broad class demands, but lost public support. By the time of the November 1946 elections, many workers abandoned the Democrats, either voting Republican or staying home.

One might ask what all this has to do with race. Quite a bit I will claim. Workers often correctly perceive broad class strategies as risky, potentially in conflict with their most pressing, immediate interests—although there exist many inspiring exceptions. In times of extensive upsurges of class activity and when workers have great confidence in their organizations and movements, overwhelming majorities of workers are willing to break with narrow, defensive, circumscribed strategies and reach for wider goals—including white workers rejecting notions of white racial identity and risking sanctions that often result from challenging the prevailing system of racial domination. When the balance of class forces is tilted overwhelmingly against workers and their organizations, as has been the case in the 1980s and most of the 1990s, when workers have low levels of confidence in their organizations and leadership, when the penalties for supporting a union organizing drive can be harsh (including likely, even if illegal, discharge), workers become understandably reluctant even actively to support unions.

Thus, demobilizing strategies by leaders and the resulting demoralization can turn workers who might have been open to supporting broad, more solidaristic, racially egalitarian approaches, to acting in a more narrow racial manner. Thus, in Detroit, racial politics was not only contradictory among whites but also evolved in a worse direction, as the UAW itself became more narrow and bureaucratized. Certain labor historians today reject such a broader understanding of racial issues and adhere to a more static analysis. Bruce Nelson, for example, in recent work in which he now claims that he is being more realistic and accurate, has evolved from one who gave a relatively nuanced analysis of racial approaches of the CIO and racial attitudes among white unionized workers, to a one-dimensional approach that now views white workers as always and forever white racists (Nelson 1996). Such an approach, however, is not borne out by the facts. In Detroit, as the UAW leadership under Walter Reuther became more bureaucratic and racially insensitive, white unionized workers often saw their immediate interests better represented by white racist neighborhood protective home owners associations, rather than by broader, more racially egalitarian approaches (see, e.g., Sugrue 1995). Although it is important to note and attempt to understand these widespread racist reactions by many white workers, it is wrong to succumb to psycho-cultural reductionism and see the reactions as inevitable, unrelated to broader questions of social and political development and the character of organizational leadership. The emerging hegemony of narrow corporatist strategies in the 1940s CIO was to have broad implications for the development of the labor movement and race relations throughout the rest of the twentieth century.

THE FAILURE OF OPERATION DIXIE

The deficiencies of the CIO's limited strategic perspective all converged to ensure one of the great tragedies for American labor and all of U.S. society: the failure of Operation Dixie, the CIO's attempt in the post–World War II period to organize the South. Operation Dixie was a campaign that might well have succeeded. The successful organization of the South by a militant, interracial, racially egalitarian CIO would have dramatically transformed not just the South but all of U.S. politics and society. Such a result would have added a decidedly positive note to the 1930s turning point. Its failure, that is, the defeat of interracial unionism in the South, on the other hand, is the most important factor on which to focus to understand all of U.S. politics from World War II up until the present time. In that sense it represents perhaps an additional, albeit negative, turning point all unto itself.

WHY THE CIO WANTED TO ORGANIZE THE SOUTH

The organization of the South had been an unfinished item on organized labor's agenda since the nineteenth century. The reasons for wanting to organize the South were numerous and interrelated, if anything having grown more urgent with the substantial union growth in all parts of the country during the previous decade and with the acceleration of industrial development in the South during World War II. The first reason was economic. As a CIO executive officer recommendation stated:

> The CIO knows full well that organized workers in the North, East and West will remain insecure until the South is solidly organized. The CIO knows full well that wage standards of unionists throughout the country remain in jeopardy as long as a North-South wage pay differential exists. The CIO knows full well that the entire nation would be better off economically if the South were organized. (Recommendations of the Executive Officers, August 30-31, 1948; Operation Dixie Papers, Box 242)

Second, many in the CIO—especially those on the left—believed that equality for African-Americans and democracy for white as well as Black citizens —especially of the lower classes—could not be achieved without labor organization throughout the South. Finally, the achievement of democracy as a result of interracial labor organization would lead inevitably to the transformation of southern politics and the ousting of many Dixiecrat politicians, who were obstacles to the broad social legislation demanded by the urban/labor/left/civil rights coalition. As an article in *The Nation* argued:

> The Consequences of C.I.O. success will benefit the whole country politically....On the day that the South is finally organized, the death knell will sound for the elective restrictions which deprive the poor white and the Negro of their votes. More information and better education will follow in the wake of unionization. The combination spells the beginning of the end of the long domination by prejudice—it means a happy goodby to the Bilbos and the Rankins. (Mezerik 1947)

THE POTENTIAL OF OPERATION DIXIE

For many union leaders 1946 seemed to be an especially propitious time to launch a new, finally successful southern-organizing campaign. As Alan Haywood stated at the March 14, 1946 CIO executive board meeting, "The South is ripe and ready" (Minutes of the CIO Executive Board, 1946:197).

The political economy of the South had been dramatically transformed during World War II. From the end of the Civil War through the 1930s, southern life and politics had been dominated by cotton agriculture, based on subsistence-level tenancy. The poverty of southern agricultural workers had set the terms for a nationally isolated southern regional labor market. The war had seen $4.5 billion invested in southern war plants, including huge ship-building facilities in Pascagoula, Mississippi, and Mobile, Alabama, aircraft-manufacturing centers in Dallas-Fort Worth and Atlanta-Marietta, along with airplane assembly plants in other cities. Nuclear facilities led by Oak Ridge, Tennessee's 40,000-employee facility, sprang up in the South. Petroleum, chemicals, steel, and various other forms of manufacturing expanded, while the war also gave a boost to traditional low-wage southern industries, including textile and apparel (Cobb 1984:51–52; Bartley 1995:10–11). National military facilities were disproportionately located in the South (35 percent of the national total, according to Cobb 1984:51) and helped inject another $4 to $5 billion into the southern economy.

Between 1940 and 1945, 4 million people left southern agriculture, representing almost a 25 percent decline. Cotton production was under intense pressure. U.S. share of the world market had declined from 72 percent in 1911 to 38 percent in 1941, as India, Brazil, China, and Egypt undercut the South's labor-intensive prices (Fite 1984:175). Domestic cotton production began to move to the more highly mechanized large farms in Texas, Arizona, and California. Finally, synthetic fibers began to successfully compete with cotton; Rayon, e.g., went from being only .3 percent of the fiber market in 1919 to 10.6 percent in 1943 (Fite 1984:175). Southern farmers began slowly to diversify to soybeans, peanuts, and livestock. These trends all signaled the lessening importance of southern agriculture, but especially of the southern cotton plantation system.

War production drew many Black and white southerners off the land and to northern industry or southern cities. By 1945, the number of southern industrial workers had increased by 800,000 from before the war (Honey 1993:214). The nationalization of the southern labor market led to labor shortages in both industry and agriculture, as southern agricultural wages tripled (Fite 1984:168; Wright 1978:241). Higher wages, however, did not always have a beneficial impact on African-American workers in the South. In metal mining, companies reversed previous policies and began disproportionately hiring white workers. Mechanization of coal mining caused the termination of a majority of the region's Black miners, many of whom were replaced by lower seniority, newly hired whites. In many modern industries such as rubber, employers began to reserve the jobs largely for whites. The most dramatic effect was in lumber and sawmills, which had been the single most important source of nonagricultural jobs for Black teenage males, who were virtually eliminated from these positions by 1960; even in 1950, the northern cities where these unskilled Black teenagers were moving presented "distinctly uninviting labor markets to them" (Wright 1978:250–51; Cogan 1982:621). Most new jobs in the region were also reserved for whites (Wright 1978:2). But this phenomemon was of little interest to the bulk of the postwar leaders of the CIO.

The entwinement of the southern economy with the federal government and the acceptance of a large amount of federal largess, including jobs, agricultural subsidies, and investment, finally led to the acceptance of certain national policies, in particular the rights of workers under the National Labor Relations Act. Though certainly not willing enthusiastically to embrace unions, southern employers by the end of World War II had largely abandoned the violence that had typified their earlier approach to labor-management relations.

Black union membership had also expanded dramatically during the war. Although only 150,000 Black workers were organized in 1935, 550,000 were by 1940, and by the war's end, 1.25 million Black workers were active union members (Marable 1991:15; Wynn 1975:58).

All in all, unions seemed to have good reasons to be optimistic. Trade union membership had increased from less than 3 million members in 1933 to more than 14 million in 1945. Thus, the commitment of enormous attention, energies, and resources to organizing the South by both labor federations seemed to promise grand results. During World War II, there had been significant union growth across the South. Industrial centers including Gadsden and Birmingham, Alabama; Laurel, Mississippi; Savannah and Atlanta, Georgia; Baton Rouge, Bogalusa, and New Orleans, Louisiana; Galveston, Texas; Memphis, Tennessee; and Tampa, Florida had all become heavily unionized. Union organizing successes ranged across the main southern industries, including coal, metal mining, oil refining, mass transit, tobacco, pulp wood and paper, and even major textile mills in the Piedmont region. In its November 1946 issue, *Fortune* magazine, no friend of unions, saw resistance to unions as weak and complete unionization of the South as inevitable. Robert R. Mason, the president of the National Association of Manufacturers, "predicted success for C.I.O.'s efforts to unionize the South" according to the June 1, 1946 issue of *Business Week*.

Now, there is considerable debate over whether or not Operation Dixie could have been successful. The reader should be advised that I occupy a pole in this discussion that answers the question in the affirmative. The prevailing orthodoxy, however, argues that Operation Dixie could not have been. There is a standard, commonly accepted argument that the South could not have been organized at any time during the 1930s and 1940s. This approach stresses the concentration of industry (particularly textile, the South's largest) in company towns dominated by an interlocking structure of factory owners, church officials, politicians, law-enforcement officers, newspaper editors, and others, with little concern for the democratic and constitutional rights of their opponents, particularly union organizers. In addition, commitment to the status quo and opposition to unionism (often by necessity interracial) was reenforced by a powerful system of white supremacy that dominated all other aspects of political and social life in the South (see, e.g., Key 1949). Opposition to unions was strengthened by an ideological hegemony rooted in southern traditionalism. Workers themselves were imbued with conservatism, generally supporting the status quo. The predominantly agrarian background of most workers helped strengthen both submissive and highly individualistic traits, judged to be intrinsic to southern character and antithetical to union membership. Though some of these features existed piecemeal in the North, there was no general parallel, so the argument goes, in other parts of the country. This explanation for the failure of unions to organize the South is put forward, by among others, Liston Pope and more recently by Barbara Griffith. Although this argument has its prima facie compelling features, it is not, in my opinion, unproblematic. There were a number of industries in the South that were successfully organized during the 1930s and 1940s. These include coal mining, metal mining, oil refining, longshore and maritime, tobacco, transportation, federal government facilities (e.g., Oak Ridge's 40,000 nuclear workers and the Tennessee Valley Authority), and a bit later telephone. Careful comparisons of these industries with textile lead one to ask a number of questions, including the degree to which these latter industries shared many of the characteristics that supposedly led union organizing to fail in textile. If the successful arenas were similar to those where unions were unsuccessful, then some additional variables must be located. Perhaps the strategies of unions and organizers were the main determinants. I argue that it was the approach of the CIO right that helped derail the labor movement in the post–World War II period.

STRATEGY OF THE CIO RIGHT

The CIO's Operation Dixie, officially declared at the CIO executive board meeting of mid-March 1946, was from the start controlled completely by the CIO right-wingers. Rather than being conceived as a militant mass mobilization campaign like many of those in the 1930s and early 1940s, the CIO right-wing wanted a corporate strategy, somewhat along the lines of the Hillman-run 1937–38 textile campaign. First, it wanted to appear completely respectable, to be seen as legitate, patriotic, and southern. Appeals were made to southern elites; arguments were made to businessmen about the benefits of unionism for their businesses. The CIO also attempted to build relations with southern politicians, newspaper editors, and religious leaders. It was in good part further constrained by its close relations with the Democratic Party, a major component of which were the racist southern Dixiecratic local, state-level, and congressional politicians.

Second, a major tenet of this strategy was to deemphasize race. The CIO chose for its point of attack the textile industry in part because it was overwhelmingly white. It downplayed those more racially mixed industries such as tobacco, transportation, and wood, whose initial prospects seemed more promising than textile. Within this context, despite the occasional rhetoric about its commitment to equality for all, the CIO deemphasized race and rarely made strong appeals to Black workers. Statewide Operation Dixie leaders even sent back national CIO literature with interracial pictures. Their racial orientation at times caused them to lose textile elections where the percentages of blacks were high, because they failed to get sufficient support from African-American workers, an almost unheard of problem for CIO unions in the mid- and late 1940s. This cautious, conservative racial strategy achieved no positive results since the CIO was attacked as communist race-mixers by the American Federation of Labor (AFL), Southern manufacturers, and other elites.[2]

Third, another component of the CIO's strategy was to exclude all left-wingers from the Operation Dixie staff, again in order to be respectable and to keep them from getting greater influence within the CIO. This approach led the CIO leadership to bypass precisely those organizers who had been most successful in the South. Because most southern Black organizers tended to be left-wingers, it also led to almost all-white organizing staffs. CIO Operation Dixie organizers were overwhelmingly white male southerners, majority veterans, almost all inexperienced in union organizing campaigns. Again the CIO gained little benefit because the composition of their staff did not keep it from being red-baited, race baited, and attacked as carpetbaggers. Even in the overwhelmingly white textile industry, inexperienced male organizers were the main organizers in an industry that was almost half female. Such was a built-in recipe for failure.

Fourth, even within this respectable corporate strategy, Operation Dixie was even more bureaucratic than Hillman's initially successful textile campaign. Operation Dixie's head, Van Bittner, had a go-it-alone approach, refusing support from other unions and even the liberal Southern Conference for Human Welfare. Because of the desire for respectability and to win acceptance with southern elites, Bittner even forced his staff members to cut their ties with the CIO's own political action committee (PAC), which was often sharply opposed to Dixiecratic politicians. Finally, in defiance of all common sense in mass organizing campaigns, particularly in cases where it was important to organize skeptical workers, Bittner demanded, sometimes in strong opposition to his own conservative lieutenants and state directors, that all workers pay a one-dollar initiation fee before joining, a position that even Hillman had rejected.

The bureaucratism and obtuseness to the importance of solidarity and worker militance, especially to questions of race, led the CIO right into a completely self-defeating strategy. The biggest successes that the CIO right had, especially in the late 1940s, were their raids on left-wing unions, which in some important instances destroyed unionism in those industries. The unions attacked were in many cases interracial and anti-racist, with varying degrees of support among white workers for racial egalitarianism. The most militantly anti-racist white workers, many of whom had large followings among whites as well as blacks and who were almost invariably leftists, were driven out of the unions in maritime, metal mining, and tobacco in the South. Such were the consequences of the CIO right's campaign, not only failing to organize new sources of support but also destroying important interracial bases of opposition to racist southern hegemony that already existed.

CONSEQUENCES

Despite the devotion of substantial resources by unions and optimistic prognoses from many quarters, Operation Dixie failed abysmally.[3] Not only did unions gain few new members and hardly any new stably organized locals, but most of the gains made during World War II were subsequently lost. By the end of the 1940s, the CIO had fewer workers organized in the South than they had at the start of the campaign. Commentator Samuel Lubell calls Operation Dixie, "Operation Fizzle." (Lubell 1952:115)

The consequences of the failure of Operation Dixie and the related narrow campaigns of 1946 and 1947 were manifold. The most obvious consequences were those that took place within the union movement itself. First, the failures and bureaucratic behavior of the CIO leadership further demoralized CIO supporters and allies, which in turn accelerated the process of bureaucratization of the unions. Second, the failure of Operation Dixie marked the end of the dramatic union growth that started in 1933; it also began the steady decline in union density that continues to the present day.[4] The 1945 high of 35 percent of the nonagricultural labor force organized into unions, although approached in 1953, has never been exceeded. Today the figure stands at less than 15 percent; substracting the more recently organized governmental employees, the figure for private-sector workers is 10 percent below the pre-depression level.

Third, unions ended up with reduced support in the population as a whole and within the Democratic Party. As a consequence, workers and their unions suffered a series of important defeats, the most significant of which was the passage of the antilabor Taft-Hartley Act in 1947, which made organizing far more difficult. Finally, the series of failures to extend their organization and develop broad popular support led to a split on tactics within the CIO. The CIO right believed that its only hope for survival was based on a further reliance on the government and the Democratic Party. They backed off even more sharply on issues of race. In order to prove its patriotism, usefulness, and subservience to the powers that be, the right broke with its critical perspective on U.S. foreign policy and became among the more ardent supporters of the Cold War, in many cases working with the Central Intelligence Agency to undermine independent left-wing labor movements in Europe and other parts of the globe. Finally, they allied with the government, businesses, and the most reactionary forces in the country, including on occasion out-and-out racists among whom were the Ku Klux Klan, to launch an all-out attack on the left to drive them out of the labor movement and out of all public life.

The demoralization of labor's ranks and its isolation from its potential allies was nationwide. Thus, those who dream of social-democratic possibilities for the United States after World War II—and support putative anti-communist, social-democratic labor leaders—miss important features of social and political life. Labor unions were isolated even in those states and areas where they were numerically strongest. Liberal racial policies, no longer an integral part of a program of class advancement, class solidarity, and class struggle, often with distinct class biases, were many times seen as alien by white workers, leading to the acceptance of narrow, defensive, racist strategies.

Anti-labor legislation passed easily in northern states that were supposedly bastions of CIO support. In New York, in the wake of the 1947 Buffalo teachers strike, the state legislature enacted the Condin-Wadlin Act, a highly repressive piece of labor legislation. In 1947 in Ohio, a highly unionized state, the strongly anti-labor Ferguson bill was overwhelmingly passed. And by 1950, most union members in Ohio either voted for Robert Taft, the author of the hated piece of legislation bearing his name, or simply stayed home (Lubell 1955:201–9). In 1948, Samuel Lubell revisited labor unions and working-class communities to which he had been in the late 1930s and after the 1940 election. In the earlier period, these CIO strongholds reflected the "dynamic near revolutionary surge" of the late 1930s. By 1948, even in the UAW, "the inner dynamics of Reuther's own union today resemble more closely the momentum of a bureaucracy than the trampling of a new social movement" (Lubell 1955:191–92).

CONSEQUENCES FOR AMERICA

The significance of the failure of Operation Dixie, combined with other events in 1946, may be viewed on deeper levels: The failure to organize the South marginalized the labor movement in national politics. Despite their important regional political influence in the Northeast, the Midwest, and to a lesser extent in California and the Northwest, unions were never able to mobilize Congressional majorities, which would have overcome the combination of the Solid South and traditional Republican and business support in other areas of the country. Nowhere was this more sharply illustrated than in organized labor's inability to stop the passage of the anti-union Taft-Hartley Act in 1947. Characterized by unions as the "slave labor act," both union federations made all-out efforts to defeat it. It was southern Democrats who provided the margin necessary to override President Truman's veto of the act. With labor's weak legislative leverage apparent for all to see, union influence within the Democratic Party declined further; union political demands became more modest.

Rather than being simply another episode in the changing fortunes of organized labor, the inability of unions to organize the South has had even wider social and political ramifications. The failure of Operation Dixie left southern Dixiecrats and the system of white supremacy with complete social, political, and economic hegemony intact in much of the South. Successful unionization was in many instances by necessity interracial and to varying degrees anti-racist. Independent organization in the South by CIO unions—the Mine, Mill, and Smelter Workers, the United Mine Workers, the tobacco workers, the longshoremen, the maritime workers, and the packinghouse workers—were often islands of opposition to racial discrimination and resources in the fight for equality, including campaigns against the poll tax and lynching. Successful unionization of the South would have most likely hastened the civil rights movement by many years.[5] It also would have insured not only more extensive involvement and support from northern unions but also a strong reservoir of southern white working-class support, largely absent from the southern struggles of African-Americans in the 1950s, 1960s, and 1970s. The unionization of the South had the potential to minimize the mobilization of white backlash, a central feature of post–World War II politics.

Southern racist Dixiecrat hegemony allowed for South Carolinian Strom Thurmond's 1948 Dixiecrat Party presidential campaign, a movement that drew its strongest support from whites in the most heavily African-American sections of the South, most notably in South Carolina and Mississippi (Key 1949:329–44). It also made possible George Wallace's 1968 presidential campaign, based on racist populist appeals to white backlash.

These originally regional appeals, however, paved the way for the Republican Party's "southern strategy," a successful attempt to win the support of southern and other whites, many of whom were traditional Democratic voters. And it is the failure of Operation Dixie, I would contend, that has allowed the Republican southern strategy, from Presidents Nixon to Bush, to be successful in shaping the more recent decades of American politics.

The consequences of labor's failure were indeed momentous.

THE 1948 ELECTIONS

On April 12, 1945, Harry Truman succeeded FDR as president of the United States. By August, he had bombed Hiroshima and Nagasaki and was presiding over the ending of World War II. The international political economy and domestic politics were tightly meshed at war's end. As the political leader of the world's dominant power, President Truman needed to play a number of interrelated roles.

Domestically, he sought to maintain social stability and business confidence in order to facilitate conversion of the wartime economy, high corporate profits, and continued economic growth. At the same time, he needed to satisfy or at least provide the political salve for a number of mobilized New Deal constituencies. This was a complicated task to which we shall turn in a moment.

Internationally, the U.S. government wished to maintain the political and economic conditions for increased U.S. trade, investments, and profits, using a wide range of tactics. The United States preached the moral imperatives of colonial independence, with the concomitant opening up of the colonial economies to U.S. trade and investment along with free trade the world over. In Japan and West Germany, U.S. occupation forces initially encouraged unionization so that American companies would not have to compete with the products of highly trained and educated yet low-paid labor forces. Most early aid from the United States to the war-torn countries was in the form of emergency relief, while the initial post-war loans usually had strict conditions attached. In this approach, as in foreign affairs later on, Truman had overwhelming bipartisan support.

At some point, the emphasis in foreign affairs began to change. Although the signal for the Cold War by the West against the Soviet Union had been given on March 5, 1946, by Winston Churchill in his Fulton, Missouri, "Iron Curtain" speech, it was formally launched in this country only on March 12, 1947. On that date, President Truman, in a speech to Congress, called for economic and military aid to Greece and Turkey. The so-called Truman Doctrine signaled that the U.S. government was willing to pull out all the stops to contain Soviet influence, including the brutal repression of a massive, communist-led guerrilla insurgency in Greece. On June 5, 1947, Secretary of State George Marshall announced a European recovery program, including extensive aid to rebuild the Western European economies. In November, a similar shift took place toward Japan, with the U.S. government joining the Japanese government in developing a plan for economic recovery (Armstrong and Glyn 1991:68, 90–91).

The reasons for the shift in U.S. policy were severalfold. First, massive debts were developing in both Europe and Japan, because of their need for U.S. imports, rising from $5.8 billion in 1946 to $7.5 billion in 1947. The U.S. export industries needed stronger development from its trading partners if their markets were to be sustained, let alone expanded. Second, in Japan and Germany, as well as in many of the Allied countries, the desperate economic conditions had helped fuel the rapid growth of radicalized working-class movements, most of which had strong communist influence. Although, as Armstrong and Glyn argue, "The European Communist parties were hardly poised to launch Moscow-inspired insurrection," the radicalization of labor movements was real (Armstrong and Glyn 1991:110). Government rhetoric gave highly exaggerated descriptions of communist insurrectionary plans and of the active role of Moscow behind them. To the ideological trappings of free trade and colonial independence, the U.S. added the rhetoric of individual rights, democracy, self-determination, and defenders of the free world, even if it meant in numerous cases (including that of Greece) supporting highly repressive, right-wing dictatorships. This demonization of the Soviet Union and the various contradictions in the new Cold War stance were challenged by the popular-front liberals, who included many former New Dealers, third-party progressives, southerners in the Southern Conference for Human Rights, and the CP.

The administration quickly branded those who opposed this new turn as themselves sympathizers and apologists for the Soviet Union, even at times traitors and fifth columnists, a tactic on which it was increasingly to rely in order to isolate its left critics. With the support of most conservatives and those to the anticommunist liberals' right, both the developing Cold War and the stigmatization of its opponents were carried off quite successfully.

The domestic situation was initially more complex and difficult for the Truman administration. President Truman appeared to have an insoluble dilemma. Unlike FDR, Truman seemed unable simultaneously to reassure both business and the key New Deal constituencies. Although initially inheriting the mantle of FDR's New Deal coalition, Truman quickly lost the support of one central group of New Deal supporters after another.

Truman was perceived by most of the urban/left/labor/civil rights coalition as being probusiness and waffling on almost every issue. The predominance of businessmen, Wall Street types, as well as conservative southerners, including James Byrne of South Carolina, in his cabinet only increased the perception that he had abandoned common people and was the pawn of big business. His early appointments were, to be sure, mixed. Initially he retained a number of New Deal liberals including Tennessee Valley Authority (TVA) head David Lilienthal, Interior Secretary Harold Ickes, Commerce Secretary Henry Wallace, and Chester Bowles as the chief of the Office of Price Administration. He also appointed liberal Paul Herzog to head the National Labor Relations Board as well as former liberal senator Lew Schellenbach as secretary of labor. Yet, as Alonzo Hamby notes, most appointments were "cronies, conservatives, and political regulars," rather than the "dynamic, imaginative, independent progressives who had served Roosevelt" (Hamby 1973:57,59). And it was the former who not only seemed to have the most influence but increasingly began to replace the latter. The more liberal New Dealers who remained with Truman were quickly replaced or resigned over policy disagreements. The departures include Ickes, whose resignation was accepted on February 13, 1946, Bowles who resigned in June, and Wallace who was fired by Truman in September over foreign-policy differences.

His waffling on price control policy, unlike the flip-flops of President Clinton in the mid-1990s, won Truman no friends. Progressive politicos saw strict price control as "the major barrier against ruinous inflation and eventual depression" (Hamby 1973:79). When the bill to continue the Office of Price Administration was eventually passed in June 28, 1946, it was filled with crippling amendments that made it ineffectual. When he vetoed the bill with a strong message, liberals were elated. After three weeks with no price controls, Truman signed another bill hardly different from the one he had vetoed. Such policies, of course, satisfied no one but had immediate consequences in the daily lives of ordinary citizens. As has been noted previously, the failure of President Truman and the Democrats to take any concerted action on inflation and meat and other food shortages was a major contributing factor to the large Democratic congressional losses in the 1946 elections.

The Full Employment Bill, more of concern for long-range than immediate policy, met a similar fate. The bill, strongly supported by members of the broad "progressive" coaliton, had been partly drafted by Russell Smith of the Farmers Union. The bill watered down significantly by the time it was passed in February 1946, but it was the failure of Truman to fill any of the positions on the Council of Economic Advisors (the strongest provision left from the old bill) by mid-July that led to strong criticism by Smith. At the same time, the Farmers Union was attacking the conservative takeover of the Department of Agriculture and the many changes in policy which it found antithetical to the interests of its members.

Truman's response to workers and their unions, however, left many aghast. When the UAW strike against GM began, the president, in his October 30, 1945, radio address seemed to back the union's demand for a substantial wage increase with no rise in prices. Yet, on December 3, he proposed new anti-strike legislation and urged autoworkers to return voluntarily to work, while asking the steelworkers to postpone their impending strike action. Philip Murray, as well as the UAW, denounced Truman and ignored the requests. Truman's response to the growing 1946 strike wave won him no friends. He quickly lost the support of unionized workers and their supporters. His attacks on many of the 1946 strikes became increasingly truculent. In May 1946, when two railway unions went ahead with their strike plans after the government had seized control of the railroads, Truman sprung to action. He went before Congress on May 25, 1946, asking for legislation to draft the strikers. Many liberals considered the plan "a species of fascism" (Hamby 1973:77). Loyal Democrats including Eleanor Roosevelt denounced the scheme. A.F. Whitney of the Brotherhood of Railway Trainmen, a long-standing political supporter of Truman, promised to use the whole $47 million union treasury to insure that Truman would not be reelected in 1948. Truman, however, also lost support among conservatives and businessmen because none of his remarks or actions seemed to have any effect on worker militancy, their support of the strikes, the course of the labor-management conflicts, or the eventual outcomes. Ultimately, Truman's inability to influence the strike wave led many potential voters to see him as in part responsible (Preis 1964:290; Lipsitz 1994:129, Brecher 1972:228–29).

Truman's seeming ineffectiveness, indecisiveness, and lack of popularity were crystalized in his stands and policies on civil rights issues. He had in part been chosen as Roosevelt's vice-presidential running mate in 1944—over the rhetorically anti-racist Henry Wallace who was for this reason unacceptable to southern politicians and the racially conservative James Byrne who was unacceptable to northern politicians and their constituents—because of his mixed record as a border-state politician. His vacillations after taking office lost him support among southern Dixiecrats as well as African-Americans and northern liberals. Although issuing rhetorically strong statements that riled many southern politicians, he refused in 1945 to fight for an extension of the Fair Employment Practices Commission (FEPC). On November 21, 1945, Truman seized the strike-bound Capital Transit Company in Washington, D.C., to restore transportation for commuters. Two days later, the FEPC prepared a directive commanding the now government-controlled company to stop denying Blacks employment as conductors, motormen, bus operators, and traffic checkers. On November 24, Truman ordered the committee not to issue its directive (Berman 1970:29–30). Although making strong statements against the largely southern violent attacks on African-American war veterans, Truman proposed no new policy or made any move to intervene.

The perception of Truman's weakness on civil rights issues and the high visibility of southern Democratic Party racists in the Senate, including Mississippi's Theodore Bilbo, led African-Americans to desert the Democratic Party en masse in the November 1946 congressional elections. After analyzing the electoral defeat, the president issued Executive Order 9008, creating a President's Committee on Civil Rights, with a number of liberal members, including four (out of fifteen) who had been recommended by the National Association for the Advancement for Colored People (NAACP) (B. Bernstein 1973:75). Yet, when the report of the committee was issued, Truman claimed to support it in principle while refusing to endorse any of the specific measures against Jim Crow. Given the high expectations of many in the urban coalition at the conclusion of the war, Truman seemed to be a nonentity, part of the problem rather than part of the solution.

In early 1947, a group of Truman's more liberal advisors, led by Clark Clifford, Truman's legal counsel and top advisor, began meeting regularly at the home of Oscar Ewing, director of the Federal Security Agency and temporary head of the Democratic National Committee (DNC), to formulate reelection strategies. They concluded quickly that Truman needed to reenergize his support among the urban/labor/civil rights coalition by making some decisive overtures to the left. This would also undercut the large growing support among workers and African-Americans for former vice president and potential third-party candidate Henry Wallace. A decision was also made to write off the concerns of the more racist Dixiecrats, who could not be ameliorated in any case and who it was thought would be unlikely to defect from the Democratic Party.

By 1948, a conservatively inclined President Harry Truman had decided that the key to his reelection chances was to abandon his attempts at conciliation of the southern Dixiecrats and appeal directly to the urban/labor/civil rights coalition, taking more liberal, pro-labor stands on a variety of issues. A key part of this strategy was a vigorous stance on civil rights issues. The overall strategy is laid out by Truman's closest advisor, Clark Clifford, in his now-famous November 19, 1947, "Memorandum for the President" (Papers of Harry S. Truman, Box 21). The specific strategy on civil rights is spelled out in some detail in Oscar R. Ewing's "Memorandum for Clark Clifford," in which he argues:

> 1. Proper handling of the Civil Rights issue is of crucial importance. It can virtually assure the re-election of the President by cutting the ground out from under Wallace and gaining the enthusiastic support of the liberal and labor groups.... 3. There is no possibility of

appeasing the southern Democrats on this issue, either by the use
of pedestrian language or by straddling on particular issues....they
will fight equally hard against any kind of move in this area....4.
There is no danger of losing the South. It will neither go Republican
nor vote for Wallace. In any event, however, it takes a considerable
number of southern states to equal the importance of such states
as New York, Pennsylvania, and Illinois. (Papers of Oscar R. Ewing,
no date, Box 52)

The early fruit of this emerging policy came on June 20, 1947, with Truman's
strong denunciation and accompanying veto of the antilabor Taft-Hartley
bill, a veto which was subsequently overridden. This veto allowed Truman
to regain the support of top labor leaders, many of whom were looking for
an excuse not to bolt.

The civil rights issue, however, initially proved more daunting for the
Truman team. On January 10, 1947, Thomas Richardson, vice president of
the left-wing United Public Workers, disclosed that there were nine federal agencies under the control of the White House which refused to hire
African-Americans. He stated that he was making this information public
because his union had so far received no reply, even though it had been
raised with appropriate White House staff. Truman continued to respond
with bold rhetoric and little policy implementation. On June 29, 1947, he
delivered a strong civil rights speech to an NAACP rally in Washington in
front of the Lincoln Memorial. Racial discrimination in the United States,
however, was not only important domestically for the Democrats. It had
begun to emerge as an international issue. On October 23, 1947, the NAACP
submitted a petition to the United Nations on human rights violations
against African-Americans in the United States; the petition had been drafted by W. E. B. Du Bois. At the UN Commission on Human Rights meeting
in Geneva on December 4, 1947, a proposal from the Soviets formally to
investigate the charges was rejected. Nevertheless, the issue received worldwide publicity and the federal government was openly embarrassed. Then,
on December 29, 1947, Henry Wallace announced in Chicago that he was
accepting the nomination of the Progressive Party to be its candidate for
president. He reaffirmed his commitment to civil rights, receiving strong
support from the African-Americian press. Truman again responded with
strong rhetoric. On February 2, 1948, Truman gave a major civil rights message to Congress that contained a plan of action and immediately had the
message sent out on the Voice of America.

None of these rhetorical gestures seemed to work for Truman; events
were rapidly passing him by. In a special congressional election in the Bronx,
the spector of the Henry Wallace candidacy emerged full blown. Wallace came

to the district on February 15, 1948, campaigning for the American Labor Party candidate (and Wallace supporter) Leo Isacson and speaking to a crowd of 8,500. Isacson won overwhelmingly two days later with 22,697 votes against less than 18,000 for his Democratic, Republican, and Liberal opponents combined. Meanwhile A. Philip Randolph and Reverend Grant Reynolds had organized a Committee Against Jim Crow in Military Service and Training, urging young Blacks to refuse to serve unless military segregation was ended (Berman 1970:97–98). Truman's ambiguity continued. In the early spring of 1948, the federal government submitted an amicus curiae against restrictive housing covenants; on May 3, 1948, the Supreme Court declared them unenforceable. But at the mid-July Democratic National Convention, the Truman forces, in order to prevent a bolt of the southern delegates attempted to have the platform's civil rights plank be vague and ambiguous. Liberal forces, including those representing big cities in the North, defeated this position and substituted one that was stronger and more specific.

Amid much evidence that his support among traditional Roosevelt constituencies was still weak, Truman moved boldly. On July 26, 1948, he issued two executive orders—9980, which set up a permanent FEPC, and 9981, which began the process of desegregating the armed forces (Berman 1970:116). And in the latter weeks of the campaign, he put special emphasis on the New Deal constituencies. On October 23, he made a visit to the Black slums of Philadelphia. On October 25, he gave a strong civil rights speech at the Chicago stadium, and on October 29, before a crowd of 65,000, he became the first U.S. president to speak in Harlem (Berman 1970:125).

These strong gestures finally began to reap dividends for Truman. In the November election in California, Illinois, and Ohio, the African-American vote was the decisive margin for victory.

These tactics, along with the successful discrediting of Wallace's anti–Cold War foreign policy and the red-baiting of him and his party, reduced the latter's vote to insignificant proportions with the exception of New York and California, although in New York, Michigan, and Maryland the Wallace vote was sufficient to deprive Truman of the electoral votes and swing them to the Republicans. The civil rights issue had been a key to the reinvigoration of support from the old New Deal supporters, triggering Truman's unexpected rise from the political dead, but after winning the election, he "demonstrated a diminished ardor for minority rights" (Bartley, 1995:95). Truman had been successful, however, because the widespread anti-racist, broad class sentiments were no longer highly organized and focused; now increasingly inchoate and diffuse, they were more easily swayed by symbols and rhetoric.

Truman's efforts to appropriate many of the left issues from Wallace and the Progressives was the result of a carefully planned strategy. What also needs to be explained—and is worthy of a detailed, lengthy analysis—is the simultaneous success of anticommunism to brand as subversive foreign policy views that had only recently been considered mainstream. Any full analysis which attempted to explain the rapid change in public opinion over the Soviet Union (our former staunch ally in the fight against fascism) and on the acceptability of communists in American life, would want to take into account a number of factors. These factors would include the heightened consciousness of world politics that emerged from World War II, the unanimity with which established leaders supported these new changes in policy, and the growing anti-communism of religious, nationalistic, Eastern European ethnics beginning with the earlier collapse of Finnish and Polish radicalism —these latter having much to do with aggressive Soviet activities in Eastern Europe. I have already mentioned some of the reasons that the Communists became isolated and lost any claims they might have had to moral ascendancy. To this must be added the numerous splits among those on the left in virtually every venue, including, of course, the labor movement, liberals, the American Civil Liberties Union (ACLU), and southern progressives.

Although Truman's election was in good part due to his renewed support from workers, African-Americans, and other components of the broad urban coalition, contradictory forces were at work within the Democratic Party and the country as a whole. Truman's strategy also initiated an organized break with the Democratic Party by southern white supremacists, which would prove to be consequential for the future development of U.S. politics. At least as significant as Truman's victory, in terms of the development of present-day politics, was the bolt of the Dixiecrats over Truman's civil rights program.

THE DIXIECRAT REVOLT

Throughout the late 1930s and the 1940s, conflicts had simmered between many southern Democratic politicans and the national Democratic Party. Much of the verbiage had centered on racial issues though economic conservatism was often at least as important. Although FDR took great pains not to antagonize southern politicians over racial matters, the substance of his policies was often the subject of bitter attacks. As we have seen, numerous conflicts took place over the rights of Blacks to have access and to have equal treatment in New Deal relief and employment programs in the South. At the 1936 Democratic National Convention, "Cotton Ed" Smith's walkout had been a star attraction. The FEPC was a particular object of attack. During the 1948 presidential campaign, Dixiecrat candidate Strom Thurmond claimed, according to a Columbia, South Carolina, newspaper, that the FEPC had been "'patterned, on a Russian law written by 'Joseph Stalin about 1920'" (Black and Black 1992:143). Eleanor Roosevelt, far more publicly assertive on civil rights issues than her husband, was the subject of widespread rumors in the South. During World War II, one had it that she had created Eleanor Clubs among Black female domestic workers—quasi unions in which Black women threatened to quit for more remunerative work unless they were given higher pay and more respect (Odum 1943:73–80). In early 1944, when the Supreme Court ruled in *Smith v. Allwright* that white primaries were illegal, there was much speculation that southern Democratic politicians might leave the New Deal coalition during the 1944 elections. The resistance to the white primary decision was "symptomatic of a new bellicosity throughout the South" (Garson 1974:90, 92). There were initial defections from Roosevelt at the 1944 Democratic National Convention when a number of southern delegates cast their nominating votes for Senator Robert Byrd of Virginia (See Bartley 1969:29). Yet, nothing decisive came of these gestures.

Opposition from many southern Democrats, of course, had been a long time in the making. When Roosevelt initially took office, southern Democrats, with only a few notable exceptions, supported him. Roosevelt himself went out of his way not to antagonize southern conservatives over racial issues, even going so far as to refuse to support antilynching legislation. As Ira Katznelson notes, from 1933 to 1953 the number of southern Democrats in Congress hardly varied, ranging from 115 to 118, while non–southern Democrats in Congress peaked in 1937 with 217 members, going as low as 73 in 1947 (Katznelson et al. 1993:285). Though southern Democrats were supportive of most New Deal legislation, this support was often conditional on accommodation of southern capitalists' special economic concerns, including the exclusion of agricultural labor from coverage of both the National Labor Relations Act and the Fair Labor Standards Act. Despite FDR's conciliatory approach, by 1937 some southerners began to suspect "Roosevelt of trying to revolutionize race relations" (Patterson 1967:97). Roosevelt's failed purge of anti–New Deal Democrats in the 1938 congressional elections was predominantly directed at southern Democrats. A growing regional split began to take place not only over race-related issues but also over labor issues. As Katznelson argues, these latter issues were not unrelated to race, because the southern economy was rooted in a separate, insulated labor market, whose calling cards were low wages and white supremacy, both of which stood to be undermined as labor became more empowered generally and especially as it became successful in organizing southern workers (Katznelson et al. 1993:292). Splits between northern and southern Democrats became apparent in a number of key congressional votes. After the 1943 wartime coal strike, Congressman Howard W. Smith of Virginia and Senator Tom Connally of Texas introduced anti-strike legislation. Only five southern Democratic congressmen opposed it, compared to eighty-one non–southern congressmen. In the Senate there were no southern opponents. After FDR vetoed the bill, the Senate overrode the veto by a 50 to 25 margin; no southern senators voted to sustain the president. In the House, the margin was 244 to 108, with only four southerners voting to sustain. More conflict arose over the Soldier's Voting bills of 1942 and 1943, which would have facilitated troops, including Blacks, voting in their home states while at war. A similar split took place in 1947 over the Taft-Hartley employer-sponsored revisions of the National Labor Relations Act. Only nine southern congressmen joined with an overwhelming majority of non-southern Democrats to sustain President Truman's veto (the small number of non-southern opponents being mostly from rural areas). Only four southern senators (Olin Johnston of South Carolina, Lester Hill and John Sparkman both of Alabama, and Claude Pepper of Florida) joined the majority of nonsouthern Democratic senators to sustain (Garson 1974:38–42; 217–19). Yet, these issues alone did not lead to a formal split.

Things, however, came to a head during 1948 in response to Truman's statements and initiatives on civil rights legislation during the course of the year. Beginning with the report of the Presidential Commission on Civil Rights, *To Secure These Rights*, in October of 1947, southern politicians began to talk of defection. By the time Truman presented his civil rights package to Congress on February 2, 1948, Dixiecrat politicians, many of whom had helped Truman become nominated for vice president in 1944, felt that Truman had betrayed them (Garson 1974:235). At the Southern Governor's Conference held in February 1948 in Wakulla Springs, Florida, a committee headed by Strom Thurmond was appointed to negotiate with the DNC and report back with a strategy.

Strong support for a separate party existed mainly in Mississippi, South Carolina, and Alabama. In May 1948, a conference was held in Jackson to launch the States' Rights Democrats, otherwise known as the Dixiecrats. Only these three states and to a lesser extent Arkansas sent official representatives (Garson 1974:262). They agreed to present a series of ultimatums to the Democratic National Convention and convene again afterwards on July 17 in Birmingham, Alabama. At the Birmingham meeting they nominated Thurmond for president and Mississippi Governor Fielding Wright for vice president.

The strategy of the Dixiecrats was straightforward. Their goal was to punish the Democratic Party and to regain their influence within the leadership of the party, particularly with respect to racial issues. They assumed, like most political analysts, that Truman could not win reelection if he did not get southern electoral votes. They assumed also that they could hold together all 127 of the South's electoral votes. By withholding them from both major parties, neither would gain a majority in the electoral college. The election would then be decided in the House, where each congressional delegation had one vote. Again, neither candidate could win outright without the South's votes. Thus, the Republicans would be forced to drop their civil rights plank in return for southern support. There was even an outside chance in Thurmond's opinion that the Dixiecrats would be seen as the lesser evil by both parties and be handed the presidency.

The short-range Dixiecrat electoral strategy failed completely. Truman, of course, won an outright majority in the electoral college in good part because his urban/labor/civil rights strategy worked. If Wallace had not been running, Truman could have won reelection without any southern states. At least as significant, however, the Dixiecrats failed to hold the South. They won only thirty-nine electoral votes from four southern states—Mississippi, South Carolina, Alabama, and Louisiana. According to V.O. Key, they probably only carried the latter two states because Dixiecrat politicians had outmaneuvered the regular Democrats and appropriated the regular Democratic party label.

The circumscribed nature of the Dixiecrat revolt may be seen from examining the new southern political economy. The main strength of the Dixiecrats was in the Black Belt counties of the Deep South, those with the highest percentage of African-Americans, whose cotton plantation owners still needed the availability of cheap, forced Black labor. Although race was central to the revolt, it overlapped with other economic interests in parts of the region, especially of employers in extractive industries who also used low-wage labor and opposed many of the New Deal social policies. In 1948, it was only in Mississippi and South Carolina where these forces clearly dominated. Truman's new policies of integrating the armed forces and of providing a token FEPC hardly impinged on the growing urban and commercial economy in southern cities or in the upper South as a whole. Even in parts of the Deep South, some elites were openly critical of the Dixiecrats. Alabama's *Hale County News* (quoted in the *Birmingham News*), on September 29, 1948, argued, "Their protestations against civil rights and for states' rights are merely a camouflage to cover their real purposes. The bolt has been led by a coalition of entrenched reactionaries who are primarily interested in maintaining their privileged positions. Their stranglehold upon the politics of their respective states has been challenged and seriously endangered by the sweep of a liberal movement across the South that is interested in progress and the development of our resources. The reactionaries have seized upon the strategy of stirring up prejudice and fomenting racial strife as a blind to their real purposes" (quoted in V.O.Key 1949: footnote 13, 329–30). When half of the Alabama delegation walked out of the Democratic National Convention in July after the passage of the civil rights plank, one Alabama paper editorialized, "The surprising thing is that the delegation was not thrown out. Never have the Democrats of Alabama been burdened with such an overstuffed bunch of obsolete and repudiated leadership" (V.O.Key 1949: footnote 31, 335).

Thus, in many states in the South, most voters and politicians refused to support the Dixiecrats. According to V.O. Key, in those states where Republican competition existed (North Carolina, Tennessee, and Virginia) or the Black population was relatively small (Florida, Texas, and Arkansas), the appeal of the Dixiecrats was minimal. Most voters, especially poor whites supported the national Democrats' economic and social policies. According to Kevin Phillips, "In the poor white counties, there was no preoccupation with white absolutism such as characterized the Black Belts, nor was there any interest in furthering the anti-New Deal economic policies of the Black Belt and urban Deep South oligarchies" (Phillips 1970:218). Finally, neither the new emerging business class nor the established political elites were willing to cut themselves off from their powerful positions of influence in the Democratic Party, nor from the federal economic largess to which these positions gained them access, merely to oppose something that did not impinge on their interests. Thus, the electoral failure of the Dixiecrats was in part, according to Key, the last gasp of a dying class. Most academic literature concurs, seeing the Dixiecrat campaign as one of complete failure.

Yet, the Dixiecrats represent the first organized opposition in the post–Roosevelt Democratic Party, opposition as well to the advancement of civil rights for Blacks and other minorities. As such it was to prove a momentous development for the future. The pooh-poohing of contemporary critics proved to be misplaced. As Numan Bartley notes, "The movement nevertheless represented a substantial regional dissent from national trends." Rather than the death throes of a terminally ill patient, "It was in a real sense a premature expression of massive resistance" (Bartley 1969:36). And here the failures of the CIO's Operation Dixie and the preoccupation of the national CIO office in fighting left-led interracial unions was to foreshadow the future. Few attacks were made in the Deep South on the Dixiecrats with respect to race and other lower-class issues, especially by unions. Alabama and Louisiana in particular had strong interracial unions that might have been mobilized. Rather than creating a counter-hegemonic pole and using the campaign for important civil rights education, the major CIO unions in the South took the cautious approach. The development of a full-scale attack against white supremacy and the politics that defended it would have to wait for the full emergence of the African-American freedom movement almost a decade later.

1. Note for example the strong statement by Harry Truman in his first major speech to the U.S. Senate after his 1934 election, so typical of the stance of the Midwestern populist-progressive tradition:

> No one ever considered Carnegie libraries steeped in the blood of the Homestead steel workers, but they are. We do not remember that the Rockefeller Foundation is founded on the dead miners of the Colordo Fuel and Iron Co. and a dozen other similar performances....It is a pity that Wall Street, with its ability to control all the wealth of nations and to hire the best law brains in the country has not produced some financial statesmen, some men who could see the dangers of bigness and of the concentration of the control of wealth...they are still employing the best brains to serve greed and selfish interest. People can stand only so much, and one of these days there will be a settlement. (Hamby 1973:44)

No longer mainstream in 1945 and 1946, consider how out of place such public utterances would be today.

2. For a fuller description of the CIO approach to race, see my forthcoming book on Operation Dixie.

3. In its October 1948 issue *Fortune* magazine observed that "The C.I.O. southern drive...[was] now grinding to a halt."

4. In an assessment with which I concur, Barbara Griffith (1988:176) states: "For American labor, Operation Dixie was, quite simply, a moment of high tragedy from which it has yet to fully recover." For detailed statistics and analysis of the decline of organized labor in the post–World War II period, see Goldfield 1989a.

5. See the similar assessment in Korstad and Lichtenstein (1988).

CHAPTER 8

The Emergence of the Civil Rights Movement

> We will not be satisfied to take one jot or tittle less than our full manhood rights. We claim for ourselves every single right that belongs to a freeborn American, political, civil and social; and until we get these rights we will never cease to protest and assail the ears of America. The battle we wage is not for ourselves alone but for all true Americans. It is a fight for ideals, lest this, our common fatherland, false to its founding, become in truth the land of the thief and the home of the Slave—a by-word and a hissing among the nations for its sounding pretensions and pitiful accomplishment.
>
> W. E. B. Du Bois, August 1906, Harpers Ferry, West Virginia (Herbert Aptheker 1968:II:907–8)

> We want freedom by any means necessary. We want justice by any means necessary. We want equality by any means necessary. We don't feel that in 1964, living in a country that is supposedly based upon freedom, and supposedly the leader of the free world, we don't think that we should have to sit around and wait for some segregationist congressmen and senators and a President from Texas in Washington, D.C., to make up their minds that our people are due now some degree of civil rights. No, we want it now or we don't think anybody should have it.
>
> Malcolm X, June 28, 1964, Organization of Afro-American Unity founding rally, New York City (*Malcolm X* 1992:47)

T he diminished concern of labor unions for the organization of African American workers and for leading the fight for racial equality left a vacuum that was initially filled by the National Association for the Advancement of Colored People (NAACP) and moderate, middle-class organizations. The next phase of the struggle for full equality would be led and fought by more militant groups, representing a cross-class coalition. Although Black workers would play an important role, they would no longer be the leaders, as they had been in the 1930s and 1940s.

The African-American freedom struggles of the 1950s and 1960s were partly an outgrowth of the civil rights struggles of the 1930s and 1940s. Nevertheless, the differences as well as the similarities between the movements of the two periods, in terms of base of support, demands, and overall perspective, provide a key to understanding the politics of the present. Thus, we shall try to pay close attention to how the modern civil rights movement emerged and to its defining characteristics.

Although social movements always begin, gather momemtum, and flourish in specific historic circumstances, they also rely on earlier traditions, struggles, victories, and defeats, as well as on the organizational support and movement experiences of their predecessors. In the twentieth century, one could easily trace the beginnings of the civil rights movement to W. E. B. Du Bois's 1905 Niagara Movement and the 1910 founding of the NAACP. Yet, Frederick Douglass, Sojourner Truth, Harriet Tubman, William Lloyd Garrison, John Brown, and other pre–Civil War abolitionists were explicit forebearers—on the minds of the early twentieth-century civil rights militants. The abolitionists themselves were in turn influenced by the Nat Turner-led 1831 slave rebellion. And for those of us who believe that the flame of freedom burns eternally in all human breasts (even if it only smolders at times), a compelling case can be made that the Black liberation movement in North America began when the first African slave got off the boat in 1619. These historic predecessors and continuities are always relevant, as this whole book tries to make clear. Yet, social movements also have an historically discrete aspect, generally going through cycles of protest, with a beginning where new generations of participants become increasingly involved and mobilized, a logic of evolution and development, an escalation of tactics and demands, and finally a tapering-off period and perhaps an endpoint (see Tarrow 1994 for an important analysis of this question).

Now, there are currently a number of important academic debates over what caused the massive upsurge of African-Americans in the South—the bus boycotts of the 1950s, the continuous wave of protests and organizing throughout the first half of the 1960s, lunch-counter sit-ins, freedom rides, mass community mobilizations and marches, the Mississippi Freedom Democratic Party, hundreds of thousands facing arrest, beatings, and murder—and why the civil rights movement was at least partially successful in attaining its demands. The underlying theoretical perspectives in these disputes are ones with which we are now familiar. Were the most important causes for the emergence and success of the civil rights movement the ideas and opinions or the activities of elites, governmental and court decisions, the emergence of a pro-civil rights southern business class, changes in the political economy of the country as a whole or perhaps the South's large-scale attitudinal and cultural changes, or mass struggle on the part of the Black population and its allies? While the debates do not precisely follow the categories which we have previously noted—and I will not try to force them to do so—the underlying perspectives are readily apparent. A brief review of the issues and positions in the debate over the causes for the emergence of the movement during the 1950s and 1960s, and of its partial success, will help us gain a sharper focus.

Perhaps the most contentious of such debates is over the role played by the evolution of legal doctrines and court decisions, especially that of the 1954 *Brown v. Board of Education* Supreme Court decision outlawing segregated schools. David Garrow, the dean of civil rights movement scholars, argues that it was *Brown* that inspired those who participated in the takeoff of the civil rights movement, particularly the 1955–56 Montgomery bus boycott led by Dr. Martin Luther King, Jr. (Garrow 1994). Michael Klarman, in contrast, argues that Brown's influence was minimal: "I believe that political, economic, social, demographic, and ideological forces, many of which coalesced during World War II, laid the groundwork for the civil rights movement, and that *Brown* played a relatively small role" (Klarman 1994:91). Mary Dudziak, on the other hand, gives priority to international factors, at least in terms of changes in public policy. She argues compellingly that "At a time when the U.S. hoped to reshape the postwar world in its own image, the international attention given to racial segregation was troublesome and embarrassing" (Dudziak 1988:62). The exposure of racial injustice at home hindered the U.S. government's ability to make political inroads in non-white, underdeveloped areas of the world. Thus, "the effect of race discrimination on international relations during the postwar years was a critical motivating factor in the develoment of federal government policy" (Dudziak 1988:66). Others look at a longer history and the dramatically altered socioeconomic structure of the South after World War II to help explain both the change in public policy as well as the increased tempo of Black protest in the South. Frances Fox Piven and Richard Cloward, for example, argue that "Changing economic circumstances, and the demographic and social ramifications that soon followed, created mounting unrest among masses of blacks, eventually culminating in a black struggle against the southern caste system" (Piven and Cloward 1977:183). The diminished importance of cotton plantations and the greater weight of southern businessmen—who, when forced to choose, preferred integration to disruption and loss of profits—also allegedly helps explain why the movement succeeded in changing public policies. Bloom and others take this approach as well, although Bloom also documents the "electric" effect of *Brown* (Bloom 1987:131). Warren Whatley, on the other hand, argues persuasively that moderate businessmen not only had minimal desire for integration but also had too little social and political power to effect things even when they wanted. Cotton planters in the late 1950s still had a strong economic need for cheap Black agricultural labor, as well as possessing the political power to dominate Southern politics. Rather, Whatley, following Doug McAdam, sees the impetus for change coming largely from the strength of the African-American freedom movement whose urban institutions, especially the Black church, were strengthened by the demographic changes of the 1930s and 1940s (Whatley 1990; McAdam 1982). Morris too emphasizes forces within the Black community. He minimizes the importance of *Brown*, highlighting instead the earlier 1953 Baton Rouge bus boycott in part because it reflects the forces he emphasizes in later years—the church, ministers, and middle-class community leaders (Morris 1984). Almost all (with the partial exception of Greenberg 1981), however, omit and seem unaware of the working-class roots of the modern civil rights movement that were its precursors, a point to which I shall return, which should hardly surprise the reader who has accompanied me this far in our journey. All these partial explanations are useful in terms of piecing together a fuller explanation and more specifically highlighting the strengths and weaknesses of the civil rights movement.

I have already sketched the dramatic changes during the 1930s and 1940s, the importance of civil rights for national politics, its centrality to the broad urban/labor/left/civil rights coalition, and the growing strength of Black labor. World War II, like the Civil War, may be regarded as a watershed period that greatly disrupted and transformed American social, economic, and political life. Its impact was especially important for race relations. So, we shall begin the story about civil rights in the 1950s and 1960s with the changes brought about by World War II. As I have argued throughout, racial practices in the United States have always been contradictory. Much racial discrimination existed in both public and private venues throughout the country. Racial stereotypes in wartime films existed alongside attempts to portray prejudice as un-American (see Koppes and Black 1986). Hate strikes, other anti-black activities on the part of whites, intense labor market discrimination, as well as a Jim Crow military, were defining characteristics of the era. Despite, or rather alongside, these widespread features of racial oppression, racial equality for African-Americans was a notion that was in ascendancy in the United States. The war had intensified trends that we have already traced during the 1930s.

Wars require the mobilization and solidification of public opinion. In the United States, World War II was portrayed universally as a war for democracy and against racism. Scientific and intellectual attitudes about race not only advanced but gained absolute hegemony as a result of the wartime attitudes. The much publicized memorial to the men who died at Iwo Jima emphasized that they were "Negroes and whites, rich and poor,... Protestants, Catholics, and Jews, together" (Dudziak 1988:70).

By the end of World War II, there was a "substantial nonsouthern consensus" that reflected worldwide attitudes on human rights. "The postwar period witnessed a surge of popular feeling against Jim Crowism" (Bartley 1995:4). Several northern and western states passed fair employment legislation, open-occupancy laws, and other civil rights measures. New Jersey voters ratified a constitutional provision making school discrimination illegal, and Indiana, Illinois, and Arizona made segregated local schools illegal. There was a cascade of civil rights decisions by the U.S. Supreme Court which progressively undermined the basis for segregation in public policy. As most political scientists and some legal scholars know, the Supreme Court, despite its claims to strict legal interpretation, tends to follow the election returns and public opinion, as well as ruling-class interests. In 1896, the Supreme Court, ratifying the white supremacist victories over interracial unions and southern populism which established the System of 1896, ruled in *Plessy v. Ferguson* that "separate but equal" facilities were perfectly legal. Beginning in the 1930s under four separate Supreme Court chief justices, the Court steadily moved to undermine this doctrine. In 1938, the justices ruled in *Gaines v. Canada* that the state of Missouri either had to admit Lloyd Gaines to the University of Missouri Law School or provide a "separate but equal" one for him and other Blacks. The "separate but equal" doctrine was all but fatally undermined in two 1950 cases, *Sweatt v. Painter*, involving the University of Texas Law School, and *McLaurin v. Oklahoma State Regents*, in which the Supreme Court ruled that the racially separate law school in Texas and the segregated facilities within the Oklahoma law school were inherently unequal. In other arenas the courts were also ruling against legalized segregation. In 1948, the court ruled in *Shelley v. Kraemer* that restrictive housing covenants were a violation of the Fourteenth Amendment. In the same year, the California Supreme Court also decided in *Perez v. Sharp* that the state's anti-miscegenation law which prohibited interracial marriages violated equal protection provisions of the constitution. And Truman's establishment in 1947 by executive order of a federal Federal Employment Practices Commission (FEPC), along with the desegregation of the armed forces, only added to the growing crescendo in public policy, which seemed to reach its grand climax in the unanimous 1954 Supreme Court ruling in *Brown v. Board of Education, Topeka, Kansas*.

As Dudziak and others have argued, the international situation placed pressure on the American government over the denial of civil rights to African-Americans. Both the tide of world and U.S. domestic opinion and the emergence of independent nonwhite countries made U.S. racial policy a visible sore point. Gunnar Myrdal saw all this clearly in the early 1940s:

> What has actually happened within the last few years is not only that the Negro problem has become national in scope after having been mainly a southern worry. It has also acquired tremendous international implications, and this is another and decisive reason why the white North is prevented from compromising with the white South regarding the Negro. The situation is actually such that any and all concessions to Negro rights in this phase of the history of the world will repay the nation many times, while any and all injustices inflicted upon him will be extremely costly.... (Myrdal 1944:1015)

> The main international implication is, instead, that America, for its international prestige, power, and future security, needs to demonstrate to the world that American Negroes can be satisfactorily integrated into its democracy. (Myrdal 1944:1016)

During World War II, German radio often mentioned the harsh treatment of Blacks in America in its propaganda broadcasts in Europe (*New York Times*, 9-2-42). According to Pearl Buck, Japan was declaring in Asia "that there is no basis for hope that colored peoples can expect any justice from the people who rule in the United States, namely the white people. For specific proof the Japanese point to our treatment of our own colored people....Every lynching, every race riot, gives joy to Japan." And Myrdal concludes, "Caste is becoming an expensive luxury of white men" (Myrdal 1944:1016, 1017).

Things were to get much worse for the United States as the Cold War began. The Truman Doctrine (1947) proclaimed to the world that the United States was leading the "Free World" in the fight for democracy and human rights. This was vigorously challenged by the Soviet bloc, whose doctrinal commitments to the rights of racial minorities and oppressed peoples were both long-standing and the opposite of those touted by the Axis powers who the United States fought in World War II. According to State Department sources, the Soviet press had detailed information on lynchings, forced peonage, deprival of the right to vote, and all the various aspects of white supremacy in the South (Dudziak 1988:88–90). The Soviet claims against the United States were given attentive and sympathetic hearings, especially by many nonwhite peoples around the world. These charges were reenforced by a variety of petitions from domestic groups presented to the United Nations which received worldwide publicity. The first such petition was presented by the National Negro Congress (NNC) in June 1946 to the United Nations (UN) Commission on Human Rights. In October 1947, the NAACP filed a petition to the same commission, which the Soviets then asked the

UN to investigate. This latter petition, written by Du Bois, created "an international sensation" and was heavily covered in the national and foreign media. U.S. Attorney General Tom Clark said, "I was humiliated...to realize that in our America there could be the slightest foundation for such a petition" (Dudziak 1988:95). On December 9, 1948, the UN adopted its Convention on the Prevention and Punishment of the Crime of Genocide. In 1951, the left-wing Civil Rights Congress (the successor to the NNC) submitted a lengthy document to the UN entitled *We Charge Genocide*, documenting hundreds of crimes of murder and terror against African-Americans which the Justice Department refused to investigate (Patterson 1951). The UN thus provided African-Americans and their organizations a worldwide forum to publicize their grievances and numerous sympathetic ears. Rather than confront the problems, however, the immediate response of the State Department to the 1951 presentation was to seize the passport of William Patterson, the editor of the document and executive secretary of the organization. Articles on the treatment of Blacks in the United States were a constant topic in newspapers in Third World countries during the postwar period. The State Department collected articles from the Philippines, including one from December 1946, appearing in the *Fiji Times and Herald*, entitled "Persecution of Negroes Still Strong in America." An Indian newspaper reported on the refusal of the Daughters of the American Revolution to allow Black pianist Hazel Scott to perform in Constitution Hall, calling it "a shameful manifestation of racial intolerance." Press reports in Ceylon, China, and closer to home, Jamaica and Haiti, scored U.S. racial discrimination (see Dudziak's excellent accounts 1988:81–92). Yet, even the U.S.'s closest allies occasionally played the race card against it. In response to criticism of Britain's policy in Palestine in 1947, a cartoon appeared in the June 8, 1947, *London Sunday Express* which showed two white men standing in front of a lynched black man and a whites-only hotel remarking, "Shameful the way the British are handling this Palestinian business" (Dudziak 1988:81).

As Dudziak convincingly documents, these foreign criticisms were a cause of great concern to the U.S. government. The impact of the international situation, however, was more complex than those who emphasize its saliency proclaim. At least as important as the international pressure on the federal government was the tremendous inspiration and strengthened resolve that it gave to African-Americans in the United States. The example of newly freed, independent, outspoken non-white peoples around the globe was telling. Indians had gained independence from Britain and were running their own affairs; the Chinese had likewise become an independent nation. And the early anti-colonial movement in Africa was a focus of attention.

Yet, what the historical record makes most clear is that there was little concern by the federal government for the substance of the criticisms, be they domestic or international. In fact, as the advertisement says, image was everything. Certainly, this was true for all U.S. presidents during this period. As numerous historians have chronicled, Truman showed little signs of concern for civil rights for African-Americans as soon as the 1948 election was over, immediately seeking a rapprochement with southern Dixiecrat politicians. Eisenhower refrained from enforcement of civil rights laws until forced to act in Little Rock in 1957 when Governor Orval Faubus directly flaunted federal authority. Kennedy's weakness on civil rights is likewise well documented. Much of the concern with U.S. image dealt with attempts to change civil rights law through the courts. The U.S. government presented numerous amicus briefs in support of plaintiffs claiming, for example, that restrictive covenants were an infringement on federal housing policy and most notably in *Brown* that school segregation undermined U.S. foreign policy. When *Brown* was announced, the State Department wasted no time, making it the top priority in Voice of America broadcasts. Even the Republican National Committee on May 21, 1954, announced that it was part of the Eisenhower administration's "many-frontal attack on global Communism" (Dudziak 1988:115).

In attempting to shore up the U.S. image abroad, the government sponsored speaking tours of African-American anti-Communists, including Max Yergan, a former leader of the NNC. They also distributed a good deal of material exaggerating the integration of African-Americans into the top levels of U.S. life. The Student Nonviolent Coordinating Committee (SNCC) activists were shocked at seeing some of the misleading material circulated by U.S. information offices in Africa. Julian Bond, for example, stated: "There were all these pictures of Negroes doing things, Negro judges, Negro policemen, and if you didn't know anything about America, like Africans would not, you would think these were really commonplace things. That's the worst kind of deceit" (Carson 1981:135). At a time when SNCC was being charged by the House Un-American Activities Committee (HUAC) and other governmental agencies with subversion and was the subject of the Federal Bureau of Investigation's deadly COINTEL-PRO, which included both misinformation and assassinations, one U.S. film in Africa was publicizing SNCC-led demonstrations in the South.

The U.S. government was at times willing to give some support to the respectable, solidly anticommunist NAACP, which had proved its patriotic mettle in numerous ways, including the firing of Du Bois, attacks on Paul Robeson, and aiding in the undermining of left-led interracial unions. Even the NAACP, however, was not immune from being caught in the anti-communist racist crosshairs as attacks on virtually all civil rights activities by government loyalty programs, HUAC, and the FBI only intensified during the course of the Cold War. Real left-wing activists and their organizations were, of course, ruthlessly repressed. W. E. B. Du Bois, after having been fired from his job as research director for the NAACP, was finally forced out of the country by the government. Benjamin Davis, the communist city councilman from Harlem, was imprisoned along with other Communist Party leaders. Paul Robeson, the leading Black cultural figure in the country, was harassed to such a degree that he was probably driven to an early death. Numerous left-wing organizations including the Civil Rights Congress and the National Negro Labor Council were hounded out of existence. Yet, government concern for civil rights did not stop there.

Working in tandem with the Cold War in international affairs, was the domestic Cold War against alleged communists. A variety of federal personnel security programs, of which loyalty oaths were only one small part, were set up throughout the federal government and the private companies that did business with it. Similar programs existed at the state and local levels, in private universities, and among private employers. Thousands were fired. In many cases, the programs were an excuse to fire without cause and with no explanation Blacks, Jews, union activists, and even those merely sympathetic to civil rights. Many of the questions asked during the security hearings indicate the equation of civil rights activity with communism and disloyalty. In one case an employee of the Department of the Interior who taught basic subjects and crafts to native peoples was asked, "What were your feelings at that time concerning racial equality?...How about civil rights?...Do I interpret your statement...that maybe Negroes and Jews are denied some of their constitutional rights at present?" (Yarmolinsky 1955:89).

At another hearing, a security agency lawyer engaged in the following dialogue:

> Agency Lawyer: "Let me say this: As I understand it, the difference between a left-winger or a Communist and conservative...in this fight which is vital to you of getting equality for the Negro, is the method of going about it." Witness: "Yes." Agency Lawyer: "But the method of going about it makes a man a left-winger or a more conservative, and the conservative says, 'Let's do it slowly and by education or by training the people to understand and be ready to accept their responsibility,' and the left-winger says, 'No, it's right now.' Is that about right?" (Yarmolinsky 1955:170).

Today, such inquisitions have an eery quality where wrong answers would result in job loss and often permanent blacklisting. History shows us, of course, that the inquisitor was clearly wrong about the conservatives. White ones, at least, by and large opposed even the slowest movement on civil rights, as is unfortunately still the case today.

At one hearing in the Department of Agriculture, a department attorney was challenged about the relevance of racial questions to a Black employee being investigated. The Department attorney replied:

> I think it is well known that the Communist Party has adopted and has fostered as one of its plans to secure membership and foster its movement, the advocacy of equality for racial and religious minorities. (Yarmolinski 1955:194).

Such hearings had disastrous consequences for Blacks, Jews, union activists and other pro-civil rights employees. Members of the Black National Alliance of Postal Employees, hardly a radical organization, claimed that the head of the Post Office Loyalty Board and its attorney were from the Deep South and the board itself was perhaps infested with Ku Klux Klanners. They presented statistics showing that "a pattern is being set to purge Negroes, Jews, and Unionists." A majority of the 129 cases were of Blacks, with 41 Jews; "Most of the men cited have been very vocal in denouncing discriminatory practices in the postal service, and very good union men" (Snow Grigsby to Walter White, January 6, 1948, Records of the NAACP microfilms, part B, series c, reel 5, courtesy of Professor Ellen Schrecker). By December 2, 1948, the NAACP had concluded, as Walter White wrote in a letter to President Truman, that there was an "increasing tendency on the part of the government agencies to associate activity on interracial matters with disloyalty" (NAACP press release, dated December 2, 1948, ibid.).

The government-sponsored loyalty purges were to get even more intense as thousands were discharged. There is much evidence to support the contention of the Marine Cooks that "Unions With Least Bias Hit Hardest By Screening" (Papers of Gladstein, Leonard, Patsy, and Anderson; Bancroft Library, University of California, Berkeley; courtesy of Professor Schrecker). Such harassment and repression continued into the 1960s with the attempts of the FBI to disrupt the more militant, but hardly communist, civil rights organizations of the modern era.

It is, of course, true that the rhetoric of the Cold War in the aftermath of World War II made white supremacy in the United States look especially hypocritical (see, e.g., Cushman in *New York Times Magazine*, 1-11-48.) Just as American presidential candidates today are considered worthy of greater scrutiny than other politicians, the activities of the Cold War's most powerful, important, and moralistic player were likewise the subject of much international discussion. Along with the growing importance of nonwhite peoples in the world and their natural concerns for the treatment of darker U.S.

citizens, the developing Cold War provided African-Americans a wider forum for their grievances and a growing sense that they had numerous new allies in their struggles for justice. Yet, the role of the government can hardly be described as salutary. Certainly, the court decisions must be included on the positive side of the ledger. But the policy of equating all concern for civil rights with subversion, and of disabling and destroying all of the most committed and militant activists and organizations, must in the end weigh the balance sheet heavily in the negative direction. What is more accurate to say in assigning weight to international factors is that it provided a more sensitive, if not supportive, context for the civil rights movement when it finally burst forth on the scene.

Let us now explore the influence that the changing political economy of the South had on the emergence and development of the civil rights movement. Six factors are especially worth examining: (1) the decline of the economic importance of southern plantation agriculture beginning in the 1930s; (2) whether the political influence of Black Belt planters also declined during this period; (3) the rise in the economic and political strength of a moderate business and professional class; (4) the growing importance of federal investments in the southern economy; (5) the effects of urbanization in general; (6) the changing demography of the Black population in the South.

Though many groups in the South contributed to the system of white supremacy, its bedrock of support I have argued was the southern plantation system. Planters installed and maintained the system of white supremacy, stretching the shadow of the plantation as far North as they could in order to maintain low-wage, Black, agricultural labor. Because agricultural labor provided the framework in which the southern labor market in general operated, planters had strong allies in traditional labor-intensive, low-wage industries, including textiles, tobacco, lumber and sawmill operations, and later paper and furniture. Let us thus briefly review the arguments about the degree to which the strength of the planters and their allies were undermined during the post–World War II period.

The takeoff in the southern economy begins in earnest during World War II. This is initially reflected in the number of people who left southern agriculture. The farm population diminished dramatically as Table 9.1 suggests.

TABLE 9.1 *Farm population in the South*

Year	1940	1945	1950	1954	1959	1964	1969
millions	16.4	12.74	11.896	9.139	7.613	5.513	4.058

Source: *Historical Statistics*: 1:448.

For a different set of figures and breakdowns by state, see Fite 1984: Table A1, p. 233.

In addition to the general decline in southern agriculture, there was also a large drop in cotton acreage. To a great extent, the dramatic historic expansion in cotton agriculture which we saw in the early nineteenth century was replayed in reverse from 1929 on. After the Civil War, there were only 7.6 million acres of cotton harvested. Subsequently, however, cotton acreage rose steadily and by 1929 there were 43 million acres devoted to cotton production. From then on there was a percipitous and continuous fall, and by 1945 total acreage had fallen to 17 million. There are a number of reasons for this decline. On the one hand, international markets were lost, initially because of the economic isolation caused by the Great Depression with its lessened demand for raw materials and its increased tariff barriers, which thwarted foreign trade. Eventually, many of these markets were lost permanently to less economically developed countries, most notably Egypt and India, where labor costs were even lower than in the plantation South. In addition, synthetic fabrics displaced cotton for many domestic uses. The proportion of rayon in the total consumption of fine fibers in the U.S. increased six and one half times in the twenty years prior to 1948, from 2.5 percent of consumption to 16 percent (Hoover and Ratchford 1951:314). Further, although national production remained in the 10 to 15 million bale range from 1945 to 1970, its locus of production underwent a major shift, moving from the traditional areas in the South to Texas, Arizona, and California (*Historical Statistics* 1975:1:517–18). In 1949, Texas, Oklahoma, New Mexico, Arizona, and California grew more than half of America's cotton (52 percent). Cotton production after 1933 kept moving westward where yields were higher and costs of production were lower (Hoover and Ratchford 1951:307–8). In 1959, cotton was the principal crop in only eleven counties in four southern states in the old cotton belt, that is where cotton represented more than 50 percent of the crops harvested (Kirby 1987:73). By the 1960s, manufacturing had become the main source of income in every southern state.

Even within the diminished cotton agriculture of the South, the demand for manual labor also began to decrease because of increased mechanization. In 1945, there was almost no mechanized harvesting of cotton in the South, still only 5 percent in 1950. By 1960, however, cotton agriculture was 50 percent mechanized, almost a done deal by 1965, 96 percent by 1969 (see Wright 1986:243–44; Whatley 1990:20). The increase in mechanization was not unrelated to the rapid growth of agricultural wages in the South and the country as a whole. U.S. farm wages, which had been relatively stagnant in previous decades, virtually tripled during World War II, going up another 20 percent by 1950, steadily climbing and multiplying severalfold again by 1970 (*Historical Statistics* 1975:I:467–68).

Yet, Warren Whatley argues convincingly that this did not initially diminish the interest of southern cotton planters in cheap labor, their commitment to maintaining the system of white supremacy, or the degree of their influence within southern politics. Increased foreign competition and more productive cotton agriculture in the Southwest put a great deal of pressure on cotton growers in the traditional areas. As a result, smaller planters in the Southeast began to drop out of cotton production during the 1950s. Larger planters in the Deep South, however, especially in the Black Belt regions, were also pressed by declining cotton prices and government restrictions but were not yet ready or able to turn to mechanization. Thus, the Deep South planters during the 1950s were still very committed to the old labor system in their region; it was only in the upper South that planter preponderance had declined. These changed economic circumstances were partly reflected in the 1948 election results and the degree and location of support for the Dixiecrats (Whatley 1990:6–13).

The planters, however, still had dominating political control in most southern states in good part a result of their control of the Farm Bureau, which directly represented their interests. The Farm Bureau in Alabama, for example, aligned itself in the 1960s with the most visibile symbols of white supremacy, including George Wallace. It was only when the industry became completely mechanized that the planters and the Farm Bureau's commitment to white supremacy lessened. As Stanley Greenberg notes, "By the late sixties, the Farm Bureau and white farmers had unobtrusively given up the race question; without sharecroppers, with machines, beef and soybeans, they could afford to" (Greenberg 1980:125). By this time, however, the civil rights movement had largely run its course and had already gained or laid the groundwork for what victories were still to be gotten. Thus, we must conclude that the weakening role of southern agriculture in general and cotton in particular played only a minor role in the undermining of resistance in the South to civil rights through the main phases of the movement.

Let us examine then the role that the rise of non-cotton-related southern business had on the emergence and success of the civil rights movement. Much, although not all, of the initial increase in southern industry after World War II was in traditional low-wage, labor-intensive employment, which itself relied on the low-wage, relatively insular southern labor market. During the decade following the war, the number of factories employing at least twenty-five workers increased by one-third. "The new industrial establishments manufactured a wide range of goods, but the majority of the new plants were traditional low-wage, usually labor-intensive operations producing textiles, apparel, furniture, lumber, tobacco, and food products. Many engaged in the first-stage transformation of raw materials from southern farms, forests, and mines and located in and around the towns where the materials were at hand and the labor was cheap and abundant. Thus from the midforties to the mid-fifties, industry expanded impressively while the value added per employee declined relative to the national average" (Bartley 1995:107).

From 1952 to 1970, the South's share of federal expenditures went up from 83 percent to near parity. Some areas were completely transformed, for example, Huntsville, Alabama, with the Redstone Arsenal and the Marshall Space Flight Center (Wright 1986:261). Beginning during World War II, southern governors and development agencies had pushed for their "fair share." Tennessee, especially the Knoxville area, which included both Oak Ridge and the headquarters for TVA, as well as the D.C. suburbs in Virginia, were heavy concentration points during World War II. Texas, however, was the premier beneficiary of the federal largess (Bartley 1995:143). Yet, even Mississippi in 1964 received $1 billion in federal funds (Wright 1986:265). What was new beginning in the 1940s compared with previous periods was the aggressive state-level political pressure for the South's share of military money and the efforts of public and private elites to encourage investment and involvement by outsiders and non-southern money (Wright 1986:240). In part it was the greater reliance of the South on federal monies during World War II and after that helped curb its frequent violent reactions to labor union organizing, placing it more in line with practices in the rest of the country during the post–World War II period.

The other supposed modernizing trend in the South was urbanization. In 1940, of the South's 41 million residents, 26 million were rural while only 15 million were classified as urban. By 1950, they were more closely divided with 24 million rural and 23 million urban residents. By 1960, the preponderance had shifted dramatically, with 32 million urban and 23 million rural; and by 1970, the 40.5 million urban residents were almost twice that of the rural ones. These trends were similar among both whites and Blacks (*Historical Statistics* 1975:I:22). In 1940, New Orleans and Houston were the only two metropolitan areas with over a half million people. After the war, Atlanta and Dallas emerged as major cities with a number of others to eventually follow. Finally, the Servicemen's Readjustment Act of 1944 was a boon to southern colleges and universities, providing economic support for a huge expansion in enrollments and the whole southern system of higher education.

Yet, there is some dispute over the degree to which these changes laid the basis, or at least allowed an opening for the civil rights movement. Samuel Lubell writing in 1952 was skeptical: "One of the more striking features of the economic revolution sweeping Dixie today is the degree to which the South has been able to transfer its traditional, agrarian-rooted racial attitudes to the new emerging industrial society" (Lubell 1952:128). Numan

Bartley, on the other hand, qualifies such an interpretation. He argues: "Advocates of economic growth were racial segregationists, but they were inclined to defend white supremacy only so far as it did not conflict with pocketbook preoccupations. Many were conscious of the South's national image and saw the danger of zealous inflexibility in race relations" (Bartley 1995:23). Yet, as Bartley also notes, in many of the rapid-growth areas, business people were among the most reactionary, including Houston, the largest metropolitan area of the South. One journalist described Houston as "with the possible exception of Tulsa, Oklahoma, the most reactionary community in the United States" (Bartley 1995:139–40). In New Orleans and Jacksonville, so-called racially moderate business people were also little in evidence. Finally, as we shall see, in not one city in the South did any businessmen take an initiative with respect to civil rights. Most, even in the 1970s, had to be taken to court or threatened by the federal government to desegregate.

The situation in Alabama, as reported by Stanley Greenberg, is indicative. "Economic growth and the changing pattern of industrialization did not immediately undermine prevailing racial practices: businessmen in manufacturing and commerce readily accommodated the customary demarcations and norms that predominated in the rural economy and the primary extractive industries. Only after these demarcations were challenged by the subordinate population and the federal government did businessmen question the costs of accommodation and consider new ways of organizing a labor force" (Greenberg 1980:220).

"In no instance that I could discover did management before the 1960s, drawing on cost calculations, business norms, or some abstract concept of justice, choose to desegregate the work place or break down job discrimination. Change came only when black civil rights organizations grew impatient with southern employment practices or, more often, when changes in law or federal policy forced it" (Greenberg 1980:231).

It was the federal Maritime Commission that ordered and then forced the breakdown of job barriers to Blacks working on the dry docks. Likewise, Interstate Commerce Commission orders forced the desegregation of railroad facilities, while Equal Employment Opportunity Commission (EEOC) complaints filed against federal contractors made the initial inroads in the construction industry. In Alabama, "in the end, virtually every major manufacturing establishment had to face the federal courts. They ordered changes in hiring practices, lines of progression, or seniority at United States Steel, Hayes International, Goodyear Tire, Scott Paper, International Paper, and Southern Bell Telephone" (Greenberg 1980:232).

During the heyday of civil rights activities, Alabama businessmen staunchly stood by the white supremacists of the Black Belts. In 1962, a court order was issued for more equal representation in the Alabama legislature. According to the Alabama state constitution of 1901 (itself a result of the system of power and racial subordination established by the System of 1896), one state senator in Black Belt Lowndes County in 1961 was found to represent 2,057 whites while one in Jefferson County, which included Birmingham, represented 130,000 registered voters. Businessmen not only fully supported the Farm Bureau's opposition to the 1962 suit but also stood with the planters in their efforts to preserve the malapportionment when the courts began redistricting in 1965 (Greenberg 1980:235).

From Montgomery in 1955 and the 1961 Freedom Rides, to the 1963 Birmingham demonstrations and the dynamiting of the Sixteenth Street Baptist Church, which killed four black children the same year, "Business concern with the course of events came slowly and unevenly." Manufacturing concerns were less worried about the impact of the civil rights movement and its worldwide publicity than those businesses that were more directly involved in the Birmingham economy; the concerns of the latter group developed as they began to lose large amounts of business. In the early 1950s, Birmingham had paced ahead of more racially progressive southern cities such as Atlanta and Memphis. After 1958, however, retail and wholesale trade in Birmingham began to stagnate. Birmingham did not participate in the early 1960s growth that characterized a number of other southern cities. Then boycotts by the Black community began to take their toll on local businesses. Attempts to remove "Bull" Connor as public safety director and Mayor Arthur Haynes failed. But by 1965, with the civil rights demonstrations in Selma, the murder of northern white housewife and civil rights volunteer Viola Liuzzo, and the burning of more churches, the whole "business community in Alabama gave up on the racial order" (Greenberg 1980:236, 237, 241). Nineteen local chambers of commerce, including those in Birmingham, Mobile, and Montgomery, plus the state Chamber of Commerce, the Alabama Bankers Association, the Associated Industries of Alabama, and the Alabama Textile Manufacturing Association, took out joint, full-page advertisements in twenty-two Alabama daily newspapers, the *Wall Street Journal,* and *U.S. News and World Report.* These changes, however, were a consequence of the civil rights movement rather than its causes.

FACTORS THAT STENGTHENED
THE BASE OF BLACK STRUGGLE
Demography

There is a compelling argument that the most important effect of southern socio-economic development for development of the the civil rights movement, was the changes it brought about in the African-American community. As I have already noted, Doug McAdam, Frances Fox Piven and Richard Cloward, and Warren Whatley all make this argument persuasively. I will be drawing on and amplifying the particulars of their work in order to paint a comprehensive sketch.

Life in the rural South was often quite repressive for many African-Americans. For those who challenged the racial order, the results were often fatal. We have seen how agricultural labor organizing in the nineteenth century after Reconstruction and during the 1930s was violently crushed. Even the NAACP was a target of Ku Klux Klan attacks. The rural Black church was small, broke, and conservative (McAdam 1982:90–91). Vast changes were to take place beginning in the 1930s. With the decline of southern agricultural employment and the concommitant growth of employment opportunities in both southern and northern cities, the location of African-Americans changed greatly. A look at Table 9.2 is instructive. The Black southern urban population more than doubled between 1930 and 1960 (McAdam 1982:78–80; Poston and Weller 1981:116–17; Bartley 1995:11; Marable 1991:15; Whatley 1990:6–8).

The arguments about the effects of the growing urban concentration of Blacks in the South parallel remarks made by Karl Marx and Friedrich Engels about the impact of capitalist development on workers. Cities, according to Marx and Engels, are more cosmopolitan, away from "the idiocy of rural life." Urban workers are both more cognizant of world and national issues and have greater concentrated power to organize and effect change (see, e.g., Marx and Engels 1969:39–43). Southern urbanization likewise led to a concentration of African-Americans in contrast to the isolated existence of rural life. One consequence was a decline in white supremacist violence, encouraging organizing efforts by southern urban Blacks (Piven and Cloward 1979:192). The Black urban churches became much larger than formerly, vastly bigger than those in rural areas, having greater resources, better paid and trained ministers, and more financial independence. Church leadership, which had been overwhelmingly accommodationist, became largely committed to civil rights advocacy (McAdam 1982:96–97, 99, 100). Southern urban NAACP branches likewise grew and increased their activities. One can see the sizable growth in some of the institutions that were to play an important role in the 1950s and 1960s civil rights struggles. Black church membership jumped by 93 percent between 1926 and 1962 (largely in the South), college enrollment increased from 15,000 in 1939 to 75,000 in 1950, and NAACP membership increased by more than 400 percent over the same period of time (McAdam 1982:95, 99, 102–3; Whatley 1990:13; Piven and Cloward 1977:205–7).

World War II also brought a number of important changes in the southern African-American community, aside from those that were directly a consequence of economic development and urbanization, especially in alter-ing Black's perceptions and expectations of American society. Between 1941 and 1945, three million Blacks, many of them from the South, served in the armed forces. Having risked their lives for the country, fought racism in the military, and traveled around the globe, the majority of Black servicemen expected conditions in this country to improve following the war's end. Neil Wynn, for example, notes that 43 percent of Black servicemen said they expected that their material and social circumstances would be improved following the war's conclusion, compared with only 19 percent of whites (Wynn 1975:29). Similar results were found in a survey by James Stiles Hadley (Yeakey 1979:135).

As Yeakey notes, many southern blacks left their homes and counties for the first time. Travel, military experience, and the war itself introduced young blacks to different perspectives. Black veterans were especially will-ing to challenge segregation when they returned home from the war. Yet, it was not only Black males who were exposed to new horizons during the war. One Black woman, for example, found that there was little racial dis-crimination when she traveled by airplane, finding no segregated restrooms in New Orleans and Miami (Yeakey 1979:134,137,138).

Thus, World War II and the postwar social and economic development transformed the southern African-American community, leaving it with more resources and better situated to take advantage of new opportunities to pursue the historic struggle for equality in North America, with a height-ened anticipation and readiness to do so.

TABLE 9.2 *Urban Population in South*

Year	1900	1910	1920	1930	1940	1950
Black Population (in thousands)	1,369	1,862	2,261	3,310	3,631	4,922

Percentage of Blacks in the South 1900-1970

1900	1910	1920	1930	1940	1950	1960	1970
89.7%	89	85.2	78.7	77	68	60	53

Source: Historical Statistics 1975:I:22

WORKING-CLASS CIVIL RIGHTS PRECURSORS

Yet, for all those who look at the background of civil rights activity, attempt-ing to discover those early activities that helped embolden, set the tone, and lay the groundwork for the later movement, few point to or even seem to know much about the scope of labor-based civil rights activities in the post–World War II period. And it was the labor organization and militancy of Black workers that was to lay the basis, broadening the horizons and expectations—energizing the vehicles of struggle—for the movement of the 1950s and 1960s.

We have already seen the importance of civil rights issues to the urban/labor/left/civil rights coalition of the 1930s and 1940s. What recent scholarship is revealing is the degree to which much of the civil rights initiatives during this period were led, not by the established, more middle-class civil rights organizations but by organized Black workers and their white working-class allies. In the 1940s, it was generally acknowledged that industrial unions were at the center of civil rights activities. A Rosenwald Fund study found to its dismay that "the characteristic movements among Negroes are now for the first time becoming proletarian," while the NAACP saw the Congress of Industrial Organizations (CIO) as "a lamp of democracy" in the South (Korstad and Lichtenstein 1988:787). W. E. B. Du Bois concluded:

> Probably the greatest and most effective effort toward interracial understanding among the working masses has come about through the trade unions. The organization of the CIO in 1935...As a result, numbers of men like those in the steel and automotive industries have been thrown together, black and white, as fellow workers striving for the same objects. There has been on this account an astonishing spread of interracial tolerance and understanding. Probably no movement in the last 30 years has been so successful in softening race prejudice among the masses (Du Bois 1948)

Beth Bates argues that the NAACP was first displaced from its traditional role in the African-American community by the left and labor groups in the 1930s, and by the end of the decade, the NAACP had reoriented itself to the new reality (Bates 1995). The instances of such activity in the North are manifold. In Detroit, the alternative Black leadership was centered in the left-wing Ford River Rouge UAW local (Stephen-Norris and Zeitlin 1996). As we have already seen, UAW militants during World War II organized thousands of Black and white members to defend Black occupancy of the Sojourner Truth Homes. They also energized the NAACP, "as almost 20,000 new members joined," making Detroit the largest local chapter in the country. A Detroit minister stated at the end of World War II that "The CIO has usurped moral leadership in the [Negro] community" (Korstad and Lichtenstein 1988:797, 798). In San Francisco, Local 10 of the International Longshoremen and Warehousemen's Union (ILWU) with its 2,000 Black members out of 9,000 total longshoremen, supported strongly by ILWU President Harry Bridges and the local's sizeable group of left-wing activists, engaged in parallel activity (Nelson 1995:3). Chicago saw similar initiatives taken by the heavily Black, left-wing packinghouse locals and activists from the Farm Equipment Union (FE) organized International Harvester Tractor Works operation. Black steelworkers and their allies in Pittsburgh and surrounding steel areas at times did likewise.

At least as impressive were the many islands of such activity throughout the South. One such center was the largely African-American, Food and Tobacco Workers of America (FTA) Winston-Salem Local 22 with its over 10,000 members in the R.J. Reynolds tobacco plant. The national union helped train and promote Moranda Smith, a Black female leader of the local, to become the director of the Southeast region (K. Korstad 1992:86). FTA was especially notable for its many Black female officers and organizers, a striking anomaly within the CIO (R. Korstad 1986:xvii:5).

FTA organizing of tobacco workers had many of the characteristics of a "crusade," with civil rights struggles occupying a central place. They had extensive educational activities involving both Black and white workers, including a large library for members of Local 22. They also held a wide array of integrated social and athletic affairs, including picnics involving thousands of workers. Local 22 was a center of oppositional cultural and political activity. Paul Robeson appeared frequently in support of strikes and major events. FTA members also received entertainment and encouragement from Zephilia Horton, Woody Guthrie, and Pete Seeger. The union attempted to gain civil rights and greater political power in Winston-Salem and in North Carolina generally, by extensive voter-registration Campaigns and by supporting "pro-labor" candidates. Hundreds of FTA members also poured into the Winston-Salem NAACP, turning it into a large branch with over 1,900 members, militantly committed to civil rights actions (R. Korstad 1986:201–2, 208, 219–30). A correspondent for the Black newspaper, the *Pittsburgh Courier* wrote in June of 1944:

> I was aware of a growing solidarity and intelligent mass action that will mean a New Day in the South. One cannot visit Winston-Salem and mingle with the thousands of workers without sensing a revolution in thought and action. If there is a 'New' Negro, he is to be found in the ranks of he labor movement" (R. Korstad 1986:230).

Other examples of high levels of labor-led civil rights activity were in Birmingham, Alabama (Hudson 1972, Norrell 1991, Kelley 1990, Huntley 1977); Memphis (Honey 1988); and Fort Worth, Texas (R. Halpern 1991). Members of the Brotherhood of Sleeping Car Porters were active in many locations. Black dockworkers in the ILA in river ports along the Mississippi from Memphis to New Orleans played a role, as did seamen connected with the NMU, Maritime Cooks, and other seafarer's and riverboat unions. In the Southwest, Hispanic workers and their allies, acting through the Mine, Mill, and Smelter workers fought for equal rights (Daniel 1992). In Columbia, Tennessee, during anti-Black riots, 150 largely African-American working-class veterans and members of Mine Mill defended the Black community from a white mob (Bloom 1987:128–29). These and other similar activities represented the leadership role of Black workers in the early civil rights movement and in politics generally.

In some few cases, unions with only small numbers of Black workers played important roles. Here, leadership was the crucial variable. A stark contrast is to be found, for example, in a comparison of the racial practice of the left-led FE with the UAW at the Louisville, Kentucky, International Harvester (IHC) plant in the late 1940s and early 1950s. FE Local 236 represented all production and maintenance workers except for those in the foundry. The plant, which opened in 1946 and was represented by the FE from the beginning, had in 1949 over 6,000 employees, approximately 14 percent of whom were African-American. Local 236 was characterized by a large, active steward system, frequent meetings, an involved militant membership, and large numbers of work stoppages. As was mentioned earlier, its leaders and members, white as well as Black, displayed an unusual aggressiveness around issues of racial equality, both within the plant and in the community at large. The context was, of course, important. The Harvester management had a rhetorical commitment to nondiscrimination and did not generally engage in the racially inflammatory tactics used by many companies; Louisville was not the Deep South, although its segregated bus lines and across-the-board Jim Crow policies distinguished it from much of the North; and there were other specific characteristics as well. The FE leadership, however, was a central ingredient. This can be seen by its contrast with the UAW leadership at the same plant. In 1949, IHC began production in its new foundry. The large facility, which would eventually employ over 1,500 workers, was a separate bargaining unit won by the UAW during that year. Unlike the overwhelmingly white plant, the foundry was one-half Black. One would have thought that there would have been even more of a base for civil rights activities in the foundry than in the main plant. There is, however, no evidence that civil rights was an important issue for the UAW local. In fact, as a 1953 study by the National Planning Association found, the foundry had racially separate locker rooms designated "White" and "Colored," which had as yet received no protest from the UAW local; the same report indicated that there were no vestiges of the original racial separation in the comparable production areas of the main plant, represented by the FE. Not only was this contrast extreme, but it is a revealing commentary on the differing priorities on racial issues of the two unions (Gilpin 1992:545–6).

The perspective of the labor left on civil rights activities—shared by large segments of the CIO during the 1930s and by most popular front liberals throughout the 1940s and 1950s—was that segregation was first and foremost supported and promulgated by powerful economic interests. The goal of these interests was to maintain a low-paid labor force. They accomplished this by depriving Blacks of their rights, most conspicuously in the Deep South, limiting their employment options, and forcing them to work for the most minimal of remuneration. Such a system had the consequence of lowering the wages of whites, who had to compete with low-paid Black workers in the labor market. Second, they encouraged racist ideas and myths in order to keep Blacks and whites separate and divided, with whites often unwilling to organize jointly with Blacks to struggle together for their common interests. Thus, racial divisions hurt white workers almost as much as they hurt African-Americans—keeping wages down for all, especially in the South, limiting social benefits (be they education, unemployment insurance, medical care, or welfare) that were widely and more fully available in those places where the labor movement was stronger and less divided.

The strategy for confronting these problems was mass solidaristic mobilization of workers, or as the old slogan said, "Black and White, Unite and Fight." Such a movement was to demand full political and social rights for Blacks (including voting, education, housing, and job opportunities) and full rights on the job. In addition, all workers were to struggle together for improvement around general class issues. In the process, and through every form of education available, including reading material, classes, lectures, and general exposure, white workers in particular were to be educated on the need for solidarity and to support full rights for Blacks. This approach, with its economic analysis, political and economic demands, and its strategy of collective struggle, was the predominant one not only for much of the CIO during the 1930s but also among civil rights groups and liberals in general.

The perspective of the 1950s and 1960s civil rights movement was somewhat different. Although not really new, and embodied in many of the early legal strategies of the the NAACP, it only emerged as a dominant perspective in the 1950s. This "new" view is exemplified and most fully articulated in Gunnar Myrdal's An American Dilemma. As Myrdal argues, the root cause of racial discrimination was not economic or structural (although these factors played a role in the vicious circle of maintaining the problem). Rather, Blacks were denied their individual rights, guaranteed by the Constitution and the American Creed because of the prejudices—irrational beliefs—held by whites, especially the less-educated, working-class whites. The remedies were twofold: First, educating whites to the irrationality of their beliefs and their inconsistencies with the American Creed, that is, moral education. Second, changing the laws in those places where the rights of Blacks were restricted. No need to mobilize people for collective struggle, no need fundamentally to challenge the social structure or economic order, no need to alter class-based governmental policies. It was merely a question of changing laws and attitudes.[1] Although the late 1950s and early 1960s civil rights movement was to drop the gradualism and reluctance to engage in mass mobilizations—harking back to the immediatism and moral urgency of the abolitionists—they were to retain much of the rights-based perspective embodied in the "new" stance.

The Black working-class and left-led civil rights orientation was to lose its hegemony, eventually being completely replaced by the new more individualistic and formal perspective in the post-World War II period. This transformation in principles and stance is perceptively analyzed by Numan Bartley:

> The concern for economic reform and for the redistribution of wealth abated as liberals identified national and international corporate expansion with the growth of democratic values. . . . As racial issues, and most especially segregation in the South, moved to the top of the agenda for national reform, what had been the nation's number-one economic problem took on the aspect of the nation's number-one moral problem and an embarrassment in Cold War diplomacy (Bartley 1995:69).

> The problem came to seem not so much the disadvantaged state of the Black American population, or even of Black southerners; it was the blatant racial prescription that was most openly practiced in the South. Southern de jure segregation marred the nation's democratic image abroad and blemished white America's sense of moral rectitude at home (Bartley 1995:69–70).

> Whatever the failures of popular-front liberals, they presented a program that offered benefits to white workers. Unless Blacks and whites alike participated in labor organizations, the unions would not have had the strength to improve working conditions and the two races could be used as strikebreakers against each other. . . . After the demise of the popular front, postwar liberals offered white workers little aside from contempt and the right to compete for scarce jobs with Black workers. By defining liberalism not in terms of the redistribution of wealth, power, and privilege, but as an issue of individual morality, the new American left sharply narrowed the liberal agenda (Bartley 1995:73)

Thus, the labor-based civil rights activity of the 1930s and 1940s, had it been successful and allowed to expand, had the potential not only to spark a mass civil rights movement a decade before it actually developed but also to do so in a manner that would have had varying degrees of support from white workers, in the South as well as in the North. The class-based approach to civil rights, however, was abandoned by various liberal forces during the late 1940s and early 1950s. Those that did not abandon it were either crushed or marginalized.

The CIO, as I have tried to show, downgraded the importance of civil rights issues of any kind in the post–World War II period; to the extent that it remained concerned, the CIO switched to the new orientation. The right-wing of the CIO abandoned efforts to sustain and expand its civil rights activities, especially after its failed Operation Dixie. By expelling the left-wing CIO unions, including the FE, FTA, Mine Mill, Fur and Leather, and others that were highly committed to civil rights demands, undermining civil rights activity in unions previously committed to it (as in the NMU), and completely destroying local unions in key venues (including the FTA in Winston-Salem and Mine Mill in Birmingham), the national CIO helped dash the potential for a labor-led civil rights movement in the 1940s. The alliance of steelworkers with the KKK in their battle against Mine Mill poisoned relations between the local NAACP and the CIO in the 1950s, for this was an activity—even in the service of anticommunism—that local activists would not forgive (Wigderson 1989:341). When racists in the union attacked the pro-civil rights United Packinghouse Workers of America (UPWA), a union that had avoided expulsion from the CIO, CIO head Walter Reuther and his assistants in 1953 "lent legitimacy to the dissidents' accusations" by supporting an investigation. Leading anti-communists in the national CIO leadership even encouraged the withholding of dues and disaffiliation of rebellious racist-led locals (Halpern 1991:175). This telling episode is another of those defining moments that is strangely missing from Nelson Lichtenstein's recent biography of Walter Reuther (Lichtenstein 1995). On the West Coast, the ILWU was acknowledged even by the stridently anti-communist Wilson Record as a defender of the rights of Black workers. After its expulsion from the CIO in 1949, the ILWU was involved in a bitter struggle with the American Federation of Labor (AFL) and several of its virulently racist unions. San Francisco NAACP members rose to support the ILWU. Not only did the national CIO side against the ILWU, but the national NAACP demanded that its local members not support the ILWU, both anti-communist organizations aligning themselves with extreme bigotry (Nelson 1995).

The marginalization of pro-civil rights left-wing unions, the purges, the move to the right on civil rights by the right-wingers, the failure of

Operation Dixie, and the unchallenged rise of the Dixiecrats, allowed southern racists to equate anti-racism and pro-civil rights stances with communism, an equation that operated, as we have seen, not only at the state level but also at the national level.

Yet, even with this national turn against civil rights, there is evidence that the the right-controlled CIO merely abandoned civil rights without a struggle, rather than having been forced from the field by McCarthyism or the overwhelming racism of white workers. This is made clear when we see those things that continued to be cultivated in small garden plots. The UPWA, the FE, Mine Mill, the less radical sleeping-car porters, remnants of the United Public Workers, as well as the several hundred member Local 1199 continued successful civil rights activity. The Communist Party (CP)-supported National Negro Labor Council (NNLC), subpoenaed, harrassed, and red-baited by the government and the national CIO, with support from only a small segment of the labor movement, carried on numerous labor-related civil rights activities in the early 1950s. In Cleveland, for example, in December 1952, the NNLC mobilized 1,500 pickets (according to official police estimates) protesting the refusal of American Airlines to hire Blacks in any but the most unskilled capacities. The demonstration was led by the UPWA's Sam Parks of Chicago. About 20 percent of the demonstrators were white (*Cleveland Plain Dealer*, December 23, 1952). In Louisville in 1953, the NNLC engaged in a year-long campaign to get the new Louisville General Electric plant to hire and upgrade Black workers; in that city they put similar pressure on Ford and General Motors and on the railroads. In all these cases they had the strong support of the FEU's International Harvester Local (Ernest Thompson Papers, Rutgers University, Box 1).

Thus, it seems likely that if the CIO had maintained or increased its commitment to Black equality and to civil rights activism, much more could have been done. Remnants of the racially egalitarian labor movement were to emerge here and there, although rarely under its own flag. Asbury Howard, a former Mine Mill official, was to play a significant role in Birmingham, while E.D. Nixon of the sleeping-car porters was to be an important leader in the Montgomery bus boycott.

Hence, by the early 1950s, although the groundwork for the second Reconstruction had already been laid, the potential for labor-based civil rights activity was lost. The NAACP regained hegemony (through its legal strategies), which it had lost in good part during the mid-1930s to the NNC, the CIO, and the CP—and in an earlier period to the Garvey organization. The abandonment of civil rights as a defining issue for the urban/labor/left/civil rights coalition meant that both Adlai Stevenson as well as Dwight Eisenhower could appeal to white southern votes and reconciliation with the racists. The return by the Democrats to their traditional conservative racial strategy was only reversed when the civil rights movement forced them to make a choice in the 1960s. This strategy, only partially abandoned by Kennedy, still trying to straddle the fence, and finally abandoned completely by Lyndon Johnson, was to hurt the Democrats dearly, because it was soon to become evident that only the modern Republicans had the flexibility to transform themselves into making consistently racist appeals.

CAUSES OF THE REEMERGENCE OF THE CIVIL RIGHTS MOVEMENT IN THE SOUTH

Despite the defeat of racially egalitarian, civil rights-oriented unionism in the South in the 1940s and early 1950s and the retrenchment of Dixiecrat rule there, the question of equality and rights for African-Americans would not disappear. Various factors contributed to the reemergence of the civil rights movement, including the international context, favorable court decisions, the increased capacities for organization and struggle of African-American communities in both the North and South, and above all the increase in Black activism. A new movement gradually began to emerge during the early and middle 1950s, with important high points of struggle. The 1953 Baton Rouge bus boycott was a short, ten-day, mass-based struggle (with movement meetings and rallies of many thousands) that functioned as a precursor to similar struggles that took place later. The 1955 Montgomery bus boycott, however, involved a fully mobilized Black community that held firm for a full year until victory was achieved, getting broad publicity, inspiring struggles across the South, including ones in Birmingham and Tallahassee. Yet, the pace of events did not appear to be moving rapidly. It is significant that no bus boycotts were successful in larger southern cities. By the late 1950s, the Southern Christian Leadership Conference was largely inactive and virtually bankrupt. After 1955, massive resistance to desegregation emerged in the South, with Arkansas Governor Oval Faubus's 1957 resistance to federal desegregation orders in Little Rock, forcing an equivocating federal government to take a stand. The years 1958 and 1959 saw various types of sit-ins with little cumulative impact (Bloom 1987:154). Thus, to a surprising extent, there was almost as much discontinuity between the protests of the middle 1950s and those of the early 1960s, as there was between the former and the labor-based civil rights struggles of the 1930s and 1940s. Yet, each wave and era of organization and struggle had left important legacies and traditions to the next.

One of the important consequences of the broad social and economic development of the South was the vast increase in the number of African-American college students there. These students were to be an important component of the next wave of civil rights struggles that began in the early 1960s. The catalyst for the fast-paced development of the civil rights movement in a multiyear cycle of seemingly continuous activity that finally shook and riveted the attention of the whole nation was the student lunch counter sit-ins that began on February 1, 1960, in Greensboro, North Carolina. The sit-ins at segregated lunch counters were to spread across the whole South and in a few short months were to involve over 50,000 southern Black students. The élan of the movement was new, with African-American youth with no jobs or homes to lose or families to support who were ready to face white mobs, police, or jail for their beliefs. Much of the protest took place in cities where intimidation often backfired. During the first week of the Greensboro protest, for example, large numbers of students proceeded to march downtown, led by the North Carolina A. and T. football team. A white gang stood in their way and tried to stop them, demanding, "Who do you think you are?" Showing a far greater appreciation of American history than Newt Gingrich or any of the current conservative pundits, they replied, "We the union army," an élan which clearly seems to capture a new spirit (Bloom 1987:161). These sit-ins made headlines and captured the imagination of youth, white as well as Black, across the nation. They led to the formation of the Student Nonviolent Coordinating Committee (SNCC), which was to set the tone, style, courage, and militancy of the civil rights movement for the whole decade.

The demands of the early civil rights movement were simple ones, to be recognized as citizens with equal rights to go to school, to eat, to ride buses, to vote. The story is told well in many places how each escalation in tactics, the Freedom Rides of 1961, the 1963 Birmingham demonstrations, the 1965 march in Selma, Alabama, saw peaceful demonstrators meet with savage local violence, shocking the majority of northern whites. The high point of such outrage was perhaps the 1964 Freedom Summer where Black and white northern students went to Mississippi to help with voter registration, education, and organizing. In the beginning of the summer, civil rights workers James Chaney, Michael Schwerner, and Andrew Goodman—one Black, two white—disappeared. The bodies were later found brutally murdered—one investigator declaring that the majority of the bones in their bodies had been broken with chains before they died. The world as well as the North was outraged, leading Congress to pass the 1964 Civil Rights Act and President Lyndon B. Johnson to sing "We Shall Overcome" on television.

In all this, organized labor was little to be seen. Support and money came, to be sure, from a number of the larger unions, including the UAW and the steelworkers. Few unions, however, attempted to mobilize their memberships to participate in the struggle, although the Packinghouse

Workers and the small Local 1199, were among the exceptions. Here and there, the tattered remnants of the old racially egalitarian unions did join the fray, but they did not fundamentally change the character of the struggle. And various white southern AFL-CIO officials bucked the tide of established southern society and often many of their own white racist members, heroically aligning themselves with the Black movement. Although some unions played a supportive role (Greenberg notes the integrationist stance of the autoworkers in Birmingham, Alabama; a number of unions with large Black memberships were aggressively active, including Hospital Workers Union 1199 and the American Federation of State, County and Municipal Employees) and even the AFL-CIO gave verbal support at times, the role of organized labor was clearly secondary.

As Malcolm X was to say, the chickens had come home to roost. Having failed to support and extend, in fact having destroyed, the most promising tendencies toward racially egalitarian, civil rights-oriented unionism, the CIO had left the 1960s civil rights movement in the South with few white working-class allies. This factor, a result of the failure of Operation Dixie and the destruction of the most promising interracial unionism, has set the terms of American politics up to the present day.

CHANGING CHARACTER

By the mid-1960s, the character of the civil rights movement was to change again and a number of splits were to take place. The demands of the early civil rights movement have sometimes been described as middle class. The reason for this is that they were directed toward equal access to lunch counters, bus service, stores, restaurants, hotels, housing, and the like—things that required money (and jobs) to utilize. These demands are, of course, in a non-pejorative sense, strictly bourgeois, what Hegel in his *Philosophy of Right* refers to as abstract right. They are the rights of the market place, where buyers and sellers are accepted irrespective of their personal characteristics (sex, race or ethnicity, royalty, status, class), merely on the basis of their ability to pay or to supply the desired goods. These bourgeois or abstract rights are a decided advance over earlier notions that restricted many categories of people from recognition as human beings who were entitled to the opportunity to participate equally in the economy and civil society. The denial of these abstract rights—abstract because they apply to everybody and are abstracted from personal characteristics—is pre-bourgeois, not in accordance with the proper functioning of capitalist markets. The demands for full citizenship, the right to vote, participation on juries, equal protection before the law, are demands for political equality, similar to abstract rights. Although the goals of the early civil rights movement may have been middle class, the movement that was demanding them was often not supported initially by many of those in the traditional Black middle class. Jack Bloom notes that most of the Black press in the South did not support the sit-ins, while established businessmen and professionals with much to lose preferred to distance themselves from confrontational tactics. As Louis Lomax stated, there was "a good deal of foot-dragging by moneyed Negroes in high places" (Bloom 1987:171).

On the other hand, the demands of the early civil rights movement had deep sympathy from all strata of the Black population because they were demands for human dignity. And in order for the early civil rights movement to achieve its goals, it had to mobilize the large numbers of lower-class African-Americans. Even the early bus boycotts in Montgomery and Tallahassee, relied largely on working-class Blacks, especially cooks and domestics (Bloom 1987:172; see also the excellent work by Yeakey 1979). As the struggle escalated, success depended on full mobilization, reaching to all strata of the Black community, most of whom were not "middle class." The changing character of the class base of the early civil rights movement may be seen by noting the difference between the participants in the 1960 sit-ins (virtually all college students) and the mass community mobilizations in Albany, Georgia, from 1962 to 1963, and in Birmingham, Alabama, in 1963. This was a contradictory mix. The demands for abstract rights, based on non-violent, respectable protest—the tactic of serving as a moral witness—required the mass involvement of people who had many other urgent needs, who did not always desire to appear respectable, and whose lifetime interactions with white authorities had left them skeptical of non-violence.

Malcolm X had been appealing to this same lower-class constituency. SNCC and even Dr. Martin Luther King shifted their appeals and tactics to stay in tune with the growing militancy and impatience spreading through Black communities. The bubble was burst by the ghetto uprisings (revolts as their supporters claimed or riots as their detractors asserted), which made clear that there were vast material problems (in addition to the questions of access to civil society and the body politic that the southern movement had emphasized) involving schools, housing, jobs, material goods—whose solution would involve huge amounts of resources and adjustments by the nation as a whole. These deeper economic and social issues—class questions —involved the redistribution of resources, questions it should be emphasized in which many white workers potentially had a large stake. That is not the way, however, that they were posed or dealt with politically at the time.

Now, these demands of access to the market and the political process, the demands for the acceptance of the abstract rights of African Americans are ones that whites have increasingly come to accept as legitimate, at least in so far as we can believe opinion polls that have been taken from the end of World War II to the present. These polls further show a growing national convergence of opinion by regions, even including southerners. Opinion polls have shown that while only 32 percent of whites in 1932 favored integrated schools, and 58 percent in 1956, over 90 percent answered favorably by 1982 (Schuman, Steeh, and Bobo 1985:74–76, table 3.1), and by 1985, the figure had reached 92 percent (Mayer 1992:369, table 3.5). By 1972, 97 percent thought that Blacks should have equal access to jobs; by 1970, 88 percent believed that transportation should be integrated, whereas only 46 percent had responded favorably in 1942. And by 1976, 88 percent felt that African-Americans had a right to live where they chose (Schuman, Steeh, and Bobo 1985:74–76). And on what was formerly the most sensitive racial taboo, 72 percent of the population in 1988 said they opposed laws against racial intermarriage (Mayer 1992:371, table 3.5). Even on school busing, which only small percentages of whites favored in the mid-1970s, the figure had risen to 32 percent in 1988, with 63 percent opposed (Mayer 1992:373, table 3.6). On the other hand, as Lou Harris has recently reported, huge majorities of whites oppose "quotas" but substantial majorities support other forms of affirmative action (a 1988 Harris poll found that 55 percent of whites favored affirmative action programs "which do not have rigid quotas;" Sniderman and Piazza 1993:130). Some of these questions will be discussed in more detail later. The civil rights movement and the response to it have played a major role in changing the opinions of whites. Even many white conservatives today say they support these types of civil rights.

As the civil rights movement evolved and went beyond the initial bourgeois demands, there were a series of different responses, much of which can be summarized succinctly. Many of the former middle-class white allies simply abandoned the civil rights movement and refused to support it any more. White middle-class (and some working-class) youth who were to become radicalized along with the militant wings of the Black movement continued to support the evolving African-American movement, but they were a distinct minority among northern whites.

SNCC and other groups turned to the slogan of Black Power. Martin Luther King went searching for other allies and new issues. Much of his new approach is represented by his support of the Memphis garbage workers strike, which was a struggle of an overwhelmingly Black workforce for increased economic security and a living wage as well as dignity and respect. King also attempted to make alliances in these struggles with organized labor, but except for some brief episodes, the overwhelming majority of unions were unresponsive (Honey 1992). Yet, white labor leaders and white-dominated unions were not the only ones to abandon the civil rights struggles of Black workers. During the school boycotts in Memphis in 1969 by Black students, the NAACP joined with the leaders of the Memphis Chamber of Congress and other prominent citizens in an interracial committee, explicitly excluding the American Federation of State, County, and Municipal Employees (AFSCME) union which represented sanitation workers. Middle-class Blacks and their organizations not only put their emphasis on increased opportunities for Black school administrators and politicians, but also refused to support a new unionization drive at the Memphis City Hospital (Faist n.d.).

Thus, as one wing of the civil rights movement became more radicalized and attempted to strengthen its ties with poorer and working-class constituencies in the African-American community, its white middle-class allies and its more middle-class Black wing began to abandon it. Unions, which should have flocked to its side, were more or less silent. The role of championing these issues fell to the growing numbers of small, radicalized Black organizations—some nationalist, some Marxist—which proliferated across the political landscape. These included the Black Panther Party, the League of Revolutionary Black Workers, the African National People's Congress, the Revolutionary Action Movement, and large numbers of groups loosely affiliated with the African Liberation Support Committee. And there were many dramatic individual instances of radicalization as, for example, when Amira Baraka (née LeRoi Jones) went from identifying as a cultural nationalist to a revolutionary Marxist. Parallel, if less pronounced, trends took place among Puerto Rican, Chicano, and Asian groups (the latter often challenging the hegemony of pro–Taiwanese Chinese business leaders in their communities).

By the early 1970s, these organizations were reduced to fractious coalitions, with only isolated mass support, usually more dependent on the skill of individual leaders than a broad, overall strategy. Yet, some of these organizations, often with public sympathy, for a time had major influence and pushed all Black leaders in more militant directions, making them pay homage to various class issues. When local, state, and federal law enforcement officials led a raid on a Chicago Black Panther Party apartment in the middle of the night, assassinating Fred Hampton and Mark Clark, two sleeping Panther leaders, every significant African-American leader in the country traveled to Chicago to eulogize the slain Panther leaders. Hundreds of thousands of Chicagoans came to view the coffins, with the neighborhood around the funeral home having to be cordoned off to traffic for many blocks in each direction.

Yet, these alliances were ephemeral. Even in Memphis (as in Atlanta), the Black political establishment and the Black middle class was often lukewarm or in opposition to the struggles of Black workers. More established

Black organizations turned to legal and electoral arenas, electing African-American congressmen and local officials throughout northern cities, whose effects, while not marginal, especially in integrating transportation services, police, and other public employment, did little fundamentally to change economic and political power and the conditions of the worst off.

In the South in the 1970s and 1980s, local mass-based civil rights movements toppled county and town power structures in what has in some ways been the most enduring triumph of the civil rights movement. Racist sheriffs and other officials were replaced with democratically controlled African-American elected politicians, largely eliminating the terror of daily life, especially in the Deep South Black Belt areas. For example, in Mississippi in 1968, there were only twenty-two Black elected officials, none of whom were county sheriffs or justices of the peace. By 1980, there were 299 Black officials, including many sheriffs and justices of the peace in Black Belt counties (Bell 1992:84; *Statistical Abstract* 1995:32). In the Deep South (Alabama, Georgia, Louisiana, Mississippi, South Carolina, and including the Upper South states of Virginia and North Carolina), the number of Black officials increased from 156 in 1968 to 1,813 in 1980 (Bell 1992:84; *Statistical Abstract* 1995:32). In hundreds of workplaces around the country, caucuses of Black workers organized for their rights, dramatically eliminating many discriminatory upgrading and supervisory practices. Some such as the League of Revolutionary Black Workers based in Detroit's auto plants or the Mahwah Black Brothers in New Jersey were rhetorically radical, while others were less so.

The official government response to poverty and the ghetto upsurges and other struggles of the poor, be they welfare rights movements, rent strikes, and other community demands, was to set up the War on Poverty. Without mass support, the War on Poverty was ephemeral and at times something of a fiasco, although it had a number of small significant successes. It also at times contributed to the heightening of inter-class tensions, some of which were racial and other aspects of which pitted the African-American poor against those Blacks already employed. Contrary to current myths being asserted today by both Democrats and Republicans, the low levels of political support for the War on Poverty led to inadequate funding, which helped contribute to its many problems. One of the most successful of its programs —one even touted as such by conservatives today—is headstart. Headstart often succeeded at giving poor children skills so that they could participate in elementary school on an equal basis. Day care centers were also provided to allow poor women on welfare to work. Yet, the income threshholds for both programs were so low (in part because of inadequate funding), that many working-class people—Black as well as white—were paying for benefits for poorer, most often Black citizens, that they themselves could have used but could not afford. Rather than the War on Poverty implementing universal programs that might have achieved broader support, it tended to, and was clearly seen as, giving public resources to the poorest Blacks. A fully mobilized labor movement might have supported these latter efforts and successfully obtained full benefits for broader sectors of the working class. The War on Poverty was not the only program that took from some needy people and gave to others. As Jill Quadagno argues, poor working people without healthcare pay a large share of Medicare for the elderly, and Black working women (who have historically participated in the labor force in far higher percentages than white women) help to subsidize Social Security for white housewives (Quadagno 1994:135, 142, 151, 108–9, 167). Medicare and Social Security, of course, have received few criticisms for these inequities, so we should be clear that it was the racial aspect of the War on Poverty that so excited many white people—and continues to make it a target for many bigots today, decades after the fact.

It is the emergence of the African-American Freedom Movement in the 1950s and 1960s that provides the key to understanding the development of American politics since. Yet, this heroic movement led by many "new abolitionists" ushering in a "second Reconstruction" of the South had both limitations as well as dramatic liberating characteristics. Any serious assessment must not only draw a careful balance sheet but also look at its specific characteristics, how they were rooted in the limitations of the 1930s and 1940s turning point, and the consequent impact of the civil rights movement on the rest of U.S. society.

First, let us begin with the liberating effects of the civil rights movement. Like the early Reconstruction struggles in the Deep South a century earlier, the civil rights movement not only developed a new self-confidence and assertiveness among individual African-Americans, but also led to an upsurge of politically conscious organization, touching virtually every aspect of U.S. society. Demands for equality and the formation of political organizations by other nonwhite minorities were stimulated. The women's movement, as had been the case during the pre–Civil War abolition movement, gained strength, involvement, and inspiration from the militant movements for equality for people of color. The student and anti-war movements were a direct outgrowth of the movement of African-Americans. The first mass campus protest, the 1964 Berkeley Free Speech Movement, was sparked by the denial of campus civil rights groups (many of whose leaders had spent the previous summer in Mississippi) from organizing on campus. Antiwar protest was propelled by the 1965 anti-war statements of the SNCC and Martin Luther King, by the courageous early draft refusals in the Deep South of SNCC activists, by the dramatic draft refusal of boxing heavyweight champion Muhammad Ali, who stated "No Vietcong ever called me nigger." The unionization of local, state, and federal level public employees (adding millions of members to unions) and the new Black caucuses at large numbers of workplaces were an outgrowth of the Black struggle. Even the renewed liberal impulses within the Democratic Party during the 1960s and 1970s owe their origins to the African-American Freedom Movement.

Yet, as I have already indicated, the civil rights movement had two related features (which were characterics of the 1930s and 1940s civil rights struggles) that were missing; these features were to create problems for the long-term success of the movement. First, as I have argued, the exclusive focus on rights led the movement largely to gloss over those class issues that were at the root of problems faced by poor and working-class African-Americans. Second, as I have argued, the main missing link from the struggles of the 1960s—in good part a consequence of the contradictory resolution of the 1930s turning point—was the organized labor movement. To be sure, one could make a long list of labor involvement, interaction, and contribution, for example, the growth of public-sector unions, the large amount of money given by many unions to mainstream civil rights groups, the verbal statements, the many individuals who participated, and the many heroisms and acts of bravery by southern AFL-CIO officials who were bucking the racist tide in the Deep South (A. Draper 1994). Yet, when comparing the 1960s with the activities of the CIO unions of the 1930s and 1940s, especially with that of many of the left-led unions, particularly in terms of active involvement and mobilization of ordinary rank-and-file members, organized labor during the second Reconstruction must be regarded as missing in action. These missing elements, I shall be arguing further in the next chapter, played a central role in how the racial politics of the last several decades has developed in the United States.

1. In a penetrating analysis, Seth Wigderson describes in graphic detail how this new orientation on civil rights was all-pervasive in the 1950s in the UAW, and how it flowed almost inevitably from the corporatist perspective of the Reuther leadership (Wigderson 1989, especially chapter 5).

CHAPTER 9

The Building of the White Racist Coalition

> I say, segregation now, segregation tomorrow, segregation forever.
>
> George Wallace in his 1963 Alabama gubernatorial inaugural address.
>
> Tactics based solely on morality can only succeed when you are dealing with people who are moral or a system that is moral. A man or system which oppresses a man because of his color is not moral.
>
> Malcolm X, June 28, 1964, Organization of Afro-American Unity founding rally, New York City (*Malcolm X* 1992:42)

An extremely broad range of writers have argued that industrial development inevitably destroys old social structures and values, especially certain narrow, provincial outlooks associated with an isolated rural existence. Marx and Engels, of course, make this argument most graphically:

> The bourgeoisie...has created enormous cities, has increased the urban population compared with the rural, and has thus rescued a considerable part of the population from the idiocy of rural life (Marx and Engels 1969:39).

Yet, Marx and Engel's attitude toward the forces of modernization was not totally sanguine:

> It has drowned the most heavenly ecstasies of religious fervour, of chivalrous enthusiasm, of philistine sentimentalism, in the icy water of egotistical calculation. It has resolved personal worth into exchange value, and in place of the numberless indefeasible chartered freedoms, has set up that single, unconscionable freedom— Free Trade. (Marx and Engels 1969:38)

Less-qualified assessments of the benefits of unfettered capitalist development are provided by a number of free-market conservatives, including Milton Friedman (1962) and W.W. Rostow (1960), who argue that such economic development leads to freedom and democracy. Such a position, of course (not held by the original free-market ideologue Fredrick Hayek, who did not associate democracy with capitalism), is amply disproved, not only by the capitalist economies of Nazi Germany and World War II Japan but also by the anti-democratic, highly repressive regime of Pinochet's Chile, whose economic policies were directed, implemented, ministered over, and overseen by Friedman's own students and coworkers.

These intellectual arguments aside, numerous southern liberals had pinned their hopes on industrial development for the South, believing that it would break down southern rural backwardness, especially its white racist character. V.O. Key, for example, asked how the South would escape from "the unfathomable maze formed by tradition, caste, race, and poverty." His hopeful conclusion was that the way forward would be through the growth of cities, which contained "the seeds of political change for the South" (Key 1949:664, 673). Key stood within a long tradition. Broadus and George Mitchell, in an earlier generation, had felt that industrial development for the South "destroys separatism, and invites and forces national and world consciousness" (Mitchell and Mitchell 1930:ix).

To many hopeful observers, the liberalization of the South after World War II, based on its economic development, recent emergence from regional isolation, and the impact of northern institutions, seemed all but inevitable. In 1944, the Supreme Court had ruled in *Smith v. Allwright,* a case from Texas, that all-white primaries were illegal. It is estimated that only about 150,000 African-Americans in the South, approximately 3 percent of the adult non-white population, were registered to vote at this time (see Garrow 1994:7 for comprehensive state breakdowns; Mathews and Prothro 1966:17, in an earlier estimate claim 250,000). By 1947, there were 595,000 Black registrants, by 1952, over one million, although almost none of this increase had taken place in the four Deep South states of Alabama, Louisiana, Mississippi, and South Carolina. So-called southern progressives, however, although clearly a minority of politicians in the South, seemed to be holding their own.[1] In 1944, progressive Senators Lester Hill of Alabama and Claude Pepper of Florida won resounding victories, while moderate Olin Johnson defeated "Cotton" Ed Smith for the Senate in South Carolina (Garson 1974:106, 125). By 1946, Texas and Virginia had accepted the *Allwright* decision and were letting Blacks vote (Garson 1974:172). In Alabama, with 25 percent of the workforce unionized and one of the few southern states where unions actually had some political influence, Congress of Industrial Organizations (CIO)-endorsed populist James Folsom won the 1946 gubernatorial election. As Robert Garson notes, "His victory was a source of encouragement to liberals throughout the South" (Garson 1974:190), leading the ever optimistic *New Republic* to declare Alabama "the most liberal state in the South" (A. G. Mezerik, April 19, 1947, "Dixie in Black and White.") The Longs in Louisiana, with a racially moderate populist appeal, continued to dominate politics in that state with Huey's brother Earl easily elected governor and his son Russell elected to the Senate in 1948 (Howard 1972:546–47). Tennessee had Senators Albert Gore, Estes Kefauver, and Governor Frank G. Clement, the latter two elected in the liberal, pro-labor, 1948 routing of the Memphis-based Crump machine. Arkansas had Congressmen Brooks Hays, Texas had Senator Ralph Yarborough, while North Carolina could boast of a host of southern liberals, including Senator Frank Graham. Not only did southern liberals appear to be thriving, but after the 1948 election, Dixiecrat fortunes seemed to be lagging even in the Deep South (Bartley 1969:36).

The first *Brown* decision (Brown I), which declared school segregation illegal, was announced on May 17, 1954, although its likely results had been anticipated in the South for months. The South, especially the Upper South, was initially quite restrained, as a number of historians and commentators have noted. In early May in the Alabama Democratic Party primaries, James Folsom was nominated for governor and John Sparkman renominated for the Senate. The latter had been aggressively attacked by his opponent as a racial liberal because Sparkman had been the 1952 Democratic vice-presidential candidate running on the party's civil rights program. These results were "hardly dictated by immediate concern for white supremacy" (Bartley 1969:56). Senator Kefauver and Governor Frank Clement also easily won renomination in August over segregationist candidates. In the South Carolina senatorial primary, Kerr Scott defeated an organization-backed incumbent while vigorously denouncing McCarthyism and racial intolerance (Bartley 1969:73; for a similar summary, see Klarman 1994:93).

Southern moderates were to have a brief heyday before being isolated, silenced, and then crushed. As Numan Bartley notes, "The long-term trend in public opinion in the South as elsewhere in the nation was clearly towards a greater acceptance of desegregation and an erosion of unfavorable images for the Negro" (Bartley 1969:14). Many southern newspapers initially supported compliance with *Brown*. Southern Baptists, Methodists, Presbyterians, and Episcopalians did likewise. Except for one district in Delaware, Washington, D.C.; Maryland; Delaware; West Virginia; and Missouri moved almost immediately toward compliance and did so relatively peaceably (McMillan 1971:8). On the day the *Brown* decision was announced, Virginia State Superintendent of Public Instruction Dowell J. Howard announced that "There will be no defiance of the Supreme Court as far as I am concerned." A few days earlier the Catholic Bishop of Richmond had announced the desegregation of Catholic parochial schools (Muse 1961:3, 4). Five days after *Brown*, the Little Rock school board announced compliance, followed shortly by similar pronouncements from Fayetteville, Arkansas; Baltimore; and Louisville. In 1955, the executive director of the Virginia Chamber of Commerce suggested that the increased purchasing power that Blacks might obtain through

integration would lead to a more prosperous South. And the Falstaff Brewing
Company, in a move that it was later to regret and retract, even purchased a
lifetime membership in the National Association for the Advancement of
Colored People (NAACP)[2]

Little of this moderate posture, however, existed in the Deep South. The
movement of massive resistance was to begin quickly in the Black Belt plantation areas in the South, and as with other reactionary movements there—
secession and the Civil War, the defeat of Reconstruction, and the crushing
of Populism—was to spread and soon dominate the whole South.

To no one's surprise, the most immediate, powerful response was to
take place in Mississippi. The main organizational vehicle was the Citizens'
Council, the first one of which was formed in July 1954, in Indianola,
Mississippi, the seat of Sunflower County in the heart of the Delta. The council was formed by the town's economic and political elites, including the
mayor, the city attorney, the manager of the town's cotton press, a Harvard-
educated lawyer, and a prominent banker. Sunflower County was dominated by cotton agriculture. It was the home of Senator James Eastland's enormous plantation. Its population was 68 percent African-American, .03 percent of whom were registered to vote. The Citizens' Councils rapidly spread
throughout the entire state, receiving support from the major newspapers
and virtually all elected officials. Even in Mississippi, the state with the highest Black population and the state most dominated by cotton agriculture,
the movement's development was uneven, drawing its greatest strength from
the cotton lands of the Delta, prospering most fully in those areas where
Blacks were 50 percent or more of the population. In the southern part of
the state, in the Sixth Congressional District where few counties were over
one-third Black, only five of the sixteen counties had organizations, a major
contrast with the Delta (McMillan 1971:18–19, 26–27). From Mississippi,
the "Mother of the Movement," Citizens' Councils quickly spread throughout much of the South.

Despite the Citizens' Council's rhetoric of eschewing violence and dis-
tancing itself from the legacy of the Ku Klux Klan, the movement of massive
resistance was accompanied by increased violence. As Jack Bloom notes, "The
Councils created an atmosphere that gave the green light to others to carry
out violence" (Bloom 1987:100). The Klan, for example, dressed in their night
sheets and regalia and made open raids on Black communities throughout
the South, injuring and killing numerous people. In Birmingham, they cas-
trated a Black handyman as part of a ceremony. In Camden, South Carolina,
they flogged a white school teacher who had allegedly made a favorable reference to desegregation. In Charlotte, the KKK attempted to blow up a Black
school. In Gaffney, South Carolina, they dynamited a white physician's

cause his wife had written an article favoring racial justice. There
bombed houses and burning crosses for those who deviated from
the racial order, as well as Blacks who were beaten and flogged for no reason at all (Bartley 1969:208–9).

The worst violence took place in Mississippi, but the effect all across
the South was to terrorize Blacks and those whites who did not support or
equivocated on massive resistance. A Black minister in Belzoni, Mississippi,
who had advocated Black suffrage, was murdered while driving his car.
Another proponent of racial justice in Mississippi was shot to death in broad
daylight near a courthouse entrance in front of several witnesses. No one
was ever prosecuted for these crimes. Several weeks later, the most infamous
murder took place, one seemingly having nothing directly to do with politics. Fourteen-year-old Emmett Till visiting from Chicago was kidnapped,
beaten, killed, and dumped in the Tallahatchie River for supposedly whistling
at a white woman (Bloom 1987:100–1). Resulting in worldwide outrage,
the Till murder served notice throughout the South that transgressions from
white supremacy were risky business. The KKK itself, however, was not as
powerful as it had been during Reconstruction. Unlike the Citizens' Councils,
it did not always have large support from southern elites and was often
involved in embarrassing situations. Its most widely publicized blunder took
place in January 1958, when the North Carolina Knights of the Ku Klux Klan
decided to teach an Indian tribe in Robeson County greater respect for white
supremacy. They burned a cross in a field near the town of Maxton, but the
only local people who showed up were a thousand armed Indians, some
with war paint, who surrounded the Klan. The Klansmen quickly decided
that the best strategy was to flee (Bartley 1969:205).

Although physical violence was frequent, it was not the main method
used in intimidating the opponents of white supremacy in the South. More
common were the tactics of the Citizens' Councils, who despite their claims
of being democratic town meetings, served as vigilante committees to suppress dissent. Their main approach was economic intimidation. A council
leader in Alabama explained the strategy: "The white population in this
county controls the money...We intend to make it difficult, if not impossible, for any Negro who advocates desegregation to find and hold a job, get
credit or renew a mortgage" (Bartley 1969:193). Numerous Blacks who
attempted to register to vote or who signed petitions for school desegregation were fired; merchants found themselves without credit and their loans
denied. Home visits were made urging the deviants to change their ways or
face the consequences (Bloom 1987:99–100; Bartley 1969:193–34). Economic
coercion, especially in the Black Belt areas, was usually quite effective, eventually however, diminishing in importance, partly because it was no longer

necessary, but also because it occasionally backfired. In Orangeburg, South Carolina, for example, when economic retaliation was taken against Blacks who had petitioned for school desegregation, the Black community—63 percent of the population of the county, responded with a boycott against white merchants who were leading the attack. And there was nothing like the loss of their business to moderate their views (Bloom 1987:103–4).

In addition to violence and the tactics of the Citizens' Councils, state power was aggressively used in the defense of white supremacy. The Mississippi legislature passed a law making it a crime to violate the state's segregation laws even when acting under federal directives. One Black man who tried to enroll at the University of Mississippi was held for ten days in the state mental hospital. Yet, as Bartley notes, "Mississippi was by no means alone in its use of law and public authority to coerce conformity. In varying degrees, all the southern states employed state power to hinder, harass, or crush dissent." The NAACP was outlawed, harassed, and immobilized by expensive and time-consuming legal suits in every state in the South (Bartley 1969:211–12).

Five states—Mississippi, Alabama, Louisiana, South Carolina, and Virginia—contained the overwhelming majority of white supremacist members and organizations. Despite variations by state in strength and popular activities, however, massive resistance spread throughout the whole South, developing a solid white racist front, which neither brooked dissenters nor eventually even found them. The unanimity that was achieved in the South is in part indicated by the remarkable Southern Manifesto, the "Declaration of Constitutional Principles," rejecting the legitimacy of the Supreme Court—signed by 101 of the 128 national legislators from the South. Of those who did not sign, most were either from Texas or the upper South. In North Carolina, two of the three congressmen who had refused to sign were defeated for reelection after a large white supremacist mobilization (Bartley 1995:96, 116, 206).

The white racist, massive resistance movement eventually destroyed the long-standing tradition of populist, economic liberalism. Racial moderate Governor James Folsom proved himself completely out of touch with the political mood developing in Alabama. In November 1955, when Harlem Congressman Adam Clayton Powell was to speak in Montgomery, Folsom had a limousine pick Powell up at the airport. Later, the two politicians drank scotch together in the governor's mansion, with this collegiality being reported in the media. In January 1956, the Alabama legislature, more in tune with the growing movement of racist reaction in the state, passed with near unanimity a resolution declaring Supreme Court racial decisions null and void in Alabama. Folsom declared it "a bunch of hogwash," finishing out his term in total isolation (Strong 1972:449–50). Governor Earl Long of

Louisiana, reelected in 1956, remained aloof from massive resistance, allowing the Louisiana State University branch in New Orleans to become the only
educational institution in the South to be substantially integrated—having
1,000 whites and 200 Blacks—and not merely desgregated on a token basis
(Bartley 1995:208). Long forces repealed the state's "right to work" law in
1956, making it the only former Confederate state without this antiunion
legislation. Although neither was an integrationist, both Long and Folsom
accorded Blacks many rights and opportunities absent in other southern
states. By the end of the decade, however, the southern progressive tradition
that both men represented was dead.

Having described the massive resistance movement, a crucial step in the
building of a national white racist coalition in the United States, it is important to attempt to understand why eventually it engulfed the whole white
South. Given the limited support for the 1948 States' Rights Democratic Party
(Dixiecrats), why was there such unanimity and so little opposition? Neil
McMillen, in his important and richly descriptive book on the Citizens'
Councils, asserts that the white South shared "a sense of solidarity that had
little foundation in fact" (McMillen 1971:5). It behooves us, however, to look
more closely.

The easiest part to explain is the strongest base of support. Desegregation
was most threatening to social and economic life in the Black Belt plantation areas of the South, where African-American majorities were disenfranchised, supplied cheap labor, and were subordinated in virtually every
aspect of life. As McMillen notes, after *Brown,* "Almost invariably, racial tensions ran highest and white intransigence was greatest in areas where the
Negro population was the most dense. Conversely, in areas where Blacks
comprised a relatively small minority, white compliance was very often
achieved with comparative ease" (McMillen 1977:6). As a first cut, it is clear
that political rights, equalizing resources, and integrating facilities would
have more effects on whites where the numbers of Blacks were greatest.

In every state the impetus and largest popular white support for massive resistance came from the Black Belt areas. In Alabama, the white Citizens'
Council began in Selma, the heart of the plantation area. This was also the
case in Louisiana, Georgia, and South Carolina, as well as the outer South,
including Florida (McMillen 1977:43, 61, 75, 81, 101). Even in Virginia, which
Muse claims was "in some ways more a Northern than a Southern state,"
the Black Belt dominated. Massive resistance there was first organized and
remained centered in the Fourth Congressional District, an agricultural area
of thirty counties, almost one-half Black that made up barely 15 percent of
the state's population. In 1831, the district had been the site of Nat Turner's
slave insurrection, and in 1888, it had elected the only Black ever to repre-

sent Virginia in Congress (Muse 1961:1–7). Race was clearly an important issue of long standing for this Black Belt area; resistance to desegregation came with the territory. It was thus no surprise that Mississippi, the state with the largest percentage African-American population had the largest, strongest council organization, with its most numerous supporters in that state's Black Belt areas. In fact, it is claimed that the Council movement throughout the South was led, organized, and to a significant degree controlled by the Mississippi White Citizens' Council (Bloom 1987:102).

Massive resistance, however, was not simply a cross-class movement supported by Black Belt whites opposed to granting equality to African-Americans because it would undermine whites political power, force them to share resources, and increase the degree of social contact between African-Americans and themselves. It was defined and led by the white economic elites of the Black Belts, planters and their allies. One important vehicle for planter influence was the Farm Bureau, a major force in many southern states. In Alabama, dominated by commercial Black Belt agriculturists, the Farm Bureau "consistently, throughout the entire civil rights period, opposed attempts by the courts, the federal government, and blacks to integrate Alabama society." Even when business groups began to waver, the Farm Bureau remained "implacable," fighting in 1961 to keep the literacy test for voting. When business groups condemned lawlessness and were prepared to make concessions, the Farm Bureau in Alabama attacked the 1964 Civil Rights Act as "unconstitutional and an infringement on the rights of property owners." They remained fervent supporters of white supremacist Governor George Wallace (Greenberg 1980:124).

As I have discussed in the previous chapter, contrary to claims made by some, the needs of planters for cheap, coerced African-American agricultural labor had not diminished in the early civil rights (and massive resistance) period. In 1957, only 17 percent of the cotton in Mississippi was mechanically harvested (peaking at 25 percent in 1956), with the highest rates that year of 35 percent in Louisiana and 37 percent in Texas (Wright 1986:244). As Warren Whatley argues in a path-breaking manuscript, the cost of harvest labor—the chief bottleneck and period of highest labor demand—for those planters still growing cotton in the late 1950s was still a major problem, made especially severe by the large declines in the real price of cotton (Whatley 1990). During the period of massive resistance (1954–59), planters were unwilling to give up on the system of white supremacy without a determined struggle.

How then did these planters proceed to gain the support, or at least the acquiescence, of the rest of the whites in the South? First, we must remember that this is what they had always done from colonial times on.

As V.O.Key explains:

The hard core of the political South—and the backbone of southern political unity—is made up of those counties and sections of the
southern states in which Negroes constitute a substantial proportion
of the population. In these areas a real problem of politics broadly
considered, is the maintenance of control by a white minority....

The black belts make up only a small part of the area of the South
and...account for an even smaller part of the white population...
Although the whites of the black belts are few in number, their
unity and their political skill have enabled them to run a shoestring
into decisive power at critical junctures in southern political history (Key 1949:5–6).

According to Numan Bartley, this is exactly what happened with the massive resistance movement (Bartley 1969:84–85). Extreme malapportionment
favoring rural areas and small towns generally, and Black Belt voters specifically, was written into the System of 1896 constitutions, existing in at least
one house in the legislature of every southern state (Bartley 1969:18). In the
previous chapter I noted the disparities in Alabama. In Georgia, there were
rural counties in 1946 where a vote for governor was worth as much as one
hundred times that of a vote in Fulton County, in which Atlanta is located;
such counties also received state representatives based on a tiny fraction of
the votes needed to elect them in Atlanta and other urban areas (Key
1949:119–20). In Lowndes County, Alabama, in the heart of the Black Belt,
one state senator represented 2,057 white voters (the 80 percent black population was completely disenfranchised), while in Jefferson County, which
included Birmingham, one state senator represented 130,000 voters. The situation was perhaps worse in Florida. The Supreme Court ordered redistricting in 1962, based on "one man, one vote," but even by the middle and
sometimes late 1960s, some states had not fully complied.

The defenders of white supremacy in the South gained confidence and
gathered increased support in part because of the apparent unwillingness
of the federal government to push the issue strongly after *Brown*. President
Eisenhower supposedly privately opposed *Brown*, and until Little Rock,
mostly expressed sympathy for the South. He never made a public statement in support of *Brown*. Whether Chief Justice Earl Warren was right when
he later wrote, "I still believe that much of our racial strife could have been
avoided if President Eisenhower had at least observed that our country is
dedicated to the principle" of racial equality, is debatable (cited in Bloom
1987:105–6; Bartley 1995:231, 234). It is clear, however, that he made the situation worse. Eisenhower even found the white supremacist-inspired

Southern Manifesto acceptable, especially because it promised to stay with-in the bounds of the law. Adlai Stevenson, Eisenhower's Democratic oppo-nent in the 1956 elections, ignored the manifesto and sought to appease white southerners, losing much of the Black vote to Eisenhower in the process (Bloom 1987:109, 151, 165).

These factors are an important beginning in our attempt to understand how the Black Belt planters were able to build such a broad and unified white racist coalition in the South, but we must still dig deeper. Planters also had convergent interests with a number of natural allies. First, the planters were involved in a dense network of economic interests, including small towns and rural areas with which they had historic ties and strong interests, whose fates rose and fell with those of the planters. Second, the southern labor market for unskilled labor was determined in good part, as Gavin Wright has convincingly argued, by the southern agricultural wage, kept artificially low by the system of white supremacy. Although industrial development had been extensive throughout the post–World War II peri-od, much of it had still taken place in the traditionally southern low-wage, labor-intensive industries. Rather than being forward looking with regard to race, such industrialists shared an interest with the planters in maintaining the system of white supremacy. Third, the elites in certain cities with either an "Old South heritage" or long-standing business plantation ties, includ-ing Shreveport and Birmingham, strongly supported the planter-led defense of racial segregation (Bartley 1969:17).

We have, at this point, come across such vexed questions before. Why did whites who were not tied directly to plantation interests go along with the most uncompromising defenses of white supremacy. We saw such acqui-escence during the Founding period, during and after Reconstruction, at the time of the establishment of the System of 1896. Massive resistance was to be sure, as Bartley and others have convincingly argued, "like the Ku Klux Klan thirty years before…a bourgeois phenomenon," yet it also served to garner at times extensive white working-class support in many cities (Bartley 1969:104). Economic development in the South had created new employ-ment opportunities, but the better jobs in the region were held dispropor-tionately by the one in ten members of the southern population who were born outside the region in 1960 (the situation was not to change substan-tially by 1980 when the better jobs tended to be held by the two out of ten from outside the South). As middle-class southerners became more affluent and gained political power, working-class whites, modestly paid in com-parison to their peers around the country, in good part a result of their lower degree of unionization, remained powerless. As Numan Bartley argues, they became "increasingly frustrated, angry, and alienated." The consumer-based taxes of most southern states hit the working class especially hard. The short-age of lower-cost housing and affordable medical care (southern working-class jobs, less unionized, were unlikely to have health benefits), combined with the relative unavailability of public services, hurt Blacks and whites alike (Bartley 1995:277–79).

Without a class-based alternative, lower-income whites were inclined and aggressively encouraged to blame African-Americans for their problems. The implementation of civil rights policies only tended to amplify these feelings. Most of the school integration and resource sharing was to be done in the cities, where most working-class whites lived. Middle-class subur-ban Birmingham whites, for example, would hardly be affected, although much of the disruption to normal patters of life would fall on less affluent whites within the city itself. In Little Rock, the class orientation of the ini-tial plan for desegregation was quite clear. Of the four city high schools, the largest and the one to be desegregated was Central High School, with its constituency of white working-class, lower-class, and middle-class fam-ilies. The brand-new Hall High School, located in an affluent, all-white sec-tion of town, would be upper status and lily-white (Bartley 1995:224). Moderate civil rights strategies were virtually guaranteed to stimulate class resentment. With traditional patterns of life being swept away by both eco-nomic development and civil rights advances, whites who were left behind, in the absense of a clear class alternative, were often attracted to the racist mass resistance movement, which reaffirmed traditional "white folk cul-ture" (Bartley 1995:200).

Finally, the lack of any viable opposition to white supremacy in the South served to strengthen the most extreme segregationists. The popular-front lib-erals had been destroyed by McCarthyism, denounced and isolated by their former liberal, intractibly anti-communist friends, including those in charge of the CIO's Operation Dixie. So-called moderates had little base and crum-bled quickly as the defenders of white supremacy mobilized. Business mod-erates were much less visible than many accounts would have us believe, especially those that use impressionistic evidence from Little Rock and Atlanta, and fail to see them as atypical cases. As we saw in the previous chap-ter, in most cities they were hardly in evidence, having little incentive to chal-lenge the established order. In many cities businessmen were among the most reactionary. The racially moderate economic liberalism represented by Long and Folsom was unable to make the transition from a rural-based, poor farmer populism to an urbanized, industrialized society. The reason for its collapse, as well as that of the popular-front liberals a decade earlier, I would argue, had to do with the failure and destruction of the racially egalitarian unionism of the 1930s and 1940s.

What might have been possible is suggested by the heroic efforts of AFL-CIO officials and their supporters throughout the South during the late 1950s and early 1960s, forces that had already been emasculated by the early 1950s (see A. Draper 1994 for a riveting account). With little to offer Black or white southern workers, the national AFL-CIO publicly supported *Brown* and denounced massive resistance and the White Citizens' Councils. Such talk was, of course, costless for those based in the North with their main offices in Washington, D.C.; along with its failure to support the 1963 march on Washington, the AFL-CIO positioned itself on the right-wing of civil rights supporters. In the Deep South, however, such stances by state AFL-CIO officials had more direct consequences. Most officials did not openly support integration. Rather, they opposed violence, stood their ground as civil libertarians, supported keeping schools open, argued their support for moderate politicians, including national Democrats on labor grounds, while opposing more militant civil rights organizations such as SNCC and the Mississippi Freedom Democratic Party. In Mississippi, such stances were nevertheless often life threatening, as state AFL-CIO head Claude Ramsey and his family were constantly under threat of attack. Less fortunate was racially moderate Laurel woodworkers official Ottis Mathews, who was dragged from his car at gunpoint by Klansmen, whipped, and had acid put on his wounds (Draper 1994:141).

What might have been is even more fully suggested by those small numbers of racially egalitarian unions that were still strong in the South in the middle 1950s, the Farm Equipment Union (FE) Louisville, the few packinghouse locals in the South. Here, the failures of the CIO stand out in sharp relief. The failure to organize the tens of thousands of integrated woodworkers in Mississippi and Alabama or the large numbers of furniture workers across the region; the reinforcement of racist job structures and racism generally by the steelworkers in Birmingham and throughout the South; the failure to organize textile workers in South and North Carolina during the 1930s and 1940s. Racially egalitarian unions might have put forward school integration plans that were city and metropolitan-wide, involving the upgrading of all education, especially those in poor and working-class neighborhoods that tended to be underfunded. They would have continued the labor traditions earlier held to by mine workers in Alabama, demanding full voting and citizen rights for all and advocating complete redistricting and an end to legislative malapportionment. Like the Louisville FE local, the fight for workplace equality might have gained large white working-class support, especially when it took place in the context of high unionized wages and broad social benefits. Yet, none of this came to pass, as massive resistance swept up the overwhelming majority of whites in its path.

Despite its meteoric rise, massive resistance had crumbled by the late 1950s, first in the outer South, then throughout the whole region. Little Rock caused the federal government to enforce court-ordered school integration, and the prospects were clear. In order to resist integration, southern whites would have to be willing to forego public schooling for their own children. For many whites outside the Black Belt, including the urban middle classes and businesses who were losing profits, fighting token integration was not worth the costs. Eventually, the movement for massive resistance posed a threat to the social stability of the region. The involvement of large numbers of Blacks throughout the South in the civil rights movement beginning with the 1960 sit-ins finally doomed the white supremacist hopes of stopping integration. Yet, the general movement of white reaction and opposition to the quest for African-American freedom, which seemed so isolated during the Dixiecrat revolt, was not only to live on but also to broaden further in support.

THE CONTINUED BUILDING OF THE RACIST COALITION

> The history of the twenty years after 1973 is that of a world which lost its bearings and slid into instability and crisis. (Hobsbawm 1994:403)

The whole of post–World War II American politics up to the present may be usefully characterized as a series of escalating and increasingly success-ful experiments in the building of a national white racist political coalition. Like the Dixiecrats in an earlier era, the appeal to racism has often served as a cover for a number of pro-business, pro-rich public policies that were designed to undermine the remnants of class solidarity and awareness that remained from the 1930s and 1940s.

In the past several decades, working-class people (even if often self-con-ceived as middle class) have been threatened by a variety of global and national economic trends, by the shipment of jobs overseas and downsiz-ing at home, by financial manipulations and mergers, junk-bond trading and financial bankruptcies, fiscal austerity and the deregulation of business, things over which they have had little control but which have occasionally affected them greatly. Many have been hurt first by the failure to expand, then the cutting, and now the elimination of many social benefits. Rather than identify the real source of their problems, many whites have been con-vinced to take the easy—if ineffectual—alternative of blaming those who were even more victimized, that is, poor Blacks and other minorities.

The putative opposition to the racist coalition has been a cross-class coali-tion of various oppressed groups and supposed enlightened interests, with little concern for the interests and problems of working people, not just white but nonwhite as well. Thus, we have had the spectacle of Black mayors in major cities, including Detroit and Atlanta, liberal Democrats all, attacking Black unionized city employees in ways similar to that done previously by white, less racially sensitive mayors. Labor organizations have had no broad class response to appeal to their followers and potential constituents. One can, of course, see the same shortsightedness by workers and their unions where race is hardly a factor. Woodworkers in the Northwest had a clear stake in taking the lead on environmental issues in ways that also took into account their job prospects. Instead, they let the initiative pass to often upper-class environmental groups and their lawyers with no sympathy for the plight of working people. Woodworkers ended up joining in a coalition with their employers, and to their own long-term detriment, opposing all environmental controls (see, e.g., Alston Chase 1995; Helvarg 1994).

But the fulcrum around which the submergence of class issues has turned and the mainspring of American politics has been race. The attempts to build a national white racist coalition have advanced with little organized working class opposition. We can pick up the main thread of the story in the sixties.

THE GOLDWATER CAPER

The 1964 presidential candidacy of Arizona senator Barry Goldwater was a pivotal event, both in the transformation of the Republican Party and the building of the white racist coalition.[3] Beginning in 1960, according to Kevin Phillips, the Republicans began to put renewed emphasis on their existing "Operation Dixie" (Phillips 1970:203). This approach was to be more aggressively attempted in 1964. Many leading conservatives today trace their political baptism to their involvement in the Goldwater campaign, which wrested control of the Republican Party from moderates and northeasterners.

Despite his electoral failure (Goldwater carried only the Deep South states of Alabama, Georgia, Louisiana, Mississippi, and South Carolina, along with his home state of Arizona), Goldwater successfully became a vehicle for projecting racism as a national issue, making it more respectable to the population in the country as a whole and tying it to conservative themes.

Whatever his personal feelings, whatever his supposed principled reasons for voting against the 1964 Civil Rights Act, there can be no doubt that his campaign, particularly in the South, was a barely veiled appeal to race hatred. Richard Rovere, who covered the campaign, reports the lily-white crowds in high-percentage African-American southern cities, including Memphis, Atlanta, and New Orleans. In staking out his anticrime position, he continually mentioned New York, Washington, and other cities that had either large African-American populations or numerous civil rights demonstrations. He preferred to talk of Washington, with its 54 percent

Black population as a high-crime area (even though it ranked fourteenth among large cities), rather than his own Phoenix, with a 95 percent white population (whose crime rate ranked it fourth among cities nationally). Rarely did he mention the three cities with the highest crime rates, Las Vegas, Los Angeles, and Miami, often preferring lower-crime cities with many civil rights demonstrations such as Philadelphia (Rovere 1965:138). As Rovere convincingly argues, "By coming south, Barry Goldwater had made it possible for great numbers of unapologetic white supremacists to hold great carnivals of white supremacy" (Rovere 1965:140).

On one level, of course, the Goldwater campaign was a dismal failure, capturing only those states in the Deep South and his own Arizona, thus leading to the reelection victory of President Lyndon Johnson and an overwhelming Democratic landslide at almost every level. As Phillips concludes, "But the party found that when it acted like the Dixiecrats, it fell into the Dixiecrat pattern. The Deep South Black Belts exalted Barry Goldwater and those of the Outer South for the most part opposed him" (Phillips 1970:223).

Much of what Goldwater said was in an Aesopian language that would be fine-tuned by succeeding generations of racist politicians. He never made any "direct racist appeals." Nevertheless, the Goldwater movement "appears to be a racist movement and very little else" (Rovere 1965:143).

THE 1968 GEORGE WALLACE CAMPAIGN

> "I say, segregation now, segregation tomorrow, segregation forever." George Wallace in his 1963 Alabama gubernatorial inaugural address. (Frady 1968:142)

Unlike Barry Goldwater, George Wallace was a direct product of the failure of southern labor organizing and the weakness of organized labor in Alabama. He started out politically as a protégé of Governor Big Jim Folsom, the "little man's friend," who ran with strong labor and poor rural support. Folsom opposed the poll tax and spoke the rhetoric of the brotherhood of all men, whatever color. Folsom, of course, had created a major furor in the state when he hosted Harlem Congressman Adam Clayton Powell for a drink of scotch in the governor's mansion. Throughout his political career, Wallace continued to emphasize many of the issues that he had espoused while a Folsom ally, with one major exception.

Wallace's biggest change came on the issue of race. Unlike Folsom, he saw in the massive resistance movement the handwriting on the wall. The AFL-CIO, weakened by its previous splits and purges and its abandonment of its early forthright activities for racial equality, was no match for the White Citizens Council in Alabama by the mid-1950s. Though attempting to position himself as a racial conservative, Wallace was defeated in the Democratic gubernatorial primary in 1958 by an arch-segregationist, who successsfully accused Wallace of being soft on the race issue. By 1962, George Wallace had repackaged himself as the most virulent exponent of race hatred and segregation. He made his name by symbolically standing up to the federal government and resisting the integration of the University of Alabama. He wholeheartedly supported the "excessess" of Police Chief Bull Connor of Birmingham in 1963 in attacking civil rights demonstrators with police dogs and fire hoses. At the same time, he also behaved as an economic liberal within the state, building many new schools, paving roads, supplying free textbooks, building medical clinics and nursing homes, increasing public welfare programs, and greatly expanding the University of Alabama, especially its Birmingham campus. Despite these economic programs, the state AFL-CIO to its credit refused to support him because of his bigotry.

In January 1964, Wallace began a national campaign against the civil rights leglislation that was then before Congress. Campaigning against pro-administration Democratic governors and senators in the 1964 Democratic presidential primaries, Wallace got 34 percent of the vote in Wisconsin, almost 30 percent in Indiana, and 43 percent in Maryland, including in the latter state a majority of the white vote (Black and Black 1992:161). These elections were among the initial reactions of many northern whites to the early thrusts of the civil rights movement and the Great Society programs in the North.

By 1968, the political landscape had changed drastically. The North itself had become the scene of school desegregation and busing fights, scores of ghetto rebellions, and numerous open-housing and hiring struggles. Without a strong labor movement, committed in fact not merely in rhetoric to equality and solidarity, a political void existed. Both Wallace and Richard Nixon attempted to fill it. Wallace, running on the racist platform of his American Independent Party, had the same strategy as the 1948 Dixiecrats, attempting to win enough votes to deny either the Republican or Democratic candidates a victory in the electoral college.

Although polls suggested that Wallace had strong support across the country at various times, by the end of the campaign, his electoral strength outside the South largely evaporated. He received 13 percent of the vote nationally, 8 percent in the North. His 34 percent in the South, however, including 40 percent of the white vote, doubled that of the Dixiecrats in 1948 (Black and Black 1992:165–66). Wallace had picked up substantial support across the region among white workers and the urban and rural poor (Phillips 1970:230). The racist coalition, its potential, and its attractiveness to major-party candidates were clearly growing.

As Kevin Phillips has argued,

> Until the national Democratic Party embraced the Negro socioe-
> conomic and civil rights revolution of the Nineteen-Sixties, the Deep
> South upcountry shunned the economic conservatism of both the
> Republicans and Dixiecrats....Although the civil rights revolution
> was straining Democratic loyalties all over the South, the poor white
> hill counties saw Goldwater as the Dixiecrat-style economic con-
> servative whose committment to New Deal farm, home loan, rural
> electrification, Social Security and other programs was minimal....
> Liberalism lost its support base in the upcountry by shifting its prin-
> cipal concern from populist economics to government participa-
> tion in social and racial upheaval (Phillips 1970:236–38).

The Wallace campaign had greatly enlarged both the southern and national base for white racist politics. It did this by developing a whole set of code
words and issues that appealed to, and purported to represent, the interests
of working-class whites, both lower and middle class. Republican strategists, in their analysis of the 1968 election and the tactics and support of
Wallace as well as their own party, whet their appetites by honing an even
more aggressive racial strategy.

NIXON'S SOUTHERN STRATEGY

Unlike Wallace, something of an economic liberal and a racist reactionary,
conservative Republicans had little sympathy for the white poor, white working people, or for trade unions. Cynically, they crafted a strategy for graft-
ing Wallace-style populist racism onto their pro-business conservative perspective. This, contrary to the self-delusions and borderline lunacy of those
such as former Reagan speechwriter Peggy Noonan, who seems to believe
that the Republicans had actually become a party representing, rather than
attempting to appeal to, certain sections of the lower classes (Noonan 1990).

In 1968, Nixon had struggled to define a middle ground that appealed
to white racist sentiment yet avoided overt racist remarks and proposals. He
stressed his opposition to busing, calling it "forced busing," and his opposition to affirmative action. By some accounts, Nixon made a deal with
southern Dixiecrats, including South Carolina's Strom Thurmond, that in
return for their active support he would, if elected, ease up on federal pressure for school desegregation. Spiro Agnew was chosen as vice president
on the ticket, both as someone acceptable to the South and as a politician
who was a master of the belligerent antiestablishment racist rhetoric used
so successfully by George Wallace. Upon their election, Nixon continued to
work on honing his southern strategy.

In 1970, Nixon was to repeat Republican Hervert Hoover's gambit by nominating two southernors for the Supreme Court: Judge Clement Haynsworth of South Carolina and Judge G. Harrold Carswell of Florida. Both were narrowly defeated in the Senate. In 1971, a journalistic account of Nixon's southern strategy deemed it a failure. The wooing of the South caused Nixon to lose popularity in a number of northern states, most notably Ohio and Illinois (Murphy and Gulliver 1971:41). Even in the South the southern strategy seemed to be failing. In attempting to get rid of Wallace in the 1970 Alabama governor's race, Republicans quietly supported his main opponent, who was nipped in a runoff election. The Republicans decided not even to run a candidate in the general election. In South Carolina, Strom Thurmond and the Republicans selected former Democratic Congressman Albert Watson for governor. Running an overtly racist campaign, Watson lost decisively to the moderate Democratic candidate John West. In Florida, a conservative Republican was defeated in the 1970 gubernatorial elections, while in Georgia, Democratic gubernatorial candidate Jimmy Carter was the one who successfully played the race card, in the process drawing on most of the supporters of Lester Maddox and George Wallace to defeat the racially moderate former governor Albert Sanders. Carter then went on to beat the conservative Republican candidate with almost 60 percent of the votes (Murphy and Gulliver 1971:193).

Yet, judgments in 1971 about the failure of the Republican southern strategy proved to be premature. In 1971 and early 1972, court orders for busing were proceeding around the country. Busing was opposed by whites nationally by margins of from five to one to ten to one.[4] On March 17, 1972, Nixon called on Congress to end busing. Much to the GOP's delight, ten Black lawyers in the Civil Rights Division at the Department of Justice denounced the president's position (Edsall and Edsall 1991:89). With this issue and his attacks on affirmative action, Nixon made great headway in building the racist coalition on a national level, winning a landslide victory in the 1972 presidential election.

THE REAGAN OFFENSIVE

Derailed by Watergate and the resignation under disgrace of President Richard Nixon in 1974, the Republicans regrouped. Democratic candidate Jimmy Carter, a southern moderate in practice who was adept at building relations with Black politicians and voters, was also skilled at using the racist lexicon of code words during his campaigns. Not the least of such examples was his speech during the 1976 presidential campaign about the importance of "ethnic purity." In his 1970 gubernatorial campaign, while attacking his Republican opponent in the general election, he stated: "The last time

the Republicans were in Atlanta was 100 years ago. They burned it down"
(Murphy and Gulliver 1971:171)—forgetting of course to add that the burning of Atlanta broke the back of the Confederacy and destroyed the slavocracy. The attempts to demonize Sherman's march through the South, one of
the most important and successful military campaigns of our nation's history, and to glorify Robert E. Lee, the military leader of the slave owners, on
a postage stamp, is both revisionist history and a needless concession to bigotry. The South has many real heroes worth celebrating. One has yet to hear
Rush Limbaugh, who claims not to have "a racist bone in his body" and asserts
that he would have opposed slavery as an "abomination," taking a stand on
these issues in his attacks on revisionist history (Limbaugh 1994:271).

The full-fledged emergence of a dominating racist coalition, however,
only took place during the presidencies of Ronald Reagan and George Bush.
Reagan, elected governor of California in 1966, had made a political name
for himself in 1964 by opposing the California fair-housing referendum,
denouncing student protesters at the University of California in Berkeley,
and in his open support for Barry Goldwater. By the time of his 1980 presidential run, he was skillful at presenting himself both as an exponent of
old-fashioned, individualistic, puritanical patriotic values, as well as a
defender of white racism against demands by African-Americans. Reagan
became the respectable proponent of a racist populism, all the while claiming that he was merely for fairness, opposing granting of special privileges
to women and racial minorities be it in hiring, college admission, busing,
or welfare. As Thomas and Mary Edsall note, one of Reagan's favorite and
most used stories was of the Chicago "welfare queen" with "80 names, 30
addresses, 12 social security cards" whose "tax-free income alone is over
$150,000" (Edsall and Edsall 1991:144,148).

Reagan's first campaign stop in the South after his 1980 presidential
nomination was in Philadelphia, Mississippi, on August 3, 1980. He told
the crowd of 10,000 fair goers there that "I believe in states' rights" (*New
York Times*, 8-4-80). The choice of Philadelphia was not an accident, as a
number of commentators pointed out at the time, for the town had been
the site of the brutal murders in 1964 of civil rights activists James Chaney,
Andrew Goodman, and Michael Schwerner. Former United Nations ambas-
sador Andrew Young claimed that Reagan was using the visit as a coded
message for the legitimacy of violent racism (*New York Times*, 10-16-80).
During the 1984 campaign, Reagan again returned to Philadelphia and
chanted that "The South Shall Rise Again," all the while Reagan claimed
that he wanted to represent everybody and was appealing to African-
Americans for support. He had perfected the use of seemingly race-neutral language to appeal to racist sentiments.

Yet, Reagan's conservative agenda was in many important parts rejected by most Americans. The Edsalls claim that most white Americans strongly supported certain types of federal social welfare programs, including Social Security, education, and health care, while opposing food stamps, Aid to Families with Dependent Children (AFDC) and other means-tested programs that disproportionately benefited poor Blacks and Hispanics (Edsall and Edsall 1991:152). Thomas Ferguson and Joel Rogers convincingly show, however, that even in these supposedly racially charged policy areas, a majority of Americans in the 1980s favored the continuation of these latter programs, including AFDC (Ferguson and Rogers 1986). Theodore Lowi more recently argues that President Reagan had problems along this line: "Every criticism of welfare expenditures depressed his ratings so consistently that he had to make widespread public reassurances that he was committed to maintaining the 'safety net'—a term he invented" (Lowi 1995:92). In response to these public sentiments, Reagan moved cautiously. David Stockman, Reagan's budget director, argues in disgust that the administration refused to abandon New Deal social policies:

> Now I was the fool, and the reasons revealed the final answer as to why the Reagan White House's anti-spending rhetoric could not be taken seriously. The Reaganites were, in the final analysis, just plain welfare state politicians like everybody else (Stockman 1986:385).

> The abortive Reagan Revolution proved that the American electorate wants a moderate social democracy to shield it from capitalism's rougher edges. (Stockman 1986:394; I was led to this quote by Lowi 1995:93).

The racist ideological offensive of the eighties allowed for a redefinition of political language. Although "special interests" had for much of twentieth-century American politics referred to the interests of the rich and corporations in opposition to those of the vast majority of people, the meaning of the term was now changed. As the Edsalls argue,

> "Special interests" were increasingly perceived...as pressing the claims of minorities, including trade unionists, blacks, Hispanics, feminists, homosexuals, AIDS victims, etc. for government preferences. These special preferences, in turn, were potentially damaging, in the minds of a significant number of voters, not only to America's overall international competitive position, but detrimental as well to the moral fibre, the personal well-being, and the security of individual "ordinary" citizens. (Edsall and Edsall 1991:203)

Increasingly, the racially charged and coded rhetoric removed the economy, corporations, and the rich as the source of people's problems, and substituted a new grouping. Under this cover, overtly regressive taxation and numerous loopholes for the rich became acceptable, if not avidly supported by masses of people.

THE BUSH CAMPAIGN

The master of racially charged rhetoric and stirring up bigotry was undoubtedly the Republican strategist Lee Atwater. Atwater learned his trade working for South Carolinian Strom Thurmond in his 1970 senatorial campaign, becoming skilful at race baiting and dirty tricks. Atwater reached his nadir as a key player in the 1988 presidential campaign of Republican George Bush. President Bush and his supporters attacked the Democratic presidential candidate Michael Dukakis as a liberal opponent of the death penalty, a "card-carrying member" of the American Civil Liberties Union, and as a governor who had vetoed a bill mandating the Pledge of Allegiance in Massachusetts schools. Atwater's special contribution was the discovery and packaging of the Willie Horton case. William R. (Willie) Horton was an African-American male who had been convicted in the murder of a gas station attendant and sentenced to life imprisonment in Dukakis's home state of Massachusetts. He was, however, granted ten weekend furloughs under a 1972 Massachusetts law. In 1976, Dukakis as governor had vetoed a bill that would have denied furloughs to first-degree murderers. On June 6, 1986, on his tenth furlough, Willie Horton disappeared. On April 3, 1987, Horton broke into a home in Maryland, bound, gagged, pistol-whipped, and stabbed a man, then raped his fiancée. Atwater orchestrated a campaign around the Horton case that bordered on racist hysteria. Horton was featured in countless Republican television commercials, campaign speeches, and leaflets throughout the course of the campaign (Edsall and Edsall 1991:222–25). Bush, in contrast to Dukakis, supposedly knew what to do with Black criminals. Atwater, in a moment of contrition on his death bed, allegedly apologized and expressed regret for his packaging of the Horton issue. But the damage, or its role in building the white racist coalition, was not to be undone; despite his dying protestations, Atwater will forever rightfully be remembered as one of the most savage architects of white racist politics.

THE DAVID DUKE CAMPAIGN

David Duke, a Ku Klux Klan leader, neo-Nazi, founder and leader of the National Association for the Advancement of White People, white supremacist, anti-Semite, and American fascist, convincingly and successfully repackaged himself as a moderately conservative Republican in Louisiana.

Exchanging his KKK white sheet and hood for a business suit, he was elected as a Republican to the Louisiana lower house from Metairie, a 99.6 percent white suburb of New Orleans. The election had an extremely high turnout, 77.8 percent of the registered voters; Duke won by a 227 vote margin out of 17,000 votes (Rose 1992:13).

Although clearly a bigot who believed in the biological inferiority of Blacks, Jews, and others, Duke claimed to be a proponent of equal rights for all and special privileges for none. He opposed high taxes, illegitimate welfare births, affirmative action, and the "Zionist control of the media." His victory was the cause for a huge celebration at the neo-Nazi Populist Party convention. He was still reputed to argue not only that African-Americans were biologically inferior but also that the Nazi Rudolph Hess was a true hero and that the existence of the Nazi death camps was a myth. Although his facist ties were quite an embarassment for the national Republicans, many of whom publicly disavowed him, his overall message was quite consistent with the coded bigotry espoused by Nixon, Reagan, Bush and others, validating the old adage that you reap what you sow.

At first, David Duke was discounted as a peculiar local Louisiana phenomenon, especially because many whites in his district had been part of the "white flight" from the increasingly Black city of New Orleans. In 1990, however, David Duke ran for U.S. Senate against the incumbent Bennett Johnson, getting 44 percent of the overall vote and 57 percent of the white vote. This gave him great visibility nationally. His race for governor the next year was the subject of continuous national media coverage, particularly in the fall runoff against the liberal populist (and accused crook) Edwin Edwards. Not surprisingly, the media did little to play up his fascist ties and beliefs, accepting at face value his lie that they were not current and had been youthful indiscretions. After an intense campaign, Edwards won by a 61 percent to 39 percent margin.[5] Thus, the Republican racist coalition, the "big tent," had room in it not only for old-fashioned, probusiness liberals but real American fascists as well. The same rhetoric and lines were sufficient to unite (even if uneasily) George Bush, Ronald Reagan, David Duke, and Newt Gingrich.

1. The term is a peculiar one; hardly any southern politicians were consistently liberal on race questions. Racially, the term is usually applied to those who did not take punitive actions toward Blacks or who did not push racial issues. Occasionally, the term was even applied to those who used racist rhetoric, but supported unions and other social reform issues, such as South Carolina's Olin Johnson, although the term was almost never used to describe pro-New Deal racist demagogues like Senator Theodore Bilbo of Mississippi.

2. This paragraph draws heavily on Bloom 1987:91–92; similar points are made by a number of other scholars. See, e.g., Garrow, 1994:153–54; Bartley 1969:53–54.

3. The term *Goldwater caper* is Richard Rovere's and was the title of his book on the subject.

4. One poll in 1970, found 13 percent favoring busing, while 76 percent opposed it; another in 1972, found only 5 percent strongly favoring it, while 70 percent opposed it; other small percentages favored it less strongly (Mayer 1992:372,373).

5. Much of the above information on David Duke is from an informative collection edited by Douglas Rose (1990).

PART III

Conclusion

CHAPTER 10

The Contours of Race and Politics in the United States

> Now I am perfectly aware that there are other slums in which white men are fighting for their lives, and mainly losing. I know that blood is also flowing through those streets and that the human damage is incalcuble. People are continually pointing out to me the wretchedness of white people in order to console me for the wretchedness of blacks....The people, however, who believe that this democratic anguish has some consoling value are always pointing out that So-and-So, white, and So-and-So, black rose from the slums into the big time. The existence—the public existence—of say, Frank Sinatra and Sammy Davis, Jr. proves to them that America is still the land of opportunity and that inequalities vanish before the determined will. It proves nothing of the sort....A few have always risen—in every country, every era, and in the teeth of regimes which can by no stretch of the imagination be thought of as free. James Baldwin 1961:58–59

> Why fight to get into a burning House? Grace Lee Boggs 1970:213.

> Mr. Rich Man, Mr. Rich Man, open up
> your heart and mind.
> Give the poor man a chance, help stop
> these hard, hard times.
> While you living in your mansion you don't
> know what hard times means....
> If it wasn't for the poor man, Mr. Rich
> Man, what would you do?
> from *Mr. Rich Man* by Bessie Smith.

In what follows, I shall try to use the historical perspective presented in the previous chapters to gain leverage and deeper insight for understanding contemporary United States politics. Before moving directly to this task, we must touch on several pertinent topics. In the previous chapter, I tried to explore the reasons for the development of the national racial politics of the preceding decades, the central feature of U.S. politics today. It would be wrong, however, to see race relations and the current racial politics as anything but contradictory.

On the one hand, many extreme racial inequities are widespread, affecting employment, housing, schools, healthcare, and other areas. Black unemployment, for example, remains twice that for whites, while unemployment for African-American youth between the ages of 16 and 19 continues to linger around 30%. In 1992, life expectancy for African-Americans was 69.6 compared to 75.8 for whites; infant mortality was 16.8 deaths per thousand in contrast to 6.9 for whites. 33.4% of Blacks live below the federal poverty-line as opposed to 11.9% of whites, while the pay of African-American workers relative to that of whites declined significantly since 1979 (*Statistical Abstract* 1995:86, 90, 400, 480; Mishel and Bernstein 1994:187-8). In Mississippi, to take one example, the legacy of slavery and the plantations is highly visible, especially in those overwhelmingly African-American, Black Belt towns, whose 30 to 40 percent unemployment rates and extreme poverty—largely a product of both the earlier labor system and the now abandoned cotton production and turpentine camps—remind one of areas in underdeveloped countries. One finds the most hardened of racist attitudes in certain isolated white communities in the South that are still defending exclusionary white churches, clubs, and even cemetaries (see, e.g., *New York Times*, 3-29-96, "Burial of Mixed-Race Baby," and *New York Times*, 3-4-96, "At Cajun Dance Hall, Race No Longer Rules"). Yet, in Mississippi, where the most extreme system of racial domination once thrived, one finds Black and white teenagers socializing together in large numbers. Along the Gulf Coast, from Louisiana through Mississippi and to Alabama, one hardly sees a non-integrated beach, yet those along Chicago's Lake Michigan lakefront remain for the most part de facto segregated. Blacks and whites are everywhere homeless together, share needles and drugs, and engage in crime together. Even the criminals who murdered Chicago Bulls' basketball star Michael Jordan's father were an interracial pair. The racial dividing line within U.S. prisons, however, is both sharp and deadly, with Black gangs and the white racist Aryan Brotherhood demanding allegiance from their respective constituencies. Jeremy Bentham once argued that the reality of a society was reflected in its prisons. Yet, it is not always clear what is reality and what is only less solidly rooted.

The civil rights movement of the 1960s brought many changes in the old Jim Crow. Certain white attitudes, at least as expressed in public opinion polls, have changed dramatically. White Americans by the 1980s overwhelmingly responded favorably to integrated schools and transportation, equal access to jobs, open housing, and even the right of people of different races to intermarry if they so chose. Earlier, as we have previously noted, most whites explicitly rejected these views. Formerly invisible to most whites (out of sight, out of mind), African-Americans are now everywhere (or so it seems to many whites). Some of the visibility is laudatory, some of it stereotypical and distortive, some of it of the subtle and not so subtle racist variety. Culturally, the increased visibility and recognition of African-American artists and entertainers in virtually every venue is immense. Black writers, especially Black female writers, including Toni Morrison, Maya Angelou, and Alice Walker have poignantly written about life behind the veil while expressing deep truths about the American experience and human existence. With respect to virtually every area of popular culture, however, the increased opportunities and visibility are coupled with stereotyping, limitations, discrimination, and unequal treatment.

Formerly excluded from all but the most menial public jobs that had contact with whites, Blacks have begun to occupy in significant numbers jobs as bus drivers, bank tellers, store clerks, food servers, police and fire-fighters, as well as positions as doctors, lawyers, and social workers. Perhaps emblematic of the arrival of a new Black middle class is the recent election of Dr. Lonnie R. Bristow as the head of the American Medical Association, an organization not known for a history of racial liberalism (*New York Times,* 6-6-95). The largest number and percentage of jobs for educated African-Americans, however, have been in local, state, and federal government. For example, between 1973 and 1991, the number of Black and Hispanic employees in state and local governments more than doubled, while the total number of jobs increased by only 70 percent (*Statistical Abstract* 1995:I:323). This being America, it would not be too farfetched to suggest that a good bit of the anti-bureacracy, anti-government sentiment of large numbers of whites since the 1960s is not unrelated to the darker complexions of many of the bureaucrats.

In sports, we have come a long way since the Mississippi State basketball team in 1963 was forced to sneak out of the state, with the school president and officials under state court restraining orders, so that they could play in the integrated NCAA basketball tournament. When Bear Bryant's all-white University of Alabama football team was defeated in the Orange Bowl in good part because of the four touchdowns scored by the University of Southern California's star African-American running back Sam "Bam" Cunningham, Bryant decided it was time to integrate the team, allegedly saying, "I've got to get me one of them." From the noble figures of track world-record holder Jesse Owens and world heavyweight champion boxer Joe Louis in the 1930s, the Harlem Globetrotters, the invisible Negro Baseball League, and the racist reception given to Jackie Robinson by white fans and fellow baseball players (*New York Times,* 10-23-95), we have arrived at the universal adulation of Michael Jordon, and African-American local professional heroes in every major sport. Black entry is only limited in those sports such as swimming, golf, and tennis, which require financial support and community commitment for coaching, travel, and facilities, making them limited to the affluent or lucky of any race. Even in sports, however, racism is rampant. The lack of opportunities for qualified African-Americans as coaches or top management, particularly in baseball and football, has been much discussed. In 1990, for example, African-Americans accounted for 60 percent of all professional football players, yet there were only two Black head coaches and two Black quarterbacks (*African American Almanac* 1994: 1259). Los Angeles Dodger executive Al Campanis and sportscaster Jimmy the Greek were fired for expressing racial prejudices shared by many others. In more subtle ways, however, sports commentators references to women and nonwhites have been shown to be less respectful and more demeaning than their references to white athletes (*Sports Illustrated*, Dec. 3, 1990:35).

Many aspects of race relations in the current period are themselves contradictory and difficult to evaluate easily. Notwithstanding its generally often misogynist, violent, and additional antisocial, reactionary themes, how does one categorize rap music? By its occasionally "progressive" socially critical, antiestablishment themes, which seem to attract broad layers of non-Black as well as Black youth? By its rebellious attempts to shock and snub bourgeois society? Or is the fascination of many white youth and others simply titillation by a new form of minstrelry? What about the brief flirtation of large numbers of white Americans with Colin Powell? Was it as some claim a sign that white Americans wanted to overcome racial stereotypes and support someone who embodied the issues of character and moderate positions on issues that they claimed to desire? Or was it really a statement that they would support (perhaps only momentarily) a Black whose background and style was sufficiently white, displaying the narrow limits of racial tolerance? I, of course, have always marveled (although no longer innocent about such things to be taken aback) at the intense reactions of many whites to the moderately liberal Jesse Jackson (whose patriotism, work with major businesses, and often ambivalence toward unionized workers, suggested most dramatically during earlier teacher union strikes in Chicago, hardly seems to qualify him as a radical), a figure who portrays a highly inclusive vision of politics. Can this be anything other than racism pure and simple?

Any adequate theory of race in the United States must be able to explain these complexities, to suggest which are part of the long-standing development of U.S. racial relations and which, however derivative and dependent on previous times as they might be, are specific to the current era. In noting these contradictory features of race relations in the United States, I make no claim here to analyzing their deepest significance. Here, it is

enough to note their existence. The contradictions stem from three things
we have explored at length: the long-standing legacy of the history of racial
domination in this country; the advances of the civil rights movement; and
the success of the white racist coalition in preserving central features of the
system of white domination and blunting the previous advances.

Before proceeding on the current leg of our journey, let us recheck our
compass. We are ultimately trying to understand what fuels racial politics in
the present period; what accounts for the intensity of feeling among many
whites; what determines the centrality of certain issues and not others. In
this attempt, we face the challenge of trying to analyze the present contours,
material basis, and prospects for change of the current system of racial domination, attempting to understand what is different and what is the same from
previous times; whether the promise of freedom for all Americans will ever
be reached; what blocks its fulfillment; what forces sustain the system of racial
domination in the present era; what is necessary to overcome and defeat it.

My plan in attempting a final assault on these issues is predictably a bit
roundabout. Hopefully, the reader will indulge me one more time in what
may seem a bit like beating around the bush. The reasons for this circuitous
approach are several. The present conjuncture is based on several related but
distinguishable features. The system of racial domination has a long-standing history that we have traced and I have argued is centrally relevant. Still,
there are also features of the present period that are unique to contemporary
life. As I have argued throughout, one must begin with the state of the economy. In these final two chapters, I will proceed in the following manner.

First, I will try to examine the current state of the world and national
economy, exploring those forces that have encouraged divisiveness, racial
and ethnic conflict, insecurity, and threats to material well being, as well as
those tendencies that suggest possibilities for greater solidarity and unity.
The forces that shape current U.S. politics and the system of racial domination are international as well as national; thus, both must be examined.

Second, I wish to look at those immediate hot-button issues on which
the white racist coalition thrives and to which many whites respond. We
wish to know which issues and reactions have a basis in recent economic
developments, which are part of the continuing hegemony of white racial
domination, and which are simply pure racism.

Finally, with this context established, in the final chapter I will look at
the contours of present politics and the state of white supremacy. In doing
this, I will attempt to draw the lessons of our historical discussions, give
some definitive answers to the questions posed at the beginning about theories of race and its role in American political development, then offer some
appropriately meager suggestions and predictions for the future.

THE INTERNATIONAL ECONOMY

The most striking and generally recognized feature of the international economy is globalization—the increased interconnectedness of the economic activities of peoples around the world. This interconnectedness is reflected in numerous dramatic figures. In the late 1970s, for example, it is estimated that approximately two-thirds of the world labor force was largely insulated from international markets; by the year 2000, less than 10 percent of workers may be disconnected from world markets. World trade has also expanded for almost all countries. The movement of goods and services across national borders has grown from 23 percent of world gross domestic product (GDP) in 1970 to 40 percent in 1990 (World Bank 1995:1). Further, as a result of developments in communication and transportation technology, production and other important functions have become much more decentralized.

These worldwide economic functions are increasingly orchestrated by multi-national corporations, which are to a large extent disconnected from their country of origin. As one executive exclaimed, "I was asked the other day about United States competitiveness and I replied that I don't think about it at all. We at NCR think of ourselves as a globally competitive company that happens to be headquartered in the United States" (Hobsbawm 1994:403). Globalization thus allows enormous and rapid economic dislocation to take place on a scale and to a degree previously unknown, making runaway shops and subcontracting around the globe much easier.

There is a tendency, on the other hand, to ascribe all problems of the present to globalization, exaggerating its impact. Not all industries are equally vulnerable to the worldwide pressures of international trade. There are many economic functions (providing employment for a large percentage of workers in a country, especially a big one such as the United States), for example, that are either not all that mobile or are largely immune from competitive pressure, especially from low-wage producers abroad. Among these activities are city services including garbage collection; transportation hubs and systems, be they railroads, trucking, airplanes; certain types of local and regional fresh-food production; industries where the costs of fixed capital are exceedingly high, or like oil and natural gas extraction in the United States, where they are dependent on the location of natural resources; industries that rely on cutting-edge technology and research and that gain an advantage from being near the most advanced intellectual centers and historic regions of innovation; healthcare; and the list could be extended. Still, the degree of mobility engendered by globalization is enormous. What is important in attempting to understand the effects of globalization is to be specific about the industries and economic functions involved and their relation to worldwide competitive pressures.

Disruptions and upheavals of communties as a consequence of global-ization have affected peoples in all countries. Globalization has also meant the loss of ability of national institutions to control more than a declining percentage of their concerns. It begins with the nation-state, but also affects nationally bounded trade unions, leaving citizens with even less leverage than before over the forces of economic change. One worldwide response, in evidence in the most developed countries as well as the most economi-cally undeveloped, is an increase in separatism and nationalism, including in such economically developed bastions as Canada (French Canadian sep-aratism), the United Kingdom (not only Ireland, but Wales and Scotland), Spain and Belgium, not to mention the former Yugoslavia. Now the agen-da of multi-culturalism has many salutary features, including the fostering of an appreciation for all peoples and cultures, rejecting the "colonializer's view of the world." Yet, to the extent that it extols ethnic identity politics —by which I mean not only the desire to retain, appreciate, and gain tol-erance for one's culture, but also the assertion that it is both superior to others and has an essential character that makes it inpenetrable to outsiders —it is problematic. For the rise in strength of separatist identity politics has a practical aura of insanity about it, because it is clear that smaller states are even less capable of dealing with the forces of globalization than larger ones. The tendency to escape rather than face the difficult task of confronting, or at least acknowledging, the overwhelmingly global forces and to retreat into narrow forms of localism and provincialism, may be seen in numerous guis-es—not only in separatism, narrow nationalism, and growing assertions of essentialist ethnic identity politics, but also in the widespread rise of reli-gious fundamentalism and traditionalism, as well as the retreat in the United States by some whites into white racist assertions of group rights.

Along with globalization, beginning in the late 1940s, has come a new international division of labor. U.S. labor productivity advantages, double that of most developed countries in 1950 (measured in GDP per hour worked) and over six times that of Japan, were largely gone by 1992 (Maddison 1995:47). The rise of Germany and now the European Community (EC), along with Japan, has reduced the United States to no more than one (even if the largest and most powerful) big player in the world economy. Further, there has been a rise in the importance of a number of developing and transitional economies, sometimes referred to as newly industrializing countries (NICs), suggested by a number of statistics. There is to be sure a debate on what coun-tries constitute the NICs, whether they should be defined by the average stan-dards of living of their citizens (which would force one to include relative-ly small countries like Taiwan, Singapore, and Hong Kong) or whether they should be defined by their international economic role, along with high rates of development. For present purposes, I shall stick with the latter rubric. Private capital flows to the NICs, broadly defined, have risen from $42 billion in 1989 to $175 billion in 1994 (World Bank 1995:1). The NICs (defined here as China, Brazil, India, Mexico, South Korea, Argentina, and Venezuela) by the 1980s consumed almost a quarter of the world's steel (Pier 1992:269). Finally, contrary to the common myth that capital always gravitates to those places with the lowest wage rates, quite a number of countries have been abandoned as sites for investment by international capital (including parts of Africa and Asia and Haiti among others); with that lack of wherewithal comes a high degree of economic and political instability and even disintegration.

The development of the world economy in the postwar period has not been of a piece. In particular, it is important to note its period of boom and its period of stagnation. As Robert Brenner points out, from the late 1940s until the middle 1960s, "the advanced capitalist economies experienced a boom of historic proportions" (Brenner forthcoming:94). Yet, the United States, whose supremacy we have already seen after World War II was extraordinary, began its relative decline even during the boom period.

The period from the late 1960s and early 1970s until the present has so far been characterized as one of economic stagnation, affecting the most economically developed countries as well as many of those not so developed (the most obvious exception being that of China). At the most human level, unemployment has soared. In the twenty Organization for Economic Cooperation and Development (OECD) developed countries, unemployment tripled between 1972 and 1982. In 1994 in the EU, the official average unemployment rate was 12 percent, twice that of the United States and four times Japan's (World Bank 1995:2; Maddison 1995:84). The 1995 International Labor Organization (ILO) World Employment Report predicts growing world mass unemployment and poverty over the next several decades. Beggars and homeless people have emerged in large numbers even in most of the richest countries during the 1980s, phenomena that were unheard of as recently as the 1970s. The statistics also tell the story. GDP growth in the OECD countries averaged less than half from 1973 to 1992 than it did from 1950 to 1973 (Maddison 1995:62). In addition, profit rates fell precipitously, averaging 40 percent lower for the seven leading industrial economies during the period from 1970 to 1990 than from 1952 to 1970 (Marglin 1991:83; Brenner forthcoming:4). Labor productivity growth slowed to less than half for the OECD countries (Maddison 1995:79) and capital investment declined. The former Soviet-bloc countries, beginning in the late 1980s, suffered not only slowing growth but also absolute declines in major economic indicators, with the exception of China and Vietnam, which did not abandon their earlier regimes or centralized planning to unrestrained market forces.

Globalization would be threatening and frightening enough to many of the world's peoples were it taking place during a period of world prosperity and economic expansion. In a period of long-term, continuing stagnation, globalization, therefore, has led to some fairly general, historically specific reactions around the globe. Marx and Engels had foreseen that the early worldwide growth of capitalism, with rapid rises in productivity, would lead to progressive, liberal global-modernizing impulses. When the growth of the world market takes place under conditions of stagnation, however, the results are hardly liberal. For one characteristic of the present period around the globe is the rejection not only of socialist and left-wing alternatives but also traditional liberal values. As jobs have become scarce there has been an increase in anti-immigrant attitudes and violence in both the United States and Europe. In many countries, ethnic and religious conflicts have led to mass slaughter—for example, Bosnia, the Indian subcontinent, Rwanda, the Middle East. Religious intolerance and the appeal of fundamentalism may be seen around the world, from the Middle East (among both Muslims and Jews) and Afghanistan to the American South, the latter the scene of the most rapid social dislocations in the United States. The growth of religious fundamentalism, with its highly structured, individually constrained, antimodern stance, is an elusive attempt to hold on to something stable in a rapidly disintegrating world. As one indicator of the degree to which many people have completely lost their bearings as their traditional worlds crumble around them, is the rise in workplace violence and mass murders, starting in the United States, the latter a nihilism perhaps reflected in the violent, often cruel television shows, movies, and songs that emerged in the West in the 1980s. Some of these centrifugal trends in the United States are clearly in an indirect way a product of the weakness of the labor movement, reflecting the failure to attain broad class forms of solidarity and stability.

THE NATIONAL ECONOMY

Beginning with the late 1940s, as the Japanese and European economies initiated their period of rapid growth, the United States slowly came to lose its total supremacy in the world market. Nevertheless, despite lower growth rates, higher unemployment, and lower levels of new investment than its international competitors, the period from the end of World War II until the late 1960s was one of respectable growth. Real gross national product (GNP) growth through 1966 averaged 3.8 percent per year. The rate of unemployment through 1970 averaged under 5 percent per year, inflation remained low (Bowles, Gordon, Weisskopf 1990:37; *Economic Report of the President* 1995:312). Manufacturing production, according to the Federal Reserve Board index, doubled between 1945 and 1965, tripling between 1945 and

1976; domestic consumption and increased standards of living for large numbers of people expanded measurably (J. Bernstein and Adler 1994:15–17).

There was, to be sure, tremendous economic dislocation during the postwar boom period. The economic expansion at this time, however, was sufficient to reabsorb most of the whites who were displaced. This was not to prove the case for many Blacks. It is important for understanding the present to look at these trends.

A phenomenon mirrored in every developed country during the postwar period (with the exception of the United Kingdom, where it was quite pronounced earlier in the century) was the immense decline in the number and percentages of people working in agriculture (Maddison 1995:39). In the United States, from the beginning of the Great Depression until the start of World War II, almost one-fourth of the population lived and worked on farms. From the beginning of World War II until 1970, over twenty million people left agriculture, leaving less than 5 percent of the population there in that year (*Historical Statistics* 1972:I:457). The trends were even more extreme in the South where the 16.4 million in 1940 represented 54 percent of the nation's farm population, yet in 1970, the four million in the South were less than 40 percent in the country as a whole (*Historical Statistics* 1972:I:458). The disproportionate impact on African-Americans, however, was even greater. Although the number of farms in the country as a whole decreased by slightly more than half between 1940 and 1969, those operated by Blacks (and other non-whites) decreased from 723,000 to 104,000, reflecting the almost complete elimination of Black cotton tenancy during this period (*Historical Statistics* 1972:I:465). John Cogan argues that the decline in the demand for low-skilled agricultural labor had a special impact on Black teenagers, 45 percent of whom in 1950 were employed in agriculture. By 1970, they had been completely displaced from this venue (Cogan 1982:621). In addition, Black youth were displaced by whites after 1950 in the lumber and sawmill industries, the most important source of jobs for them outside of agriculture. Both Cogan and Gavin Wright argue that federal minimum-wage policies encouraged employers to switch to white labor when employers were forced to pay higher wages (Wright 1986:250; Cogan 1982:627). Numerous Black youth forced to leave the South with the elimination of low-paid unskilled workers in agriculture and rural industries ended up in northern cities where they already had friends and relatives. Rather than finding economic opportunity, many joined the growing ranks of the urban Black unemployed.

More skilled and stably employed Black workers were also displaced from the coal mining industry in West Virginia and Alabama where they had made up a large percentage of the labor force. From 1930 to 1950, with only a small decline in the total number of coal miners in the country, the number of Black miners decreased from 55,000 to 30,000. African-American workers were also disproportionately forced out of the coal mining industry during the postwar period. Mechanization caused large-scale reductions in employment (until the brief miniboom in the industry in the 1970s). From over half a million coal miners in 1950, the total number dropped to barely 130,000 in 1970. The numbers of Blacks in that field, however, plunged to less than 3,700, virtually eliminating them from the industry (Lewis 1987:167, 180).

Like their white counterparts, Blacks who were displaced from mining, agriculture, and low-wage southern industries such as lumber and timber during the postwar boom period, were sometimes absorbed into the expanding economy. Yet, there were trends in the North that made it more difficult, if not impossible, for many Blacks to make this transition, making their employment much more problematic. It was these trends of the postwar period which began the expansion of the modern urban Black ghettos, a phenomenon that was to accelerate as the boom period came to an end.

The greater difficulties faced by Blacks in obtaining suitable employment in urban areas existed along numerous dimensions. First, there were a number of white preserves from which they were excluded by employers and occasionally by white workers and their unions. The venues are familiar. Among construction workers, they were virtually absent from skilled jobs before the 1960s, with the unions often playing a major role in continuing the exclusion. Industrial skilled jobs were equally discriminatory. In 1960 in Detroit, for example, when 25.7 percent of Chrysler workers and 23 percent of General Motors workers were Black, African-Americans made up only 24 of 7,425 skilled workers at Chrysler, and only 67 of 11,125 at General Motors (Sugrue 1995:106–7). These figures are typical. Even in less-skilled jobs in many industries, however, it was more difficult for Blacks to find employment. Not only in mining but in railroad and aircraft, jobs were hard to come by if one were not white. In Detroit, Blacks were unlikely to obtain jobs in small automobile parts plants and in machine-tool companies, which were most often located in the suburbs. In both 1950 and 1962, the Detroit Urban League found hardly one percent of the brewery jobs there occupied by Blacks (39 out of 3,300 in 1950; less than 120 out of 12,000 in 1962; Sugrue 1995:108). Such situations were mirrored in numerable other occupations and industries, including fire fighters and police, high-level public employment, professional jobs including university teachers, lawyers, and doctors. These white exclusionary sources of employment were regarded by many whites as entitlements, privileges that went along with their skin color. These factors made the urban labor market far less hospitable for newly arrived displaced Black workers than for newly arriving whites.

Second, there was a tendency in the post-war period to move factories and build new ones outside the central cities. Part of the push for this was technical and economic, although the racial implications were immense. Improved transportation (especially highway systems) and a preference for single-story operations led employers to seek "green field" construction. There was also a strong desire to expand production in areas that were removed from traditional centers of union militancy. New auto plants were in addition often placed in rural areas or in parts of the country where they were remote from centers of large African-American populations. When manufacturing plants were built in urban areas, they were invariably built outside the cities themselves. In Chicago, International Harvester phased out its Chicago-based operations (eliminating its last plant there in 1970)—its historic center of operations—building its new plants either in the Chicago suburbs or in other parts of the country. As Sugrue notes, between 1947 and 1958, Detroit's three largest automobile manufacturers built twenty-five new plants in the Detroit area, all in the suburbs (Sugrue 1993:103–4). The likelihood of Blacks finding employment in these plants, usually far from the central city, was low, as is suggested by the number of Blacks who found employment in the General Motors plant in Livonia, a western suburb of Detroit; in 1960, they were only 20 out of the 2,384 employees (Sugrue 1993:109). Third, it was the proliferation and strengthening of segregation with the growth of the suburbs that intensified the above factors, encouraged not only by racist white homeowners and unscrupulous discriminatory realtors, but also by federally enforced Federal Housing Authority (FHA) and Veterans Housing Administration (VHA) home financing and mortgage policies, which as we noted previously began under the New Deal period.

The situation for white, as well as Black, working-class and poor people was to worsen as the world economic boom came to an end and stagnation began to deepen in the 1970s. That there has been economic stagnation in this country and the rest of the developed world since the late 1960s or early 1970s is, of course, indisputable. Before looking at the impact on people's lives, race relations, the system of racial domination, and the politics of the United States, it is instructive first to look at some general indicators.

The annual growth of GNP in the United States, which averaged a respectable 4.0 percent per year from 1960 to 1973, fell to 1.8 percent per year from 1973 to 1982 (Bernstein and Adler 1994:17). Profits declined substantially, productivity rates dropped, inflation rose, while unemployment worsened (Bowles, Gordon, Weisskopf 1990:37; Bernstein 1993:17; *Economic Report of the President* 1995:312, 320). Much of what was happening to the U.S. economy was also happening to other developed economies. Yet, there were a number of indications that the U.S. position in the world economy

was also deteriorating relatively. The percentage of a number of key manufacturing goods that were imported increased dramatically between 1967 and
1977, including steel, automobiles, rubber tires, chemicals, and apparel
(Bernstein and Adler 1994:21). The trade deficit soared after 1970, when it
was only $2.7 billion to $24.1 billion in 1980, until it spun almost out of control in the 1980s, reaching $132 billion in 1985 (*Statistical Abstract* 1983:833;
Statistical Abstract 1996:814). During the 1980s, the United States went from
being the largest creditor nation in the world to being the largest debtor nation
(Glyn and Sutcliff 1992:89–90). U.S. trade was partly sustained by the country becoming a major exporter of raw materials, more characteristic of underdeveloped countries than developed countries. By 1988, the major export from
the West Coast was waste paper (Bernstein and Adler 1994:22); most of the
timber from the Northwest was shipped abroad as unprocessed logs. Finally,
the largest export for the country as a whole continued to be raw grains—
though the value of this export declined from 46.4 percent of the total in
1980 to 36.5 percent in 1990 (*Statistical Abstract* 1995:684).

Although not constituting an economic collapse or depression, the economic stagnation, combined with technological advances and globalization,
has led to many uneven and dramatic dislocations. It is, of course, true that
service jobs have increased significantly and manufacturing jobs have declined
as a percentage of the labor force. Yet, the loss of U.S. manufacturing jobs in
absolute numbers tends to be exaggerated (see, for example, Gordon
1996:188). In general, since 1965 the absolute number of manufacturing jobs
has remained in the 18 to 20 million range. What has happened, however,
is that there have been enormous shifts in the number of employees within particular industries and big changes in the location of operations. The
most dramatic declines were those in the iron and steel industry where the
number of workers has been cut in half between 1980 and 1994 (*Statistical
Abstract* 1995:426). Coal mining and railroads have also lost significant numbers of workers. Certain industries such as shoes and televisions have largely abandoned the United States. Yet, these have been for the most part offset by increases in other industries such as construction, which has gained
a million and a half employees since 1970. In addition, the decline in railroad employment has been more than offset by more substantial increases
in employment in air transportation and trucking and warehousing, with
the latter going from 1.28 million to 1.75 million employees from 1980 to
1994 (*Statistical Abstract* 1983:298; Statistical Abstract 1995:428).

None of this is meant to argue that deindustrialization is not real or
without a substantial impact. The rapidity with which large multinationals
can shift their investments, resources, and sites of business is dramatic.
Deindustrialization and disinvestment in the 1970s, 1980s, and 1990s has

affected wide strata of the population. The loss of jobs and the destruction of large parts of major cities in the Northeast and Midwest are clear consequences of postwar plant location strategies. The decline of steel has destroyed large, formerly stable working-class communities, from the now largely Black city of Gary, Indiana, whose 30,000 jobs at U.S. Steel were virtually all lost as that corporation abandoned the area, to the largely white steel towns in Pennsylvania along the Monongahela Valley, where unemployment and shattered lives are the norm. Similarly, in 1995, Bethlehem Steel closed its historic mill in Bethlehem, on the banks of the Lehigh River, dismissing the last 1,800 workers, most of whom faced uncertain prospects (*New York Times,* 10-21-95). The economy of the whole state of Louisiana has yet to recover from the loss of oil production, on which the state economy was highly dependent, one effect of which was to provide fuel for the appeals of the David Duke campaigns discussed in the previous chapter. In all these areas, suicide, divorce, crime, and murder have increased, suggesting that conservative solutions that place the moral onus on the failures of individuals are more than a little off base.

What is also especially pronounced in this period of stagnation, global competition, and rapid change is the substantial decrease in the wages of nonsupervisory employees, especially in traditionally unionized industries. Between 1979 and 1994, real wages per hour have dropped 10 percent in manufacturing, 12.4 percent in mining, 15 percent in transportation and public utilities, and 20.7 percent in construction (Gordon 1996:191). Declining wages are often seen as evidence of global competition, but there is some reason to question this analysis. On the one hand, in manufacturing, most of the global competition with the United States comes not from low-wage countries (such as Mexico, South Korea, and China) but from Japan and European countries where manufacturing wages are now often substantially higher than in the U.S. On the other hand, some of the biggest declines in wages are in those industries that are the least exposed to international competition. These changes are less the result of global competition, but of the several decades-long assault on unions in this country, itself a result of trends we have already discussed. Thus, it is indicative that the most severe declines in wages have taken place in construction, an industry largely insulated from international competition. In the 1960s, this was an industry that was highly unionized. By the early 1980s, the assaults on the union, led by the industry organized Business Roundtable had effectively destroyed unionization in the bulk of the construction industry (see Goldfield 1989:191–92). Likewise in trucking, the demise of the Teamsters' Master Freight Agreement, spurred by deregulation of the industry, has not only encouraged a proliferation of non-union shippers but also undermined union leverage.

The former privileged job preserves of less-educated white males has declined noticably, while the level of job security of even the more educated has been greatly constricted. Prior to the mid-1960s, Blacks were virtually excluded from a number of skilled white preserves, particularly in the South. In 1960, for example, of the 1,120 apprentice carpenters in the South, there were no minorities; there were only two Blacks among the 978 apprentice electricians (Marshall 1967:30–31). Between the 1960s and the 1980s, however, these white preserves came under attack. The success of these challenges can be seen in a variety of industries. In iron and steel in 1963, for example, Blacks held only 5.9 percent (555 of 9,431) of all skilled positions in the South and 7.6 percent (3,503 of 46,063) in the Midwest. Only three years later, however, Black workers held 7.4 percent (664 of 8,991) and 8.5 percent (3,903 of 45,821) of all skilled positions (Rowan 1968, 124–35). Similarly, in 1970, Blacks occupied only 6.9 percent of all over-the-road trucking jobs, yet by 1983, they held 12.3 percent of such positions (Hill 1985:254). In certain industries however, one can see a reversal of these trends in the late 1980s and 1990s, most notably urban construction (see T. Bates 1997).

The undermining of the white preserves was exacerbated by the post-1973 decline of the economic status of many white male workers. First, the real average weekly earnings for the bottom 80 percent of production and nonsupervisory workers fell by 19 percent between 1973 and 1995 (Bluestone 1995:1). Second, medium family income remained stagnant from 1973 to 1989—that it did not drop substantially was in good part due to the increase in the average number of wage earners per family. Between 1973 and 1989, real family wages increased 1.5 percent for families with both parents in the paid labor force, while wages for families with only one working parent declined .6 percent. A downward trend, however, developed for all families between 1989 and 1993 as wages of two-income families declined .7 percent. Finally, and possibly most disturbing, is the decline of wages for single-income families by 2.5 percent, while real weekly income in 1993 fell below what it was in 1959 (*Economic Report of the President* 1995:326; Mishel and Bernstein 1994:34).[1] Wage inequality, more extreme in the United States than in any other economically developed capitalist country, has also increased dramatically, while family and individual wealth have followed even more sharp tendencies (Freeman 1994; *Human Development Report* 1996:13). There was at one time a debate over the existence of these trends, with some conservative economists denying their existence. This is no longer the case. Currently, the main debates are over their causes (see Levy and Murnane 1992 for a summary and analysis).

These trends have been further compounded by declines in healthcare benefits and pension coverage, along with the rising real costs of obtaining a college education and the greater financial obstacles and difficulties faced by first-time home buyers. Costs for college education have increased each year during the past several decades much more rapidly than the rate of inflation. At elite schools, where the average cost of room, board, and tuition in the 1960s was typically in the $2,500 to $3,000 range, costs in the late 1990s are ten times that, while the cost of living index has barely quadrupled. Even public college education has increased substantially, although not nearly so fast as that at private colleges. In 1996, the average cost of an education at a four-year public university (for tuition, room, and board) was $7,118 per year (*New York Times* 9-26-96). In 1970, a similar education cost $1,362 annually, a little more than a fifth as much, while the cost of living had barely tripled (*Statistical Abstract* 1995:185; *Statistical Abstract* 1982–83:163). Similarly, the cost of home ownership has increased substantially. In 1950, a thirty-year-old white male with an average income had to pay 14 percent of his wages for the average home mortgage. By 1973, it required 21 percent of his income, but by 1984, this amount had more than doubled to 44 percent (Levy 1988:68). Finally, mortgage rates for both existing homes and new homes almost doubled between 1975 and 1982 (*Statistical Abstract* 1995:523; Statistical Abstract 1982–83:763). As a result, the so-called American Dream has slipped further from the reach of many white Americans. Needless to say, for large numbers of African-Americans, the conditions of life have worsened even more as the creation of growing areas of concentrated poverty have become a major feature of life in virtually all U.S. cities. An especially alarming example is New York City. In 1996, the poorist fifth of the population, whose median annual income amounted to only $5,800, were forced to pay 79 percent of their meager earnings to secure increasingly dilapidated rental units (see the series on housing in the *New York Times* 10-6-96 through 10-10-96; and Wilson 1987).

I have argued that early post–World War II anti-Black attitudes and activities on the part of white workers were fueled by a number of factors. These include, of course, the long history of white racism and scapegoating that have existed throughout U.S. history. Further, despite the postwar economic boom, most white workers, even those who worked in the automobile industry in Detroit, felt correctly that their hold on reasonable paying jobs, home ownership, and the material wherewithal to support their families was rather tenuous. White workers sometimes perceived that their lives were threatened by the advances in employment and the integration of previously all-white neighhoods by African-Americans. The retreat of the labor movement from offering broad class solutions to the effects of racial domination and the general problems of all workers implicitly encouraged the adoption of narrow, defensive strategies on the part of whites that were at times

. Their sense that they were being both ignored and victimized, with their feeling of white entitlement, which seemed to be dis- is an important reason why the racist attitudes are often presented with such moral fervor.

The emergence and successes of the civil rights movement only accentuated the perceived threat seen by some white workers. Ghetto riots, the women's movement, flag burning and draft board refusals, accentuated the danger seen, especially by the most racially conservative segments of the labor movement. The high point of political expression of such activities were the so-called hard-hat demonstrations of construction workers in 1970, ostensibly in support of the war in Vietnam. These demonstrations were hardly spontaneous, being in good part organized by former construction union leader and Nixon Secretary of Labor William Brennan. On May 8, construction workers physically assaulted peace demonstrators and students in New York City; on May 20, 100,000 demonstrated in support of the Nixon administration and the war. Similar events took place in St. Louis (aside from contemporary newspaper reports, see Cook 1970; Freeman 1993). These attitudes and activities among workers, while fixated on by the popular media, were not the only tendency. According to polls at the time, most white workers actually opposed the war in Vietnam by 1970. I can remember going to basketball games in Chicago during 1970 and 1971 with my coworkers. These events, when tickets were easy to obtain and good seats could be had for three dollars, were largely working class, highly integrated affairs, if still majority white. When the national anthem would be played, no one in the stadium would rise. The combination of militancy on civil rights and opposition to the war had made antipatriotism the hegemonic view. One only has to contrast this situation with the reception received in 1996 by former Denver Nuggets star Mahmoud Abdul-Rauf to see how times have changed New York Times, 3-3-96). Never, to my knowledge were such commonplaces of the early 1970s discussed in the media. Yet, we must keep the whole picture in mind when trying to assess working-class stances.

Unlike the period of postwar expansion, the era of stagnation brought with it a significant deterioration in the material conditions of large numbers of white working people. Without a labor movement that supported the struggles of Blacks, that put forth solutions to the problems of racial domination that would help raise the circumstances of all workers, it was to prove easy for those politicians building the white racist coalition to convince many white workers that the reasons for their problems were two polar opposite trends occurring in the Black community, both of which seemed to be a consequence of the civil rights movement itself. On the one hand were the growing number of poor Blacks receiving welfare, characterized as unwilling to work, potentially violent, propagating out-of-wedlock children, supported by the taxes of hard-working—white—workers. On the other hand, more directly a result of civil rights victories was a growing Black middle class, people who were seen by many whites as thriving in jobs that they had obtained, not through hard work or merit, but through affirmative action —jobs that under any fair system of competition would have rightfully gone to whites. Thus, the interaction of the decades-long period of economic stagnation with the gains of the civil rights movement, provided a fertile field for the growth of white racist reaction.

NOTES ON THE VEXED ISSUES

It is perhaps appropriate that we now take a look at the substance of the micro issues that have fueled the white racist coalition that has developed over the past several decades. I wish initially to distinguish between two types of questions. First, are the ones which provide a legitimate basis of concern for those who are upset about them and for people in general. However distorted the responses, there is underneath some substance to people's concerns. Second, there is another set of issues which, though there may be some grain of truth buried within, the issues themselves are largely a smoke screen for racist attitudes and the perpetuation of the racial subordination of Blacks.

Among the first set, I would include crime and neighborhood and school deterioration. Crime, whether it be auto theft, car jacking, home burglary, assault, rape, or murder is a concern of all who live in the United States. Although whites have valid reasons to be concerned, in general their fears, particularly those who live in suburbs, tend to be exaggerated; many whites such as those who I have encountered in the metropolitan suburban areas of cities such as Detroit and Chicago frequently express irrational fears about visiting even the relatively safe downtown areas. On the other hand, worry over crime is an issue of equal concern for numerous Blacks, many of whom do often live in high-crime areas and have greater cause to be afraid than whites. Similar arguments might be made about neighborhoods, schools, and the decline in the availability of decent jobs. The narrow racist response of some whites to these issues belies the broad solutions that are the only way to solve these problems. A more adequate strategy would, of course, involve rebuilding U.S. cities, developing public transportation, building extensive and affordable housing, and providing greater degrees of parks, recreation facilities, and cultural opportunities.

One part of the implementation would be the creation of a vast system of public jobs, for which large numbers of the unemployed would be trained and educated. Approaches that would improve the education system involve its expansion, more teachers, smaller class sizes, improvement of facilities, involvement of parents in education and learning, and much more. There are not, contrary to popular political lore, easy cheap answers. Real race-blind solutions to social problems would include the extension of healthcare, nutrition, and early supplementary education to the whole population with special emphasis on those of all races from impoverished and low-educational backgrounds. Whether these programs might be accomplished without a massive political upheaval that overcame the opposition of many entrenched interests is, of course, dubious. Still, it is perhaps the only realistic goal toward which to strive. For what is most clear is that campaigns against busing have rarely improved schools; building more jails and invoking harsher penalties have not reduced crime. Yet, these are among the solutions toward which many people gravitate when there are no broad strategies being offered.

There is another series of issues, however, whose substance is less well rooted and which ultimately serve merely as fronts for expressing racial antagonism. Let us start by considering the most contentious of issues, that of affirmative action—and the opposition to it.

AFFIRMATIVE ACTION

Affirmative action, an ambiguous term which refers to a number of social policies, has been under attack in recent years. Before the election of Ronald Reagan in 1980, it was hardly controversial, at least among politicians of the two major parties. Since then, it has been disavowed first by conservatives, later by large numbers of Republicans and Democrats, more recently by many liberals. The issue played a central role in the successful 1990 Senate campaign of right-wing Republican Jesse Helms. The advertisement designed by former Clinton aide and political strategist Richard Morris, which supposedly cemented Helms' victory against Black Democrat Harvey Gantt, showed white hands holding a rejection slip for a job that was filled by an allegedly less-qualified minority. Affirmative action is also the subject of the California Civil Rights Initiative, which seeks to ban it. Affirmative action was even conceived by Republican strategists in 1995 as the ultimate wedge issue to defeat President Bill Clinton and the Democrats, supposedly being *the* issue that would separate the angry white males who supposedly powered the 1994 Republican congressional takeover further from the Democrats.[2]

Although affirmative action never quite achieved this exalted status in the 1996 campaign, it is still a key hot-button issue. Social scientists and public-opinion analysts have written dozens of books and hundreds, perhaps thousands, of articles on the subject. The most disputed question has been whether opposition to affirmative action policies is based on principle and legitimate concerns or whether it is merely a new vehicle for whites to express racism, either of the old-fashioned type or of a newer, more modern variety. In general, analysts attempt to distinguish between what they argue are two quite different types of policies. First, there is encouragement in the training, seeking out, recruitment, and hiring of underrepresented minorities and women. Often this involves only outreach, the development of new networks, and advertising, all supposedly to replace the old-boy network, previously dominated by an in-group of certain white males (which had excluded many other white males as well as minorities and women). These are activities that take place before the selection process (for jobs, universities, contracts, etc.), and in general seem to be supported by large numbers of whites (for one summary of such results see the op-ed piece by pollster Louis Harris in the *New York Times*, 7-31-95). This type of affirmative action may or may not merge into or be combined with the setting of quotas, goals, and timetables, a putatively quite different type of affirmative action. It is this latter feature that has led to claims of "reverse discrimination," the victimization of white males, and violation of the norms of fairness and equal opportunity, and is opposed by large numbers of whites when general questions are posed to them by pollsters.

One of the better summaries of existing studies, and itself an example of careful, nuanced work, is a piece by Laura Stoker (1995). Stoker reports on answers to questions that attempt to distinguish between different situations in which remedial action is proposed. She finds, not surprisingly, that those who adhere to old-fashioned white supremacist views oppose remedies for Blacks, no matter how harsh the discrimination that they face may be. She also finds that people who regard the disadvantages faced by Blacks a result of white racism and discrimination virtually always support affirmative action even with racial quotas, no matter what the context may be. Where Stoker finds great variance is among that majority of whites who do not believe that the disadvantages faced by Blacks are general or require across-the-board remedies. Her study does find, of course, as do many others that whites support the first type of affirmative action described above. She also finds, however, that many of these whites would support even quotas and timetables when they are clear, specific remedies for injustices and discrimination caused by a particular employer or institution. From this, she concludes that the broad opposition of many whites to quotas and strong forms of affirmative action is not necessarily based on racist attitudes but on a conception of fairness that differs from the views of the hard-core racists. Among the more striking results of her study is that—after controlling for a large number of other variables—opposition to affirmative action is greater among those with higher incomes and higher levels of education, exactly the opposite of what politicians and political pundits would have us believe. Also, quite surprisingly, Stoker finds support for affirmative action slightly stronger among those residing in southern or border states.

Given the assault on affirmative action, quotas, and the attempts to blame the victims for their plight that has been in high gear since the early 1980s, such results may even give us some marginal reason for encouragement. Any attempt to deal reasonably with the sources of and remedies for the long history of racial subordination faced by Blacks, however, must look not only at the effects of this broad propaganda on the general public, but also at the arguments of the critics of affirmative action who have gotten broad publicity and have been promulgated far and wide. Their positions must, I am tempted to say, be deconstructed.

First, it is important to underscore that the catchy term *reverse discrimination* is misleading. In the "worst case," whites may face stiffer competition for a smaller number of jobs or even partial exclusion because of minority quotas, as was the case with the affirmative action program in the Birmingham, Alabama fire department—eventually overturned by the Supreme Court. The idea that even the most extreme of such cases are the same as (or even similar to) the complete historic exclusion of African-Americans from many jobs, housing, and educational opportunities, or to the historic indignities and threats of white supremacy, is a forced metaphor at best. The term *reverse discrimination* is thus a perversion of the language, comparable to the use of the term "holocaust" to refer to a variety of mishaps. Still, victimization of innocent white males is both possible and does undoubtedly take place. Two recent studies, however, suggest that the problem is hardly widespread.

An internal study by the Labor Department, reported by the Bureau of National Affairs, analyzes 3,000 cases of claimed employment discrimination from 1990 to 1994. Between one and three percent were ones of so-called reverse discrimination. Few of these claims by "disappointed" white job applicants were found to have merit, that is, the complainants were found by courts, in fact, to have been less qualified than the women or minorities actually hired. The report of the Federal Glass Ceiling Commission, appointed by President George Bush, in examining the top, highest-paying corporate jobs, found that women and minoritiies, rather than getting preferences, are still largely excluded; at least 95 percent of these jobs are still occupied by white males (Glass Ceiling Commission 1995:12). It is easy to get cynical about the claims of large-scale reverse discrimination. Tom Wood, the executive director of the conservative California Association of Scholars and one of the authors of the anti-affirmative action California Civil Rights Initiative, once claimed to *USA TODAY* that he "blamed affirmative action programs for being passed over for a teaching job in favor of a 'diversity hire,' even though he was told he was the most qualified." Wood later admitted that he did not actually apply for the job, that what he had been told about qualifications "may not have been accurate" (*USA TODAY*, 4-4-95). Black history Professor Roger Wilkins reports a similarly fabricated story where a white history professor wrote that Wilkins' job was about to be given to him, when it was taken away and given to an unqualified Black (Wilkins 1995:409). In fairness, complete evidence is difficult to come by. Both proponents and critics claim large-scale results (including increases in the numbers of African-American firefighters, police officers, bank tellers, and pharmacists) since 1970, more rightly attributed to the general gains of the civil rights movement than any one particular program (Taylor 1995). The most careless and irresponsible assertions, however, are made by critics of affirmative action. One, for example, argues that increases in the presence of women and a few minorities in sociology departments since 1969 are clear evidence of reverse discrimination—a sign not only of illogic but of the blinding bigotry of the scientific racists (See Lynch 1989:132). Of course, one of the legacies of the several centuries of white supremacy in this country is that many whites often continue to perceive Blacks as less qualified even when they are equally qualified or more so; the existence of an African-American in a responsible job is a sure sign to some whites that they were given some special preference.

The most persistent argument, however, made by many conservative critics is that affirmative action violates the ideals of equal treatment and selection by merit. This is an objection that one must examine extremely carefully because it is a principle that is at the core of the demand for civil rights. On the other hand, there is also the lurking suspicion that those who raise such objections to affirmative action are doing so in bad faith, that is, they have no interest in seeing African-Americans and other minorities receive equal treatment. The way to tell whether someone is using a principle hypocritically or is an honest critic, is to examine his or her consistency—do they apply the same principle when it does not involve African Americans? Some examples are instructive.

Let us start with university admissions, a subject around which there has been much debate, a fair amount of research, and in which I have had a small amount of experience. While a professor at Cornell University, for a year I worked on undergraduate admissions. The number of African-American students at Cornell (similar to the number reported in the *New York Times* for the University of California) was around 3 to 4 percent[3] Admission criteria at Cornell were similar to those at other prestigious schools. Anywhere from 5 to 10 percent of the acceptances at such schools (and exact figures are hard to come by and may at times even be higher) are "legacies," students with parents who were alumni, most of whom might not have made the cut based on academic qualifications alone. We thus find affirmative action for the rich. Hence, the number of legacy cases was much more than the number of Black undergraduates, many of whom might well have been admitted without regard to race (for discussions of Harvard, Princeton, and Yale, see, e.g., Lamb 1993 and Megalli 1995).

Which conservatives, or liberals for that matter, have raised protests against this long-standing violation of the merit principle, or are we to be less worried when standards are lowered for affluent, advantaged whites than for more disadvantaged Blacks? There are even more extreme quotas, however, at most elite schools. Cornell, like many other U.S. universities, has quotas by geographical region. Thus, hundreds of students with college board scores well over 700, with virtually all As and many advanced courses, are rejected over others, perhaps "less qualified"—if one believes in the validity of the grades and scores—with scores a hundred points lower and grade averages in high school barely above Bs. The most extreme cases of the geographically excluded were those students from the New York City area, especially Long Island, largely Jews and to a lesser extent Catholics, in preference for students from other parts of the country, especially the West and the South. Who among those who argue for the merit principle are publicly denouncing these quotas, which certainly affect a far larger percentage of undergraduate admissions than affirmative action for minorities, especially at many elite schools?

To ask such questions is to know the answer, for the silence as the old cliché goes is deafening. To raise a public ruckus on supposed principle about the small percentage of African-American students receiving affirmative action, and not get equally if not more excited about the larger violations of one's principles is, of course, hypocrisy. In this case, it is racial bigotry pure and simple. Other examples abound.

For many federal civil-service jobs people are given tests that supposedly determine their qualifications. Veterans have historically been given extra points. For other jobs without tests, they get other types of preferences, often over better-qualified—or at least more highly rated—employees. Why have the critics of affirmative action not criticized this clear violation of their principles? Or do the critics accept the argument that some valid public interest is being served in giving preferences to veterans, yet there is no interest being served in giving preferences to Blacks?

Contrary to the claims of critics, quotas and preferences abound throughout the society. They may be right, they may be wrong, but they are rarely attacked. The Constitution, for example, says that each state is entitled to two senators, clearly an undemocratic quota because citizens in New York State and California have a far smaller fraction of the influence in choosing their senator than more favored citizens in Wyoming. Who has been making an issue of this quota? We have seen the even more extreme legislative preferences that existed in most southern states for the first two-thirds of this century, quotas that were often accepted by many of the same people who now oppose all forms of affirmative action.

Still more common than affirmative action for women and minorities, of course, is affirmative action in reverse. Historically, at least since they were driven out of these occupations in the nineteenth century by force and violence, African-Americans have been excluded from most skilled construction jobs. In St. Louis in the 1960s, civil rights leaders found that apprenticeship applicants whose fathers were already journeymen received a ten-point bonus on exams. In Philadelphia, Blacks were excluded by the verbal administration of tests. More common today is the use of informal kinship and friendship networks for jobs. Whatever the mechanism, they all add up to the exclusion of African-Americans on the basis of race, clear violations of the merit principle. What solution do critics of affirmative action propose for these violations of the merit priniciple that they supposedly oppose, and where are their indignant expressions of protest?

During the 1960s, the Johnson Administration attempted to work with American Federation of Labor and Congress of Industrial Organizations (AFL-CIO) construction unions to increase the number of African-American skilled construction workers. In trying not to offend either constituency, the results were minimal. Republican President Richard Nixon decided he had the perfect wedge issue to turn these white workers against civil rights. On June 27, 1969, Labor Secretary George Schultz announced the Philadelphia Plan—setting targets (dare we say quotas) of between 19 percent and 26 percent for minority hiring along with timetables—applicable to all government construction projects there. Despite the politically opportunist reasons for the targets, quotas, and timetables, according to Jill Quadagno, "the Philadelphia Plan worked." Whereas in 1967 minorities accounted for less than 6 percent of apprentices, by 1979, minorities represented 17.4 percent of the construction labor force (Quadagno 1994:81). Comparable gains, however, were not made nationally, because the Philadelphia Plan was not pursued elsewhere with the same degree of dilligence. Yet, despite the extensive affirmative action program, informal mechanisms have reasserted themselves in the Philadelphia construction labor market. With the current decline in urban labor market demand, skilled and qualified African-American construction workers are not hired as frequently or consistently as comparable white workers. A white foreman interviewed by the New York Times admits that he invariably hires white workers, even though he knows some African-Americans to be highly skilled (New York Times, 7-9-95). What are the upholders of the principle of merit advocating and trying to do about these violations of their sacred principles?

The answers, of course, are simple. None of us has read or met anyone who opposes affirmative action on the merit principle who is concerned with any of the above violations. Therefore, any fair-minded person must accept their arguments for what they really are—a hypocritical smoke screen for bigotry.

Let us take one more focal point of controversy surrounding affirmative action—minority business set-asides. A good bit of current hiring is done by small businesses, although the exact percentage is a matter of some dispute (see T. Bates 1994:115, for a summary of differing studies). It may be that over half of all new jobs created are in businesses with less than 100 employees. As Bates argues and the Philadelphia situation suggests, white small business owners tend not to hire minority workers, including Blacks, Asians, and Latinos, while Black small business owners tend to hire many minority workers, even when their businesses are located outside minority communities. Affirmative action is little help in overcoming the attitudes of white small business owners. Thus, the increase in minority small business set-asides for government contracts has led to the hiring of more minority workers where they would not have otherwise been hired. In the growing concern of both the courts and politicians that white small businessmen are being disadvantaged by the minority set-aside programs, who is proposing to do something to ensure that qualified minority workers are not excluded from jobs? One sees no concern on the part of the critics of these programs. And so the argument goes.

Whatever the pros and cons on affirmative action, to attack quotas and goals as a violation of one's principles and to say little, pay lip service to, or not make greater noise about the far greater violations of one's supposed principles that affect minorities and women is pure and simple hypocrisy.

What's Behind It?

The reason that so many whites can be mobilized against affirmative action is simple. Although cases of so-called reverse discrimination are few, the decline in living standards and the contraction of job prospects for a large percentage of the population are quite real. As has been true historically in this country, the political alternatives are stark. One can attempt to understand the broad economic trends and organize for more justice, greater union organization, and a larger safety net. This puts people in sharp conflict with the most powerful forces in the country. Or one can pick a scapegoat. When collective organization is weak, the latter alternative is the one usually tried. Politicians defending the prerogatives of the rich are quick to seize on this alternative.

WELFARE

The politics of welfare reform are not so dissimilar to the politics of affirmative action. Here, however, the recent initiatives to attack welfare, and by not-so-subtle implication African-American women, have come initially from the Democrats. Social welfare, especially Aid to Families with Dependent Children (AFDC) has been used as a scapegoat for high taxes and budget deficits, the rise in illegitimate births and single female-headed households, poorly educated children, drugs, crime, and the decline in the work ethic. Most of this causal chain falls apart on initial examination. AFDC in 1995 made up perhaps one percent of the federal budget, less than many other forms of federal government dependency and largess, including home mortgage tax exemptions (over 3 percent), farm subsidies, the savings and loan bailout, and defense contract overruns and rip-offs of the federal treasury. Studies have shown that the rise in illegitimate births is a worldwide phenomenon, the increases being no higher in numbers or percentages among young, single Black women than among other sectors of the population. Higher welfare payments do not seem to be an accompaniment of this trend. In fact, those states with the lowest AFDC payments (for example, Mississippi) seem to have had higher increases in out-of-wedlock births than those that have the highest payments (including New York). And so the argument goes.[4]

The attack on welfare is a diversion from the real causes of budget deficits and the more complex realities of poverty, crime, drugs, and social dislocation. That the moves to eliminate "welfare as we know it" and to blame these problems on the poorest African-Americans are a political hoax are made clear in the remedies. Despite the fact that there is a declining labor market for low-educated, unskilled workers—labor market characteristics of the majority of welfare recipients—women are to be kicked off of welfare and told to get jobs with little provisions for training, upgrading of skills, and taking care of their children. The only substantial proposals that have been implemented are to use welfare recipients to do the work of unionized public-sector employees, thus undermining their job security and bargaining leverage (New York Times 9-20-96, 9-23-96).

IMMIGRATION

The furor over immigration is another such issue with racial overtones. Epitomized by the xenophobic, racially charged book by Peter Brimelow, Alien Nation, and fueled by the campaign that passed California's Proposition 187, victims are again easy targets for scapegoating. Even some conservative Republicans denounced the California campaign as divisive and illogical. The truth remains that immigrants have historically been brought to this country as sources of cheap labor; in times of economic expansion—as in the mid-1960s when the 1965 immigration law was passed—there is hardly any worry about immigrants. California agribusiness has for at least a century been the leader in efforts to ensure the availability of cheap immigrant labor. Even today throughout the border areas and immigration gateways to the United States, hundreds of thousands of illegal immigrants toil in illegal and below minimum-wage conditions, barely disturbed by immigration authorities. Although many rightly denounce prison labor in China and slave camps in Brazil, newspaper reports reveal the enslavement of seventy Thai immigrant workers (some for as long as seven years) "stitching together American name brand clothes" in a factory in southern California. The garments had labels from retailers such as Macy's and Filine's. Some economists and labor union officials estimate that one-fifth of the garment workers in Los Angeles work in illegal sweatshops. Federal immigration officials acknowledged that they knew about the conditions of the Thai workers nearly three years before the factory was raided and the enslaved workers were freed (*New York Times*, 8-5-95)! The penalties for employers of this slave labor are minimal. One hears little sense of outrage among the advocates of the death penalty and heavy sentencing. It is, again, a question of values, where the class and race of the victims lead many to regard their kidnapping and enslavement as minor offenses. The solution to these problems, as proposed by some politicians, is not to punish the employers, but to deny schooling, medical care, and social support to the victims, usually non-white.

When good jobs are disappearing and real wages are falling, many whites fall back on the claims of their ethnic identity to assert their special privileges. As Howard Winant argues, "In this situation, the Right is ascendant, because it can express the anxieties and reiterate the familiar national-popular themes, which the center and the left cannot so easily assert" (Winant 1995:1). The reason is that the anti-immigrant proposals are essentially undemocratic, of no problem for the right, but of varying degrees of ideological concern for the left, those in the center, and even for some conservatives. As Winant argues, taken far enough, anti-immigrant politics moves toward fascism.

Racism provides the framework in which virtually all of today's vexed political issues exist. If those touting the values of fairness and equal opportunity were at all sincere, one might expect them to vehemently oppose the present application of the death penalty, for it is one of the few areas in our society where African-Americans really do get preferential treatment. Blacks are far more likely to get the death penalty than whites. The race of the victim, however, is even more important. Nationally, killers of whites are nearly three times more likely to be sentenced to death than the killer of an

African-American. In Dallas, twenty-seven killers of whites were sent to death row from the time of the enactment of the death penalty statute in 1973 until 1986, but none who were convicted of murdering Blacks even *faced* the death penalty. In Louisiana, a review of 504 cases showed that 14.5 percent of the men who killed whites were sentenced to die, while no whites received the death penalty for killing a Black. Equal opportunity for all, no preferences, yet Democrats and Republicans alike scramble to see who can come up with the greatest number of crimes for which the death penalty is applicable.[5]

Race is even involved in many of those public issues where it is seemingly absent. Take the articles sympathetically detailing the life and adventures of the white supremacist, fascist murder suspect, convicted terrorist Timothy McVeigh. The mass media and politicians have been unusually kind to him. It is a toss-up over whether the reason is that he is a right-winger or that he is a white racist. Rarely are the above, quite accurate adjectives part of his description in the media; his racism is often only mentioned as an afterthought. Geronomo ji Jaga (Pratt) and Mumia Abu-Jamal are always mentioned as former Black Panthers; Jamal always as a convicted cop killer. Jamal's supporters are defamed and ridiculed throughout the mainstream press, although they include labor unions, civil rights organizations, and well-known entertainers. McVeigh's supporters are never mentioned. How strange yet so typical. McVeigh was a "troubled…teenager," a loner, who tried to be a "perfect soldier." As an aside, never mentioned as an integral part of his ideology or motives, he was an open racist who routinely gave the worst assignments to his Black subordinates (*New York Times*, 5-4-95). In the in-depth coverage of the indictments for the Oklahoma bombings, the defendant's racism and fascist proclivities are not even an issue (*New York Times*, 8-13-95). For those who claim the system of white supremacy has been dismantled and that equality of opportunity exists for those who wish to take advantage of it, one must only wonder about their lack of perception and the shortness of their attention spans.

As always in the United States, the situation is contradictory. We must be clear that the current period is not like the early part of the century, where white supremacy exerted uncontested hegemony. Further, like in many other periods of time—even those that were not historic turning points—one finds numerous examples of solidaristic behavior and a refusal on the part of at least some whites to accept their designated roles in the system of racial domination. In the concluding chapter, I will try to put these questions in perspective, looking at the state of white supremacy today, and attempt to finish the historical and theoretical agenda promised at the beginning of this chapter.

1. Recent census data for 1995 show a slight increase in family income in some categories, although the general multiyear trend still remains downward. See *Money Income in the United States: 1995,* U.S. Department of Commerce 1996:vii.

2. For an analysis of the 1994 election results, which casts doubt on this view, see Ruy A. Teixeira and Joel Rogers 1996.

3. Exact figures are often difficult to ascertain because universities tend to distort the figures upward, including many categories of minority or non-white foreign and domestic students that obfuscate the reality. See Cohen and Gates 1987.

4. For a lucid analysis, see Frances Fox Piven, "Poorhouse Politics"; for a definitive analysis of the welfare system and its origins, see Piven and Richard Cloward, *Regulating the Poor.*

5. For a review of evidence, see Ronald J. Tabak 1986.

CHAPTER 11

Concluding Remarks

> The country will not change until it reexamines itself and discovers what it really means by freedom....It is a terrible, an inexorable law that one cannot deny the humanity of another without diminishing one's own: in the face of one's victim one sees oneself. Walk through the streets of Harlem and see what we, this nation, have become.

James Baldwin, *Nobody Knows My Name*, 1961:66

> The American Negro has the great advantage of never having believed that collection of myths to which white Americans cling: that their ancestors were all freedom-loving heroes, that they were born in the greatest country the world has ever seen, or that Americans are invincible in battle and wise in peace, that Americans have always dealt honorably with Mexicans and Indians.

James Baldwin, *The Fire Next Time*, 1963:101

> I left America because I doubted my ability to survive the fury of the color problem here....In my necessity to find the terms on which my experience could be related to that of others, Negroes and whites, writers and non-writers, I proved to my astonishment, to be as American as any Texas G.I.

James Baldwin, *Nobody Knows My Name*, 1961:17

> Someone once said we never know what is enough until we know what's more than enough.

Billie Holiday, 1956:155.

In this concluding chapter, I summarize a number of the continuing themes of this essay. These include the implications of the preceding analysis for theories of U.S. political development; the relevance of the historical material for understanding contemporary U.S. society; what the analysis suggests for theories of race in the United States, and hence, what it implies for the present state of racial domination and race relations; the prospects for the racial egalitarianism that has been advanced at certain of the critical moments in U.S. history; and finally, what needs to be done about it.

RACE AND U.S. POLITICAL DEVELOPMENT

I have argued that present American politics has largely been shaped by at least five great historical turning points. For each, race and racial issues have been central and are the key to understanding U.S. political development. There are several reasons why this has been the case. First, for most of the nation's history, the system of racial domination has been central to the economic interests of an important segment of the U.S. ruling class. The system of racial domination allowed southern plantation owners to obtain and base their profits on cheap, coerced Black labor from the 1680s until the 1960s. The struggle to ensure the continuance of the system of racial domination and its ideological supports—often in defiance of federal laws, often in conflict with putative U.S. values, sometimes in conflict with other parts of the nation, including other fractions of the ruling class—has been a defining character of U.S. political development from colonial times until the late 1960s.

Second, at critical junctures, the interests of other segments of the North American ruling class have come into conflict with the implications of the system of racial domination, if not the system itself. I have tried to trace some of these conflicts throughout U.S. history.

Third, conflicts over race, however, have not been only the province of elites. Among more ordinary people, particularly laborers, U.S. politics and the degree of class formation and class influence in politics have largely revolved around the degree of unity or conflict across racial lines, for the most part the degree to which white workers have understood that their ultimate success has depended on their ability and willingness not only to unify with nonwhite workers but also to take up the fight against the special grievances of minorities as their own. Thus, the high points of working-class struggle and class political initiatives have come at times when steps have been taken toward such unity. Most important, the character of each historic turning point is to a large part a reflection of the degree to which working people have been able to assert themselves on an independent class basis; here, questions of race have always proved primary.

Fourth, the issue of freedom, justice, and equality for African-Americans in particular, as well as other subordinate groups, is the great litmus test and moral barometer of virtualy every major political initiative in this country. The most enobling moments in the nation's history have been closely tied to the high points of racial egalitarianism. The universalism implicit in the Declaration of Independence and its widespread attractiveness around the world, I have argued, are closely tied to the universal character of the prerevolutionary colonial mobs and the growth at the time of abolitionist sentiment among broad segments of the population. I have made similar arguments about the abolitionist movement, the Civil War and Reconstruction, perhaps the apex of moral authority achieved by the United States. The point is also true for the 1890s, the 1930s, the industrial union movement, and the civil rights movement. Conversely, the retreat from these commitments and perspectives have characterized the United States as morally defective in the eyes of the world.

LEGACIES OF HISTORIC TURNING POINTS FOR TODAY

Each historic turning point has played an important role in shaping the present system of racial domination as well as the structure of U.S. politics and social relations. One can summarize these legacies in shorthand form for each historic moment.

The turn to African slavery as the predominant form of agricultural labor in the South during the 1680s led to the creation of the peculiar, unique U.S. color line. For one group of people alone, one drop of blood, one forebearer of African or African-American descent, defined a person as Black; no intermediary groups existed. This result of the colonial period remains with us today at least as strong as during earlier centuries. The differential legal system, with differing punishments for the same or similar crimes (be it loitering, drug offenses, or murder), established during the colonial period still exists de facto, even if no longer fully inscribed in the law. This feature of present U.S. society is a major part of the explanation for the highly divergent reactions to the O.J. Simpson verdict. Whites dismissed the central involvement of a virulently racist cop and any questions of doubt it raised. Their indignation at the acquittal was not matched by similar concerns for the acquittals of white defenders with equally highly paid technical and legal support. On the other hand, many Blacks decided that equality before the law means the acquittal of a prominent Black—guilty or innocent—in circumstances in which a similarly placed white would have gotten off. Another legacy of the colonial period, reenforced, developed, and changed but still very much alive, is the differential labor market, of which I will be saying more, but whose origins help explain its existence and present character. The divide-and-conquer approach to Black and white labor and the far more extreme penalties applied to Black revolutionaries than to white racists or even white radicals also began during this period. Finally, we have the suppressed legacy of interracial struggle that suggests that racial oppression and white racist attitudes are not a necessary concomitant of the human or even the American condition.

The American Revolution accentuated the importance of slave revolts, the legitimacy of interracial struggles, and the centrality both of issues of Black freedom and of slavery. The founding period suppressed all of these advances, inscribing the non-citizen slave population into the Constitution, successfully turning the issue of slavery into a central national issue and the focal point of sectional conflict.

The struggle over slavery during the first six-and-a-half decades of the nineteenth century, the final emancipation, the Civil War, and Reconstruction were the most violent and contentious events in U.S. history. The two political parties forged in this period are still with us today. The struggle against slavery was the most inspiring episode in the nation's history and was implicitly and sometimes explicitly recognized as such at the time. It provides a rich legacy on which North Americans can still draw for moral strength and inspiration. It destroyed the system of chattel slavery. It inspired, shaped, and colored numerous struggles throughout the nineteenth century. Its incomplete resolution, however, left the bulk of the African-American population in a state of semifeudal oppression, which was not finally eliminated until the civil rights movement of the 1960s. The complex legacy of this period remains with us today.

The resolution of the contradictory transition period created the System of 1896, based on electoral fraud, lynching, and violence, ending in the further suppression of the African-American population. The complete disenfranchisement of the southern Black population and the large-scale disenfranchisement of poor whites in the South were mirrored in the North by an enormous decline in voting. The depoliticization of electoral politics, the low levels and the class skew in voter turnout, are a heritage of this turning point that is alive and well today. It was also during this period that more aggressive, successful attempts were made to drive African-Americans out of many skilled positions in the labor market which they traditionally held, exclusions that are in many areas still the rule. In contrast to the earlier period, this turning point marks the initiation of one of the more unsavory periods in U.S. social and political life.

Numerous strictures of the System of 1896 were challenged during the Depression/New Deal era. Here we have inspiring examples of interracial, racially egalitarian struggles on a scale never seen before nationwide in the United States. Despite the racial conservatism of the national Democratic Party, civil rights burst forth as a central public political issue in both the national and international arenas, where it still remains today. The 1930s also marked the national entry of the African-American working class as a central political and industrial actor, playing leading roles in the organization of meatpacking, tobacco, coal and metal mining, steel, auto, food processing, southern longshore, maritime, and in numerous other venues north and south. As the quote from James Baldwin suggests, Black workers had many reasons for being among the most farsighted and class-oriented segment of the working class, where they remain today. The crushing and abandonment of racially egalitarian unionism, the undermining of the Black working class, the failure of Operation Dixie, and the transformation of the labor movement in a corporatist direction have set the contours of politics from the 1930s and 1940s up to the present. These developments help explain many of the positive characteristics and limitations of the 1950s and 1960s civil rights movement, and why a white racist political coalition was able to emerge and dominate U.S. politics for much of the post-civil rights period. It is the historical legacy of racial domination and race relations, the power relations on which they were based, and the new systems that emerged out of the resolution of various critical periods, that help us to understand what is going on in the United States today.

THEORIES OF RACE

I have argued and tried to show throughout this book that racial attitudes and the systems of racial domination of which they are a part are not based on inherent features of the human psyche, unshakeable cultural legacies, or unchangeable racial identities. Although various pieces of other theories are part of the general explanation, at the root of the historic oppression of Black people in the United States has been their use as cheap, forced agricultural labor in the plantation areas of the South from the 1680s until the 1960s, almost three hundred years. The interests that benefited from the conditions of Black people have been in large part responsible for the attending legal, social, cultural, and ideological trappings of white supremacy throughout the country. None of which is to argue that interests and privileges of white workers, divide-and-conquer strategies by employers, white identities and belief systems, and much more have not played an important role, simply that to be understood they must be put in perspective and their relationship to the root that nourished and sustained them traced.

In addition to the interests of southern planters, there have always been other economic actors and interests that have benefited from the system of white supremacy in fairly direct ways, hence supporting the maintenance and extension of important aspects of racial domination. Even after slavery, Blacks performed as low-paid laborers in lumber, mining, tobacco, southern longshore, steel, and other industries. Black women, in addition to their work in agriculture, tobacco, and elsewhere, also provided a disproportionate number of the maids, housekeepers, and washer women, especially in the South. Black workers who migrated North during the World War I and after were to be found concentrated in the lowest-paying, dirtiest, most unhealthy, hardest of jobs in foundries, coke plants and blast furnaces, on killing floors of slaughterhouses, in the bottom-rung jobs in the hotel and restaurant industry, as maids and porters, and in food processing, the heritage of which one can still see in the chicken and catfish industries today.

Despite the existence of an increasing prosperous middle class and the growth of inner-city areas of concentrated poverty, African-Americans today are still overwhelmingly concentrated in the working class, in its lowest, most exploited sectors and occupations. One should note that those who argue that the growth of ghettos and dehumanizing conditions of life shows that the Black population is being marginalized and therefore being made dispensible, are proven wrong by the facts. Black workers are first of all increasingly concentrated in those unionized jobs, particularly in the industrial sector, which are still vital to the operation of the economy. In the growing and important healthcare industry, African-Americans are located in the lowest but still highly essential occupations. Although in 1994, they made up only 4.2 percent of doctors and 3.7 percent of dentists (a slight increase from 1983), they made up 9.3 percent of registered nurses, 18.7 percent of licensed practical nurses, and almost 30 percent of nurses aides, orderlies, and attendants. They made up 21.7 percent of telephone operators, 28.2 percent of postal clerks, 20.8 percent of janitors and cleaners, and 27.9 percent of maids and housemen, all vital, continuing economic functions. Blacks made up only 5 percent of university teachers and 8.9 percent of school teachers, but were 14.3 percent of teachers aides, also being well represented in a variety of administrative support positions from bank tellers, data entry key-punchers, and statistical clerks. They are disproportionately represented in the armed forces and also make up over a quarter of the correctional officers in the nation's prisons, sadly one of the fastest-growing U.S. industries (*Statistical Abstract* 1995:411–13). The story could be told in greater detail, but the fact remains that African-Americans are highly integrated into the central economic institutions of the country, albeit in general at the lowest levels of society. These patterns are a continuation of long-standing labor market patterns (given the degree of discrimination), but also something new in the pervasiveness of the occupations and economic sectors in which African-Americans labor.

If, as I have argued, the key to understanding the system of racial domination and the racial attitudes of whites is located in the socioeconomic system, then the question that ought to be asked is the following: If the historic system of racial domination and white racist attitudes were rooted in the southern plantation economy—and that economy has largely disappeared—what keeps African-Americans suppressed and what explains the continued virulence of white racism?

The economic interests that benefit from the continuing racial domination of African-Americans and their availability as a lower-priced segment of the labor force are, of course, still substantial. Yet, their specific availabily is neither as absolute nor indispensible as was the case with southern plantation owners. This role could just as well be filled by other nonwhites, as well as the bottom layers of lower-class whites, and particularly by the large number of legal and illegal immigrants. In part, the system of racial domination continues because of the weight of tradition, habit, and culture, and the attendant vested privileges and interests that reap advantages from the present arrangements. Although neither as powerful nor incorrigibly resistant as the earlier planters, at a time of economic stagnation the costs and stakes are high. In an economy that is not generating new resources and where the standards of living for the vast majority are not rising, resources used for one area must be diverted from others. The resources necessary to train, educate, and elevate the present, disproportionately minority, unskilled workforce and unemployed at the bottom of the occupational and earnings structure would be tremendous. It would require a massive redistribution of resources and income at a time when the trend both in terms of private income and public spending is going in the opposite direction. For those whose program is to siphon more of the diminishing wealth to the rich, a political agenda that blames the nonwhite poor for their own plight, pandering to the racism and occasionally legitimate fears of many whites, is highly self-serving. It is clear that the current agendas of both major parties, which eschew substantial redistribution of resources and major structural changes in the system of power—and accept the current system of racial domination and white racial attitudes as a given —can provide us with no source of hope.

In this context, the maintenance and continual regeneration of white racist attitudes rests on several bases. The first is the continued existence of segregation in housing, schools, and many other aspects of daily life. Separation rather than familiarity tends to breed fear and contempt. Second, for numerous African-Americans, segregated life in poor urban areas has many dehumanizing aspects. As Frederick Douglass noted, racist attitudes find fertile soil when whites see the degraded conditions of life under which many African-Americans are forced to live. We thus have something of a vicious circle, where the system of racial domination and its historic effects help reenforce racial prejudice, which in turn makes it more difficult for many whites to envision broader, more structural solutions to the problems of poor Black urban areas. As a consequence, Blacks at all levels of society in all circumstances continue to be stigmatized by many whites. On the other hand, African-Americans are more integrated into the occupational structure, many workplaces, and the visible national culture than ever before. This situation generates tendencies to break down traditional patterns of racial prejudice.

It is the existence of these differing structural features of society that provide the basis for the many contradictory features of current race relations that I have noted and that appear around us every day in the United States.

Yet, structural features alone can hardly determine social relations directly. In a period when the groups and movements advocating racial egalitarianism are weak, the field remains dominated by politicians appealing to whites on racial issues and those who would use divide-and-conquer tactics to keep the people who least benefit from current arrangements from uniting in common cause. Thus, the present period is one of both instability and flux for the system of racial domination and race relations, with the looming possibility for the increasing dominance of racial scapegoating.

THE CURRENT PROSPECTS

It is, of course, tempting to try to end this discussion on an optimistic note, citing all the hopeful signs for the future and looking for every instance of interracial comity, no matter how small or idiosyncratic. In a contradictory period such as the present, it is easy to find many such events and phenomena. There is also the tendency quite prevalent among the more pessimistic to cite all the arenas of conflict, mistrust, and racial antagonism by whites, seeing no signs of hope for change now or forever after. In contrast to these approaches, it is more appropriate, in trying to strike the right note, to evaluate the unique features of the current conjuncture and what possibilities they suggest for the future.

First, as I have already tried to document, a large percentage of white male workers who seemed to be doing so well as a group several decades ago, are clearly not doing well now. Workers laid off by the millions in basic industry in the late 1970s and early 1980s either remain unemployed or have obtained new jobs at significantly lower income levels. High-wage unionized workers have made concessions across the board. In other industries, including coal, trucking, construction, and meatpacking, unions have been driven out of large parts of the industry, with wages and working conditions declining dramatically. The numbers and percentages of white workers who are defending privileged positions have diminished greatly.

Further, the working class has been reconstituted, its composition changed dramatically since the early 1960s. White male workers, not many decades ago the overwhelming majority of the non-agricultural workforce, are now a distinct minority. They are almost matched by an equivalent number of white female workers, themselves routinely excluded from the traditional white male privileged jobs. Black, Hispanic, Asian, and Asian-American workers now make up over one-fourth of the labor force and are approaching majority status in certain geographic areas (*Statistical Abstract*

1995:399).To recover their standards of living, working conditions, and dignity, white workers will be even more in need of allies in a broad struggle.
The many nonwhite and female workers, concentrated in the lowest paid
jobs, have the traditional grievances of all workers who are forced to struggle to obtain minimally acceptable remuneration and working conditions.
They also have special grievances because of oppression based on their ethnicity, race, and gender, integrally linked to the historic structures of white
and male supremacy. For workers to unite and find common cause for struggle, all workers—and especially white male workers—will have to act in
solidarity and mutual support, giving central attention to the grievances of
the most oppressed groups.

None of these broad trends automatically lead to greater solidarity. No
system of oppression ever falls without a struggle. So far, most of what one
finds in the United States as well as in many other countries are large amounts
of electoral volatility and increases in outrage and alienated behavior. Here,
there has been a large decrease in the number of people who identify with
either of the two major parties and a large increase in the number who say
they would prefer a third party. According to one recent poll, as many as 62
percent of the electorate say they would welcome a third party (New York
Times, June 6, 1995). Much of this political volatility has to this point grav-
itated toward the right. It has either focused on dead-end panaceas such as
cutting government spending, balancing the federal budget, and imposing
term limits on politicians. Or it has led people to look for scapegoats among
nonwhite immigrants or Blacks through the issues of welfare reform, crime,
immigration, or affirmative action.The main beneficiaries of this right-wing-
supported public policy have been big business and the rich, savings and
loan institutions, military contractors, and unregulated industries.

Yet, some small yet intriguing signs in other directions have appeared
as well. In a political act, not totally devoid of significance, white workers
during 1988 in Michigan,Wisconsin, California, and other places joined with
their African-American brethren to vote enthusiastically for Jesse Jackson.
Jackson gained support from these white workers by putting forward a program that, although hardly radical, nevertheless based its appeal on broad
class issues, symbolizing his allegiance by appearing on the picket lines of
scores of strikes and at numerous demonstrations. He did not back off on
his identifcation with many so-called Black issues. In Michigan, Jackson won
the 1988 Democratic presidential primary, beating Michael Dukakis, the eventual nominee by 54 percent to 29 percent. Jackson, of course, got a large
Black vote, even though Detroit Mayor ColemanYoung and other Black elected officials, and Michigan Democratic Senator Donald Reigle, were supporting Dukakis.The official position of most unions, particularly the United

Auto Workers International, was to back Representative Richard Gephardt. As *Newsweek* noted, the Jackson campaign had very little money compared to its rivals, yet "For weeks Jackson had drawn enthusiastic throngs 10 times —even 100 times—larger than those of his white rivals. The winning combination featured heavy Black support, backing from Michigan's large Arab-American community and a surprising number of high-income white liberals who in other states supported Dukakis" (*Newsweek*, 4-4-88).

What the national media did not note, but which was apparent in Michigan from newpaper reports and by examining the voting returns, is that large numbers of overwhelmingly white union locals around the state, many in auto, were defying their national leadership and campaigning for Jackson. The large amount of white working-class support for Jackson around the country, but especially in Michigan, is clear from looking at the overwhelmingly white, heavily working-class congressional districts that he carried. Of course, he won easily in Congressmen John Conyers' and George Crockett's majority-black districts. But he also won in other Democratic congressional districts including Michigan's Third Congressional District (Kalamazoo, 9 percent black), Michigan's Sixth (including Lansing and Pontiac, 7 percent black), Michigan's Seventh (including Flint, 15 percent black), Michigan's Eighth (including Bay City and Saginaw, 7 percent Black), Michigan's Fifteenth (southwestern Wayne County, 6 percent black), and in Michigan's Seventeenth (Northwest Detroit and Southeast Oakland County, 6 percent black), districts that include many of the largest industrial areas of the state. In addition, Jackson won three of Michigan's Republican-held districts, also overwhelmingly white (Second, Fourth, and Ninth, these latter victories possibly reflecting a reputed Republican crossover vote; see *Congressional Quarterly*, July 8, 1988: 1893 for details). Jesse Jackson's campaign, with little money but large numbers of volunteers and large attendance at mass rallies, did well in a large variety of other overwhelmingly white districts, including liberal college towns (such as Ithaca, New York) and white Republican-dominated decaying industrial areas (as in Binghamton and Syracuse, New York).[1]

The recent period has also not been without its share of struggles by low-paid minority workers as well as integrated unions. Though the 1990s saw many defeats, unions also held their own in a number of venues. Catfish farmworkers in Mississippi successfully unionized across the state, receiving widespread support from their largely African-American communities. The 1990–91, five-month New York City newspaper strike by the *Daily News* workers had the active support of several of New York's unions and the mobilization of thousands of supporters. Though inadequately supported by national unions and even many city unions, the New York strike was one of the few where newspaper employees managed to keep their unions intact and avoid huge concessions. In 1994 in Flint, Michigan, 11,500 General Motors workers struck against heavy workloads and too much forced over-time (the combination of the two sending over a thousand workers onto disability with repetitive motion injuries); they succeeded in lowering some workloads and in having between 700 and 800 new workers hired. In 1995, 32,000 northern California supermarket employees carried out a successful nine-day strike, whose most important victory was the company with-drawing a proposal that would have gutted or eliminated healthcare for many workers. One finds the United Electrical Workers in Milwaukee with strong community support and assistance from a Mexican labor cadre, successful-ly organizing numerous manufacturing plants in the city, while workers in South Carolina's Hilton Head area have succeeded in organizing one of the major resorts there. Many new types of organizations and tactics have also emerged. Justice for Janitors, affiliated with the Service Employees International Union (SEIU), has successfully organized large numbers of immigrant janitors in large office buildings on the West Coast, while Black Workers for Justice, centered in North Carolina, has focused its attention on the special problems of Black workers in the South. In addition, the SEIU, representing government employees in Washington, D.C., has reponded to proposals for large budget cuts that would lead to heavy layoffs and increased workloads there, by having a sit-in at Newt Gingrich's Atlanta office and engaging in big demonstrations along Washington-area expressways.[2]

La Mujer Obrera (LMO), a labor organization for Mexican-American women garment workers, is located in the U.S. border town of El Paso, Texas. They operate in a declining industry that is highly labor intensive and com-petes with garment manufacturers whose operations are in underdeveloped countries that pay extremely low wages and have substandard working con-ditions. LMO grew out of the successful union organizing of the 4,000-work-er Farah textile manufacturing company in 1974. LMO was established in 1982, in good part because many of the women were dissatisfied with the lack of attention to women's issues by the male-dominated International Ladies Garment Workers Union (ILGWU). Many of these shops not only pay subminimum wages but also cheat their workers by the nonpayment of wages. With little leverage in the small sweatshops, LMO turned to broad-er political activities and met with some degree of success. "The group has recovered unpaid wages, confronted employers with workers' grievances, provided limited legal help, and reported workplace health and safety vio-lations to the state." They acted in conjunction with the ILGWU to run a strike against four local garment makers, picketing, calling press conferences, engaging in hunger strikes to successfully dramatize the issues to the broader community. As a result of the widespread publicity, the mayor of El Paso appointed a commission to investigate the local garment industry; several prominent politicians joined the hunger strike. LMO also won a number of economic issues including a 25 cents-an-hour wage increase and addition-al benefits. Equally important, the strike helped push a bill through the state legislature that made nonpayment of wages a felony (Marquez 1995).

Another major trend that affects the possibilities for unified struggle is globalization. Practical needs force many unions to look for allies in other countries, laying the basis for broader, more solidaristic perspectives. Some small steps have been taken in this direction, developing those ties that are indispensable for workers in the new international economy.

During the 1990s, there has been an increase in cooperation between Canadian, U.S., and Mexican unions. There has also been new support for cross-border organizing of workers who are engaged in joint production on both sides of the U.S.–Mexican border. During a 1990 strike at a Ford plant in Cuautitlán, Mexico, a worker was killed by goons from the gov-ernment-controlled Mexican Confederation of Labor (CTM). Responding to calls for solidarity, American and Canadian autoworkers held meetings and marched on Ford showrooms. Similar issues and demands have been raised by workers at the Ford plant at Hermosillo, Mexico, which has also received much international attention (*Los Angeles Times*, 3/8/93). An arti-cle in the *Los Angeles Times* on September 7, 1992, describes successful coop-eration between communication workers and autoworkers unions in the three North American countries, where previously those in the United States and Canada were decidedly uninterested. Since the passage of the North American Free Trade Agreement (NAFTA) in 1994, communication worker unions have been cooperating further to develop strategies to deal collec-tively with the telecommunication industries in the three countries. The International Longshoremen and Warehousemen's Union (ILWU) has been working with Mexican longshore workers, while the California Teamsters have been Supporting a Campaign by FAT (Autonomous Labor Front) to organize Green Giant operations in Irapuato. The United Electrical Workers (UE) has developed extensive relations with FAT, subsidizing eight orga-nizers in maquilladora assembly plants along the U.S.–Mexican border, all of which are U.S.- owned companies with which the UE has contracts in the United States. The UE and FAT also have a strategic organizing agree-ment focusing on fifteen General Electric plants in Mexico (Ross 1994; McGinn 1994). Finally, the United Mine Workers of America (UMWA) has been aiding 4,000 Columbian miners who work for Exxon in the largest export coal mine in the world (McGinn 1995). These are small developments, to be sure, but trends of enormous potential for the future. And the development of international ties, requiring a broader sensitivity to the special concerns of other workers, particularly those in less economically developed countries, provides a more fertile soil for the growth of solidarity at home.

THE LESSONS OF HISTORY — AGAINST ABANDONMENT

If the lessons of history are any reasonable guide, then they should help us measure various strategies for the future against past performances. Two types of approaches are currently popular among those claiming to be concerned with the issues we have discussed here. One approach, that of the liberal pessimists noted in the first chapter, argues that white people as a group, and in particular white working-class people, will always be racist. Either the fight against racial domination is to be abandoned completely (and replaced by various self-helf and community development schemes) or it is to be carried on without any attempt to enlist white working people in the struggle. This approach makes pessimistic assumptions about the permanence of human attitudes toward race that may have strong resonances in the present moment, but are not borne out by historical analysis. Not only is such an approach self-defeating, it allows its proponents to be morally smug, seemingly very realistic, while in practice abandoning the struggle for racial egalitarianism in the society at large.

A second approach, however, is by far the most common among whites who claim to be concerned about the issues. It is to be found among some conservatives and moderates, as well as among liberals and others much farther to the left. This approach involves a theory of stages. In the first stage, one must first abandon the demands for equality for African-Americans because the demands are divisive and might inflame whites. Rather one must emphasize, if not focus exclusively on, at least initially, only those issues that have "broad appeal." At some future stage, when everyone is unified in their quest for the lowest-common-denominator issues, one can slowly bring in the special demands for racial egalitarianism—of course, in a gingerly way so as not to offend the racial sensibilities of whites. The most cynical of such views is the version offered by the Democratic Party, particularly its neo-conservative wing, as represented by Bill Clinton and the Democratic Leadership Council (DLC), which tries to offer a kinder and gentler version of the Republican strategy but mimics their coded racial rhetoric. They claim to be for affirmative action but against quotas. Their solution to the crime problem is, like the Republicans, to be tough on crime, build more prisons, hire more police, and expand the use of the death penalty, with the one difference being the addition of certain neighborhood programs such as midnight basketball for inner-city youth. On welfare, they have outdone the Republicans with their proposals for five-year limits, repeating all the misinformation about the extent of welfare dependency, including the stigmatization of African-American women.

Although the official documents of the DLC occasionally often appear quite modest, their more extreme positions may be found in articles in their publication *The New Democrat*. In one piece, for example, New York Republican Mayor Rudy Guiliani is congratulated for running in his successful 1993 campaign as a "New Democrat." Yet, as the *Village Voice* makes clear in a special section with numerous articles—entitled "A Divided City" —Guiliani ran a racially charged, divisive campaign, dubbed in one article "Code White" (See *Village Voice*, November 16, 1993). In another *New Democrat* piece, Mario Cuomo—their favorite whipping boy—is attacked for not separating himself sufficiently from the Reverend Al Sharpton, seemingly a greater enemy than the Republicans, largely because he is an immoderate African-American. And so it goes. The New Democrats seem to believe that if they can pass themselves off as fellow travelers of the Republicans, in bigotry and conservatism, they will be able to make social progress— including on racial issues—behind the scenes only confirming the Republican accusations that they are opportunists with a secret agenda. Yet, as Harry Truman once quipped, when people have a choice between a Republican and a Republican, they tend to choose *the* Republican. And in 1994 that is what 52 percent of the electorate in an exceedingly low turnout did. In 1996, despite the reelection of Democrat Bill Clinton, a Republican House and Senate was selected. Other less unsavory versions of this approach dot the landscape of the putative left. The argument, however, is always the same: Drop those issues that might alienate *the* white workers, by which is meant those most wedded to the racial status quo rather than those who show signs of a readiness to abandon it.

Now, as I have argued throughout, interracial struggles against common grievances have often proved enobling and unifying—the struggles of colonial mobs against impressment and the Crown, the campaigns of Populist farmers, the 1930s unemployed battles, the industrial union movement organizing. Yet, these movements, certainly in their best moments, did not submerge the issues of racial equality. As the history of the abolitionists underscores for us, and the 1930s racially egalitarian unions and the 1950s and 1960s civil rights movement only confirms, white people's attitudes will only be changed substantially on racial matters when a determined group that is uncompromising and relentless on the issues, proselytizes, organizes, and refuses to go away. The only hope for unifying the overwhelming majority of people of various races, ethnic groups, and people of both sexes in the United States, in a movement for a just, equitable society, is by placing the principle of racial egalitarianism on the top furl of our marching banner.

1. For in-depth analysis of the Jackson campaign in these three upstate New York areas, see the highly informative thesis by David Reynolds 1994, and the continuing discussion in his *Democracy Unbound* (1997). It is noteworthy that Allen Hertzke (1993) also fails to understand the degree of white working class support for Jackson.

2. Most of the information about strikes and new organizing has been obtained from *Labor Notes,* an invaluable source of information if one wants to follow developments within the labor movement.

Bibliography

African-American Alamanac, 1994. Detroit: UXL Publishing, 1994.

Allen, Theodore William. *Can White Workers (Radicals) Be Radicalized?* Pamphlet. Ann Arbor, Michigan: Radical Education Project, 1968.

———. "Class Struggle and the Origin of Racial Slavery—The Invention of the White Race." *Radical America* (May-June 1975); Expanded version with fuller footnotes reissued as a pamphlet. Hoboken, N.J.: H.E.P., n.d.

———. "Slavery, Racism, and Democracy." *(1975). Monthly Review* 29 (March 1973):10.

———. *The Invention of the White Race.* New York: Verso, 1994.

———. *The Kernel and the Meaning.* New York: Verso, forthcoming

Allswang, John M. "The Chicago Negro Voter and the Democratic Consensus: A Case Study, 1918–1936." In *The Negro in Depression and War, Prelude to Revolution, 1930–1945,* edited by Bernard Sternsher. Chicago: Quadrangle Books, 1969.

Andreano, Ralph L. *The Economic Impact of the American Civil War.* New York: Schenkman Publishing Company, 1967.

Aptheker, Herbert. *Documentary History of the Negro People in the United States.* New York: Citadel Press, 1968.

———. *Racism, Imperialism and Peace: Selected Essays.* Minneapolis: MEP Publications, 1987.

———. *Abolitionism: A Revolutionary Movement.* Boston: Twayne Publishers, 1989.

Armstrong, Philip, and Andrew Glyn. *Capitalism Since 1945.* Cambridge, Mass: Basil Blackwell, 1991.

Arnesen, Eric. *Waterfront Workers of New Orleans: Race, Class and Politics, 1863–1923.* New York: Oxford University Press, 1991.

———. "'Like Banquo's Ghost, it Will Not Down': The Race Question and the American Railroad Brotherhoods, 1880–1920." *American Historical Review.* 99 (December 1994).

Ashbaugh, Carolyn. *Lucy Parsons: American Revolutionary.* Chicago: Charles H. Kerr, 1976.

Ashby, Steven. "Shattered Dreams: The American Working Class and the Origins of the Cold War. 1945–1949." Ph.D. Diss., University of Chicago, 1993.

Avrich, Paul. *The Haymarket Tragedy.* Princeton, N.J.: Princeton University Press, 1984.

Bailyn, Bernard. *The Ideological Origins of the American Revolution.* Cambridge, Mass.: Belknap Press of Harvard University Press, 1990.

———. *Pamphlets of the American Revolution, 1750–1776.* Cambridge, Mass.: Belknap Press of Harvard University Press, 1965.

Baldwin, James. *Nobody Knows My Name; More Notes of a Native Son.* New York: Dial Press, 1961.

———. *The Fire Next Time.* New York: Dell, 1963.

Baldwin, Peter. *The Politics of Social Solidarity.* Cambridge, U.K.: Cambridge University Press, 1990.

Baron, Harold M. *Building Babylon: A Case of Racial Controls in Public Housing.* Evanston, Ill.: Northwestern University, 1971.

———. "The Demand for Black Labor." *Radical America.* (March/April 1971).

Barone, Michael. *Our Country: The Shaping of America from Roosevelt to Reagan.* New York: Free Press, 1990.

Bartley, Numan V. *The Rise of Massive Resistance: Race and Politics in the South during the 1950s.* Baton Rouge: Louisiana State University Press, 1969.

———. *Southern Politics and the Second Reconstruction.* Baltimore: Johns Hopkins University Press, 1975.

———. *The Creation of Modern Georgia.* Athens: University of Georgia Press, 1990.

———. *The New South, 1945–1980.* Baton Rouge: Louisiana State University Press, 1995.

Bates, Beth T. "Old Guard Versus New Crowd: Black Workers Challenge Agenda of NAACP 1935–1941." *American Historical Review.* 102:2 (April 1997).

Bates, Edward C. "Eli Whitney and the Cotton Gin," in Stuart Brouchey ed., *Cotton and the Growth of the American Economy, 1790-1860*. NY: Harcourt, Brace and World, Inc., 1967.

Bates, Timothy, and David Howell. "The Declining Status of Minorities in the New York City Construction Industry," *Economic Development Quarterly*, 1997 (forthcoming).

Beard, Charles A., and Mary R. Beard. *A Basic History of the United States*. New York: Doubleday Doran and Co., 1944.

Beck, E.M. "Discrimination and White Economic Loss: A Time Series Examination of the Radical Model." *Social Forces* 59, no. 1 (September 1980):148–68.

Becker, Carl. *The History of Political Parties in the Province of New York*. Madison: University of Wisconsin Press, 1909.

Becker, Gary. *The Economics of Discrimination*. Chicago: University of Chicago Press, 1971.

———. "National History Standards: Clintonites Miss the Moon," Circular released by the Family Research Council, 1996.

Bell, Daniel. *The End of Ideology*. New York: The Free Press, 1960.

Bell, Derrick. *Faces at the Bottom of the Well: The Permanence of Racism*. New York: Basic Books, 1992.

Bennett, Lerone, Jr. *The Shaping of Black America*. Chicago: Johnson Publishing Co., 1975.

Bennetts, David P. "Black and White Workers: New Orleans, 1880–1900." Ph.D. Diss., University of Illinois, 1972.

Bensel, Richard. *Sectionalism and American Political Development*. Madison: University of Wisconsin Press, 1987.

———. *Yankee Leviathan: The Origin of Central State Authority in America, 1859-1877*. New York: Cambridge University Press, 1990.

Berk, Gerald. *Alternative Tracks: The Constitution of American Industrial Order, 1865-1917*. Baltimore: Johns Hopkins Unviersity Press, 1994.

Berlin, Ira. *Slaves Without Masters: The Free Negro in the Antebellum South*. New York: Pantheon Books, 1974.

Berman, William C. *The Politics of Civil Rights in the Truman Administration*. Columbus: The Ohio State University Press, 1970.

Bernal, Martin. *Black Athena*. London: Free Association Books, 1987.

Bernstein, Barton. *Towards a New Past: Dissenting Essays in American History*. New York: Pantheon Books, 1968.

———. "The Truman Administration and Minority Rights." *The Journal of Ethnic Studies* 1, no. 3 (Fall 1973): 66–77.

Bernstein, Iver. *The New York City Draft Riots: Their Signicance in American Society and Politics in the Age of the Civil War*. New York: Oxford University Press, 1990.

Bernstein, Irving. *The Lean Years*. Boston: Houghton Mifflin, 1960.

———. *The Turbulent Years*. Boston: Houghton Mifflin, 1969.

Bernstein, Jared. "Rethinking Welfare Reform." *Dissent*, (Summer 1993): 277–79.

Bernstein, Michael and David Adler. *Understanding American Economic Decline*. New York: Cambridge University Press, 1994.

Blackburn, Robin. *The Overthrow of Colonial Slavery, 1776-1848*. London: Verso, 1988.

Black, Earl and Merle Black. *Politics and Society in the South*. Cambridge, Mass.: Harvard University Press, 1987.

———. *The Vital South*. Cambridge, Mass.: Harvard University Press, 1992.

Black, Isabella. "American Labour and Chinese Immigration." *Past and Present*, no. 25 (July 1963): 59–76.

Blassingame, John W. *Black New Orleans, 1860-1880*. Chicago: University of Chicago Press, 1973.

Blaut, James M. *The Colonizer's Model of the World: Geographic Diffusionism and Eurocentric History*. New York: Guilford Press, 1993.

Block, N.J., and Gerald Dworkin, eds. *The IQ Controversy*. New York: Pantheon Books, 1976.

Bloom, Jack. M. *Class, Race, and the Civil Rights Movement*. Bloomington: University of Indiana Press, 1987.

Bluestone, Barry, and Lawrence Mishel. " 'Is the Technology Black Box Empty?' An Imperical Examination of Technology on Wage Inequality and the Wage Structure." *The American Prospect*, no. 20. (Winter 1995):81–93.

Boggs, Grace Lee, and James Boggs. *The Awesome Responsibility of Revolutionary Leadership.* Detroit: Advocators, 1970.

Bonacich, Edna. "A Theory of Ethnic Antagonism: The Split Labor Market." *American Sociological Review*, 37, no. 5 (October 1972):547–59

———. "Advanced Capitalism and Black/White Relations in the United States: A Split Labor Market Interpretation." *American Sociological Review* 41, no. 1 (February 1976):34–51.

———. "Class Approaches to Ethnicity and Race." *The Insurgent Sociologist*, 10, no. 2 (Fall 1980):9–23.

Boorstin, Daniel J. *The Americans.* New York: Vintage, 1958.

Bowles, Samuel, David Gordon, and Michael Reich. *After the Waste Land: A Democratic Economics for the Year 2000.* London: M.E. Sharpe Inc., 1990.

———. *Beyond the Waste Land: A Democratic Alternative to Economic Decline.* Garden City, N.Y.: Anchor Press/Doubleday, 1983.

Boyle, James. "A Process of Denial: Bork and Post-Modern Conservation." *Yale Journal of Law and the Humanities*, 3 (1991): 263–314.

Brandeis, Louis. *The Words of Justice Brandeis.* New York: H. Schuman, 1953.

———. *The Unpublished Opinions of Mr. Justice Brandeis: The Supreme Court at Work* Cambridge, Mass.: Belknap Press, 1957.

Brecher, Jeremy. *Strike.* San Francisco: Straight Arrow Books, 1972.

Breen, T. H. "A Changing Labor Force and Race Relations in Virginia, 1660–1710." *Journal of Social History*, 7, no. 1 (1973).

Breen, T. H., and Stephen Innes. *Myne Own Ground: Race and Freedom on Virginia's Eastern Shore, 1640–1676.* New York: Oxford University Press, 1980.

Brenner, Robert. *Uneven Development and the Long Downturn: The Advanced Capitalist Economies from Boom to Stagnation.* New York: Verso, forthcoming.

Bridenbaugh, Carl. *Cities in Revolt: Urban Life in America, 1743–1776.* New York: Knopf, 1955.

Bridges, Tyler. *The Rise of David Duke.* Jackson: University Press of Mississippi, 1994.

Brier, Stephen. "The Career of Richard L. Lewis Reconsidered: Unpublished Correspondence from the National Labor Tribune." *Labor History* 21 (Summer 1980): 3.

Brimelow, Peter. *Alien Nation.* New York: Random House, 1995.

Brinkley, Alan. *Voices of Protest, Huey Long, Father Coughlin, and the Great Depression.* New York: Random House, 1983.

Broadus, Mitchell and Mitchell, George. *The Industrial Revolution in the South.* Baltimore: The Johns Hopkins Press, 1930.

Brodkin, Evelyn Z. "The War Against Welfare." *Dissent,* (Spring 1996):211–20.

Brody, David. *The Butcher Workman: A Study of Unionization.* Cambridge, Mass.: Harvard University Press, 1964.

———. "The Old Labor History and the New." *Labor History,* 20, no. 1 (Winter 1979):111–26.

Brophy, John. *A Miner's Life.* Madison: University of Wisconsin Press, 1964.

Brown, Michael. "Divergent Fates: The Antinomies of Race and Class in the New Deal." Paper presented at the Annual Meeting of the American Political Science Association, Chicago, Ill., 1992.

Bruce, Robert V. *1877: Year of Violence.* Chicago: Quadrangle, 1970.

Bruchey, Stuart Weems. *Cotton and the Growth of the American Economy, 1790–1860.* New York: Harcourt, Brace, and World, 1967.

Burnham, Walter Dean. *Critical Elections and the Mainsprings of American Politics.* New York: W.W. Norton and Co., 1970.

———. "The Appearance and Disappearance of the American Voter." In Burnham, Walter Dean, *The Current Crisis in American Politics.* Oxford: Oxford University Press, 1982.

———. "Periodization Schemes and the 'System of 1986' as a Case in Point," *Social Science History,* Vol. 10, No. 3, Fall 1986, 263-314.

Burns, James MacGregor. *Roosevelt: The Lion and the Fox.* New York: Harcourt Brace Jovanovich, 1956.

Cannon, James. *Notebook of an Agitator.* New York: Pathfinder Press, 1973.

Capeci, Dominic J. *Race Relations in Wartime Detroit: The Sojourner Truth Housing Controversy, 1937–1942.* Philadelphia: Temple University Press, 1984.

Carmines, Edward G., and James A. Stimson. *Issue Evolution: Race and the Transformation of American Politics.* Princeton: Princeton University Press, 1989.

Carson, Clayborne. *In Struggle: SNCC and the Black Awakening of the 1960s.* Cambridge, Mass.: Harvard University Press, 1981.

Carter, Dan. *The Politics of Rage: George Wallace, the Origins of the New Conservatism, and the Transformation of American Politics.* New York: Simon and Schuster, 1995.

Cayton, Horace R., and George S. Mitchell. *Black Workers and the New Unions.* Westport, Connecticut: Negro Universities Press, 1939.

Chase, Alston. *In a Dark Wood: The Fight Over the Forests and the Rising Tyranny of Ecology.* Boston: Houghton Mifflin Co., 1995.

Cheney, Lynne V. *Telling the Truth.* Washington, D.C.: National Endowment for the Humanities, 1992.

———. "The End of History," *Wall Street Journal,* 20 February 1994.

———. *Wall Street Journal,* October 20, 1994.

Clark, Paul E., Peter Gottlieb, and Donald Kennedy, eds. *Forging a Union in Steel: Philip Murray, SWOC, and the United Steelworkers.* Ithaca, N.Y.: ILR Press., 1987.

Cleveland Plain Dealer, 23 December 1952.

Cloutier, Norman R. "Who Gains from Racism?: The Impact of Racial Inequality on White Income Distribution." *Review of Social Economy,* 45, no. 2 (October 1987):152–62.

Cobb, James. *Industrialization and Southern Society, 1877–1984.* Lexington: University Press of Kentucky, 1984.

Cochran, Bert. *Labor and Communism: The Conflict that Shaped American Unions.* Princeton: Princeton University Press, 1977.

Cochran, Thomas C. "Did the Civil War Retard Industrialization?" in Ralph Andreano ed., *The Economic Impact of the American Civil War.* Cambridge: Schenkman Publishing Co., 1967.

Cogan, John. "Decline in Black Teenage Employment, 1950–1970." *The American Economic Review,* 72 (September 1982): 621–38.

Cohen, Joshua. "Do Values Explain Facts?—The Case of Slavery." Paper presented at the Annual Meeting of the American Political Science Association, *Washington, D.C., 1986.*

Cohen, Lizabeth. *Making a New Deal: Industrial Workers in Chicago, 1919–1939.* New York: Cambridge University Press, 1990.

Cohen, Walter, and Henry Louis Gates. "The Crisis of Minority Faculty at Cornell," Unpublished essay, 1987.

Coleman, McAlister. *Men and Coal.* New York: Ferrar and Rinehart, Inc., 1943.

Collum, Danny Duncan, and Vitor A. Berch. *African Americans and the Spanish Civil War: 'This Ain't Ethiopia, But It'll Do".* New York: G.K. Hall., 1992.

Collins, Ernest M. "Cincinnati Negroes and Presidential Politics." In *The Negro Depression and War, Prelude to Revolution, 1930–1945,* edited by Bernard Stershner. Chicago: Quadrangle Books, 1969.

Commons, John R. and Associates. *History of Labour in the United States.* vol. 2. New York: The Macmillan Company, 1951 (1946).

Congressional Quarterly. "Presidential Elections, 1789–1992." Washington, D.C.: Congressional Quarterly, 1995.

Conway, M. Margaret. *Political Participation in the United States.* Washington, D.C.: Congressional Quarterly Press, 1991.

Cook, Fred J. "Hard Hats: The Rampaging Patriots." *The Nation, (*15 June 1970):712–19.

Corbin, David, A. *Life, Work, and Rebellion in the Coal Fields—The Southern Wester Virginia Miners, 1880–1992.* Chicago: University of Illinois Press, 1981.

Council of Economic Advisors. *Economic Report of the President.* Washington, D.C.: United States Government Printing Office, 1984.

Council of Economic Advisors. *Economic Report of the President.* Washington, D.C.:

United States Government Printing Office,

Cowley, Malcolm, and Daniel Pratt Mannix. *Black Cargoes: A History of the Atlantic Slave Trade 1518–1865.* New York: Penguin Books, 1962.

Cox, Oliver C. *Caste, Class, and Race.* New York: Modern Reader, 1970 (1948).

Cramer, M. Richard. "Race and Southern White Workers' Support for Unions." *Phylon 39:* (December 1978): 311–21.

Crew, Spencer R. "The Great Migration of Afro-Americans, 1915–1940." *Monthly Labor Review,* 110, no. 3 (March 1987):34–36.

Critchlow, Donald T. "Communist Unions and Racism: A Comparative Study of the Responses of the United Electrical Radio and Machine Workers and the National Maritime Union to the Black Question During World War II." *Labor History,* 17, no. 2 (Spring 1976).

Cronon, William. *Changes in the Land: Indians, Colonists, and the Ecology of New England.* New York: Hill and Wang, 1983.

Crosby, Alfred W. *Ecological Imperialism: The Biological Expansion of Europe, 900–1900.* Cambridge: Cambridge University Press, 1986.

Daniel, Cletus E. *Bitter Harvest, A History of the California Farmworkers, 1870–1941.* Berkeley: University of California Press, 1981.

———. *Chicano Workers and the Politics of Fairness.* Austin: University of Texas Press, 1992.

Daniel, Pete. *The Shadow of Slavery: Peonage in the South, 1901–1969.* Chicago: University of Illinois Press, 1972.

Darby, Michael R. "Three-and-a-Half Million U.S. Employees Have Been Mislaid: Or, an Explanation of Unemployment, 1934–1941." *Journal of Political Economy,* 84, no. 1 (February 1976):1–16.

Darity, William A. "The Class Character of the Black Community." *The Black Law Journal* VII, no. 1 (1982): 21–31.

———. *The Question of Discrimination: Racial Inequality in the U.S. Labor Market.* Middletown, Conn.: Weslyan University Press, 1989.

Davin, Eric Leif. "The Littlest New Deal: SWOC Takes Power in Steeltown, A Possibility of Radicalism in the Late 1930s." Unpublished manuscript, 1989.

———. "Carthage Burning: The Very Last Hurrah of the Labor Party Idea: 1934–1936." Unpublished manuscript, 1995.

Davin, Eric Leif, and Staughton Lynd. "Picket Line and Ballot Box: The Forgotten Legacy of the Local Labor Party Movement." *Radical History Review,* 22 (Winter 1979–80) 42–63.

Davis, Angela Y. *Women, Race, and Class.* New York: Vintage, 1983.

Davis, David Brion. *The Problem of Slavery in Western Culture.* Ithaca, N.Y.: Cornell University Press, 1966.

———. *The Problem of Slavery in the Age of Revolution, 1770–1823.* Ithaca, N.Y.: Cornell University Press, 1975.

Davis, Horace B. *Labor and Steel.* New York: International Publishers, 1933.

Davis, James F. *Who Is Black.* University Park: Pennsylvania State University Press, 1991.

Davis, John P. "A Survey of the Problems of the Negro Under the New Deal." *The Journal of Negro Education.* 5 (1936): 3–12.

Davis, Mike. *Prisoners of the American Dream.* London: Verso, 1986.

Dawley, Alan. *Class and Community: The Industrial Revolution in Lynn.* Cambridge, Mass.: Harvard University Press, 1976.

de Tocqueville, Alexis. *Democracy in America.* 2 vols. New York: Vintage, 1956 (1835).

Degler, Carl. *Out of Our Past: The Forces that Shaped Modern America.* New York: Harper, 1959.

———. *Neither Black nor White: Slavery and Race Relations in Brazil and the United States.* New York: MacMillan, 1971.

De Waal, Frans. *Good Natured: The Origins of Right and Wrong in Humans and Other Animals.* Cambridge, Mass.: Harvard University Press, 1996.

Diamond, Sigmund. "Labor History vs. Labor Historiography: The FBI, James B. Carey, and the Association of Catholic Trade Unionists." In *Religion, Ideology and Nationalism in Europe and America.* Jerusalem: The Historical Society of Israel and the Zalman Shazam Center for Jewish History, 1986.

Dickerson, Dennis C. *Out of the Crucible: Black Steelworkers in Western Pennsylvania, 1875–1980*. Chicago: University of Illinois Press, 1986.

Dinwiddie, Robert C. "The International Woodworkers of America and Southern Laborers, 1937–1945." Masters thesis, Georgia State University, 1980.

Dobbs, Farrell. *Teamster Rebellion*. New York: Monad Press, 1972.

Douglass, Frederick. *Life and Times of Frederick Douglass*. New York: Collier, 1962 (1892).

———. *The Life and Writings of Frederick Douglass*. five vols., edited by Philip S. Foner. New York: International Publishers, 1950–1975.

Draper, Alan. "A Sisyphean Ordeal: Labor Educators, Race Relations and Southern Workers 1956–1966." *Labor Studies Journal*, 16, no. 4 (Winter 1991): 3–19.

———. *Conflict of Interest*. Ithaca, N.Y.: ILR Press, 1994.

Draper, Theodore. "Communists and Miners, 1928–1933." *Dissent* (Spring 1972):371–392.

Du Bois, W. E. Burghardt. *Dusk of Dawn: An Essay Toward an Autobiography of a Race*. New York: Schocken Books, 1940.

———. "Race Relations in the United States, 1917–1947." *Phylon* IX (third quarter 1948).

———. *John Brown*. New York: International Publishers, 1962(1909).

———. *Black Reconstruction in America 1860–1880*. Cleveland, Ohio Meridian Books, 1964(1935).

———. *The Souls of Black Folk*. New York: New American Library, 1969(1903).

Du Bois, W. E. B., and Augustus G. Dill, eds. *The Negro American Artisan*. Atlanta:The Atlanta University Press, 1912.

Dubofsky, Melvyn. *We Shall Be All*. New York: Quadrangle, 1969.

Dubofsky, Melvyn, and Warren Van Tine. *John L. Lewis*. New York: Quadrangle, 1977.

Dyson, Lowell K. *Red Harvest: The Communist Party and American Farmers*. Lincoln: University of Nebraska Press, 1982.

Dudziak, Mary L. "Desegregation As a Cold War Imperative." *Stanford Law Review*, 41,

no. 1 (November 1988):61–120.

Edsall, Thomas Byrne, and Mary D. Edsall. *Chain Reaction: The Impact of Race, Rights, and Taxes on American Politics*. New York: W.W. Norton and Co., 1991.

Edwards, Bryan. *History, Civil and Commercial, of the British Colonies in the West Indies*. Dublin: L. White, 1793.

Elkins, Stanley M. *Slavery: A Problem in American Institutional and Intellectual Life*. New York: Grosset and Dunlap, 1959.

Engerman, Stanley L. "The Economic Impact of the Civil War," in Ralph Andreano ed., *The Economic Impact of the American Civil War*. Cambridge: Schenkman Publishing Co., 1967.

Esping-Anderson, Gøsta. *The Three Worlds of Welfare Capitalism*. Cambridge, U.K.: Polity Press, 1990.

Ezorsky, Gertrude. *Racism and Justice: The Case for Affirmative Action*. Ithaca, N.Y.: Cornell University Press, 1991.

Farrand, Max. *United States Constitutional Convention (1787)*. New Haven: Yale University Press, 1911.

———, ed. *The Records of the Federal Convention of 1787*. New Haven: Yale University Press, 1966.

Faue, Elizabeth. *Community of Suffering and Struggle: Women, Men, and the Labor Movement in Minneapolis, 1915–1945*. Chapel Hill: University of North Carolina Press, 1991.

Feeley, Dianne. "In Unity There Is Strength: The Struggle of the Unemployed Throughout the 1930zs". Unpublished manuscript, 1983.

Fehrenbacher, Don Edward. *Slavery, Law, and Politics: The Dred Scott Case in Historical Perspective*. New York: Oxford University Press, 1981.

Ferguson, Thomas, and Joel Rogers. *Right Turn: The Decline of the Democrats and the Future of American Politics*. New York: Hill and Wang, 1986.

Fields, Barbara Jeanne. "Slavery, Race and Ideology in the United States of America." *New Left Review*, (May/June 1990):181.

Filler, Louis. *Crusade Against Slavery: Friends, Foes, Reforms, 1820–1860*. Algonac, Mich:

Reference Publications, 1986.

Fink, Gary M., and Merl E. Reed, eds. *Essays in Southern Labor History*. Westport, Conn.: Greenwood Press, 1977.

Finkelstein, Joseph. *The American Economy from the Great Crash to the Third Industrial Revolution*. Arlington Heights, Ill.: Harlan and Davidson, 1992.

Fischer, Claude S. et al., *Inequality by Design: Cracking the Bell Curve Myth*. Princeton, N.J.: Princeton University Press, 1996.

Fite, Gilbert. *Cotton Fields No More: Southern Agriculture, 1865–1980*. Lexington, Ky.: University Press of Kentucky, 1984.

Fitzgerald, Michael W. *The Union League Movement in the Deep South: Politics and Agricultural Change During Reconstruction*. Baton Rouge: Louisiana State University Press, 1989.

Fligstein, Neil. *Going North*. New York: Academic Press, Inc., 1981.

Foner, Eric. *Free Soil, Free Labor, Free Men*. London: Oxford, 1970.

———. *Politics and Ideology in the Age of the Civil War*. New York: Oxford University Press, 1980.

———. *Reconstruction*. New York: Harper and Row, 1988.

———. "The Meaning of Freedom in the Age of Emancipation." *Journal of American History*, 81, no. 2 (September 1994): 435.

Foner, Philip S. *The Fur and Leather Workers Union*. Newark: Nordan Press, 1950.

———. *History of the Labor Movement in the United States*, vol. 1. New York: International Publishers, 1962.

———. *History of the Labor Movement in the United States*, vol. 2. New York: International Publishers Co. Inc., 1955.

———. *History of the Labor Movement in the United States*, vol. 4. New York: International Publishers, 1965.

Foster, William Z. *The History of the Communist Party of the United States*. New York: International, 1952.

Franklin, John Hope. *From Slavery to Freedom, A History of Negro Americans*. 3rd edition. New York: Random House, 1969.

Fraser, Steven. *Labor Will Rule*. New York: The Free Press, 1991.

Fredrickson, George M. *Black Image in the White Mind: The Debate on Afro-American Character and Destiny, 1817–1914*. New York: Harper and Row, 1971.

———. *White Supremacy: A Comparative Study in American and South African History*. New York: Oxford University Press, 1981.

———. *The Arrogance of Race: Historical Perspective on Slavery, Racism, and Social Inequality*. Middletown, Conn.: Weslyan University Press, 1981.

———. "Land of Opportunity." *New York Review of Books*, 4 April 1996.

Freeman, Joshua B. "Hardhats: Construction Workers, Manliness and the 1970 Pro-War Demonstration." *Journal of Social History*, 26, no. 4 (1993).

Freeman, Richard B. *Working Under Different Rules*. New York: Russell Sage Foundation, 1994.

———. "Why Do So Many Young American Men Commit Crimes and What Might We Do About It?" *Journal of Economic Perspectives*, vol 10, no. 1, (Winter 1996): 25-42.

Frey, Sylvia R. *Water from the Rock: Black Resistance in a Revolutionary Age*. Princeton, N.J.: Princeton University Press, 1991.

Friedman, Milton. *Capitalism and Freedom*. Chicago: University of Chicago Press, 1962.

Galenson, David. *White Servitude in Colonial America: An Economic Analysis*. Cambridge: Cambridge University Press, 1981.

Galenson, Walter. *The CIO Challenge to the AFL: A History of the American Labor Movement. 1935–1941*. Cambridge, Mass.: Harvard University Press, 1960.

Garfinkel, Herbert. *When Negroes March*. New York: Free Press, 1959.

Garrett, Geoffrey, and Peter Michael Lange. "Political Responses to Interdependence: What's 'Left' for the Left?" *International Organization*, 45 (Autumn 1991).

Garrow, David J. "Hopelessly Hollow History: Revisionist Devaluing of *Brown v. Board of Education*." *Virginia Law Review*, 80, no. 1 (February 1994): 151–160.

———. *Protest at Selma: Martin Luther King, and the Voting Rights Act of 1965*. New

Haven, Conn.: Yale University Press, 1994.

Garson, Robert A. *The Democratic Party and the Politics of Sectionalism, 1941–1948*. Baton Rouge: Louisiana State University Press, 1974.

Genovese, Eugene D. *The Political Economy of Slavery*. New York: Vintage, 1967.

———. *Roll, Jordan, Roll*. New York: Vintage, 1976.

———. *In Red and Black: Marxian Explorations in Southern and Afro-American History*. Knoxville: University of Tennessee Press, 1984.

Gilbert, Alan. *Democratic Individuality*. Cambridge: Cambridge University Press, 1990.

Gilpin, Toni. "Left by Themselves: A History of the United Farm Equipment and Metal Workers Union, 1938–1955." Ph.D. Diss., Yale University, 1992.

Gingrich, Newt. Course transcripts from *Renewing American Civilization*, Taught at Reinhardt College, January 7–March 11, 1995.

Glaberman Martin. "Black Workers and the Labor Movement." *New Politics* 1, no. 4 (Winter, 1988): 115–23.

Glass Ceiling Commission, U.S. Department of Labor. *Good for Business: Making Full Use of the Nation's Human Capital*. Washington D.C.: U.S. Government Printing Office, 1995.

Glickstein, Johnathan A. "'Poverty Is Not Slavery': American Abolitionists and the Competitive Labor Market." In *Antislavery Reconsidered: New Perspectives on the Abolitionists*, edited by Lewis Perry and Michael Fellman. Baton Rouge: Louisiana State University Press, 1979.

Glyn, Andrew, and Robert Sutcliff. *Capitalism in Crisis*. New York: Pantheon Books, 1972.

———. "Global but Leaderless? The New Capitalist Order." *Socialist Register*, 1992.

Goldfield, Michael. "The Decline of the Communist Party and the Black Question in the U.S.: Harry Haywood's Black Bolshevik." *Review of Radical Political Economics*, 12, no. 1 (1980): 44–63.

———. "Recent Historiography of the Communist Party U.S.A." In *The Year Left* vol. 1, edited by Mike Davis, Fred Pfeil and

Michael Sprinker. London: Verso, 1985.

———. *The Decline of Organized Labor in the United States*. Chicago: University of Chicago Press, 1989.

———. "Worker Insurgency, Radical Organization, and New Deal Labor Legislation." *American Political Science Review*, 83, no. 4 (December 1989): 1257–82.

———. "Class, Race, and Politics in the United States." *Research in Political Economy*, vol. 12 (1990).

———. "Race and the CIO: The Possibilities for Racial Egalitarianism During the 1930s and 1940s." *International Labor and Working-Class History*, 44 (Fall 1993): 1–32.

———. "The Failure of Operation Dixie: A Critical Turning Point in American Political Development." *Race, Class, and Community in Southern Labor History: Selected Papers, Seventh Southern Labor Studies Conference, 1991*, edited by Gary M. Fink and Merl E. Reed Tuscaloosa, Alabama: University of Alabama Press, 1994.

———. "Race and the CIO: Reply to Critics." *International Labor And Working-Class History*, 46 (Fall 1994): 142–60.

———. *Race, Class, and the Nature of American Politics: The Failure of the CIO's Operation Dixie*. Forthcoming.

———. "Race and the Reuther Legacy." *Against the Current*, vol. xii, no. 1 (March/April 1997).

Goldstein, Robert Justin. *Political Repression in Modern America*. Cambridge, Mass.: Schenkman Publishing Co., 1978.

Gompers, Samuel. *Seventy Years of Life and Labor*, Nick Salvatore ed. New York: ILR Press, 1984.

Goodwyn, Lawrence. *Democratic Promise: The Populist Movement in America*. New York: Oxford, 1976.

Gordon, Colin. *New Deals: Business, Labor, and Politics in American, 1920–1935*. New York: Cambridge University Press, 1994.

Gordon, David. *Fat and Mean: The Corporate Squeeze of Working Americans and the Myth of Managerial 'Downsizing.'* New York: Martin Kessler Books, 1996.

Gould, Stephen Jay. *The Mismeasure of Man.* New York: Norton, 1981.

Gray, Lewis C. *History of Agriculture in the United States.* 2 volumes. Washington, D.C.: Carnegie Institute of Washington, 1933.

Green, James R. "The Brotherhood of Timberworkers, 1910–1913: A Radical Response to Industrial Capitalism in the Southern U.S.A." *Past and Present,* 60 (1973):161–200).

Greenberg, Stanley B. *Race and State in Capitalist Development.* New Haven, Connecticut: Yale University Press, 1980.

Greene, Felix. *The Enemy: What Every American Should Know About Imperialism.* New York: Vintage Books, 1970.

Greene, Lorenzo J., and Carter G. Woodson. *The Negro Wage Earner.* Washington, D.C.: The Association for the Study of Negro Life and History, 1930.

Gregory, Charles O. and Harold A. Katz. *Labor and the Law.* New York: W. W. Norton and Company, 1979 (1946).

Griffith, Barbara S. *The Crisis of American Labor: Operation Dixie and the Defeat of the CIO.* Philadelphia: Temple University Press, 1988.

Giffler, Keith P. *What Price Alliance?: Black Radicals Confront White Labor, 1919–1938.* New York: Garland, 1995.

Gulliver, Hal and Reg Murphy. *The Southern Strategy.* New York: Scribner, 1971.

Gutman, Herbert G. "The Negro and the United Mine Workers of America. The Career and Letters of Richard L. Davis and Something of Their Meaning: 1890–1900." In *The Negro and the American Labor Movement,* edited by Julius Jacobson. Garden City, N.Y.: Anchor Books, 1968.

Hahn, Steven. *The Roots of Southern Populism.* New York: Oxford University Press, 1983.

Halpern, Eric B. "Black and White Unite and Fight": Race and Labor in Meatpacking, 1904–1948." Ph.D. Diss., University of Wisconsin, 1989.

Halpern, Rick. "Interracial Unionism in the Southwest: Fort Worth's Packinghouse Workers, 1937–1954." In *Organized Labor in the Twentieth Century,* edited by Robert H. Zeiger. Knoxville: University of Tennessee Press, 1991.

Hamby, Alonzo L. *Beyond the New Deal: Harry S. Truman and American Liberalism.* New York: Columbia University Press, 1973.

Handbook of Labor Statistics, 1978. Washington, DC: US Department of Labor, Bureau of Labor Statistics, 1978.

Handlin, Oscar, and Mary F. Handlin. "Origins of the Southern Labor System." *William and Mary Quarterly,* 3rd series, VII, no. 2 (April 1950): 199–222.

Hanks, Lawrence J. *The Struggle for Black Political Empowerment in Three Georgia Counties.* Knoxville: University of Tennessee Press, 1987.

Harris, Abram L. *The Black Worker: The Negro and the Labor Movement.* New York: Antheneum, 1968.

———. *Race, Radicalism, and Reform.* Edited by William Darity, Jr. New Brunswick, N.J.: Transaction, 1989.

Harris, Marvin. *Patterns of Race in the Americas.* New York: Walker and Company, 1964.

Hartz, Louis. *The Liberal Tradition in America.* New York: Harcourt, Brace, and World, 1955.

Havard, William C., ed. *The Changing Politics of the South.* Baton Rouge: Louisiana State University Press, 1972.

Haywood, Harry. *Negro Liberation.* New York: International Publishers, 1948.

———. *Black Bolshevik: Autobiography of an Afro-American Communist.* Chicago: Lake View Press, 1978.

Hegel, G.F.W. *Philosophy of Right,* translated by T.M. Knox. New York: Oxford University Press, 1962.

———. *Philosophie des Rechts.* edited by Dieter Henrich. Frankfurt: Suhrkamp Verlag, 1983.

Helvarg, David. *The War Against the Greens: The 'Wise-Use' Movement, the New Right and Anti-Environmental Violence.* San Francisco: Sierra Club Books, 1994.

Herbst, Alma. *The Negro in the Slaughtering and Meat-packing Industry in Chicago.* New York: Arno Press, 1971.

Herrnstein, Richard J., and Charles Murray. *The Bell Curve: Intelligence and Class Structure in American Life.* New York: Free Press, 1994.

Hertzke, Allen D. *Echoes of Discontent: Jessie Jackson, Pat Robertson, and the Resurgence of Populism*. Washington, D.C.: Q Press, 1993.

Hevener, John W. *Which Side Are You On? The Harlan County Coal Miners, 1931–39*. Chicago: University of Illinois Press, 1978.

Higgs, Robert. "The Boll Weevil, The Cotton Economy, and Black Migration, 1910–1930." *Agricultural History*, 50, no. 2 (April 1976):335–50.

Hill, Herbert. "Anti-Oriental Agitation and the Rise of Working-Class Racism." *Society* (January/February 1973).

———. "Race and Ethnicity in Organized Labor: The Historic Sources of Resistance to Affirmative Action." *Journal of Intergroup Relations*, xii, no. 4 (Winter 1984):5–49.

———. *Black Labor and the American Legal System*. Madison: University of Wisconsin Press, 1985.

———. "Myth-making As Labor History: Herbert Gutman and the United Mine Workers of America." *International Journal of Politcs, Culture, and Society*, 2, no. 2 (Winter 1989):132–200.

———. "Black Labor and Affirmative Action: An Historical Perspective." In *The Question of Discrimination*, edited by Steven Schulman and William Darity, Jr. Middletown, Conn.: Wesleyan University Press, 1989.

———. Rejoinder to Symposium on "Myth-making As Labor History: Herbert Gutman and the United Mine Workers of America." *International Journal of Politics, Culture, and Society*, 2, no. 4 (Summer 1979): 587–96.

Historical Statistics of the United States: Colonial Times to 1970, 2 volumes. Washington, D.C.: United States Bureau of the Census, 1975.

Hobsbawm, E. J. *The Age of Extremes, 1914–1991*. New York: Pantheon Books, 1994.

Hoerder, Dirk, Gary B. Nash, and Billy Smith. *American Labor and Immigration History, 1877–1920s*. Urbana, Ill.: University of Illinois Press, 1983.

Hofstadter, Richard. *The Age of Reform*. New York: Vintage Books, 1955.

———. *The American Political Tradition and the Men Who Made It*. New York: Vintage, 1989.

Holiday, Billie with William Duffy. *Lady Sings the Blues: The Searing Autobiography of an American Musical Legend*. New York: Penguin Books, 1956.

Holt, Michael F. *The Poltical Crisis of the 1850s*. New York: Wiley, 1978.

Honey, Michael. "The War Within the Confederacy: White Unionists of North Carolina," *Prologue*, (Summer 1986).

———. "Labor and Civil Rights in the South: The Industrial Labor Movement and Black Workers in Memphis, 1929–1945." Ph.D. Diss., Northern Illinois University, 1988.

———. "Coalition and Conflict: Martin Luther King, Civil Rights, and the American Labor Movement," 1992.

———. *Southern Labor and Black Civil Rights: Organizing Memphis Workers*. Urbana, Ill.: University of Illinois Press, 1993.

Hoover, Calvin and Benjamin Ratchford. *Economic Resources of the South*. New York: Macmillin, 1951.

Horowitz, Roger. "The Path Not Taken: A Social History of Industrial Unionism in Meatpacking, 1920–1960". Ph.D. Diss., University of Wisconsin, 1990.

Howard, Donald S. *The WPA and Federal Relief Policy*. New York: Russell Sage Foundation, 1943.

Huber, Evelyn, Leonard Ray, and John D. Stephens. "The Welfare State in Hard Times," Paper given at the American Political Science Association, New York, 1994.

Huber, Evelyn, and John D. Stephens. "Economic Internationalization, the European Community, and the Social Democratic Welfare State," Paper presented before the American Political Science Association Annual meeting, Chicago, Ill, September 3-6, 1992.

Hudson, Harriet D. *The Progressive Mine Workers of America: A Study in Rival Unionism*. Urbana: University of Illinois, 1952.

Hudson, Hosea. *Black Worker in the Deep South*. New York: International Publishers, 1972.

Hughes, Jonathan R.T. *American Economic*

History. Glenview, Ill.: Scott, Foresman, 1990.

Human Development Report, 1996. New York: Oxford University Press, 1996.

Huntley, Horace. "Iron Ore Miners and Mine Mill in Alabama: 1933–1952". Ph.D. Diss., University of Pittsburgh, 1977.

Ignatiev, Noel. *How the Irish Became White.* New York: Routledge, 1995.

Irons, Janet. "Testing the New Deal: The General Textile Strike of 1934". Ph.D. Diss., Duke University, 1988.

Jacobson, Julius. *The Negro and the American Labor Movement.* Garden City, N.Y.: Doubleday Publishers, 1968.

Jacoby, Russell and Naomi Glauberman, eds. *The Bell Curve Debate.* New York: Times Books, 1995.

James, C.L.R. *The Black Jacobins: Toussaint L'Ouverture and the Santo Domingo Revolution.* New York: Vintage, 1963.

Janoski, Thomas H., and Alexander Hicks. *The Comparative Political Economy of the Welfare State.* New York: Cambridge University Press, 1994.

Jensen, Vernon H. *Lumber and Labor.* New York: Farrar and Rinehart, Inc., 1945.

———. *Nonferous Metals Industry Unionism, 1932–1954. A Story of Leadership Controversy.* Ithaca, N.Y.: Cornell University Press, 1954.

Johannsen, Robert Walter. *Lincoln-Douglas Debates of 1858.* New York: Oxford University Press, 1965.

Jones, Leroi. 1963. *Blues People.* New York: Morrow Quill, 1963.

Jordan, Winthrop D. *White Over Black: American Attitudes Toward the Negro, 1550–1812.* New York: W.W. Norton, 1977.

Joyner, Charles. *Down by the Riverside: A South Carolina Slave Community.* Urbana: University of Illinois Press, 1984.

Judd, Dennis R. "Coalitional Politics and Urban Policies: How African Americans Got so Little from the Democrats." Unpublished manuscript, 1993.

Karabel, Jerome. "The Failure of American Socialism Reconsidered." *The Socialist Register* (1979):204–27.

Karsh, Bernard, and Phillips Garman. "The Impact of the Political Left." In *Labor and the New Deal,* edited by Milton Derber and Edwin Young. Madison: University of Wisconsin Press, 1957.

Katznelson, Ira. *Black Men, White Cities, Race, Politics, and Migration in the United States, 1900–30, and Britain, 1948–68.* New York: Pantheon, 1976.

———. "Considerations on Social Democracy in the United States." *Comparative Politics* 11, no. 1 (October 1978):77–99.

———. *City Trenches.* New York: Pantheon, 1981.

Katznelson, Ira, and Margaret Weir. *Schooling for All: Class, Race, and the Decline of the Democratic Ideal.* New York: Basic Books, 1985.

Katznelson, Ira and Bruce Pietrykowski. "Rebuilding The American State: Evidence from the 1940s." *Studies in American Political Development,* 5 (Fall 1991): 301–39.

Katznelson, Ira, Kim Geiger, and Daniel Kryder. "Limiting Liberalism: The Southern Veto in Congress, 1933–1950." *Political Science Quarterly,* 108: no. 2 (Summer 1993):283–306.

Katznelson, Ira and Aristide R. Zolberg, eds. *Working Class Formation.* Princeton, N.J.: Princeton University Press, 1986.

Keech, William R. *The Impact of Negro Voting: The Role of the Vote in the Quest for Equality.* Chicago: Rand McNally, 1968.

Keeran, Roger. *The Communist Party and the Auto Worker's Unions.* Bloomington: Indiana University Press, 1980.

Kelley, Robin D. G. *Hammer and Hoe: Alabama Communists During the Great Depression.* Chapel Hill: University of North Carolina Press, 1990.

———. "Notes on Deconstructing 'the Folk'." *American Historical Review,* vol. 97 (December 1992).

Kerr, Clark, and Abraham Siegel. "The Interindustry Propensity to Strike—An International Comparison." Arthur Kornhauser, Robert Dubin, and Arthur M. Ross, eds. *Industrial Conflict.* New York: McGraw Hill Press, 1954.

Kerr, Clark et al. *Industrialism and Industrial Man.* Cambridge, Mass.: Harvard University Press, 1960.

Key, V.O., Jr. *Southern Politics in State and Nation.* Knoxville: University of Tennessee Press, 1984 (1949).

Kifer, A.F. "The Negro Under the New Deal, 1933–1941". Ph.D. Diss., University of Wisconsin, 1961.

Kirby, Jack Temple. "The Southern Exodus, 1910–1960 : A Primer for Historians." *The Journal Of Southern History,* 49 (February 1983):585–601.

————. "Black and White in the Rural South, 1915–1954." *Agricultural History,* 58, no. 3 (July 1984):411–22.

————. *Rural Worlds Lost: The American South, 1920–1960.* Baton Rouge: Louisiana State University Press, 1987.

Kirby, John B. *Black Americans in the Roosevelt Era: Liberalism and Race.* Knoxville: University of Tennessee Press, 1980.

Klarman, Michael. "*Brown v. Board of Education*: Facts and Political Correctness." *Viginia Law Review* 80, no. 1 (February 1994):185–200.

————. "How *Brown* Changed Race Relations: The Backlash Thesis." *The Journal of American History* 81, no. 1 (June 1994):81–118.

Klehr, Harvey. *The Heyday of American Communism: The Depression Decade.* New York: Basic Books, 1984.

Klehr, Harvey, and John Earl Haynes. *The American Communist Movement: Storming Heaven Itself.* New York: Twayne, 1992.

Kleppner, Paul. *Who Voted?: The Dynamics of Electoral Turnout, 1870–1980.* New York: Praeger, 1982.

Kolchin, Peter. *American Slavery: 1619–1877.* New York: Hill and Wang, 1993.

Kolko, Gabriel. *The Politics of War: The World and United States Policy, 1943–1945.* New York: Random House, 1968.

Koppes, Clayton R., and Gregory D. Black. "Blacks, Loyalty, and Motion-Picture Propaganda in World War II." *Journal of American History,* 74 (September 1986):383–406.

Kornblith, Gary J., and John M. Murrin. "The Making and Unmaking of an American Ruling Class." In *Beyond the American Revolution: Explorations in the*

History of American Radicalism. Dekalb, Ill.: Northern Illinois University Press, 1993.

Korstad, Karl. "Black and White Together: Organizing in the South with the Food, Tobacco, Agricultural & Allied Workers Union (FTA–CIO), 1942–1952." In Rosswurm, 1992.

Korstad, Robert R. "Daybreak of Freedom: Tobacco Workers and the CIO, Winston-Salem, North Carolina, 1943–1950". Ph.D. Diss., University of North Carolina, 1987.

Korstad, Robert, and Nelson Lichtenstein. "Opportunities Found and Lost: Labor, Radicals, and the Early Civil Rights Movment." *The Journal of American History.* 75, no. 3(December 1988):786–811.

Kousser, J. Morgan. *The Shaping of Southern Politics: Suffrage Restriction and the Establishment of the One-Party South, 1880–1910.* New Haven: Yale University Press, 1974.

Kraditor, Aileen. *Means and Ends in American Abolitionism; Garrison and His Critics on Strategy and Tactics, 1834–1850.* New York: Pantheon Books, 1969.

Kramnick, Isaac. "Jefferson vs. the Religious Right," *New York Times,* August 29, 1994.

Kulikoff, Allan. *Tobacco and Slaves: The Development of Southern Cultures in the Chesapeake, 1680–1800.* Chapel Hill: University of North Carolina Press, 1986.

Kulikoff, Alan. "The American Revolution, Capitalism, and the Formation of the Yeoman Classes." In *Beyond the American Revolution: Explorations in the History of American Radicalism,* edited by Alfred Young. DeKalb: Northern Illinois University Press, 1993.

Lakatos, Imre. "Falsification and the Methodology of Scientific Research Programmes." In *Criticism and the Growth of Knowledge,* edited by Imre Lakatos and Alan Musgrave. London: Cambridge University Press, 1970.

Lamb, John D. "The Real Affirmative Action Babies: Legacy Preferences at Harvard and Yale." *Columbia Journal of Law and Social Problems,* 26 (1993):491.

Laslett, John H. M., and Seymour Martin Lipset, eds. *Failure of a Dream? Essays in the*

History of American Socialism. Garden City, N.Y.: Doubleday, 1974.

Laurentz, Robert. "Racial Conflict in the New York City Garment Industry, 1933–1980". Ph.D. Diss., State University of New York, Binghamton, 1980.

Lawrence, Ken. *Marx on American Slavery.* Tougaloo, Miss: Freedom Information Service, 1976.

Lax, John, and William Pencak. "The Knowles Riot and the Crisis of the 1740's in Massachusetts." *Perspectives in American History,* X (1976):163–216.

Lembcke, Jerry. *Capitalist Development and Class Capacities.* New York: Greenwood Press, 1988.

Lembcke, Jerry, and William M. Tattam. *One Union in Wood.* New York: International Publishers, 1984.

Lemisch, Jesse. *Towards a Democratic History.* Ann Arbor: Radical Education Project, 1967.

———. "Jack Tarr in the Streets." *William and Mary Quarterly.* XXV, no. 3 (July 1968):371–407.

———. *On Active Service in War and Peace.* Toronto: New Hogtown Press, 1975.

Lemann, Nicholas. *The Promised Land: The Great Black Migration and How It Changed America.* New York: A.A. Knopf, 1991.

Leo, John. *U.S. News and World Report,* 10 October 1994.

Levine, Bruce et al. *Who Built America: Working People and the Nation's Economy, Politics, Culture, and Society.* New York: Pantheon Books, 1989.

Levine, Bruce. *Half Slave, Half Free: The Roots of the Civil War.* New York: Hill and Wang, 1992.

Levy, Frank. *Dollars and Dreams: The Changing American Income Distribution.* New York: W.W. Norton, 1988.

Levy, Frank, and Murnane Richard J. "U.S. Earnings Levels and Earnings Inequality: A Review of Recent Trends and Proposed Explanations." *The Journal of Economic Literature.* 30 (September 1992):1333–81.

Levy, Leonard W. *The Establishment Clause, Religion and the First Amendment.* Chapel Hill: University of North Carolina Press, 1994.

Lewis, Ronald L. *Black Coal Miners in America —Race, Class, and Community Conflict, 1780–1980* Lexington: University of Kentucky Press, 1987.

Lewontin, Richard. *The Genetic Basis of Evolutionary Change.* New York: Columbia University Press, 1974.

Lewontin, Richard, Steven Rose, and Leon J. Kamin. *Not in Our Genes: Biology, Ideology, and Human Nature.* New York: Pantheon Books, 1984.

Leuchtenberg, William Edward. *Franklin D. Roosevelt and the New Deal, 1932–1940.* New York: Harper and Row, 1963.

The Liberator, January 1, 1933.

Lichtenstein, Nelson. *Labor's War at Home.* Cambridge: Cambridge University Press, 1982.

———. *The Most Dangerous Man in Detroit: Walter Reuther and the Fate of American Labor.* New York: Basic Books, 1995.

Limbaugh, Rush. *See, I Told You So.* New York: Pocket Star Books, 1994.

Lipset, Seymour Martin. "Why No Socialism in the United States?" in *Sources of Contemporary Radicaliism,* edited by S. Bailer and S. Sluzard. Boulder, Colo.: Westview Press, 1977.

———. *The Confidence Gap: Business, Labor, and Government in the Public Mind.* New York: Free Press, 1983.

———. "Trade Union Exceptionalism: The United States and Canada." *The Annals of The American Academy of Political and Social Science* 538 (March 1995):115.

———. *American Exceptionalism: A Double-edged Sword.* New York: W.W. Norton and Company, 1996.

Lipset, Seymour Martin and Bendix, Reinhold. 1964. *Social Mobility in Industrial Society.* Berkeley: University of California Press.

Lipsitz, George. *Rainbow at Midnight, Labor and Culture in the 1940s.* Chicago: University of Illinois Press, 1994.

Litwack, Leon. *North of Slavery: The Negro in the Free States, 1790–1860.* Chicago: University of Chicago Press, 1961.

Los Angeles Times, March 8, 1993.

Lott, Eric. *Love and Theft: Blackface Minstrelry*

and the American Working Class. New York: Oxford University Press, 1993.

Lotta, Raymond. *America in Decline: An Analysis of the Development Towards War and Revolution in the United States and World Wide in the 1980s.* Chicago: Banner Press, 1984.

Lowi, Theodore J. "Why Is There No Socialism in the United States? A Federal Analysis." *International Political Science Review* 5, no. 4 (1984):369–90.

———. *The End of the Republican Era.* Norman: University of Okalahoma Press, 1995.

Lubell, Samuel. *The Future of American Politics.* New York: Harper and Brothers, 1952.

———. *The Revolution in World Trade and American Economic Policy.* New York: Harper, 1955.

Lynch, Frederick R. *Invisible Victims: White Males and the Crisis of Affirmative Action.* New York: Greenwood Press, 1989.

Lynd, Staughton. *Class Conflict, Slavery, and the United States Constitution.* New York: BobbsMerrill Company, 1967.

Mackie, Thomas T., and Richard Rose. *International Almanac of Electoral History.* London: McMillan, 1994.

Maddison, Angus. *Monitoring the World Economy, 1820–1992.* Paris: Development Center for the Organization for Economic Cooperation and Development, 1995.

Magdol, Edward. *Antislavery Rank and File: A Social Profile of the Abolitionists Constituency.* Westport, Conn.: Greenwood Press, 1986.

Maier, Pauline. *From Resistance to Revolution: Colonial Radicals and the Development of American Opposition to Britain, 1765-1776.* New York: Norton and Norton, 1972.

Majak, Linda C. and Theo J. *Farmworkers, Agribusiness, and the State.* Philadelphia: Temple University Press, 1982.

Mandel, Bernard. *Labor: Free and Slave; Workingmen and the Anti-Slavery Movement in the United States.* New York: Associated Authors, 1955.

Mannix, Daniel P., and Malcom Cowley. *Black Cargoes, A History of the Atlantic Slave Trade.* New York: Viking Press, 1962.

Marable, Manning. *Race, Reform, Rebellion: The Second Reconstruction in Black America,* *1945–1990.* Jackson: University of Mississippi, 1991.

Marglin, Stephen A. and Juliet B. Schor. *The Golden Age of Capitalism: Reinterpreting the Postwar Experience.* Oxford: Clarendon Press, 1991.

Markovits, Andrei S. "The Other 'American Exceptionalism': Why Is There No Soccer in the United States?" *Leviathan, Zeitschrift fuer Sozialwissenschaft,* 15, no. 4 (December 1987):486–525.

Marshall, Ray F. *The Negro and Organized Labor.* New York: John Wiley and Sons, 1965.

———. *Labor in the South.* Cambridge, Mass.: Harvard University Press, 1967.

Martin, Charles H. "Southern Labor Relations in Transition: Gadsden, Alabama, 1930–1943." *The Journal of American History.* 67, no. 4(November 1981):545–68.

Marquart, Frank. *An Auto Worker's Journal: The UAW from Crusade to One-Party Union.* University Park: Pennsylvania State University Press, 1975.

Marquez, Benjamin. "Organizing Mexican-American Women in the Garment Industry: La Mujher Obrera." *Women and Politics* 15, no. 1(1995):65–87.

Matthews, Donald R., and James Warren Prothro. *Negroes and the New Southern Politics.* New York: Harcourt, Brace and World, 1966.

Marx, Karl. *The Poverty of Philosophy.* Moscow: Foreign Languages Publishing House, (1847).

———. *Capital* vol. 1, translated by Samuel Moore. New York: International Publishers, 1967 (1867).

Marx, Karl, and Frederick Engels. *Selected Correspondence.* Moscow: Foreign Language Publishing House, 1953.

———. *Selected Works.* New York: International Publishers, 1968.

———. *The Civil War in the United States.* New York: International Publishers, 1969 (1861–1866).

———. *The Communist Manifesto.* New York: International, 1982 (1848).

Mayer, William G. *The Changing American Mind.* Ann Arbor: The University of Michigan Press, 1992.

McAdam, Doug. *Political Process and the Development of Black Insurgency, 1930–1970.* Chicago: University of Chicago Press, 1982.

McColoch, Mark. "The Shop-Floor Dimension of Union Rivalry: The Case of Westinghouse in the 1950s." In Rosswurm, 1992.

McCormick, Richard L *The Party Period and Public Policy: American Politics from the Age of Jackson to the Progressive Era.* New York: Oxford University Press, 1986.

McElvaine, Robert S. *The Great Depression: America, 1929–1941.* New York: Times Books, 1984.

McGerr, Michael E. *The Decline of Popular Politics: The American North, 1865–1928.* New York. Oxford University Press, 1986.

McGinn, Mary. "Honeywell, G.E. Fire Mexican Workers for Organizing Union." *Labor Notes,* (January 1995).

———. "Miners' Cross-Border Solidarity Extends to Columbia." *Labor Notes,* (February 1995).

McLaurin, Melton A. *The Knights of Labor in the South.* Westport, Connecticut: Greenwood Press, 1978.

McMath, Jr., Robert C. *Populist Vanguard, A History of the Southern Farmers' Alliance.* New York: W.W. Norton and Company, 1975.

McMillen, Neil. *The Citizens' Council: Organized Resistance to Second Reconstruction, 1954–1964.* Urbana: University of Illinois Press, 1971.

Megalli, Mark. "So Your Dad Went to Harvard: Now What About Lower Board Scores of White Legacies?" *Journal of Blacks in Higher Education* (spring 1995):71–73.

Meir, August, and Elliot Rudwick. *Black Nationalism in America.* Indianapolis: Bobbs-Merrill, 1970.

———. *From Plantation to Ghetto.* New York: Hill and Wang, 1976.

———. *Black Detroit and the Rise of the UAW.* New York: Oxford University Press, 1979.

———. "Communist Unions and the Black Community: The Case of the Transport Workers Union, 1934–1944." *Labor History.* 23, no. 2 (spring 1982):165–97.

Menard, Russell R. "From Servants to Slaves." *Southern Studies,* xvi, 1977.

———. *Economy and Society in Early Colonial Maryland.* New York: Garland Publishing, Inc., 1985.

Menard, Russell R. and Mckusker, John J. *The Economy of British North America, 1607–1789.* Chapel Hill: University of North Carolina Press, 1985.

Menard, Russell R., Lois Green Carr, and Lorena Seebach Walsh. *Robert Cole's World: Agriculture and Society in Early Maryland.* Chapel Hill: University of North Carolina Press, 1991.

Messer-Kruse, Timothy. "The Yankee International: Marxism and the American Reform Tradition, 1831–1876". Ph.D. Diss., University of Wisconsin, 1994.

Mezerik, A. G. "The CIO Southern Drive." *The Nation,* 11 January 1947.

———. "Dixie in Black and White." *The Nation,* 19 April 1947.

Miller, Richard. *Fact and Method.* Princeton: Princeton University Press, 1988.

Miller, William Lee. *Arguing About Slavery: The Great Battle in the United States Congress.* New York: Alfred A. Knopf, 1996.

Milward, Alan S. *War, Economy, and Society, 1939–1945.* Berkeley: University of California Press, 1977.

Mink, Gwendolyn. *Old Labor and New Immigrants in American Political Development.* Ithaca, N.Y.: Cornell University Press, 1986.

Mishel, Lawrence, and Jared Bernstein. *The State of Working America, 1994-95.* Armonk, N.Y.: M.E. Sharpe, 1994.

Mishel, Lawrence and Simon, Jacqueline. *The State of Working America.* Washington, D.C.: Economic Policy Institute, 1988.

Mitchell, George and Broadus Mitchell. *The Industrial Revolution in the South.* Baltimore: The Johns Hopkins Press, 1930.

Money Income in the United States, 1995. Washington, DC: US Department of Commerce, 1995.

Montgomery, David. *Beyond Equality: Labor and the Radical Republicans, 1862–1872.* New York: Vintage, 1967.

Moon, Henry Lee. *Balance of Power: The Negro Vote.* Garden City, New York: Doubleday and Company, 1948.

Moore, Barrington. *Social Origins of Dictatorship and Democracy: Lord and Peasent in the Making of the Modern World.* Boston: Beacon Press, 1966.

Morgan, Edmund S. *The Birth of the New Republic, 1763-1789.* Chicago: University of Chicago Press, 1956.

————. *American Slavery, American Freedom: The Ordeal of Colonial Virginia.* New York: Norton, 1975.

Morris, Aldon D. "The Rise of the Civil Rights Movement and Its Movement: Black Power Structure, 1953–1963". Ph.D. Diss., State University of New York, 1980.

————. *The Origins of the Civil Rights Movement: Black Communities Organizing for Change.* New York: Free Press, 1984.

Morrison, Toni. *Beloved.* New York: Knopf, 1987.

Murphy, Reg, and Hal Gulliver. *The Southern Strategy.* New York: Scribner, 1971.

Murrin, John, ed. *Colonial America: Essays in Politics and Social Development.* New York: McGraw-Hill, 1993.

Muse, Benjamin. *Virginia's Massive Resistance.* Bloomington: Indiana University Press, 1961.

Myrdal, Gunnar. 2 vols. *An American Dilemma: The Negro Problem and Modern Democracy.* New York: Harper, 1964 (1944)

Naison, Mark. *Communists in Harlem During the Depression.* Chicago: University of Illinois Press, 1983.

Nash, Gary B. *Class and Society in Early America.* Englewood Cliffs, N.J.: Prentice-Hall, 1970.

————. *Urban Crucible: Social Change, Political Consciousness, and the Origins of the American Revolution.* Cambridge, Mass.: Harvard University Press, 1979.

————. *Race, Class, and Politics: Essays on American Colonial and Revolutionary Society.* Urbana, Ill.: University of Illinois Press, 1986.

————. *Red, White, and Black: The Peoples of Early North America.* Englewood Cliffs, N.J.: Prentice-Hall, 1992.

Nash, Gary B. and Richard Weiss. *The Great Fear: Race in the Mind of America.* New York: Holt, Rineheart and Winston, 1970.

National Center for History in the Schools. *National Standards for United States History.* Los Angeles: University of California Press, 1995.

Nelson, Bruce. "Mobile During World War II: Organized Labor and the Struggle for Black Equality in a 'City That's Been Taken by Storm." Unpublished manuscript, 1991.

————. "Class and Race in the Crescent City: The ILWU, from San Francisco to New Orleans." In Rosswurm, 1992.

————. "Harry Bridges, The Law, and Race Relations in the CIO Era." *Working Papers in Labor Studies.* University of Washington: Center for Labor Studies, 1995.

————. "Class, Race, and Democracy in the CIO: The 'New' Labor History Meets the 'Wages of Whiteness'." *International Review of Social History,* 41, no.3 (December 1996).

New York Times. September 9, 1942.

————. August 8, 1980.

————. October 16, 1980.

————. May 4, 1995.

————. June 6, 1995.

————. July 9, 1995.

————. July 31, 1995.

————. August 5, 1995.

————. August 13, 1995.

————. October 21, 1995.

————. October 23, 1995.

————. February 16, 1996.

————. February 17, 1996.

————. February 23, 1996.

————. March 3, 1996.

————. March 4, 1996.

————. March 29, 1996.

————. August 11, 1996.

————. September 20, 1996.

————. September 23, 1996.

————. September 26, 1996.

————. October 6, 1996.

————. November 2, 1996.

New York Times Magazine. January 11, 1948.

Noonan, Peggy. *What I Saw at the Revolution, A Political Life in the Reagan Administration.* New York: Ivy Books, 1990.

Norrell, Robert J. "Caste in Steel: Jim Crow Careers in Birmingham, Alabama." *Journal of American History.* 73(1986):3.

————. "Labor Trouble: George Wallace

and Union Politics in Alabama." In *Organized Labor in the Twentieth Century South*, edited by Robert H. Zeiger. Knoxville: University of Tennessee Press, 1991.

North, Douglas C. *The Economic Growth of the United States, 1790–1860*. New York: Norton, 1966 (1961).

Northrup, Herbert R. "The Tobacco Workers International Union." *Quarterly Journal of Economics*. 56(August 1941):4.

———. *Organized Labor and the Negro*. New York: Harper and Brothers Publishers, 1944.

Northrup, Herbert R., et al. *Negro Employment in Southern Industry*. Philadelphia: University of Pennsylvania, 1970.

Novick, Peter. *The Noble Dream*. Cambridge: Cambridge University Press, 1988.

Nyden, Paul. *Black Coal Miners in the United States*. Occasional Paper No. 15. New York: American Institute for Marxist Studies, 1974.

Oakes, James. *The Ruling Race: A History of American Slaveholders*. New York: Knopf, 1982.

Odum, Howard W. *Race and Rumors of Race: Challenge to American Crisis*. Chapel Hill: University of North Carolina Press, 1943.

Omi, Michael, and Howard Winant. *Racial Formation in the United States*. New York: Routledge and Kegan Paul, 1986.

Operation Dixie Papers. Box 242 "Recommendations of the Executive Officers," 30–31 August 1948.

Operation Dixie Papers—Executive Officers Records.

Orfield, Gary. *The Reconstruction of Southern Education: The Schools and the 1964 Civil Rights Act*. New York: Wiley-Interscience, 1969.

Orren, Karren. *Belated Feudalism: Labor, the Law, and Liberal Development in the United States*. New York: Cambridge University Press, 1991.

Oshinsky, David M. *Worse Than Slavery: Parchman Farm and the Ordeal of Jim Crow Justice*. New York: Free Press, 1996.

Papers of Harry Truman, Harry S. Truman Library, Independence, MO, Box 21.

Papers of Harry Truman, Harry S. Truman Library, Ind., MO, Box 52. Clark Clifford Memorandum.

Papers of Oscar Ewing, Harry S. Truman Library, Ind., MO, Box 52.

Patterson, James. *Congressional Conservatism and the New Deal*. Lexington: University of Kentucky Press, 1967.

Patterson, William L. *We Charge Genocide: The Crime of Government Against the Negro People*. New York: Emergency Conference Committee, 1970. (1951)

Pease, Jane, and William Pease. *Antislavery Thought*. Indianapolis, Ind.: Bobbs-Merrill, 1965.

Perkins, Frances. *The Roosevelt I Knew*. New York: The Viking Press, 1946.

Perlo, Victor. *The Negro in Southern Agriculture*. New York: International, 1953.

Phillips, Kevin P. *The Emerging Republican Majority*. New Rochelle, New York: Arlington House, 1970.

Piel, Gerard. *Only One World: Our Own to Make and Keep*. New York: W.H. Freeman and Company, 1992.

Piven, Frances Fox. "Poorhouse Politics." *The Progressive*, 22 (February 1995):4.

———. "Welfare and the Transformation of Electoral Politics." *Dissent*, (Fall 1996).

Piven, Frances Fox, and Richard Cloward. *Poor People's Movements: Why They Succeed How They Fail*. New York: Pantheon Books, 1979. (1977)

———. *Why Americans Don't Vote*. New York: Pantheon, 1988.

———. *Regulating the Poor*. 2nd ed. New York: Random House, 1993.

Post, Charley. "Rural Class Structure and Economic Development: The Transformation of the Northern U.S. Countryside Before the Civil War." Unpublished manuscript, 1996.

Poston, Dudley L., and Robert H. Weller. *The Population of the South: Structure and Change in the Social Demographic Context*. Austin: University of Texas Press, 1981.

Potter, David M. *The Impending Crisis, 1848–1861*. New York: Harper and Row, 1976.

Powell, Thomas. *The Persistence of Racism in America*. New York: University Press of America, 1992.

Preis Art. *Labor's Giant Step: Twenty Years of the CIO*. New York: Pioneer, 1964.

Putnam, Hilary. *Meaning and the Moral Sciences*. London: Routledge and Kegan Paul, 1978.

Quadagno, Jill. *The Color of Welfare*. New York: Oxford University Press, 1994.

Quam-Wickham, Nancy. "Who Controls the Hiring Hall? The Struggle for Job Control in the ILWU During World War II." In Rosswurm, 1992.

Quarles, Benjamin. *The Negro in the Making of America*. New York: Collier Books, 1964.

Rachleff, Peter. *Black Labor in Richmond, 1865–1890*. Chicago: University of Illinois Press, 1989.

Rawick, George P., ed. *The American Slave: A Composite Autobiography*. Westport, Conn.: Greenwood Press, 1977 (1972).

Rawley, James A. *Race and Politics: "Bleeding Kansas" and the Coming of the Civil War*. Philadelphia: Lippencott, 1969.

Rediker, Marcus. *Between the Devil and the Deep Blue Sea: Merchant Seamen, Pirates and the Anglo-American Maritime World, 1700–1750*. Cambridge: Cambridge University Press, 1987.

———. "A Motley Crew of Rebels: Sailors, Slaves, and the Coming of the American Revolution." Unpublished manuscript.

Rediker, Marcus and Peter Linebaugh. "The Many-Headed Hydra: Sailors, Slaves, and the Atlantic Working Class in the Eighteenth Century," in *Gone to Croatan: Origins of North American Dropout Culture*, Ron Sakolsky and James Koehpline eds. Brooklyn, NY: Autonomedia, 1993.

Reed, Merl E. "The FEPC, the Black Worker, and the Southern Shipyards." *The South Atlantic Quarterly*. 74(1975):446–67.

Reed, Merl E., Leslie S. Hough, and Gary M. Fink, eds. *Southern Workers and Their Unions, 1880–1975*. Westport, Conn.: Greenwood Press, 1981.

Regensburger, William E. "Ground Into Our Blood": The Origins of Working Class Consciousness and Organization in Durably Unionized Southern Industries, 1930–1946". Ph.D. Diss., UCLA, 1987.

Reich, Michael. *Racial Inequality*. Princeton: Princeton University Press, 1981.

Reid, Ira De A. *Negro Membership in American Labor Unions*. New York: Negro Universities Press, 1930.

Reidy, Joseph P. *From Slavery to Agrarian Capitalism in the Cotton Plantation South: Central Georgia, 1800–1880*. Chapel Hill: University of North Carolina Press, 1992.

Reston, James. "Bush's Choices: Quayle, Hucksters." *The New York Times*, 26 October 1988.

Reynolds, David B. "Movement Politics: Grassroots Progressive Political Activism as Seen Through Jessie Jackson's 1988 Campaign," Ph.D. Diss., Cornell University, 1993.

———. *Democracy Unbound*. Boston: South End Press, 1997.

Richard, Leonard. *Gentlemen of Propterty and Standing: Anti-Abolition Mobs in Jacksonian America*. New York: Oxford University Press, 1970.

Richards, Paul David. "The History of the Textile Workers Union of America, CIO, in the South, 1937 to 1945". Ph.D. Diss., University of Wisconsin-Madison, 1978.

Rochester, Anna. *Labor and Coal*. New York: International Publishers, 1931.

Robinson, Cedric. *Black Marxism: The Making of the Black Radical Tradition*. London: Zed Press, 1983

Robinson, Donald. *Slavery in the Structure of American Politics, 1765–1820*. New York: Norton, 1979.

Roediger, David. *Haymarket Scrapbook*. Chicago: C. H. Kerr Publishing Co., 1986.

———. *The Wages of Whiteness: Race and the Making of the American Working Class*. London: Verso, 1991.

———. *Towards the Abolition of Whiteness: Essays on Race, Class, Politics and Working Class History*. London: Verso, 1994.

Roediger, David, and Philip S. Foner. *Our Own Time: A History of the American Labor and the Working Day*. New York: Greenwood Press, 1989.

Roemer, John E. "Divide and Conquer: Microfoundations of a Marxian Theory of Wage Discrimination." *Bell Journal of Economics* 10, no. 2 (Autumn 1979):695–705.

Rose, Douglas. *The Emergence of David Duke and the Politics of Race.* Chapel Hill: University of North Carolina Press, 1992.

Rosenberg, Daniel. *New Orleans Dockworkers: Race, Labor, and Unionism, 1892–1923.* Albany, N.Y.: State University of New York Press, 1988.

Rosenstone, Steven J., and John Mark Hansen. *Mobilization, Participation, and Democracy in America.* New York: MacMillan, 1993.

Ross, John. "Labor Pains." *Mexico Business,* November/December 1994.

Rosswurm, Steve, ed. *The CIO's Left-led Unions.* New Brunswick. New Jersey: Rutgers University Press, 1992.

Rostow, W. W. *The Stages of Economic Growth: a Non-Communist Manifesto.* Cambridge: University Press, 1960.

———. *The World Economy: History and Prospect.* Austin: University of Texas Press, 1980.

Rovere, Richard H. *The Goldwater Caper* New York: Harcourt, Brace, and World, 1965.

Rowan, Richard L. *The Negro in the Steel Industry.* Philadelphia: University of Pennsylvania Press, 1968.

Rubin, Lester, William S. Swift, and Herbert R. Northrup. *Negro Employment in the Maritime Industries.* Philadelphia: University of Pennsylvania, 1974.

Said, Edward W. *Orientalism.* New York: Vintage, 1979.

Saville, Julie. *The Work of Reconstruction: From Slave to Wage Laborer in South Carolina, 1860–1870.* New York: Cambridge University Press, 1994.

Saxton, Alexander. *The Indispensable Enemy: Labor and the Anti-Chinese Movement in California.* Berkeley: Univerity of California Press, 1971.

———. *The Rise and Fall of the White Republic: Class Politics and Mass Culture in Nineteenth-Century America.* London: Verso, 1990.

Schattschneider, E.E. *The Semisovereign People.* New York: Holt Rinehart, and Winston, 1960.

Schatz, Ronald W. *The Electrical Workers—A History of Labor at General Electric and Westinghouse, 1923–60* Chicago: University of Illinois Press, 1983.

Schiff, Michel. *Education and Class: The Irrelevance of IQ Genetic Studies.* New York: Oxford University Press, 1986.

Schlesinger, Arthur M. *The Age of Jackson.* Boston: Little, Brown and Company, 1950.

———. "Political Mobs in the American Revolution." *Proceedings of the American Philosophical Society,* vol. 99, 1955.

Schluter, Herman. *Lincoln, Labor, and Slavery: A Chapter in the Social History of America.* New York: Russell and Russell, 1965.

Schrecker, Ellen. *No Ivory Tower, McCarthyism and the Universities.* New York: Oxford University Press, 1986.

Schuman, Howard, Charlotte Steeh and Lawrence Bobo. *Racial Attitudes in America.* Cambridge, Mass.: Harvard University Press, 1985.

Schwartz, Michael. *Radical Protest and Social Structure, The Southern Farmers' Alliance and Cotton Tenancy, 1880–1890.* Chicago: University of Chicago Press, 1976.

Sellers, Charles Grier. *The Market Revolution: Jacksonian America, 1815–1846.* New York: Oxford University Press, 1991.

Shapiro, Bruce. "One Violent Crime." *The Nation,* April 3, 1995, 445-452.

Shover, John L. *Cornbelt Rebellion: The Farmer's Holiday Association.* Urbana: University of Illinois Press, 1965.

Shugg, Roger W. "The New Orleans General Strike of 1892." *The Louisiana Historical Quarterly.* 21, no. 2 (April 1938): 547–60.

Shulman, Steve. "Racial Inequality and White Employment." *Review of Black Political Economy.* Forthcoming.

Sims, George E. *The Little Man's Big Friend: James E. Folsom in Alabama Politics, 1946–1958.* University of Alabama: University of Alabama Press, 1985.

Sitkoff, Harvard. *A New Deal for Blacks.* London: Oxford University Press, 1978.

Skowronek, Stephen. *Building a New American State.* New York: Cambridge University Press, 1988.

Slaughter, Thomas P. *The Whiskey Rebellion: Frontier Epilogue to the American Revolution.* New York: Oxford University Press, 1986.

Slotkin, Richard. *The Fatal Environment: The*

Myth of the Frontier in the Age of Industrialization. Middletown, Conn.: Wesleyan University Press, 1986.

Smith, Douglas L. *The New Deal in the Urban South.* Baton Rouge: Louisiana State University, 1988.

Smith, Warren B. *White Servitude in Colonial South Carolina.* Columbia: University of South Carolina Press, 1961.

Sniderman, Paul M., and Thomas Piazza. *The Scar of Race.* Cambridge: The Belknap Press of Harvard University Press, 1993.

Sobel, Mechal. *The World They Made Together.* Princeton: Princeton University Press, 1987.

Sombart, Werner. *Why Is There No Socialism in the United States?* White Plains, N.Y.: M.E. Sharpe, 1976 (1905).

Sosna, Morton. *In Search of the Silent South: Southern Liberals and the Race Issue.* New York: Columbia University Press, 1977.

Spero, Sterling D., and Abram L. Harris. *The Black Worker.* New York: Atheneum, 1968 (1931).

Sports Illustrated. 72, no. 23 (December 3, 1990): 35.

Staples, Brent. *New York Times,* April 18, 1995.

Starobin, Robert S. *Industrial Slavery in the Old South.* New York: Oxford, 1970.

Starr, Raymond. "Historians and the Origins of British North American Slavery." *Historian* 36, 1973.

Statistical Abstract of the United States, 1983. Washington, DC: US Bureau of the Census, 1983.

Statistical Abstract of the United States, 1995. Washington, DC: US Bureau of the Census, 1995.

Stein, Judith. 1991a. "Race and Class Consciousness Reconsidered." *Reviews in American History,* 19 (1991a):551–60.

———. "Southern Workers in International Unions, 1936–1951." In *Organized Labor in the Twentieth Century South,* edited by Robert H. Zieger. Knoxville: University of Tennessee Press, 1991b.

Stepan-Norris, Judith, and Maurice Zeitlin. "Insurgency, Radicalism, and Democracy in America's Industrial Unions." Working Paper Series 215. Institute of Industrial

Relations, University of California, Los Angeles, 1991.

———. *Talking Union.* Urbana, Ill.: University of Illinois University, 1996.

Stephens, John D. "The Scandinavian Welfare States: Development and Crisis." Paper given at the World Conference of Sociology, Bielfeld, Germany, 1994.

Sterner, Richard. *The Negro's Share: A Study of Income, Consumption, Housing, and Public Assistance.* New York: Harper and Brothers, 1943.

Stewart, James Brewer. *Holy Warriors: The Abolitionists and American Slavery.* New York: Hill and Wang, 1976.

Stockman, David A. *The Triumph of Politics, Why the Reagan Revolution Failed.* New York: Harper and Row, 1986.

Stoker, Laura. "Understanding Whites' Resistance to Affirmative Action: The Role of Principled Commitments and Racial Prejudice," Unpublished manuscript, 1995.

Streater, John B., Jr. "The National Negro Congress, 1936–1947". Ph.D. Diss. University of Cincinnati, 1981.

Strong, Donald S. "Alabama: Transition and Alienation." In *The Changing Politics of the South,* edited by William C. Harvard. Baton Rouge: Louisiana State University, 1972.

Sugar, Maurice. *The Ford Hunger March.* Berkeley: Meiklejohn Civil Liberties Institute, 1980.

Sugrue, Thomas J. "Crabgrass-roots Politics: Race, Rights, and Reaction Against Liberalism in the Urban North, 1940–1964." *Journal of American History,* 82 (September 1995): 551–86.

Sullivan, Patricia A. "Gideon's Southern Soldiers: New Deal Politics and Civil Rights Reform 1933–1948." Ph.D. Diss., Emory University, 1983.

Sundquist, James L. *Dynamics of the Party System.* Washington, D.C.: Brookings Institute, 1983.

Sydnor, Charles A. *The Development of Southern Sectionalism, 1819–1848.* Baton Rouge: Louisiana State University Press, 1948.

Szymanski, Albert. "Racial Discrimination and White Gain." *American Sociological Review* 41, no. 3 (June 1976):403–414, 1976.

Tabak, Ronald J. "The Death of Fairness: The Arbitrary and Capricious Imposition of the Death Penalty in the 1980s." *Review of Law and Social Change.* 14(1986):797.

Taft, Philip. *Organizing Dixie: Alabama Workers in the Industrial Era.* Westport, Conn.: Greenwood Press, 1981.

Takaki, Ronald. *Iron Cages: Race and Culture in Nineteenth-Century America.* New York: Knopf, 1979.

Tarrow, Sidney G. *Power in Movement: Social Movements, Collective Action, and Politics.* New York: Cambridge University Press, 1994.

Taylor, Alan. "Agrarian Independence: Northern Land Rioters After the Revolution." In *Beyond the American Revolution: Explorations in the History of American Radicalism,* edited by Alfred Young DeKalb, Ill.: Northern Illinois University Press, 1993.

Taylor, William. "Affirmative Action: The Questions to Be Asked." *Poverty and Race,* 4 no. 3 (May/June 1995):2–3.

Teixeira, Ruy A. *Why Americans Don't Vote.* Westport, Conn.: Greenwood, Press, 1987.

———. *The Disappearing American Voter.* Washington, DC: The Brookings Institute, 1992.

Teixeira, Ruy A., and Joel Rogers, "Volatile Voters: Declining Living Standards and Non-College Educated Whites." Economic Policy Institute Working Paper, 1996.

Terkel, Studs. *Race: How Blacks and Whites Feel About the American Obsession.* New York: The New Press, 1992.

Thernstrom, Abigail M. *Whose Votes Count: Affirmative Action and Minority Voting Rights.* Cambridge: Harvard University Press, 1987.

Thernstrom, Stephan. *Poverty and Progress.* New York: Atheneum, 1975.

Ernest Thompson Papers, Rutgers University. Box 1, Folders, "The Louisville Story"; "GE Discrimination Against Negro Woman"; and "Let Freedom Crash the Gateway to the South Campaign."

Tindall, George B. *The Emergence of the New South, 1913–1945.* Baton Rouge: Louisiana State University Press, 1967.

To Secure These Rights: The Report of the President's Committee on Civil Rights. Washington, D.C.: Government Printing Office, 1947.

Todes, Charlotte. *Labor and Lumber.* New York: International Publishers, 1931.

———. *William H. Sylvis and the National Labor Union.* New York: International Publishers, 1942.

Tribe, Laurence H. *American Constitutional Law.* Mineola, N.Y.: Foundation Press, 1978.

Trotsky, Leon. *The Basic Writings of Trotsky.* edited by Irving Howe. New York: Vintage Books, (1938) 1963.

Trotter, Joe W., Jr. *Coal, Class and Color, Blacks in Southern West Virginia, 1915-32.* Chicago: University of Illinois Press, 1990.

Turner, Frederick Jackson. *Frontier and Section. Selected Essays.* Englewood Cliffs, New Jersey: Prentice-Hall, 1961.

Tyler, Alice Felt. *Freedom's Ferment: Phases of American Social History From the Colonial Period to the Outbreak of the Civil War.* New York: Harper and Row, Publishers, 1944.

USA Today. April 4, 1995.

Usner, Daniel. *Indians, Settler, and Slaves in a Frontier Exchange Economy: The Lower Mississippi Valley Before 1783.* Chapel Hill: Unviersity of North Carolina Press, 1992.

Valelly, Richard M. *Radicalism in the States: The Minnesota Farmer-Labor Party and the American Political Economy.* Chicago: University of Chicago Press, 1989.

Vaughan, Alden T. "The Origins Debate: Slavery and Racism in Seventeenth-Century Virginia." *Virginia Magazine of History and Biography,* (July 1989).

Vidal, Gore. *Matters of Fact and Fiction: Essays, 1973–1976.* New York: Random House, 1977.

Village Voice, 16 November 1993.

Voss, Kim. *The Making of American Exceptionalism: The Knights of Labor and Class Formation in the Nineteenth Century.* Ithaca, N.Y.: Cornell University Press, 1993.

Wald, Alan. "Search for a Method: Recent Histories of American Communism." *Radical History Review.* 61(1995):166–74.

Walsh, J. Raymond. *C.I.O.: Industrial Unionism in Action.* New York: Norton and Company, 1937.

Washburn, Wilcomb E. *The Governor and the Rebel: A History of Bacon's Rebellion in Virginia*. Chapel Hill: University of North Carolina Press, 1957.

Weaver, Robert C. *Negro Labor*. New York: Harcourt, Brace and Company, 1946.

Wellenreuther, Herman. "Labor in the Early American Revolution." *Labor History*, 22, (1981).

———. "Rejoinder," *Labor History*, 24, (1983): 440-454.

Wesley, Charles H. *Negro Labor in the United States, 1850–1925*. New York: Russell and Russell, 1927.

West, Cornel. "Race and Social Theory: Towards a Genealogical Materialist Analysis." In *The Year Left 2: Towards a Rainbow Socialism*, edited by Mike Davis et al. London: Verso, 1987.

Whatley, Warren. "Getting a Foot in the Door: 'Learning,' State Dependence, and the Racial Integration of Firms." *Journal of Economic History*, (March 1990).

Widgerson, Seth. "The UAW in the 1950s". Ph.D. Diss. Wayne State University, 1989.

Wiener, Johnathan M. *Social Origins of the New South, Alabama 1860-1885*. Baton Rouge, LA: Lousiana State University Press, 1978.

Wilentz, Sean. *Chants Democratic: New York City and the Rise of the Working Class, 1788-1850*. New York: Oxford University Press, 1984.

———. "Against Exceptionalism: Class Consiousness and the American Labor Movement." *International Labor and Working Class History* 26 (Fall 1984):1–24.

Wilhot, Francis M. *The Politics of Massive Resistance*. New York: George Braziller Inc., 1973.

Wilkins, Roger. "Racism Has Its Priviledges: The Case for Affirmative Action." *The Nation*, 27 March 1995: 409–16.

Willis, William S. "Divide and Rule: Red, White, and Black in the Southeast." *Journal of Negro History*, XLVIII, 1 (July 1963) 157–76.

Williams, Eric. *Capitalism and Slavery*. New York: Capricorn Books, 1966.

Williams, T. Harry. *Huey Long*. New York: Knopf, 1969.

Williams, Rhonda M. "Capital, Competition, and Discrimination: A Reconsideration of Racial Earnings Inequality." *Review of Radical Political Economics*, 19, no. 3 (Summer 1987):1–15.

Williams, William Appleman. *The Contours of American History*. Cleveland: World Publishing Co., 1961.

Wills, Gary. *Detroit Free Press*, 19 February 1995.

Wilson, William Julius. *The Truly Disadvantaged: The Inner City, the Underclass, and Public Policy*. Chicago: University of Chicago Press, 1987.

Winant, Howard. *Racial Conditions: Politics, Theory, Comparison*. Minneapolis: Unviersity of Minnesota Press, 1994.

———. "The New International Dynamics of Racism." *Poverty and Race*, 4, no. 4 (July/August 1995).

Winkler, Alan M. "The Philadelphia Transit Strike of 1944." *The Journal of American History* 59, no. 1 (June 1972) 73–89.

Wolfe, Alan. *America's Impasse: The Rise and Fall of the Politics and Growth*. Boston: South End Press, 1981.

Wolfe, F.E. *Admission to American Trade Unions*. Baltimore: Johns Hopkins Press, 1912.

Wolman, Leo. *Ebb and Flow in Trade Unionism*. New York: National Bureau of Economic Research, 1936.

Wood, Gordon. "A Note on Mobs in the American Revolution." *William and Mary Quaterly*, XXIII, no. 4 (October 1966): 635–42.

———. *The Creation of the American Republic, 1786–1787*. New York: Norton, 1969.

———. *The Radicalism of the American Revolution*. New York: A.A. Knopf, 1992.

Wood, Peter. *Black Majority: Negros in Colonial South Carolina from 1670 Through the Stono Rebellion*. New York: W.W. Norton and Company, 1974.

———. "The Changing Population of the Colonial South: An Overview by Race and Region, 1685–1790." In *Powhatan's Mantle: Indians in the Colonial Southwest*, Peter

Wood, Gregory A. Waselkov, and H. Thomas Hatley eds. Lincoln, NB: University of Nebraska Press, 1989.

———. "'Liberty Is Sweet:' African-American Freedom Struggles in the Years Before White Independence." In *Beyond the American Revolution: Explorations in the History of American Radicalism*. Dekalb, Ill.: Northern Illinois University Press, 1993.

Woodward, C. Vann. *Tom Watson: Agrarian Rebel*. New York: Rinehart and Company, Inc., 1955. (1938)

———. *The Strange Career of Jim Crow*. New York: Galaxy, 1964.

———. *Reunion and Reaction: The Compromise of 1877 and the End of Reconstruction*. Boston: Little, Brown, 1966.

———. *Origins of the New South, 1877–1913*. Baton Rouge: Louisiana State University Press, 1971.

———. "The Seige." *The New York Review of Books*, 25 September 1986.

World Development Report 1995. New York: Oxford University Press, 1995.

Wright, Gavin. *The Political Economy of the Cotton South*. New York: Norton, 1978.

———. *Old South, New South: Revolutions in the Southern Economy Since the Civil War*. New York: Basic, 1986.

Wye, Christopher G. "The New Deal and the Negro Community: Toward a Broader Conceptualization." *The Journal of American History* 59, no. 3 (December 1972):621–39.

Wynn, Neil. *The Afro-American and the Second World War*. New York: Homes and Meir Publisher, 1975.

X, Malcolm. *The Autobiography of Malcom X*. New York: Ballintine Books, 1992 (1965).

———. *Malcolm X Speaks*, edited by George Breitman. New York: Grove Press, 1996 (1965).

Yarmolinsky, Adam, ed. *Case Studies in Personnel Security*. Washington, D.C.: Bureau of National Affairs, 1955.

Yeakey, Lamont B. "The Montgomery, Alabama Bus Boycott, 1955–56," Ph.D. Diss., Columbia University, 1979.

Zangrando, Robert L. "The NAACP and a Federal Anti-lynching Bill," *Journal of Negro History* 50 (April 1965):106–17.

———. *The NAACP Crusade Against Lynching*. Philadelphia: Temple University Press, 1980.

Zolberg, Aristide R. *Working Class Formation: Nineteenth Century Patterns in Western Europe and the United States*. Princeton, N.J.: Princeton University Press, 1986.

Index

Abbott, Josiah, 143
Abdul-Rauf, Mahmoud, 336
Abolitionism: during American Revolution,
61-68; in Constitutional Convention, 70;
working-class and, 76; in antebellum
period, 76-83, 87-111; during American
Revolution, 56-62; impact of American
Revolution on, 68-73; repression of,
87-91, 94-95; support among free Blacks
and, 88, 103; northern antebellum societies, 87; northern mob violence and, 94,
97, 101; southern opposition to, 98; anti-
union sentiment and, 96; growth of in
antebellum North, 96-108; historical
debate over, 96-97; working-class opposition to, 101, 108-111; women and, 102,
106; working-class support of, 102-111;
advocacy of equal rights, 103; middle-class
basis of, 103; radical abolitionists, 103;
as pawns of northern capital, 104; involvement with the First Interantional, 106
Academic Freedom, 151
Adams, Abagail, 61
Adams, John, 52, 61
Adams, John Quincy, 79-80
Adams, Samuel, 54, 60, 61, 72
Affirmative Action: failure of, 47, 79;
present day attacks upon 5, 7, 147,
338-344, 361; hypocrisy of attacks on
racial quotas, 340-342
AFL-CIO, 289, 295, 307, 343
African-Americans (see also African-
American working-class, Blacks, civil
rights movement, Depression-New Deal,
Reconstruction, slaves, slavery, and white
supremacy): abolition movement and,
97,100-101; affirmative action and, 47, 79,
147, 338-344; American Revolution and,
51, 54-60; Black Codes and, 88, 120; Civil
War Troops and, 115; Communist Party
and, 191-194, 214; Democratic Party
and,179, 201 203, 212 213; Republican
Party and, 166-168, 179-180, 201-203,
212-213; Depression-New Deal and, 184,
190-199, 202-218; disenfranchisement and,
90-91, 127, 164-165, 167; emancipation
and, 114-116; Great Migration and,
209-211, 242; labor movement and, 30-31,
108-111, 130-134,142, 144-146, 191-192,
193-198, 213-215, 235, 252-253, 289; military service and, 115, 206-207, 266, 279;
post-World War II changes and, 272-279;
pre-Civil War restrictions on, 87-89, 90-92,
FDR and support of, 202-203; Scottsboro
case and, 192-193, 209, 214; suffrage and,
90, 126-128; Truman and, 252-256, 258;
unemployment movements and, 183-185;
violence against, 126-127, 160, 161, 190,
208, 253, 278, 288, 292, 299-300; voter
turnout and, 121-122, 135, 297; post-Civil
War political mobilization, 121-123;
impact of Depression-New Deal on,
190-199; Communist Party and, 190-194;
voting and, 212-214; post-Reconstruction
disenfranchisement of, 164-167; growth
of Black middle-class, 336, 354; Scottsboro
case and, 192-193, 209, 214
African-American working-class: during
American Revolution, 52, 58-61; exclusion of antebellum waterfront jobs, 92;
role of during the Depression-New Deal
period, 214-218; expansion of in post-
World War II period, 243-244; role of in
formation of civil rights movement, 265;
role in civil rights movement, 279-287;
Populists and, 155-167; exclusion from
white job preserves and skilled trades,
330-331, 334; Southern Tenant Farmers
Union and, 186
African Black Brotherhood, 191
African Liberation Support Committee, 292
Agnew, Spiro, 312
Agricultural Adjustment Act, 201-202
Aid to Families with Dependent Children
(AFDC): present day attacks on, 6-7 , 345
Alabama, 86, 276-277, 297, 298, 301;
Birmingham, 277, 286; Montgomery
Bus Boycott, 264, 286-287
Alcott, Louis May, 83
Alexander, Will, 203
Alger, Horatio, 26
Ali, Muhammad, 295
Allen, John, 62
Allen, Theodore, 12-13, 38, 40, 43-45, 118
Atgeld, John Peter, 158, 163